SMELTER WAR
A Rebellious Red Trade Union Fights for its Life
in Wartime Western Canada

In 1938, the Congress of Industrial Organizations (CIO) sent communist union organizer Arthur "Slim" Evans to the smelter city of Trail, British Columbia, to establish Local 480 of the International Union of Mine, Mill and Smelter Workers. Six years later the local was recognized as the legal representative of more than 5,000 workers at a smelter owned by the powerful Consolidated Mining and Smelting Company of Canada. But the union's fight for survival had only just begun.

Smelter Wars unfolds that historic struggle, offering glimpses into the political, social, and cultural life of the semi-rural, single-industry community. Hindered by economic depression, two world wars, and Cold War intolerance, Local 480 faced fierce corporate, media, and religious opposition at home. Ron Verzuh draws upon archival and periodical sources, including the mainstream and labour press, secret police records, and oral histories, to explore the CIO's complicated legacy in Trail as it battled a wide range of antagonists: a powerful employer, a company union, local conservative citizens, and Co-operative Commonwealth Federation (CCF) leadership.

More than the history of a union, *Smelter Wars* is a cultural study of a community shaped by the dominance of a world-leading industrial juggernaut set on keeping the union drive at bay.

(Canadian Social History Series)

RON VERZUH is a writer and historian. His previous books include *Radical Rag: The Pioneer Labour Press in Canada* and *Underground Times: Canada's Flower-Child Revolutionaries.*

Canadian Social History Series

ISBN 978-1-4875-4111-8 (cloth)   ISBN 978-1-4875-4112-5 (paper)
ISBN 978-1-4875-4114-9 (EPUB)   ISBN 978-1-4875-4113-2 (PDF)

Library and Archives Canada Cataloguing in Publication

Title: Smelter wars : a rebellious red trade union fights for its life in
wartime Western Canada/Ron Verzuh.
Names: Verzuh, Ron, 1948– author.
Series: Canadian social history series.
Description: Series statement: Canadian social history series |
Includes bibliographical references and index.
Identifiers: Canadiana (print) 20210303042 | Canadiana (ebook) 20210303107 |
ISBN 9781487541118 (cloth) | ISBN 9781487541125 (paper) |
ISBN 9781487541149 (EPUB) | ISBN 9781487541132 (PDF)
Subjects: LCSH: Labor unions – British Columbia – Trail – History. | LCSH: Iron
and steel workers – Labor unions – British Columbia – Trail – History. | LCSH:
Industrial relations – British Columbia – Trail – History. | LCSH: Subsidies –
British Columbia – Trail – History. | LCSH: Smelting – British Columbia –
Trail – History. | LCSH: Trail (B.C.) – History.
Classification: LCC HD6529.B8 V47 2022 | DDC 331.87/097116241–dc23

We wish to acknowledge the land on which the University of Toronto Press
operates. This land is the traditional territory of the Wendat, the Anishnaabeg,
the Haudenosaunee, the Métis, and the Mississaugas of the Credit First Nation.

This book has been published with the help of a grant from the Federation for the
Humanities and Social Sciences, through the Awards to Scholarly Publications
Program, using funds provided by the Social Sciences and Humanities Research
Council of Canada.

University of Toronto Press acknowledges the financial support of the Government of Canada and the Ontario Arts Council, an agency of the Government of
Ontario, for its publishing activities.

Canada Council
for the Arts

Conseil des Arts
du Canada

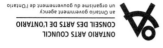

ONTARIO ARTS COUNCIL
CONSEIL DES ARTS DE L'ONTARIO
an Ontario government agency
un organisme du gouvernement de l'Ontario

Funded by the
Government
of Canada

Financé par le
gouvernement
du Canada

MIX
Paper from
responsible sources
FSC C016245
www.fsc.org

Smelter Wars

A Rebellious Red Trade Union
Fights for Its Life in Wartime
Western Canada

Ron Verzuh

UNIVERSITY OF TORONTO PRESS
Toronto Buffalo London

For Leola and for the men and women who built the smelter city

While the acts of kings and governments provide the great brush strokes on the canvas of human experience, it is the strivings and aspirations of ordinary people, and day-to-day events, that complete the picture and give it meaning. A careful reading of the history of the Kootenay district clearly demonstrates this fact. In the lives of the early fur traders, miners and lumbermen, we find thought and action which has left its imprint upon our times.

– H.W. "Bert" Herridge, member of Parliament for Kootenay West in his column "Jottings From Ottawa," published in Mine-Mill Local 480's *Commentator*, June 1954

Contents

Acknowledgments

I wish to acknowledge the assistance of Gregory S. Kealey, who commented on an early draft of *Smelter Wars* and recommended it to the University of Toronto Press. I also owe much to the patience and perseverance of UTP acquisitions editor Len Husband and other staff members who guided me through the publication process. *Smelter Wars* is based on my Simon Fraser University doctoral dissertation "Divided Loyalties: A Study of a Communist-Led Trade Union's Struggle for Survival in Trail, British Columbia, 1943–1955." I am indebted to dissertation committee members Joseph Taylor III, senior supervisor; Allen Seager, supervisor; Kendra Strauss, internal examiner; and the late John H. Thompson, external examiner. I also want to acknowledge Mark Leier for his many years of support and encouragement. His invaluable advice, guidance, and friendship added much to the writing of this book. In addition, I am grateful to the many labour historians, scholars, researchers, librarians, archivists, fellow students, and trade unionists who offered suggestions and encouragement in the research and writing of this book. I owe a further debt of gratitude to United Steelworkers Local 480 for giving me access to its files and to the retired members and leaders of the local who shared their stories with me. I am also indebted to the Canadian Union of Public Employees, my former employer, for funding a sabbatical leave during which I was able to refine my research skills as well as rekindle my interest in labour history. Greg Nesteroff, Ronald Shearer, and Jamie Forbes are also to be thanked for their assistance. The depth of research could not have been achieved without the help of the Trail Historical Society, BC Archives, the University of British Columbia's Rare Books and Special Collections division, Library and Archives Canada, and other agencies. Sean Griffin also proved a valuable resource regarding the history of the Communist Party of Canada. I also benefitted from the formatting expertise of Dave Chokroun at Simon Fraser University's Bennett Library. Further thanks to the friends, peer readers, and others who offered many thoughtful comments and suggestions. Finally, to my wife Leola Jewett-Verzuh, to whom I owe renewed life, I dedicate this book. All errors and omissions in *Smelter Wars* are mine alone.

Preface

Writing *Smelter Wars* was driven as much by a personal interest in discovering the history of my birthplace as by my historian's curiosity about what influenced the social and political attitudes and subsequent actions of the smelter city workforce of the 1940s and 1950s. In deciding to write it, I knew that I would need to supply answers to several questions. Why write a book about a small band of radical trade unionists struggling to survive in a relatively remote would-be company town far from the mainstream of national and world affairs? What could a locally based study of the seventeen years covered here – turbulent years marked by economic depression, war, and Cold War intolerance – add to our understanding of labour's role in shaping society? Could a detailed examination of shifting social relations and conflicts offer new insights to an audience of trade union leaders, labour historians, students, and smelter workers? Also, would a study of one union's struggle for survival seventy-five years ago provide new directions for today's labour movement as it battles against the persistent conservative view that unionism is dead? My search for answers took me on a scholarly journey stimulated by intellectual curiosity about the historic struggle of the working people who built Trail, British Columbia.

I was born in Trail in January 1948, riding the first wave of the post-war baby boom, and grew up among the thousands of other smelter workers' kids who lived in the surrounding communities that made up the West Kootenay District of British Columbia's southern interior. I started working full-time at the Consolidated Mining and Smelting Company of Canada (CM&S and then Cominco) when I was eighteen, following in the footsteps of my father and his brothers, all second-generation immigrant Canadians. They were of Croatian background, as I was to learn much later. My mother had worked as a secretary for the company at its Marine Building offices in Vancouver before transferring to Trail, where she met and married my father. My first job at the smelter was as a labourer in the notorious phosphate plant in Warfield, the small village above Trail where the company produced its lucrative Elephant Brand fertilizer. My father worked in the plant next door. Thus the smelter had played a significant role in my life from as early as I can remember.

During my first work experience with Cominco, I lived the shift-work life of a smelterman, climbing aboard the old workers' co-op bus at 5:30 a.m. to arrive at the plant gate for a dayshift starting at 6 a.m., or at 10:30 p.m. for the graveyard shift. Dozing men occupied the back seats, snatching the last half hour of rest before starting their work day. The driver would shift gears to slow the bus as he negotiated the twisting section of road to Trail known as the Columbia River Bluffs. As we reached the outskirts of town, we could see the smoke pouring from what was once said to be the world's largest lead and zinc smelter. The Big Stack, 300 metres high, polluted the skies as far south as Stevens County in Washington State. Then came the unmistakable stink of rotten eggs. It was sulphur from the giant expanse of factory plants that shadowed downtown Trail. By the time the bus edged into the parking lot we could see the mountain of slag discarded from the lead refinery. Getting off the bus, I walked into a world that would later seem to me not that different from the factory scenes in Fritz Lang's famous silent film *Metropolis*.

The day before my first shift, I had attended the company's basic orientation course. Later that day, after a brief examination, a company nurse declared me fit for work. Nothing, however, could have prepared me for what was to come. The next day, I was steered to the plant office, where the foreman and shift boss sat behind a large window looking into the lunchroom. We "new starts" were fresh victims for Paddy the Rat and his sidekick Eagle Beak, the pejorative nicknames we workers gave to these bosses. I did not fully realize at the time that I was protected from such zealous managers by one of the most radical trade unions in North American labour history, the International Union of Mine, Mill and Smelter Workers (Mine-Mill). I would soon be sworn in as a member in good standing and receive the basic information about my rights under the collective agreement, a document that had been renegotiated, at first annually, since Mine-Mill Local 480 signed the first such agreement in 1944.

My first assignment was cleaning out a sulphuric acid silo several storeys high. John, my work partner, was a short, stocky Italian immigrant whose real name was Giovanni. When we finished the shift, I hung up my work clothes, showered, and went home exhausted. The next day, I got a rude surprise: my pants had been reduced to a pair of shorts; the acid fumes had eaten away my pant legs. When I lined up to punch the ancient time clock to start the shift, I heard the sniggers of men dressed in many different types and colours of work clothes and sporting all manner of headwear from engineer's hats to baseball caps and hardhats. "New kid," said one. "He'll learn," said another. "It won't take long for him to see that school is the best place for him." At the end of the shift, the foreman issued me acid-proof material with which my mother would sew me new work clothes.

Working with Immigrants from "Up the Gulch"

Like many newly arrived Italian immigrants, Giovanni took up temporary residence at the Kootenay Hotel at the head of the Trail Gulch, an immigrant enclave where my father's family also lived. My grandmother took in some of the overflow of immigrant boarders, some of them of Austro-Hungarian origin like herself. In the days and weeks to come, I tried to keep up with Giovanni as we did many other mindless, muscle-challenging jobs together. We were supplied with jackhammers to clean hardened fertilizer from giant cylinders and eighteen-pound sledgehammers to pound rocks through metal screens called grizzlies. Giovanni's work ethic did not win him any friends. The dominant rule was to work at a reasonable pace and be safe. Truth be told, the union also had to discipline a few slackers who would search out dark, quiet places where they could nap away as much of the shift as possible. Giovanni, with his bull-like approach and his willingness to accept any task, no matter how dirty or dangerous, ran counter to the thinking of some active members of the union. In their view, such work behaviour gave managers like Paddy the Rat and Eagle Beak an excuse to work the men harder.

Giovanni's poor English meant he did not understand his work-mates' concerns. It was in his nature to work hard. But no matter how hard he worked, we still both earned $2.24½ cents an hour, a decent labourer's wage in the mid-1960s. We joked that it was the cost of a twelve-bottle case of beer, so we earned eight cases of beer a day. My pay grade rose slightly when I was transferred to the other "worst shithole," the lead furnaces in the main smelter at Tadanac. (The name combined Canada spelled backwards with a *T* for Trail.) Tadanac included a model village reserved for top company managers and their families – a clear symbol of class divisions in the smelter city.

If ever there was a workplace that would persuade me to return to school, it was the lead furnaces, a blistering hot, fiery, cavernous place that seemed the modern equivalent of the "dark satanic mills" I had read about in high-school English class. Mysteriously, I was advised to wear long johns under my work pants because the lead furnaces got so hot, especially in summer, that my pants could easily get burned into my skin. After a year, I was transferred to the indium plant, a kind of purgatory that was my reward for surviving without succumbing to a debilitating and often deadly condition called "leading" that occurs after too much exposure to lead fumes. At the end of my first two-year stint with Cominco, I had graduated to a wage rate of $3.12½ an hour as a light equipment operator. The cost of beer had stayed about the same.

Growing up in a smelter household, workplace fatalities were a regular topic of conversation, with my father noting the number of "lost-time" accidents the company had recorded on the "Elmer the Safety Elephant" billboard outside the Tadanac plants. I often heard the names of Mine-Mill leaders spoken around the dinner table. Sometimes the comments were angry denunciations, other times there was a recognition of union efforts to address the health and safety situation or the negotiation of a good contract. Al King and union negotiator Harvey Murphy, both Communists, were prominent among the leaders who had won many benefits for the Mine-Mill members of Local 480, including me. By the time I started at the smelter, they were getting set to move on to higher-level union jobs. King, the tough-minded local president, became the Mine-Mill regional director when Murphy, a shrewd organizer and a tireless negotiator, became a vice-president of Mine-Mill in Canada. He "lived out of a suitcase," my father used to say, and I detected a begrudging tinge of respect for Murphy. He would become a hero of sorts for me and all shift workers at the smelter partly because he had negotiated an extra day off known, not surprisingly, as a "Murphy Day." That was the first time I had heard the name Harvey Murphy, and it became the source of endless anecdotes about a man my family knew only by reputation and seemed to alternately admire and dislike.

An even more notable topic during our family's dinnertime conversations was the memory of former company president Selwyn G. Blaylock. Mr. Blaylock, and it was always "Mr.," was cherished by some for his benevolent management style. He died three years before I was born, but well into my adulthood I heard stories about the great industrialist. One story about how he intervened in a hockey dispute to force players back on to the ice – he was a strong supporter of the world champion Trail Smoke Eaters – highlighted his power. I soon learned, however, that the union did not fully share the public's admiration, and in some cases adoration, of Mr. Blaylock. Some Local 480 leaders remembered him as a hard-nosed dictator of company policy with a keen eye for fresh profits. Rumour had it that you could not enlist in the Army or even get married without his permission.

A Second Stint up the Hill

My second stint at Cominco occurred in the early 1970s. I had completed an undergraduate degree at Simon Fraser University, then one of the more radical campuses in the country, and returned to the smelter workplace brimming with notions of class consciousness and class struggle. I was anxious to use my book learning in a naive attempt to apply theory to practice. For my efforts the bosses, and some of my fellow workers, told me to "shove your ivory tower ideas where the sun don't shine." But some of the younger men were interested in discussing Mine-Mill's history as a progressive union, a force for resistance against injustice in the workplace and society. Some old-timers were stirred to remember the early struggles to build and maintain Local 480 as their bargaining agent. Some of them were also Communists or left-wing New Democrats. This environment fed my intellectual curiosity about how much our lives were influenced by the company and the union that challenged it.

As a writer and historian, I wanted to explore that history and try to shed some light on the social forces that shaped it. My curiosity had deep roots and could be triggered by childhood memories. Giovanni, for example, piqued my interest in the immigrant community that coalesced around the Gulch, including the search for my own family's origins in Croatia. Working at the smelter engendered concerns about workplace health and safety as well as environmental safety. When I joined a group of dissident Steelworkers protesting low strike pay in the early 1970s, I overheard some recall the early 1950s when Mine-Mill had to fight off a Steelworker raid. The rebellious actions of the dissident group prompted discussions about the long tenure of Blaylock's company union and the role it played in stifling union organizing. The absence of women in the workforce hid the fact that women, some of them my friends' mothers, had been smelter war workers. Lunchroom conversations about politics revealed old rivalries on the left and the role Communists had played in forming the smelter union. Finally, there was the presence in Warfield of a multi-storied tower that few people seemed to know anything about other than it was the "heavy water plant." I later learned of the plant's secret role as a producer of material used in making the atomic bomb.

When I left the smelter for the last time, all of these personal experiences stimulated me to research and write articles, speak at conferences, and make short documentary films about the rivalries, political intrigues, industrial civil war, and battle of the sexes within a male breadwinner culture. Trail's history from the 1930s to the 1950s, a period of world-changing events, shaped my parents' attitudes, their politics, and their understanding of how things worked. It dictated what they would become and provided the wherewithal to live relatively safe and comfortable lives.

With *Smelter Wars* I have attempted to put historical events in a local, regional, and national context and draw some conclusions about their significance to North American labour and social history. I hope readers will enjoy journeying into the past with me and will benefit from reading the story of Local 480 as it struggled to be born in the late 1930s and to survive the anti-union and anti-Communist attitudes that plagued it from the long organizing drive that began in 1938 through to the McCarthyism of the 1950s.

Ron Verzuh
September 2021

Acronyms

ACCL	All-Canadian Congress of Labour
ACTU	Association of Catholic Trade Unions
AFL	American Federation of Labor
AIMM	American Institute of Mining and Metallurgy
AUC	Amalgamated Union of Canada
BCFL	British Columbia Federation of Labour
CAIMAW	Canadian Association of Industrial, Mechanical and Allied Workers
CBC	Canadian Broadcasting Corporation
CCF	Co-operative Commonwealth Federation
CCL	Canadian Congress of Labour
CCU	Canadian Congress of Unions
CIO	Congress of Industrial Organizations
CLC	Canadian Labour Congress
CLDL	Canadian Labour Defense League
CMA	Canadian Manufacturers' Association
CM&S	Consolidated Mining and Smelting Company of Canada
CPC	Communist Party of Canada and Canadian Peace Congress
CSU	Canadian Seaman's Union
CWU	Canadian Workers' Union
DOCR	Defence of Canada Regulations

HUAC	House Un-American Activities Committee
IATSE	International Association of Theater and Stage Employees
IBEW	International Brotherhood of Electrical Workers
ICA	Industrial Conciliation and Arbitration Act (BC)
IFLWU	International Fur and Leather Workers
IJC	International Joint Commission
ILWU	International Longshore and Warehouse Union
ISWU	Independent Smelter Workers' Union
IUMMSW	International Union of Mine, Mill and Smelter Workers (Mine-Mill)
IWA	International Woodworkers of America
IWW	Industrial Workers of the World (Wobblies)
LA	Ladies Auxiliary
LAC	Library and Archives Canada
LPP	Labor-Progressive Party (Communist)
LRB	Labour Relations Board
MWUC	Mine Workers' Union of Canada
NFB	National Film Board of Canada
NWLB	National War Labour Board
OBU	One Big Union
PPBAA	Pullman Porters Benefit Association of America
SPC	Socialist Party of Canada
SWOC	Steel Workers' Organizing Committee
TBT	Trail Board of Trade
TDT	*Trail Daily Times*
TLC	Trades and Labor Congress
UFLWU	United Fur and Leather Workers' Union
UE	United Electrical Workers
UMWA	United Mine Workers of America
UPW	United Public Workers of America
USWA	United Steel Workers of America
WUL	Workers' Unity League
YCL	Young Communist League

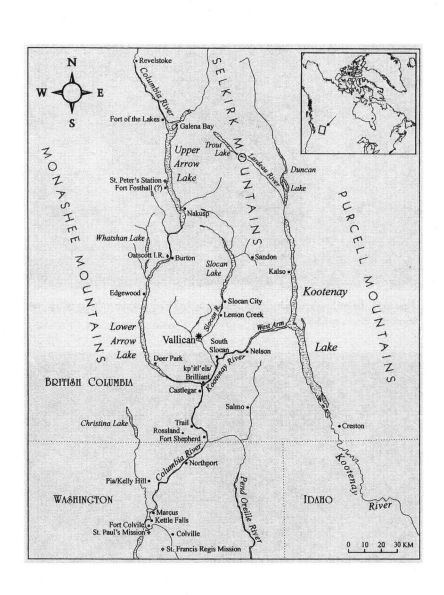

Map from Paula Pryce, *Keeping the Lakes Way: Reburial and the Recreation of a Moral World among an Invisible People* (Toronto: University of Toronto Press, 1999).

SMELTER WARS

Introduction: A Smelter City Is Born

It was a hot July day in 1899 when a dapper-looking young man newly graduated from Montreal's McGill University stepped onto the platform of the red-washed Canadian Pacific Railway (CPR) station at Trail Creek Landing. The train had slowly snaked its way down into the mining camp nestled deep in the British Columbia interior a few kilometres from the Canada–United States border. As the train crawled through an immigrant community called Dublin Gulch, the young man noticed a few wooden houses beside the station, a large stable, some shops, and "a very unpretentious one storey building."[1] From the station, he could see the sternwheeler SS *Lytton*, one of at least three that docked at the landing. They plied this broad section of the Columbia River, bobbing up and down as men unloaded cargoes of lead and zinc ore from the surrounding mines destined for the CPR's newly purchased smelter. On the *Lytton*'s deck, a new crop of workers might have been disembarking to join the growing workforce that would build the landing into a town and then a lively interior city. The young man, just twenty years old, was Selwyn Gwillym Blaylock. About six hundred workers then employed at the smelter were unlikely to have noticed the tall, sportive-looking Blaylock, but in time he would have a profound impact on the labour-management relations that would surface many years later. Those relations and their influence on the social, economic, and political development of Trail, as it was called when incorporated as a city in 1901, are the main focus of this book.

Blaylock, the son of an Anglican minister of British heritage, had been hired soon after completing his science degree in mining and metallurgy at McGill and was about to start his career in the assay office of the Canadian Smelting Works, later called the Consolidated Mining and Smelting Company of Canada (CM&S). Four years earlier, another young man, thirty-year-old Butte, Montana, copper king F. Augustus Heinze, already a wunderkind in the mining and smelting industry, had erected the smelter in record time under the corporate name the British Columbia Smelting and Refining Company. Rumour had it that after unsuccessfully trying to persuade the CM&S's first smelter manager, Walter H. Aldridge, to play poker for the property, Heinze eventually sold it to the CPR in 1898 for more than $800,000. The deal included a narrow gauge railway to the nearby mining mecca of Rossland, constructed to ward off rival mining and rail baron Daniel Chase Corbin of Spokane, WA.[2] The CPR also inherited some of the workers who had followed Heinze north.

By the time Blaylock arrived, Trail Creek Landing was shedding some of its rough-hewn image as "a boom town of labourers and smelter men who worked long 12-hour shifts" and was emerging as a permanent industrial centre with growing influence on the BC political economy.[3] It also shed part of its name, becoming Trail Creek, and soon enough it was proudly displaying the trappings of a booming metropolis. As Blaylock settled in, he could soon attend a show at the new opera house, order a case of local beer at the brewery, stay at any one of seventeen hotels (the law only allowed liquor sales in such establishments), visit one of five churches, and become a member of the local Trail Board of Trade, and the Masonic Lodge. Other service clubs, such as the Owls, the Eagles, the Knights of Pythias, and a "hive" of the Ladies of the Maccabees were also present. Local historian Elsie G. Turnbull describes the Trail Creek that Blaylock would have seen as he entered "a typical frontier mining town": "Rectangular frame hotels were perched on stilts along the waterfront to avoid river flooding while modest shops hid behind false fronts on Bay Avenue, Cedar Avenue and Spokane Street. Five little churches clustered on Pine Avenue, bells in Anglican and Methodist towers calling worshippers to service.

Peaked-roof cottages covered the lower slopes of Lookout Mountain in tiers, veranda and living room looking down on the chimney of the house below."[4]

About three hundred Italian immigrants, many of them living in Dublin Gulch below Smelter Hill, were employed at the CM&S, along with other eastern and southern Europeans eager to find work in the job-rich West Kootenay District. An influx of Americans had migrated across the international boundary during the regional rush for precious metals, and many stayed to work at the smelter. Indeed, the new city's founding fathers, Colonel Eugene Sayre Topping and Frank Hanna, were American. Another American, W.F. Thompson, founded the new city's first weekly newspaper, the *Trail Creek News*. In fact, there were so many Americans at Trail Creek by the time Blaylock came to town that residents celebrated the Fourth of July instead of Dominion Day. Some of the American workers had migrated from Heinze's operations in Anaconda and Butte, and they carried their patriotism along with the experiences of belonging to a militant trade union. They were joined by what CM&S historian Lance Whittaker describes as a "conglomerate lot." He notes, "Very largely they were Americans.... [But] they came of almost every racial strain ... Cousin Jacks (Cornishmen) and the Irish of Butte and Anaconda had sent their quota: Spanish, Serbian, Croatian and Scandinavian names were more common than Anglo-Saxon ... and several prolific Italian families were among the earliest employees of the British Columbia Smelting Company."[5]

Miners' Union Would Bring "Violence, Strikes, and Bloodshed"

Trail's workforce no doubt heard migrants talk of the Western Federation of Miners (WFM), one of the founding unions of the radical Industrial Workers of the World (IWW or Wobblies). "Most of the mining officials in Rossland were graduates of the Montana and Nevada schools of union procedure," wrote Whittaker, hinting that they were well schooled in "violence, strikes, and bloodshed."[6] The WFM had already made inroads at Rossland by 1895 when

Local 38 was established to represent local miners. By 1896, Local 38 was well known in Trail for its annual picnics, and smelter workers held meetings in the Rossland Miners' Union Hall, an impressive four-storey edifice that the miners had completed in 1898. As Whittaker notes, there were "efforts to unionize [the] smelter ... and endeavours of the union to establish the eight-hour day in the smelting industry."[7] There were calls for higher wages, better working conditions, and a safer workplace, with the *News* regularly reporting workplace fatalities at the notoriously hazardous smelter. Editor Thompson also occasionally reported on a strike, usually in the United States, but he, like future editors, was quick to criticize unions if they interfered with operations that might threaten progress or profits in the smelter city.

It is not clear exactly when the WFM chartered the Trail Mill and Smeltermen's Union Local 105, but in August 1899 the *Trail Creek News* reported on "the greatest social event in the history of Trail." A ball had been organized "under the auspices of the union miners."[8] The weekly also regularly reported on the union's popular "smokers" (men-only social events). In one such report, the *News* praised the union's "splendid musical program" and highlighted the reading of a poem that "brought down the house." The poem described the smelter's "heat and gaseous fumes" and being "begrimed in dust and sweat." One stanza even seemed to reveal an inchoate militancy:

> With unity and stable minds, the workman should progress.
> And arbitrate all grievances, which leads to sure success.
> Be loyal to your order, to each brother lend a hand.
> Like true men strive to aid, cement the federation band.[9]

Union elections were announced in the *News*, and short blurbs noted union settlements reached in other parts of Canada or signalled the success or failure of union organizing drives elsewhere.[10] Thompson, a Trail Board of Trade member, and William K. Esling, who eventually replaced him as editor, tended to browbeat workers to spend their "seventy five dollars a month" at local businesses, blaming them for any downturn in the local economy.[11] In one of many editorials written to entice more people to join the growing population of "at least 2,000," the *News* listed Trail's virtues: "What other city in the world has no poverty, no liability, no famines, pestilences, floods, blizzards, cyclones, earthquakes, or rainy seasons, no Sunday laws, debts, boodlers [political grafters], advertising doctors, Doweites, or other brands of religious cranks, mediums, faith cureists, spiritualists, business men doing business in their wife's names in order to defraud creditors, fad foodists, anarchists, christian scientists, or patent medicine men."[12] It was Trail as seen through rose-tinted spectacles, to be sure, boosterism being the editors' stock in trade. Despite their claims, many of the characters listed would eventually visit the smelter city.

Local trade unionists were noticeably missing from the list; perhaps they were accounted for as "anarchists." But if Trail workers did have a militant streak, as the earlier poem might suggest, initially it was not obvious. The *News* did report on a carpenters' strike at the brewery, the founding of a "Servant Girls' Union" in New Jersey, and Local 105's contributions to striking unions.[13] There was also ample evidence of the need for some sort of worker protection. On 1 February 1896, for example, the *News* reported that "Harry Fay had the ends of his two fingers on his left hand cut off while examining the blower to [*sic*] close." George Quyle "tore a great hole in the fleshly part of his thigh while being lowered for an elevation."[14] Initially, though, there was little evidence of the radicalism that marked the local's parent union or that of Local 38.

In one of the most famous conflicts in early BC mining history, the Rossland local struck in 1900–1, bringing WFM leaders north to Canada, including William "Big Bill" Haywood, the hard-drinking, tough-talking leader of the Wobblies.[15] Much later, local lore holds that Rossland miners hid Wobbly troubadour Joe Hill in the union hall, helping him to evade the Pinkerton private police – or so claims a plaque at the hall's entrance today. These and other labour luminaries were instrumental in engendering a working-class consciousness throughout the West Kootenay. As this book shows, their experiences educated workers of the district over long periods, informing their class consciousness and fuelling future attempts to mobilize.

S.G. Blaylock Meets Ginger Goodwin

By 1906, when the Trail smelter began operating officially under the CM&S banner, Blaylock's career was on a trajectory that continued straight up the corporate ladder, not just because of his assaying skills, but also because he shared the company's paternalistic attitude toward immigrant labour and eschewed any trade union attempting to organize workers. The following year, Blaylock was assigned to close down Hall Mines in Nelson. His success, much to the chagrin of laid-off workers, led to his promotion to superintendent of the CM&S's St. Eugene Mines property at Moyie, BC. There he had his first encounter with a labour dispute when mine workers organized as the WFM's Moyie Miners' Union threatened to stop work if the food the company supplied did not improve. Blaylock apparently handled a difficult situation deftly when he convinced the workers to stay on the job while he fixed the food problem.[16] His success at averting a strike fostered his interest in cooperation between employers and workers, but it was not until 1918 that he initiated the concept in the smelter workplace. The notion gained currency after the first strike in the smelter's history, in 1917.

Despite its earlier signs of complacency, Local 105 did eventually become radicalized, but it took the arrival of another newcomer, Albert "Ginger" Goodwin, in 1915 to lead the way. Goodwin ran for provincial election the following year as a West Kootenay candidate of the Socialist Party of Canada. His fellow workers at the smelter were impressed with his oratorical abilities and organizing skills, and he had won both friends and enemies for his strong anti-war stance. A pacifist, he opposed the conscription policy of Conservative Prime Minister Sir Robert Borden, and he stood firm against Blaylock, who was by then the CM&S's assistant general manager. By 1917 smelter working conditions and pay were suffering under the weight of three years of world war and the accompanying long work hours, food rationing, and other wartime restraints. The strike issues were better pay and almost as importantly an eight-hour workday, but Blaylock as chief company negotiator refused to bargain with Goodwin. With an ample stockpile and substantial demand from Allied forces he was able to force the strikers to capitulate. The work stoppage lasted thirty-five days, ending as the harshness of a Kootenay winter increased in late December.

Goodwin and Local 105 were fighting an unwinnable war against an enemy who had no intention of engaging in collective bargaining. Blaylock certainly rejected the union's view. That was clear. "Each settlement only puts us further away from getting what we want, that is, cheaper production," he told the smelter's second general manager, James J. Warren.[17] Strike historian Stanley Scott summarizes the outcome: "Union solidarity quickly vanished; soon the union lost its International Mine, Mill, and Smelter Workers affiliation. Workmen's Co-operative Committees organized instead, 'to help management run the plants fairly and safely,' according to Blaylock. Record production, no strikes, and the workingman's paradise followed. Unfortunately, for the men, wages did not rise correspondingly. The base rate remained the same until 1930 and the bonus system fluctuated wildly. Blaylock got his efficiency bonus, as he had suggested in 1917, in 1922. The men got the eight-hour day when it became law."[18]

The 1917 strike left a lingering bitter memory of the union's failure and an ongoing concern among potential union organizers that no union could succeed by confronting Blaylock. A key factor assuring that anger against unionism would persist was the decision of International Mine-Mill President Charles Moyer (the WFM had changed its name in 1916) to end financial support for the strike. The sense of abandonment that striking workers surely must have felt worked in Blaylock's favour as he pursued his dream of a cooperative workplace.

Following the strike, Goodwin was mysteriously declared fit for military service. He had been rejected for service previously after several illnesses. The reverse decision saw him flee to Vancouver Island, where he found refuge with his former mining friends, including Joe Naylor, who had served with Goodwin on the BC Federation of Labour executive. The refuge was cut short in July 1918, when a special police constable shot and killed him in the island woods. Several accounts, including two biographies, suggest that the local enlistment board's politics hastened the tragic end of Goodwin's short life. He was thirty years old. Unsubstantiated rumours claim Blaylock orchestrated Goodwin's death. Remembrances of old-timers who participated in the 1917 strike and other battles for workers' rights, particularly the martyring of Goodwin that precipitated Canada's first general strike, would later influence the trend toward left-wing politics among Trail workers at a time when Communist ideas were in the ascendency. The 1917 strike was in essence the first smelter war. Many were to follow, starting with the long struggle to wrest control of the workforce from Blaylock's paternalistic grip.

From "Workingman's Paradise" to Radical Action

The Trail strike came on the front end of what historians have called the Western Labour Revolt. At the other end were the 1919 Winnipeg General Strike, the brief but spectacular rise and fall of the One Big Union (OBU), and the founding of the Communist Party of Canada (CPC). Throughout the 1920s, a quiescence fell on Trail, and the image of a "workingman's paradise" was propagated to bolster Blaylock's industrial empire as he rose to managing director and eventually CM&S president.[19] Despite strike losses and growing corporate power, workers in the West Kootenay and elsewhere in BC "remained the most militant in the Canadian labour movement." A. Ross McCormack further suggests that the rebels of the revolt period "left a heritage" and "engraved into the collective memory of the working class a residual solidarity."[20]

Trail smelter workers embraced that solidarity slowly, but they failed to activate a new union drive until another newcomer, a one-time OBU organizer named Arthur "Slim" Evans, arrived to lead the second smelter war in the late 1930s. It is with him that our story begins, for Evans's arrival began the long struggle to build a legitimate union in Trail. The struggle involved many combatants, some of them hard-line Communists like Evans and others espousing strong anti-Communist views. They engaged in bloodless class warfare that would shake the community to its roots.

We meet Evans and accompany him on his organizing rounds, his frequent stops at Trail's many watering holes, and we observe his strategies and tactics in organizing the smelter's 5,000 workers. We also meet his fiercest opponents, with Blaylock being the most determined to stop him.

Anti-union since his earliest days with the CM&S, Blaylock was aided in his anti-union activities by the Workmen's Co-operative Committee (WCC), the company union that he formed and financed after the 1917 strike. The WCC leadership shared Blaylock's growing anti-Communism and it willingly colluded with him. The WCC's attacks against the new Mine-Mill Local 480's Communist leadership illustrate fundamental challenges of unionizing in a remote company town. The pro-company *Trail Daily Times*, which had replaced the weekly *News* in the early 1930s, reported and editorialized on what the WCC cited as the negative aspects of unionism and the positive attributes of Blaylock's cooperative management approach. When Evans arrived, some smelter workers began to see the possibility of a more democratic workplace. How did they respond to Evans and Local 480's Communists? How would they react to the predictable confrontations with the employer and the employer-cowed WCC? Would a successful bid to represent the smelter workforce stop a dissatisfied segment of the smelter population from continuing to reject Mine-Mill Local 480 in favour of a second company union, the Independent Smelter Workers' Union (ISWU)? The wait for answers would be long, arduous, and fraught with difficulties.

Some Trail women were among the opponents to Evans's drive and some were its strongest supporters. We first meet the mothers, sisters, daughters, spouses, and girlfriends of smelter workers as they join a domestic army of lesser-paid industrial war workers who replaced males fighting fascism in Europe and the Pacific. Women workers adapted to the traditionally male workplace. Not all of them appreciated Local 480's leftist politics and some disagreed with its bargaining policies. Some viewed Local 480 as a hindrance to winning a more prosperous and fulfilling future, while others embraced the union vision. Gender issues challenged male smelter workers' vision of that future. Communists knew that the Mine-Mill constitution called for gender equality, but the membership's male breadwinner values complicated their ability to honour that goal. Takaia Larsen notes that the local ignored "the voices of the almost 2,000 women workers who were employed at the plant."[21] Even members of the local Mine-Mill ladies auxiliary who supported the union refused to be reduced to a mere adjunct of the male organization. The auxiliary had its "own political agenda including women's emancipation," Elizabeth and Andrea Quinlan explain, but it was not obvious how Communists on the auxiliary executive committee could encourage the male leadership to support gender equality.[22]

Trail's immigrant workers and their families also included both opposition to the union and significant pockets of support. The different cultural background and political inclinations of immigrant families posed special problems for Local 480 organizers. Not least was their strong adherence to the anti-Communist Catholic Church. Many churches opposed what newspapers dubbed the "Red" union, but members of the Catholic clergy were the most forceful antagonists. Early immigrants continued to follow the teachings of the church and Old Country–based religious belief systems as they adapted to the New World. During the war, Local 480 worked to attract second-generation smelter workers, but they had to overcome the anti-union church doctrine of the older generation. This was a particular problem for the atheistic leaders of Local 480, especially when some priests' "talents could be easily adapted to the needs of North American capitalists," as Donald Avery notes.[23] What Local 480 leaders were contending with, Steve Rosswurm explains, was a church view, supported by national and international labour leaders such as Congress of Industrial Organizations (CIO) President Phillip Murray, that "radicalism of any sort became increasingly suspect and procapitalism became a political and religious litmus test."[24] What were the possibilities that immigrant workers, some of them members of the Communist Party, would join Evans and the Local 480 Reds in continuing the struggle?

Roadblocks Threaten to End the Organizing Drive

An endless clash of ideologies also created roadblocks for the Local 480 organizing drive. The Catholic Church was but one force of anti-Communism facing the Trail union. Joining the church were national unions, the predominantly Protestant social democrats under the Co-operative Commonwealth Federation (CCF), and the CM&S itself. The CCF and the CPC may have shared a common goal – representing the class interests of the workers – but there were major differences between them. Local 480's leaders had a way of closing the resulting divisions or at least skirting them when a local concern demanded non-ideological attention. To do so, they had an ally and a liability in the guise of another newcomer to the West Kootenay, the mercurial Harvey Murphy, life-long Communist and seasoned union organizer. Murphy would inspire the workers and lead Local 480 to victory as the smelter's legal bargaining agent, but his open espousal of Communism would also unlatch the door to anti-Communist attacks within Mine-Mill and in the broader labour movement. In his notorious "underpants speech" in April 1948, for example, a drunk Murphy lambasted the BC labour leadership assembled at a banquet during the annual lobbying of politicians. As described later, the impromptu speech presented Local 480's numerous adversaries with an obvious opportunity to shun Murphy and other Communists.

  To the media, Murphy epitomized the evil Communist labour leader, and he exposed Mine-Mill to angry anti-Reds in the Canadian Congress of Labour (CCL) and the CCF. How did the local try to mitigate the damage as they faced a national union movement leadership pressing to purge its ranks of Red troublemakers like those at Local 480? As Benjamin Isitt notes, CCF leaders were "desperate to distance themselves from Soviet Communism" and were adamantly opposed to the idea of "unity with Communist and non-Communist workers against a common enemy."[25] What was the stimulus behind the smelter anti-Communism that nearly wiped out the old Communist guard that built Local 480? How did Local 480 contend with the anti-Communist strategy driving the ISWU? When the US Congress passed the anti-Communist Taft-Hartley Act in 1947, how did Local 480's Communists address this new threat? How did they cope with the increased level of fear that McCarthyism would generate in Canada and even in the remote West Kootenay region?

The CCL embraced the Taft-Hartley-inspired notion that Red union purges would solve the union movement's problems. On the heels of Murphy's underpants speech, the national union moved swiftly to neutralize Communists and Communist sympathizers within union leadership ranks. Trail's leading anti-Red, Claire Billingsley, once hired by Murphy as a Mine-Mill representative, was elected Local 480 president in 1947. As the self-appointed arch-enemy of local Communists, Billingsley began courting the United Steelworkers of America (USWA). His goal was total demolition of the Communist-led local. How did Trail Communists deal with this internal existential threat? What strategy was needed to combat subsequent external attacks by the USWA, a union that was in the vanguard of labour movement anti-Communism in North America?

The Steelworkers manoeuvred to "liberate" Trail's smelter workers, using anti-Communist propaganda as the main raiding tactic to motivate workers to abandon their Labour Relations Board (LRB)–certified union. Billingsley worked hard to deliver them into the hands of the waiting Steelworker raiders. His leadership was a cornerstone of the USWA's Red-baiting strategy. Another pillar of support was lingering company loyalty among workers who had long supported company unionism. Did a spring 1951 *Maclean's* article by noted journalist Pierre Berton influence workers to side with the raiders? How did Local 480 stalwarts, some charter members of the union, battle to maintain a hold on the union they helped to found? This was a struggle amidst vast anti-Red hostility. As former Local 480 President Al King recalled, "All the preachers were preaching ... and the paper [the *Times*] was flailing away at us and the company was putting out garbage ... warning people to beware the evil Communists."[26]

McCarthyite Tactics Mark the Raiders

The story of the Steelworker raids that threatened to undo Mine-Mill Local 480 dominated the Trail labour scene throughout the early 1950s. Local 480 leaders, encouraged by Murphy, continued to defy the McCarthyite tactics of the raiders. Perhaps borrowing on the successes of the Industrial Workers of the World with their *Little Red Song Book* and troubadours like Joe Hill, Local 480 employed culture as a weapon of defence. First, despite mounting Cold War hysteria, the local supported the famous American singer–civil rights activist Paul Robeson in his efforts to regain his passport after having had it confiscated by the US government. To assist Robeson and draw attention to the causes he and Mine-Mill espoused, Local 480 leaders actively worked to launch an annual series of four Robeson concerts at the Canada-US border.

As Laurel Sefton McDowell explains, a "radical minority remained loyal to Robeson" and Local 480 was a member of it.[27] As we explore the motives of local members to support the popular singer, widely but falsely thought to be a Communist or Red sympathizer, we see the roots of Trail's class-conscious activism come alive. A second instance of that activism appeared with the local's public airing of the banned Mine-Mill-sponsored film *Salt of the Earth*. As we will see, by supporting *Salt*, Local 480 became part of a broad movement of resistance as well as defiance. Produced by members of the Hollywood Ten, a group of blacklisted filmmakers, the film was a moving depiction of class struggle and worker solidarity in New Mexico. As Ellen Schrecker notes, the union had fallen victim to the "injustice of McCarthyism."[28]

Fighting that injustice is part of Local 480's legacy, and it marked the historic Communist versus anti-Communist struggle that preoccupied the smelter city from the start of the organizing drive in the late 1930s through to the Cold War 1950s. As the local regrouped following the Steelworker raids, the CCL and CCF declared a moratorium on anti-Communist actions. The two would soon join forces to form the Canadian Labour Congress (CLC). The lull gave Communist Mine-Mill leaders, who were celebrating the founding of a fully autonomous Canadian Mine-Mill union, a false sense of security. World events had overtaken McCarthyism, but while Local 480 survived the worst of the Cold War excesses, further raiding would plague Mine-Mill locals elsewhere. How did Trail's tribulations affect the modern labour movement? How did it help shape that movement when its leadership made significant compromises, encouraged by the new labour laws of the post-war era?[29] Local 480's leaders rejected the CCF in the early 1950s, but King, Murphy, and others would also leave the CPC. How did these actions influence the local's dedication to a progressive heritage? Would Local 480 continue to dissent and militantly introduce capitalist-challenging alternatives to the mainstream business unionism that emerged in the late 1940s?

Some of the answers will surface as we examine the remnants of the smelter wars in today's Trail. The CM&S, for example, is now the property of Teck Resources Ltd., a multinational company whose corporate managers, unlike Blaylock, live far away. Local 480 has been transformed into a local of the United Steelworkers (USW). Looking back, we might ask, Does the Local 480 experience recounted here contain any lessons for twenty-first-century unionism?

Local Class War Pits Worker against Worker

In the chapters that follow, we review this brief historical moment in the story of the Canadian mining West and Trail's role in shaping it. The story is set in a secluded place far from Canada's major industrial centres. In this introduction, we tracked back to some of the history of the smelter city. In chapter 1, we retrace the beginnings of Local 480. Chapter 2 examines the role of the Workmen's Co-operative Committee, the company union formed after the 1917 smelter strike. Chapter 3 recalls how Trail's women joined a domestic army of lesser-paid industrial war workers that replaced male smelter workers fighting fascism in Europe and the Pacific. Chapter 4 looks at the cultural background and political inclinations of Trail's immigrant workers and their families, with special emphasis on the influences of the anti-Communist Catholic Church. Chapter 5 documents the seemingly endless clash of ideologies between Local 480 and the forces of anti-Communism, including the churches, national unions, the predominantly Protestant CCF, and the CM&S itself. Chapter 6 explores the "Red" union purges that the Canadian Congress of Labour (CCL) orchestrated in the post-war period. Chapter 7 discusses the Steelworker raids that threatened to undo Mine-Mill Local 480 and the tactics Local 480 used to fight off the raiding union. The concluding chapter highlights the legacy of the Communist versus anti-Communist struggle that preoccupied the smelter city from the start of the organizing drive through to the Cold War 1950s. The epilogue returns us to Trail and we see the smelter city as it is today.

At the start of this history, Trailites along with everyone else were just emerging from the Great Depression, and some would soon be fighting in the bloodiest conflict the world had ever seen. It is a story of high passions, fierce verbal and written combat, and the occasional fist-fight. It is also the story of a class war that pitted workers against each other. For some Trailites it was also an ethnic war where immigrants fought nativism and discrimination. For still others, it was the story of a gender war in which many of the women of Trail sought a better, fairer world.

What follows is the portrayal of how trade unionism was revived in Trail after twenty years of employer-controlled worker committees, and shows that the working-class consciousness that existed from the building of the first Trail smelter in 1895 was instrumental in that revival. In *Smelter Wars* we find a detailed account of the battles that took place as the revival grew. These wars were not fought with bombs and bullets, but rather were driven by competing ideologies. They were wars fought on radio, in the pages of newspapers, and in the meeting rooms where Trail's future would be debated. Either side's proponents were armed with rhetoric that filled speeches, newspaper articles, radio broadcasts, and submissions to government commissions, labour relations boards, and occasionally the courts.

There were casualties in these wars, but not in the normal sense. Workers died in hazardous workplaces. Children were subjected to massive amounts of lead in the soil and water. Farmers lost crops. Family members found themselves on opposite sides of the ideological divide. These tragedies were the collateral damage of almost twenty years of clashes between the CM&S and Mine-Mill Local 480, between local institutions, political parties, and workers themselves. *Smelter Wars* tells this story with the intent of exploring the roles of ordinary people in shaping that future. It offers a view of the social, economic, and political battlegrounds that came to preoccupy the smelter city, even as it was enduring the hardships of the period. To give social context to the smelter wars, we visit Trail's cinemas, sports arenas, theatres, city hall meetings, Labour Day Picnics, and sometimes witness beer parlour brawls. The views of Trailites themselves are intermingled with those of historians, politicians, and journalists. Previous conclusions are applied and tested here. Views about the role of immigrants are critically examined, as are those about women and their role in society and the union. Union policies are questioned and sometimes found wanting. Corporate decisions also come under scrutiny.

Trail, and the vast smelter that still dominates its skyline today, was once the battlefield for those wars. They occurred in fraternal societies, social clubs, and churches, at union meetings, and most vociferously in the *Trail Daily Times* and its union protagonists, the *Commentator* and the *B.C. District Union News*. A glimpse of the smelter city today shows little sign that it was such a battlefield. What is revealed is a sleepy mountain town whose history as a mining and smelting community is tucked away in library archives, mining journals, local newspapers like the *Trail Creek News* noted above, and the memories of a few old-timers. With the help of those memories, the years of confrontation between a trade union once led by Communists and a powerful industrial empire take shape here.

Visitors to modern-day Trail – a tranquil, sports-loving, church-going community of about eight thousand – founded on the rich mining resources of the late nineteenth century, might ask how it became the scene of the raucous trade union battles that are recalled in the pages to come. More questions will arise about the history of this relatively obscure corner of North America whose lead and zinc smelter was once considered the largest in the world. Some of the answers hopefully will be revealed here. Others will remain as locked in the past as the carefully constructed old stone walls that are still to be found in Trail. Nevertheless, in the pages ahead, we probe for explanations for why and how the smelter wars occurred and to understand the changes they foreshadowed.

A Handful of Determined Activists Faced Divided Loyalties

More than a hundred years after young Selwyn Blaylock stepped off that CPR train at Trail Creek Landing, his legacy and that of Local 480 continue to resonate as part of the smelter city's vibrant history. As we will see, Local 480's battles left their small mark on labour history, and it is a reminder that labour's struggle in Trail and elsewhere is a celebration of the capacity of working people – with a handful of determined activists in the lead – to sustain themselves despite the odds. In the smelter city, the fight tested the long-gestating working-class political roots of Trail workers for the first time in a quarter century. In the aftermath, Trail's working-class identity would be further transformed, and smelter workers would continue to shape the distinctive social fabric of the small city in the BC interior. The clashes resulting from conflicting values and ideologies – from divided loyalties – would mould the community's future, influencing local businesses, civic politics, churches, ethnic associations, working-class cultural institutions, and family life. The union's response to changing economic, cultural, social, and environmental circumstances would have an impact on Trail and surrounding environs far beyond the years covered here.

In recounting this story, *Smelter Wars* tries to present a balance of views and information about the company and other institutional participants, but the book knowingly features a bias toward a democratic labour movement, one that is open to a diversity of progressive ideas, regardless of their source. That does not mean avoiding Local 480's mistakes and misjudgments. However, in the interest of fully declaring a bias, *Smelter Wars* is wholly in sympathy with the working people who built Trail and helped it to thrive. Sympathy of historians who are tasked to be fair and accurate is a much-debated issue, but as Bryan D. Palmer has suggested, "It is this sympathy that enables the social historian to grasp the impor-tance of cultural continuities in the midst of economic transforma-tion, to glimpse the tenacity of common people struggling against increasingly harsh realities."[30] What follows was written in this same spirit.

Now, rewinding to 1938, we begin our journey into how that history unfolded and what it wrought.

1

A Red Union Comes to Town

When Arthur H. "Slim" Evans drove his union-supplied vehicle into the secluded citadel of the powerful Consolidated Mining and Smelting Company of Canada (CM&S) in the autumn of 1938, he might have been forgiven for thinking that he had been sent on a fool's errand endorsed by the Communist Party of Canada (CPC).[1] His assignment grew out of a June trade union conference in Vancouver, where delegates instructed him to organize the miners and smelter workers of the province into locals of the International Union of Mine, Mill and Smelter Workers (Mine-Mill), an affiliate of the Congress of Industrial Organizations (CIO). His first mission, as reported in the *Union Bulletin*, the newly founded official organ of Mine-Mill Local 289 in Vancouver, was to establish Mine-Mill Local 480 at Trail.[2]

Evans was a good choice. He had a solid organizing background. Three years earlier he had led the famous On to Ottawa Trek to protest Conservative Prime Minister R.B. Bennett's treatment of unemployed workers in relief camps.[3] Before that he was jailed for his role in organizing a miners' strike in Princeton, BC, where the local Ku Klux Klan threatened to drive him out of town.[4] As a younger man, he had been involved in labour disputes, some of them violent. Now he would need all his skills to persuade about five thousand workers at the CM&S lead, zinc, and fertilizer smelter to join what many claimed was a Communist union.

At least two others – Ora L. Wilson, a Mine-Mill organizer from Spokane, Washington, and George Price, an organizer with Local 289 – had come before him.[5] But Trail was "virtually impenetrable for union organizers in the 1930s."[6] In fact, although socialist Albert "Ginger" Goodwin had strengthened the smelter's Mine-Mill Local 105, active but not militant since the early 1900s, the failure of the 1917 strike for a shorter workday led to a long dormancy of union activism in Trail.[7] That bitter dispute persuaded CM&S President S.G. Blaylock to form his company union, the Workmen's Co-operative Committee (WCC), in an effort to avoid any future strike threats. As we will see in the next chapter, the WCC would remain the smelter workers' illegitimate bargaining agent for the next twenty-five years and become a highly manipulative labour-management tool for Blaylock. Evans called on Trailites to reject the company union and to support Local 480, warning in the *Union Bulletin*, "The operators must face the fact that they cannot forever suppress the growing demand for collective bargaining and job security."[8] The call resonated loudly with some workers, but not with many others. Ultimately, it was the opening battle cry in a series of smelter wars that would change the history of the small interior city over the next seventeen years.

Trail in the late 1930s was somewhat insulated from the worst of the Great Depression. But while it might have escaped some of the severest wartime troubles, as Jeffrey Keshen explains, elsewhere in Canada there were some undesirable and even shameless responses to wartime rationing, restrictions, and higher taxation. In some communities, he writes, the "rapidly accelerating demands of the war created much criticism and many Canadians appeared unwilling to make needed sacrifices." He adds, "Perceptions of crumbling social structure" surfaced with signs of increased prostitution, exploitive attempts to make windfall profits, juvenile delinquency, and evidence of "excessive cheating."[9] Graham Broad further notes that "petty politics, regional tensions, self-interest and greed, skepticism, and outright cynicism existed side by side with genuine patriotic self-sacrifice in wartime Canada."[10] Trail's wartime consumer experience included some of these extremes. Trailites also read wartime advertisements that "encourage patriotic shoppers

to part with their paycheques – ads whose essential message was
that buying, under the correct circumstances, was neither wasteful
nor unpatriotic but a meaningful contribution to the war effort,
at times even a sacrifice that consumers made for freedom." But
as Broad stresses, "Local and temporary shortages, brought on by
panic buying or delayed deliveries ... became an everyday fact of
life" that included Trail families.[11]

No Patience for "Communist Agitators"

Even so, "by the standards of the day, we were well paid," recalled
former Local 480 President Al King in his memoir *Red Bait!*[12] He
started work at the smelter as a labourer in 1937 and remembers
that benefits included a company dairy, a pension plan, a mortgage
program, a subsidized coal-buying system, a garden-allotment
program, and a family health plan. "In 1937, a job at the Trail
smelter instantly elevated your status from deprivation to one of
relative economic security," King wrote.[13] The *Trail Daily Times*
agreed. It focused on the good fortune of Trail workers, thanked
the company for its generosity, and had no patience for "Communist agitators" like Evans.[14] As early as winter 1934–5, *Times* editor
William Curran had printed warnings of the arrival of "Red agitators," often supplemented with tirades about them roaming the
nation "preaching Communism without hindrance."[15]

Under Blaylock, the company had maintained a high profit
level, even through the worst of the Depression. But it did so at the
expense of its workers, according to David Michael Roth, who cites
record company profits in 1937. And "while earnings 'corrected'
somewhat the following year," he added, "profits still remained
solid."[16] As one Trail city councillor told the *Times*, Trail was "sitting atop of the world," and the increasing need for smelted metals
and fertilizer promised to keep it that way.[17] So impressed was one
visitor that he told the newly formed Trail Canadian Club that the
smelter was like "the wonders of the world," and he likened the vast
smelter to the Pyramids of Egypt.[18]

Meanwhile, as if by comparison, the newspaper regularly
reported on rising tensions worldwide. Benito Mussolini's fascist

Italian armies occupied Ethiopia and threatened Libya in North Africa. Such reports of Il Duce's aggressive actions gave Trail's large Italian population pause to consider their plight. General Francisco Franco continued to drive his fascist forces deeper into Republican Spain with aid from Adolf Hitler, leading some Trailites to contribute financially to the largely Communist contingent of Canadian volunteers called the Mackenzie-Papineau Battalion (Mac-Paps).[19] In another Second World War warm-up act, this one well hidden on the other side of the world, Japan bombarded Chinese cities in its undeclared aggression against Chiang Kai-shek, including the unspeakable atrocities committed during what became known as the Rape of Nanking. The city once served as the ancient Chinese capital. These events spurred University of British Columbia professor F.H. Soward to suggest that the world war had already begun. Clearly, fascism and Nazism were on the march across Europe and Asia, and across the front page of the *Times*.[20]

Despite these faraway concerns, smelter workers and their families enjoyed some distractions from the Depression. In the smelter city, that meant hockey for many of the men and some of the women. Trail had been a big hockey town as far back as the late 1890s, when Butte copper king F. Augustus Heinze built the first smelter on the banks of the Columbia River, and the sport enjoyed community as well as company support. The Smokies won the national Allan Cup in 1938, establishing them as a sports leader throughout Canada. As the *Times* effusively reported, "Men working on shift at night drove cars equipped with radios into the plants beside the humming wheels of industry to follow closely the triumphant march of the Smelter City puckmen." These "dashing gentlemen of the steel blades" won the right to represent Canada in the World Amateur Hockey Championships in 1939.[21]

If Evans had been a hockey fan in 1938, he might have spurned the game for distracting workers from fighting for their rights. But still other distractions hindered his efforts. For example, the Liberty and Rialto Theatres featured the films of Hollywood stars like Joan Blondell, Spencer Tracy, Errol Flynn, Melvyn Douglas, and funny man Jimmy Durante. A promised third "moving picture palace" called the Strand would soon offer three shows a week to smelter families, including features like Walt Disney's *Snow White and the Seven Dwarfs*. The vaudeville comedy team of Laurel and Hardy appeared in *Swiss Miss*, Fred McMurray got top billing for *Coconut Grove*, dubbed "the best musical of 1938," Shirley Temple was *Rebecca of Sunnybrook Farm*, and Tyrone Power appeared with Don Ameche in Irving Berlin's *Alexander's Ragtime Band*. Major Hoople was the main attraction of the daily *Our Boarding House* cartoon in the *Times*, and the lives of the Dionne Quintuplets regularly appeared in the news and social pages. On *Night Shift*, a popular Canadian Broadcasting Corporation radio show, Trail listeners could hear the smelter's zinc refinery described in detail.[22]

Lest these distractions lull smelter families into complacency regarding the Depression, Blaylock regularly lectured Trailites on the profligate spending habits of Canadians. At Canadian Club meetings, reported in the *Times*, he called on governments to tighten their belts, chastised corporate managers, and criticized BC Labour Minister George Pearson for meddling in business affairs.[23] He also admonished Prime Minister William Lyon Mackenzie King for his Liberal government's "orgy of public expenditure." He advocated "a relatively small tax on the larger number," proposing that this would be "more equitable." However, he did not consider a higher tax on the wealthy few, a proposal that would soon be coming from Evans and Local 480. "I am not a pessimist, an alarmist, or a politician," Blaylock stressed, "but a Canadian who has no axe to grind unless to clear away obstructions which might wreck Canadian progress."[24] His self-assessment in the *Times* struck home for one prominent listener. "I long for the day when S.G. Blaylock stands at the head of this country," the Reverend Dr. J.S. Henderson, grand master of the BC Freemasons, told the daily.[25] The *Times* also aligned itself with Blaylock on the question of obstructions, issuing increasingly shrill warnings about threats to the free-enterprise system, especially from Communism.

Locals Steal CIO Organizer's Truck, Burn It

A few Trail workers, some of them Communists, joined Evans to begin the work of building a union base. Soon, however, they ran into trouble. A gang of hooligans stole Evans's truck, set it ablaze, and ran it into a ravine at nearby Stoney Creek. The *Times* reported no arrests, but "there was no doubt in Evans's mind that it was a joint company-police operation." He filed a complaint with BC Attorney General Gordon S. Wismer, but the court dismissed the charges.[26] Meanwhile, Evans sought legal permission to carry a gun as a "protective measure," and he declared that "a small Fascist group in Trail" was out to get him. He also told the *Times* that he was asking Wismer to assign special investigators to deal with his case.[27] In the wake of these allegations, Blaylock, perhaps sensing that Evans could make inroads into his workforce, warned smelter workers against joining a union.

In his 1938 year-end message, the CM&S managing director would also announce a Christmas bonus of fifty dollars for married employees and the usual free turkey. Single men would get thirty-five dollars and a two-dollar voucher for the Company Store.[28] Blaylock also boasted that the company had hired more employees in Trail than ever before, a total of 4,290. He further explained that even with the recent layoffs – about 150, with at least 100 more to come – "the force will be higher than the average of any previous year." He ended with the hope that in the coming year "conditions will not be any worse."[29] He had good reason for his optimism. Depression misery was slowly abating, profits were up, and a metal-hungry European war was on the horizon, as regularly predicted in the *Times*.

Evans knew he must counter the rosy picture Blaylock and others had painted of the smelter city if he was to revive interest in a union at the Trail smelter. With Blaylock on the offensive and anti-Communism seething inside the national labour movement, he had one albeit weak legal advantage: BC's 1937 Industrial Conciliation and Arbitration Act (ICA). With its miniscule fines for non-compliance, employers like Blaylock were not bound to either recognize or bargain with a trade union, but it was enough to give Evans a slight edge. Yes, his job would have been easier had the ICA been stronger, and he would have been aided immensely by Canada's first national labour code, Order-in-Council PC1003, which eventually legalized unions' right to collective bargaining.

Unfortunately for him, that law was still years away. He would have to rely on his faith in radical CIO tradition and the tendency, as Nelson Lichtenstein described it, "to create and sustain a sense of common identity among the membership and transform the union into a close-knit working-class political community."[30] That sense fuelled the organizing efforts of Evans and other Communist trade unionists north of the border, especially in BC and most especially in the East and West Kootenays, where many American workers had been crisscrossing the international boundary since gold, silver, copper, and other precious ores were first discovered in the late 1800s.[31]

At the start of 1939, the *Times* reported on "Labor's World-Wide Crusade" to free Tom Mooney in the United States.[32] Unionists everywhere cheered the left-wing labour leader's release from a California prison after more than two decades for a murder he did not commit. On tasting freedom, Mooney pledged to devote the rest of his life to union organizing. The news encouraged Evans and the men he had recruited to help organize Local 480, but the effort he had spearheaded the previous autumn to found the union was clearly stalled. The smelter workforce, long non-union, was wary of Evans, Mine-Mill, and the CIO. News reports of impending war in Europe further exacerbated their wariness about what the future might hold. Although Blaylock had been more cautious in his year-end statement the previous week, there were still predictions of a good year ahead. Those who made them may have been overlooking the fact that war was a virtual certainty. Perhaps in an effort to reject that reality, Trailites continued to enjoy their usual pastimes.

Trailites Enjoy Sports, Movies as War Threatens

Local radio station CJAT highlighted the NBC comedy show *Fibber McGee and Molly*. Tough guy Jimmy Cagney was *The Oklahoma Kid* at the new Strand. Betty Grable, child star Jackie Cooper, and cowboy Roy Rogers and his horse Trigger also made frequent appearances on Trail's silver screens. The Trail cricket team was a summer alternative to the Smoke Eaters. Cricket was a symbol of home for the many smelter workers who had migrated from the British Isles or other parts of the British Empire. *Times* readers could follow the exploits of Becky Gibson in "The Runaway," the latest serialized story by American author Kathleen Norris, a devout Catholic. *Alley Oop* was among the popular cartoon strips of the day. Homemakers were pleased to learn that a new Co-op Meat Market would soon open with pot roast at fifteen cents a pound, eggs at thirty cents a dozen, and butter at eighty-nine cents for three pounds.

Times readers mourned the death of former CM&S President James J. Warren, who had taken the helm as smelter general manager during the First World War, heavily relying on Blaylock to oversee daily plant operations. Under Warren, Blaylock crushed the 1917 strike, discussed elsewhere. The Doukhobors, a local sect of Russian immigrants described in a later chapter, prayed for the soul of their spiritual leader Peter "Purger" Verigin. And Trailites decried the death of yet another smelter worker in a workplace explosion. For Evans, the fatality was reason enough to press on with his organizing drive. *Times* editor Curran remained confident that he was winning the war to stop the union, but Evans soon raised the editor's ire by calling Blaylock and his company allies "a greedy minority" with "an unquenchable appetite for dividends." He added, "You are paid fat salaries, you perform your ornery duties zestfully regardless of the injustice of or ill effects those duties are to others." Was he referencing the fatality? In the "open letter," he chided Blaylock for his "friendly little chats, [that] skilfully put over company desires." He then delivered a potential knockout punch: "You have your 'stooges' who, like 'Judas Iscariot,' keep you well informed."[33]

On 14 May, a Sunday, some of Blaylock's loyalists attended a gathering of smelter workers at the city's Butler Park, where Evans planned to explain "the program and policy of the union," as he told Mayor E.L. Groutage. The mayor granted permission to hold the event, then returned to preparations for the royal visit of King George VI and Queen Elizabeth.[34] In a letter to Blaylock days before the Butler Park rally, Evans told the CM&S manager that the employees are "deciding in greater numbers each day to become members of Mine-Mill," and he proposed setting up a meeting to lay "the basis for future peaceful negotiations and amicable relationships." Blaylock waited ten days to respond, then wrote, "I have read most issues of your 'Commentator' and 'Union Bulletin' and through them I am forced to the conclusion that no useful purpose could be served by interviews or correspondence with you."[35]

Perhaps the brisk dismissal added fire to Evans's mission when he addressed up to two thousand workers at Butler Park, for he struck squarely at all the sore spots in Blaylock's cooperative labour-management program. First he charged that the CM&S "made an annual profit of $256,000" on its in-house pension plan. Then he moved on to other payroll issues, claiming, for example, that deductions for medical and hospital treatment were unjustified. Though a labourer was said to be paid $4.91 a day, he argued, these deductions meant he received far less. "If I were an ex-member of the CM&S Co.," he told the crowd, "I'd sue the Company for back wages." Evans also praised the CIO, arguing that strikes were "a last resort," and he lashed out at capitalism in general with particular emphasis on the "50 big shots" who control the "country's industries and the press." The charge of "Red" has been hurled at the CIO, Evans said, but if "the work and program of the union was 'Red,' then I'm a 'Red' and I'm proud of it." Evans said he planned to stay in Trail until a union was formed. "Fullest democracy would reign under unionism," he added. "Wages would be raised, working conditions improved, and hours of work reduced. Seniority rights, too, would be recognized." Then Evans told the crowd, "Lacking economic power, workers are powerless in the face of corporations." He ended his speech saying that he "saw a new day dawning for local workers."[36]

The CIO organizer probably did not know it at the time, but this was to be his swansong speech. Not long after the park rally, Corporal Gordon Lennox arrested him for "proceeding along Columbia Avenue ... under the influence of liquor." The *Times* reported that Constable W. McCulloch had asked Evans to turn his vehicle around because of heavy crowds attending a Saturday night band concert. "In turning, Evans struck the rear fender of another car at the curb and Corporal Lennox took him to the police station."[37]

Evans spent a restless night in jail, making such a racket that the police officer in charge and the firefighters upstairs were happy when some of the union members arrived to calm the prisoner down. But "Art insisted on raising hell," according to Gar Belanger, another Communist and Local 480's first president.[38] After being arraigned, Evans was granted a temporary adjournment. At the subsequent trial in mid-June, Evans opted to defend himself, but he was no match for prosecuting counsel Eric Dawson. After hearing more than a dozen witnesses, Magistrate R.E. Plewman found Evans guilty and, when he failed to appeal the decision, sentenced him to seven days in jail.[39]

CIO Organizer Goes to Jail, Leaves Town

The guilty verdict surely undermined Evans's effectiveness as a CIO organizer and vocal Blaylock critic. By Dominion Day, 1 July, he had resigned, stating his reason as "continuing ill health."[40] Perhaps Evans's old union battle injuries were acting up. Perhaps he was running out of steam, given the intense pace of his activities over the previous nine months, although most who knew him would have rejected those reasons. He may also have worn out his usefulness by capturing so much public attention through his vitriolic attacks in the *Times*. The drunk-driving verdict was the final straw. It was no secret that Evans liked to drink with the workers, and he may have found some comfort in the many hotel beer parlours of the Trail-Rossland area. Perhaps it was a way of releasing some of the tensions of leading such a difficult drive. One observer saw the arrest as "an act of harassment aimed at interfering with his [Evans's] organizing work and at destroying his credibility."[41] In any event, the circumstances led to him leaving town, and after being chastised by even the CPC, his days of organizing a Mine-Mill local in Trail were over.

Blaylock, no doubt pleased at Evans's departure, announced that there would be no more layoffs in addition to the 580 that had already occurred since October 1938. He now calculated that the total smelter workforce had been reduced to 3,708.[42] The announcement, wrote editor Curran, should "quiet the wagging tongues of those pessimists and rumor mongers who, without founding of fact, have aroused undue fear in the minds of many with their false statements."[43] Undoubtedly, this was a reference to Evans and perhaps a more direct one to his band of fellow Reds at Local 480. The absence of such a well-known Communist organizer as Evans might have given Blaylock reason to think the workers of Trail would return to complacency. Now he had finally reached the pinnacle of his career, and he was more convinced than ever that his company union, the Workmen's Co-operative Committee, was the best way to maintain Trail smelter workers as an obedient workforce. But Local 480 was not dead yet.

With Evans out of the picture, a local machinist named John McPeake took over as leader of the drive. McPeake had worked on the Hill for three years, and the *Commentator*, the newspaper Local 480 founded in late 1938, considered him "a capable and brilliant" leader. But the paper warned that smelter workers should not expect him to be a "Houdini" who could say "Presto" and create a union.[44] Still, with McPeake at the helm, the battle to form a union carried on with Blaylock allowing his WCC loyalists to do most of the Red baiting. By then the civil war in Spain had been lost to Franco's fascists, Hitler and Mussolini had retooled for world war, and young Trail workers were clamouring to enlist for overseas combat duty. Blaylock, who would become the city's biggest Allied booster, was getting set to make record war-time profits on metals, such as lead and zinc, and other materials used in munitions production. These included fertilizer needed to assure accelerated food growth to meet soldiers' needs, as well as being used in bomb production.

Meanwhile, Trail's political environment was about to feel the heat generated by the smelter war Evans had instigated. While still much would remain mysterious about the CIO's main obstacles in Trail, McPeake and other organizers knew well the kind of community Blaylock had admired in other towns around North America. What founding fathers Eugene Topping, Frank Hanna, Fritz Heinze, and other fortune-seekers had put in place were the corporate foundations of a phenomenon called the company town.

As Jean Barman has noted, "Through the inter-war years company towns would remain worlds unto themselves, their circumstances reflecting the deference of the provincial government towards capitalism in its various guises."[45] The smelter city, although not by strict definition a company town, still exhibited many of those same characteristics.

As McPeake and the Local 480 organizers pondered how they might prepare for the next phase of their smelter war with Blaylock, British Prime Minister Neville Chamberlain announced that his country was at war with Germany. The *Times* devoted its front page to Hitler's destruction in Poland and Stalin's in Finland. Inside, the daily linked Communism to fascism and Nazism and reiterated the charge that the CIO was a Communist organization. Local enlistments to the 109th Field Battery had started to create staff shortages at local businesses, and Trailites began to experience the "jitters" that Blaylock had earlier warned them against. Yet perhaps there was cause to be jittery. Veterans of the First World War, among them veteran James Melvin, warned that there were "Nazis in Trail" and that they needed to be carefully watched.[46]

On 10 September, Canada declared war on Germany and Trail city council immediately ordered more guards posted at water reservoirs and pipelines.[47] The Mackenzie King government set a wartime budget of $100 million. Editor Curran now expressed concern over war profiteering. "Just as 'our boys' must sacrifice their lives in the front lines of battle," he wrote, "so must those who stay behind be prepared to accept the sacrifice of the pocket book."[48] Blaylock predicted that there would be "no profiteering" and offered this view: "One of the most annoying things to a soldier was the thought that while he was at war the man at home was 'robbing the roost.'" He also reminded members of the Smelter Social Club that "every dollar of excess profit 'comes out of the taxpayers' jeans – yours and mine.'" Characteristically, Blaylock provided fiduciary evidence. For the First World War, the company had produced about 500 tons of zinc a day. In 1939, production had reached 3,000 tons daily.[49] He assured smelter employees that their jobs were safe and would be waiting for them when they returned from the war. "It is natural that men wishing to join the army should want to know as much as possible about their future employment," the *Times* reported.[50] Once again the CM&S president had earned the loyalty of Trail's smelter workforce, potentially further undermining the union drive as it contended with the loss of Evans.

By autumn 1939, the Mine-Mill position against the war had grown complicated with the signing of the Nazi-Soviet non-aggression pact, the two-year deal that sowed confusion in Red ranks everywhere. Local 480 declared its full support in the fight to defeat fascism. However, the support came with a proviso: "Canadian labor in giving its wholehearted support to the war against Hitler Fascism also demands the conscription of wealth before the conscription of manpower and the complete elimination of profiteering on the war by individuals and Corporations."[51] The war would also sow confusion among Trail's Italian Catholic population, which was regularly reminded of the horrors of Communism and fascism, "the two great enemies of Christendom," according to the *Times*.[52] Trailites were also frequently warned to beware the CIO's "Communistic drive" in BC. Strikes in the mining industry, particularly Pioneer Mines in Bralorne, a gold-mining community near Lillooet, had provided the *Times* with another reason to condemn the union as being strike prone.[53]

In his first wartime year-end message, Blaylock told Trailites that they had "a lot to be happy about." He once again focused on his theme of "keeping down profiteering" and "intensifying our agricultural and industrial activity to the greatest possible extent." He looked to the future when "a great influx of immigrants" would arrive in Canada after hostilities ended.[54] One immigrant, a Yugoslavian named Danielo Dosen, was part of an earlier influx, but he was not the type of immigrant Blaylock meant. He had sworn his allegiance to Canada a few weeks after the war began, but his allegiance to Blaylock would soon be tested.[55] While some immigrant workers on the Hill were weighing the decision to also swear allegiance to the union, Dosen felt no hesitation in doing so. The charter member of Local 480 was a sworn member of the Communist

Party and a strong believer in trade unionism. Still, persuading the other immigrant workers to follow his lead posed a complex problem for the Red union's organizers.

Dollar-a-Day Wage Demand Spurned

As the war escalated in 1940, Trail families were grateful not to have seen any war dead or wounded at that early point in the hostilities. They might also have been buoyed by the fact that the company's wartime profits were on the rise. Blaylock seemed confident that the loyalty of a predominantly immigrant work force was assured. McPeake visited smelter plants trying to convince a divided workforce that forming a Mine-Mill local was in their best interest. Though he was no Evans, he bombarded Blaylock with demands for a fifty-cent wage increase.[56] Meanwhile, Trailites learned that there could be traitors among them, when police arrested three people in an alleged sabotage plan at the smelter. Three "enemy aliens" had been arrested at Nelson, BC, after police seized correspondence disclosing the plot planned for Christmas Day 1939.[57] The *New York Times* reported the plan to "wreck the biggest smelter of its kind in the British Empire." The *Ottawa Journal* wrote of "Nazi chemists caught red-handed in nefarious aims" that "disclose a web of Nazi intrigue and dastardly espionage."[58] A *Times* letter signed "Vigilant" demanded that "strict military guards" be posted at "important national points" to ensure the "fullest support of our boys in uniform."[59]

Though home-front spirits were increasingly shaken, Trailites could still soften the barrage of bad news with a night out at the Strand, where Greta Garbo starred in her Oscar-nominated role as Ninotchka, a Russian woman who undermines Stalin's Communist Soviet state. John Howard reprised his role as Bulldog Drummond, the First World War veteran turned gentleman adventurer. And the *Times* published instalments of American mystery writer Helen McCloy's 1938 book *Dance of Death*. Diners at the Bluebird Cafe could enjoy a "Special Sunday Dinner" for sixty cents. The Kline Brothers furniture store was selling five-piece bedroom sets for $69.50. To help defer wartime costs, the company issued 2,043 bonuses to its employees in the form of shares valued at $42.25 for a total of about $91,000.[60]

Smelter workers' hopes were raised when five smeltermen, under the Local 480 banner, drafted and presented the rationale for a dollar-a-day pay raise.[61] At that time, the employees had been working on three-quarter-time, having taken "a cut in their earnings to enable their fellowmen to continue in employment." This reduced household income even more.[62] Blaylock reacted badly to the initiative and expelled four of the drafters from his WCC in what the *Commentator* called "a deliberate and traitorous attempt to scuttle the drive for a wage increase and to smother in the committee all attempts at a zealous prosecution of the smeltermen's rights."[63] When the five-month-old Pioneer miners' strike plodded on in BC's Bridge River Valley, near Lillooet at the confluence of the Fraser and Bridge Rivers, frustrated Local 480 organizers told smelter workers, "If Pioneer is defeated smeltermen may as well put away their hopes for an increase until a greater structure of unionism is built in B.C."[64]

Trailites were advised to be vigilant as the war progressed, but the war news was shattering. Belgium had capitulated, France was falling, and Italy was entering the war as an ally of Nazi Germany. Those announcements increased fear among Trail's Italian families and added force to *Times* warnings that "there are certain persons throughout Canada who would foment uprisings."[65] The "persons" no doubt included McPeake, several Local 480 Reds, and Communist union organizer Harvey Murphy, a person of interest whom police had continued to watch as he appeared at strikes and protests across the country throughout the 1930s and early 1940s.

That May, a police officer reported that Murphy had told a Young Communist League (YCL) gathering in Ontario that the war was "a predatory imperialist war which the workers and common people will pay for." Constable Murray Black further quoted Murphy: "Big financial interests were placing the war burden on the backs of the poor through higher prices, taxes and longer working hours. It was natural for resistance to spring up from factory workers and demands for higher wages to be made."[66] Such statements were among a growing list of reasons the political mainstream and the police had long viewed Murphy as a troublemaker. In future, Blay-lock would find out just how much of a troublemaker he could be.

Kootenay newspaper pioneer William K. "Billy" Esling was campaigning for federal re-election in the spring of 1940. A Con-servative, he had long held the Kootenay West seat. The socialist CCF had nominated H.W. "Bert" Herridge, a Kaslo, BC, farmer who would perennially challenge Esling's political throne. Her-ridge campaigned on an anti-capitalist platform, with the *Times* reporting that he said, "Capitalism could offer the people nothing but wars abroad and poverty at home."[67] Herridge would lose the election and wait until 1945, when Esling retired before winning the federal seat. Perhaps the loss was due partly to a Liberal MLA's charge that the CCF was tied to the Communists.[68]

It would not be long before Herridge and Local 480 joined forces. Meanwhile, CIO founding leader John L. Lewis, who had hired Communists like Evans to rapidly build the CIO in the mid-1930s, now began to weed out those same organizers as he adopted a rigorous anti-Red posture. His actions triggered a similar drive to defang the Communist unions in Canada. As Irving Abella states, leaders like Silby Barrett of the United Mine Workers (UMW), United Steelworkers of America (USWA) leader Charles Millard, and Steelworker lawyer David Lewis, later the federal leader of the New Democratic Party (NDP), "felt that merger with the strongly anti-Communist ACCL [All-Canadian Congress of Labour] would dilute the Communist element which, for three years, had domi-nated CIO activity in Canada."[69]

Trail Says Farewell to Its Smeltermen Soldiers

The federal government assisted their cause with a ban on the CPC and affiliated organizations such as the Canadian Labour Defence League (CLDL), the League for Peace and Democracy (LPD), and the YCL.[70] All had supporters in Trail. On the same day, the *Times* reported that Blaylock was sending twenty-three German employ-ees to Great Slave Lake in the far north "to carry on prospecting work for the company."[71] Trail families, meantime, said a second farewell to soldiers climbing aboard a CPR train to join the BC regiment in Vancouver. The Trail pipe band played "martial Scottish airs and the Veteran's home guard cheered as relatives, friends and well wishers crowded around the coaches, bidding farewell with a final handshake, kiss and embrace," as the *Times* reported.[72] The previous October the Trail-Rossland 109th Field Battery had been recalled to active service. Soon another thirty-four Trail men enlisted, bringing the total to 126 since recruitment began.

A few weeks later, federal Justice Minister Ernest Lapointe called for the arrest of eleven Communists "with a view to preventing these persons from acting in a manner prejudicial to the safety of the public or the safety of the State."[73] Harvey Murphy, still working his way west into BC's Crowsnest Pass region and eventually to Trail, would be apprehended in late 1941, eliminating him temporarily from Blaylock's concerns. Meanwhile, the CM&S president strived to steady the increasingly troubled labour-management situation on the Hill. Going against him were letters from soldiers supporting Local 480's bid for a raise. "While I am in the army fighting against this mad movement which is devastating Europe," wrote C. Lilydale, "I expect that smeltermen remaining in Trail will do what they can in the way of bringing about a more decent Canada and world and particularly in the way of bringing about a better deal for themselves in Trail." Local 480 member Morvin Reid, commenting on the First World War, noted that "last time there were quite a few millionaires made out of the soldiers and the people and it is only concerted action of the people that will stop it." He added that he wholeheartedly supported Local 480.[74]

Also a possible impediment to Blaylock was the previously mentioned merger that year of the ACCL with several smaller unions to form the Canadian Congress of Labour (CCL). The union marriage might have strengthened Local 480's resolve, since the 100,000-member CCL was the CIO counterpart in Canada, and Mine-Mill was an affiliate. But ACCL President Aaron Mosher, who had ruled the union since its founding in 1927, would soon become a vocal Mine-Mill detractor as CCL president.

Regardless of visible wartime stress and strain, an autumn visitor to Trail opined that war abroad had not affected the smelter city's appeal, calling it "picturesque" in spite of its "grim, bare cliffsides." He suggested that it "fills the imagination as being some colossal amphitheatre."[75] The article appeared in the *Times* on the heels of news of another workplace fatality. This time the cause was an explosion and fire at one of the smelter plants. A week later, and following Blaylock's rejection of yet another Local 480 demand for a wage increase, a federal Labour Department official told smelter workers there was no point in low wage earners expecting a wage increase. At a gathering at the Knights of Pythias Hall in Rossland, the official supported this contention, telling the *Times* that the "C.M.&S. Co. pays as high for ordinary labor as any industry in Canada."[76] When a WCC questionnaire asked if smelter workers were in favour of a strike, 2,026 said they were against it and 754 were for it.[77] Local 480 had asked its members to boycott the vote, and the union was counting on support from International Mine-Mill Vice-President Reid Robinson. Unfortunately, he was stopped at the border, incensing McPeake, who declared unpatriotic the border's refusal to let him pass. Robinson, also a vice-president of the CIO, was to address a public meeting at the Strand Theatre. Instead McPeake stood alone to berate the authorities for barring the CIO man.

The Battle of Britain came to an end in October 1940, but Nazi bombers continued to pummel London hard, also striking the Midlands. The incessant bombings threatened to interrupt funeral services for former Prime Minister Neville Chamberlain. The prime minister who had once promised "Peace in Our Time" died on 9 November. Events on the labour front at home seemed calmer as smelter city workers awaited their company turkeys, Christmas bonuses, and hockey season.[78] The BC legislature continued to debate implementing a provincial health care insurance scheme.[79] The CCF called for a tax on "monopolistic business, speculative land-holdings and alienated natural resources" as well as other measures to "protect the people of B.C. against the injustices of the profit system."[80] And the company earned a warm tribute from George C. Bateman, the controller of metals for Canada, for "its fine productive effort to assist the empire."[81]

Blaylock's year-end message was a "cheery" one. "In spite of all the trouble in the world," the *Times* reported him saying, "we members of the British Empire have every reason to be cheerful and thankful. Our people have resisted the German onslaught and are slowly but surely turning it back on Germany itself."[82] Neither he nor anyone else could predict that the war would go on for another five years. Renewing the fight for a raise would preoccupy McPeake, who characterized 1940 as "a year of tragedy and disasters, of hardships for labor and attacks upon the organizations and leaders of the working class in many parts of the world." The *Commentator* predicted that 1941 "will probably be the most significant in all history," and it feared that "the Canadian worker, including the Trail smeltermen, will find himself impoverished at the end of the war."[83] That possibility energized the organizing drive, but the union's prediction might also have added to smelter workers' wartime sense of insecurity.

Local 480 Leaders Oppose "Imperialist" War

Throughout 1941, Blaylock pressed his employees ever harder to invest in Victory Loans, the Canadian government's appeal for war funding, and he took umbrage at the popular union slogan "Soak the Rich."[84] Later, he told the Associated Boards of Trade of Southeastern BC that further taxes should not come from "the wealthy men of Canada" who are "already pretty well milked."[85] Instead, "if much more money is required through taxation, it will have to come in the main from the incomes below $15,000."[86] During a six-week swing through eastern Canada, Blaylock conducted a personal survey and found that Canadians "were engaged in luxury and non-essential production who might otherwise be engaged and should be engaged in war work." He told local Rotarians that "every citizen of the country should expect and be prepared to dedicate as much of his or her income to the government as was the case in Great Britain where moderate incomes of $3,000 a year or more were taxed 10s [shillings] on the pound or 50%."[87] Such messages surely grated on McPeake and Local 480 leaders who were calling for a wage increase to pay for essentials during wartime.

As the CM&S president travelled the country with a pro-conscription message, McPeake likened him to "Humpty Dumpty in

Alice in Wonderland" for his proposal "to conscript everyone" and suggested that he "means that the people of this nation should be dragged out by the heels and slammed into the army or industry; there to be enslaved at least for the duration." Indeed, he concluded, "Mr. Blaylock's 'conscription' of 'everyone' means – profits for industry and slavery for the Canadian people."[88] It was near to his last act as leader of the Local 480 drive. By August 1941, he had left Trail to take up duties in Dawson City, Yukon Territory.

At the Trades and Labor Congress (TLC) convention in Calgary in September, delegates called for a "conscription of wealth to the same extent as man-power."[89] They also wanted changes to Defence of Canada Regulations and assurances that Order-in-Council PC 7460, establishing a cost-of-living bonus in industry, would remain in effect. The TLC, Canada's oldest and largest labour body, along with other labour organizations, had long fought against wage controls, and this order at least promised to mitigate what they saw as possible wage losses.

In early October, the war took one of Local 480's most effective organizers when Recording Secretary Gordon Martin resigned to join the Royal Canadian Air Force. On parting, he offered a counter-argument to those that say unions "promote strife and are, therefore, unpatriotic." Men fighting overseas "look to all those they left behind to keep up the struggle to make Canada the kind of country they want to live in," he wrote in the *Commentator*. "And the kind of country they want is one in which the workers have more say and the Blaylocks less."[90]

The Communist leaders of Local 480, once anxious to oppose the war, in keeping with the party view that it was an imperialist war, now fully supported the Allied war effort. The 1939 non-aggression pact signed by Nazi Germany and the Soviet Union had fuelled their opposition, but it was dissolved in June when the Russians faced devastating attacks under Hitler's Operation Barbarossa. Local 480 leaders and others were concerned about the failure of the Allies to open a second front to assist the Soviet Union, now an ally. In mid-October, the *Commentator* noted that there are those "who spend their time debating whether communism is an evil or a blessing, consciously or unconsciously aiding those who support fascism and a fascist victory." The editorial stressed, "Bombs when they drop, KILL and they don't care who they kill."[91]

In November, police arrested Harvey Murphy as he left a downtown Toronto movie theatre. It was perhaps ironic that *Citizen Kane* was showing, given that Blaylock, Murphy's future adversary, had sometimes been compared to Kane, a quintessential capitalist. The Defence of Canada Regulations advisory committee that had jailed Murphy after a vigorous grilling judged him a "danger to the state" who would be "prejudicial to public safety."[92] He entered the Hull internment camp, where he would remain until early September of the following year. He was identified anonymously as "Internee No. H.6."[93] The arrest merited only cursory news coverage next to an impending strike at Mine-Mill Local 240 in Kirkland Lake in Northern Ontario that would change labour relations in Canada. Soon Mine-Mill officials were reporting that all eight mines in the mining region were "at a complete standstill."[94] Late in the month there were rumours of a general strike to support the miners, but these were quickly denied.[95] Local 480 supported the strike, as did many unions and even some church officials. Nevertheless, the strike was eventually lost, but as Laurel Sefton McDowell and others have explained, it led to the adoption of a kind of Canadian Wagner Act, the short name for the New Deal's National Labor Relations Act. Like Wagner, the long-promised Order-in-Council PC1003 seemed to guarantee "the right of collective bargaining" to Canadian workers.[96]

In his 1941 year-end message, Blaylock was less sanguine than in 1940, pressing everyone to "do everything we can to help them win this gigantic struggle."[97] For Trail families, sending their young men and women to fight overseas and possibly die there, the reality of war began to hit home. Escape from that reality was impossible but there was momentary relief at the local theatres where British actor James Stephenson starred in *Shining Victory* at the Rialto. He had appeared two years earlier in the Edward G. Robinson hit *Confessions of a Nazi Spy*. Citizens could dance to the music of the Silvertone Swingsters at the Trail Armouries on Saturday nights, and the Trail Ladies Choir provided a "Quiet Hour of Music" on Sundays at Knox Church.[98] The CM&S Company Store was selling

Corn Flakes two boxes for fourteen cents. Kootenay Breweries Ltd. introduced its "Kootenay Rainbow," claiming that some people "(ladies particularly) prefer a sweeter, milder smoother beer."[99] The *Times* now provided a "Peek at the Week" in which *Times* illustrator Glen Lehman accompanied his cartoons with poetic impressions of political events. For example,

> Adolf should have learned by now
> Bear traps get you anyhow.
> Stooge Benito now is weeping,
> For Libya he'll not be keeping.
> The little men of the rising sun
> Rattled their sabres and picked up the gun.
> Now they are singing a different tune –
> They may back down again very soon.[100]

And for those curious to know what their uncertain future might hold, "Madame Levoi" was reading tea leaves at the Bluebird Cafe.

Smelter Workers to the European Front

No one needed a fortune teller to know that 1942 was likely to breed more of the same, but the New Year also brought some good news. Premier John Hart's new Liberal-Conservative coalition government in Victoria announced a five-dollar increase in old age pensions, raising monthly cheques to twenty-five dollars.[101] Some of that money might go to Victory Loan contributions. As the war wound down, it might also come out of mother's allowance or "baby bonus" cheques that women started receiving under the Mackenzie King government's Family Allowance Act. Regular reports of local soldiers missing or killed in action were starting to appear and, adding to Trailites' concerns, the federal government announced that a plebiscite on expanding conscription was in the offing.[102] If passed, more smelter workers were sure to be sent overseas.

By the end of February, Canadian authorities were seizing "forbidden" possessions from Japanese families in BC. Under a change in the Defence of Canada Regulations, a curfew was imposed, restricting their movements to daytime only, and most severe of all, the regulations now permitted "the removal of all Japanese, men, women and children numbering 24,000 from the protected areas" of BC.[103] Conservative Kootenay West MP William K. Esling called for protection for Trail in the event of a Japanese attack, but none was to come. Local 480 entered the conscription debate that spring with the *Commentator* demanding "labor be recognized as a partner in the war effort."[104] A letter from membership "Card 10" argued, "Canadian industrialists, in making more profits[,] have increased the exploitation of Canadian workers while refusing their democratic rights."[105]

Founding CCF leader J.S. Woodsworth died in March, still adamantly holding to his pacifist principles while his party chose another course. American labour radical Tom Mooney also died. Mackenzie King introduced his new National Selective Service program in April "to record the movement of labour" and to "move the people to the work or the work to the people."[106] The *Times* considered that "the duty of labor in this emergency is plain. An Axis victory would be the greatest calamity that has befallen the working classes of the world."[107] Mine-Mill's McPeake, back from his northern assignment, told a poorly attended rally at the high school auditorium that organized labour would support conscription. The former Local 480 organizer spoke of "those brave men who had died at Dunkerque [*sic*], Norway, Crete and the Philippines, of the heroic fight put up by the Chinese and the Russians." He declared that these events were what motivated him to vote yes.[108] When the 27 April "plebiscite vote was counted, West Kootenay citizens favoured the 'Yes' side by 10,364 to 3,653."[109]

Soon Blaylock would begin hiring women to replace soldiers, joining other employers who were doing so across Canada, as detailed elsewhere. He would no doubt also encourage his new female employees to contribute to Victory Loans, despite paying them at 80 per cent of the male salary rate. In August, the *Commentator* applauded a parliamentary committee recommendation to "legalize all anti-fascist organizations," and Local 480 passed a resolution calling for the release of interned anti-fascists, including

J.B. Salsberg, the Communist Party's Ontario labour organizer.[110] Murphy was not named, however, suggesting that he was still unknown to Trailites. But that would soon change.

Trail celebrated its fourth wartime Labour Day with some hope of what the *Times* called a "brightened domestic labor front."[111] CCL President Mosher spoke of labour's commitment to the war effort and called for further sacrifices from workers. "Not a single day's production of war materials should be lost through any action on the part of workers," he told the CCL's annual convention.[112] Elliott M. Little, director of the National Selective Service program, reminded delegates of the massive need for more workers in war industries, the importance of less "sniping and hostility between management and labor," and the necessity of reducing "our civilian standard of living to the bare minimum."[113] In a rousing statement reported in the *Times*, federal Labour Minister Humphrey Mitchell called on workers to "think of your fellow workers in the navy, the army and the air force, ready to lay down their lives that our country shall be free. They depend on you to give them the tools of war."[114]

The American Federation of Labor (AFL) held its sixty-second annual convention in Toronto, where delegates heard Prime Minister Mackenzie King reiterate a familiar theme as he spoke of the role of labour in a post-war world: "A new order must be based on faith leading to co-operation between the parties in industry."[115] Even Mitchell Hepburn, Ontario's notoriously anti-labour premier, told the AFL that he would introduce compulsory collective bargaining. Later, the archbishop of Canterbury preached cooperation in the rebuilding of a post-war world. A long-time leftist supporter, the primate had often "urged the rank and file toward a goal of partnership in industries in which they serve and has called for limitation of the profits of capital."[116] There was also a hue and cry in October for the release of Communist leaders, and federal Justice Minister Louis St. Laurent seemed to hear the protests, for he ordered the release of the sixteen detained Reds. A third Victory Loan subscription drive brought a CM&S pledge of $5 million, with Trailites pledging $372,900.[117]

In November, Local 480 again led the charge in support of a second front in Europe. "Only with blood can we Canadians and

Americans write the tribute we owe the Soviet people," the *Commentator* stated.[118] As winter set in, the local edged closer to its organizing goal when BC Labour Minister George Pearson stated that he was ready to consider amendments to the law compelling employers to bargain with duly elected workers' representatives. The law would also force employers to recognize a bona fide union.[119] Finally there was some light at the end of the organizing tunnel for Local 480. There was also some relief for Italian and German "enemy aliens," who would soon be told that if they were naturalized citizens of Canada before 1922 they would no longer be subject to wartime restrictions. However, Japanese Canadians got no similar Christmas news from the External Affairs Department.

In an earlier than usual Christmas message, Blaylock, who was soon to be elected a director of the CPR, saluted the Canadian war effort and expressed pride in the company's role, revealing that it employed 7,728 men at the end of October and that "1,463 men were wearing his majesty's uniforms."[120] Absent was any discussion of Murphy, who had been released on 9 September 1942 after serving eleven months in a Toronto jail and subsequently at the wartime internment camp in Hull, Quebec. Now he planned to return to the West to continue the organizing work he had started among the hard-rock miners of Alberta and BC. It would not be long before he would arrive in Trail to take up his duties as Local 480's chief negotiator, and when he came he would be well prepared to face the anti-union CM&S and its war-preoccupied president. In 1943, it would become Murphy's war as well and he, like Blaylock, would find himself fighting on at least two fronts.

Local 480's Organizing Drive Stalled

Months before Murphy arrived in the smelter city, the *Times* reported on the Soviet Union's Red Army and its deadly combat against Hitler's invading forces in January 1943. That winter Japan fought to secure Guadalcanal, and Iraq declared war on the Axis nations, while Royal Air Force fighters engaged in dogfights high above Tunisia. Strikes saw 12,500 Canadian steelworkers crowding onto picket lines in spite of a Labour Ministry ruling that all strikes were illegal. The *Times* railed against the work stoppages: "The steel strike is to be deplored by all who would see the United Nations victorious."[121] The *Commentator* laid the blame for the strikes at the foot of Labour Minister Mitchell and called for his resignation. "No one can deny the wages received by the steelworkers are far below what they should be for such an industry," the union argued. "Those who say the wages should not be raised now, only contribute to the injustice of these conditions, which means that steelworkers cannot give the maximum to increasing production for the war."[122] At the same time came some positive news from the eastern front: the Siege of Leningrad, the brutal Nazi starvation campaign initiated on 21 August 1941, had finally ended.

It was unlikely that Murphy's arrival in Trail would soften the *Times* editorial approach to unions or Communism, but smelter workers might have expected more from the labour movement. In an early signal that Communist unions were in trouble with the CCL, President Mosher suspended the boilermakers' and iron shipbuilders' unions after a report charged that the "outlawed Communist party had 'concentrated their numbers and strategy inside practically all shipyard workers' unions in Vancouver.'" Murphy had once worked at those same shipyards and was active in the union. The CCL also suspended the BC district council of the International Woodworkers of America (IWA).[123] With Murphy and other Local 480 leaders politically close to the IWA leadership of Harold Pritchett, it also could have been viewed as a forewarning of the anti-Communist labour purges to come. Time was running out for Local 480, and by most measures they were losing the smelter wars.

Five years had passed since Slim Evans first brought the CIO to the smelter city and it seemed as if little had changed substantially. There was still no legal union and the voices of anti-Communism were louder than ever. The old WCC had been part of Blaylock's dream, his design for how industry could produce in harmony. In his vision, everyone, from the workers down in the lead furnaces to the business-suited managers in the offices above the Tadanac commissary, would get along like one big happy family. For the Red leaders of Local 480, it was a dream waiting to be dismantled, as the union developed its strategy for the continuation of the smelter wars. Blaylock, however, was not about to succumb to a Communist union and there was still plenty of fight left in the Blaylock loyalists. Even after the BC legislature declared company unions illegal in 1943, WCC leaders would regroup under the banner of a new challenger with Blaylock still in full control. The battle was about to escalate.

2

Battling Blaylock's Company Union

When BC's amended Industrial Conciliation and Arbitration Act (ICA) officially became law in March 1943, Local 480's *Commentator* dubbed it a "'Bill of Rights' for labor" that "will increase war production."[1] Displeased with the act, Blaylock and other mining and smelting employers met with government officials soon after the bill was introduced that February, asking them to protect "what are known as company unions."[2] When his Workmen's Co-operative Committee (WCC) was declared illegal, the CM&S president was so furious he called Premier John Hart to demand "proper leeway in paying the expenses of the Co-operative Committee," and he reminded Hart that "Mr. [George] Pearson [the labour minister] had promised me to take care of our committee situation."[3] The *Commentator* countered the employer group's arguments, saying that such protections "would mean companies could continue to oppose labor's rights – block their efforts to organize and once again precipitate all over again, the struggle of the workers to organize their own unions."[4]

The lobbying attempt failed to end the company's ICA difficulties, but neither did the ICA dictate a ceasefire in the WCC's continuing war against the Mine-Mill local. As David Michael Roth noted in his assessment of the situation, the "new act served as a catalyst, pushing union activism to the forefront in the company town." Still, impediments to legitimizing Local 480 were many and varied. Blaylock saw the danger and had the WCC issue bulletins soon after the ICA amendments were adopted. For the company president, the new labour law had the potential to make it "illegal to accept financial assistance from the company." Nevertheless, he continued to allow the old WCC leaders to meet on company time and company property, which Roth viewed as an additional "element of quiet coercion."[5] In a speedy attempt to circumvent the new law, WCC leaders formed the Independent Smelter Workers' Union (ISWU) to replace the WCC. The new body sent a delegation to Victoria to protest changes that would "prevent the company from dominating, interfering with or financing any worker's organizations." This, the *Commentator* asserted, "shows that they intended not only to sell out the interests of the workers here, but of organized labor elsewhere."[6]

While the WCC fought a hopeless battle for its life, Trail families coped with increasing household shortages, and rationing was enforced as the war against fascism moved through its fourth year. As in the past, some relief from the strain could be had at local cinemas, whose marquees enticed Trailites to see George Sanders in W. Somerset Maugham's *The Moon and Sixpence* at the Rialto, Humphrey Bogart and Ingrid Bergman in *Casablanca*, Basil Rathbone playing Arthur Conan Doyle's super-sleuth Sherlock Holmes, and Grand Forks, BC-born director Edward Dmytryk's *Hitler's Children*, an exposé of Hitler's youth corps. Edward G. Robinson was on the rise as a tough guy star, but Congressman Martin Dies's anti-Communist committee called the actor out as a Red sympathizer. Women had started to replace soldiers the previous summer, and an advertisement in the *Times* noted that Trail's "worker girls" could purchase Dr. Chase's Nerve Food as "a 'pick-me-up' when they are tired, nervous and jittery" as a result of leaving the "comforts of home life to take on work which is both interesting and strenuous."[7] Trailites who turned to liquor to cope with the war were disappointed when the BC government agreed to a 30 per cent cut in the amount of hard liquor that could be purchased.[8] To divert the mind, CJAT radio listeners could tune in to the Ogden Playhouse's version of Charlotte Bronte's *Jane Eyre*, among other radio plays. In the *Times*, they could read the occasional anecdote by celebrated Canadian humourist Stephen Leacock.

Canadians were buoyed that spring by the promise of a minimum income law as recommended by Dr. Leonard C. Marsh. The Marsh Report, as it became known, was commissioned by Mackenzie King and was to be similar to Britain's Beveridge Report, the document that laid the groundwork for a post-war welfare state.[9] Marsh, once president of the League for Social Reconstruction, a key founding policy body for the Co-operative Commonwealth Federation, also proposed social assistance, social insurance, and public welfare programs. Local 480 welcomed these measures and cheered the introduction of draft legislation for a national health insurance bill that would give every Canadian "medical and dental services, hospital care and drugs as necessary at a cost of not more than $26 a year to each adult."[10] Blaylock preferred his private health scheme. Meanwhile in Ottawa, Stanley Knowles, a young Winnipeg parliamentarian, earned applause from Trail smelter workers who read in the *Times* that he stood in the House of Commons to call for "a new attitude toward the workers of Canada."[11] The new CCF member had won the Winnipeg seat vacated by the death of CCF founding leader J.S. Woodsworth the previous March.

On the local political scene, MLA Bert Herridge added new ammunition to Local 480's bid to represent smelter workers when he alleged that the CM&S was involved in a tax evasion scheme. The CCF MLA called for a public inquiry after learning from S.H. Kyle, a former Tadanac municipal clerk, that the CM&S had received an "amazingly conservative assessment for tax purposes."[12] Herridge complained that the company had apparently failed to pay appropriate taxes.[13] Tadanac, incorporated in 1922 as a separate municipality within Trail city limits, served as a *Better Homes & Gardens*-style village for CM&S managers, including a lavish residence for Blaylock to use when he was not staying at the even more palatial Blaylock Mansion near Nelson, BC. The *Times* came to the company's defence with a front-page editorial that recapped the history of happy relations between Trail and Tadanac and tangentially suggested that Herridge's complaint was unwarranted, opportunistic, and a "political smoke screen." The daily further opined, "Attacks on corporations or anything closely allied to big business generally appear to be excellent political ammunition these days."[14]

The passage of the amended ICA and Herridge's exposé provided only a short breathing space before Local 480's anti-Communist detractors began to erect new roadblocks to the local's advance as an affiliate of Mine-Mill. The parent union was still considered one of the most progressive unions in North America, with a constitution that insisted its locals adopt democratic principles and promote equality of race, gender, and the right to choose political beliefs. But it would soon be under sustained attack as a Communist-led organization. As we have seen, Blaylock was among the local's most virulent adversaries, and his chief weapon was the WCC, now in the guise of the ISWU. Indeed, Blaylock and his company union would prove strong anti-union allies in the next skirmishes in the ongoing smelter wars.

A Powerful Corporate Adversary Rallies Its Defences

As CM&S president, Blaylock was a cautious and methodical business executive unlikely to expend company funds before commissioning a thorough scientific research plan. He might risk plunging the CM&S into what Jonathan Levy called the "economic-chance world of capitalism," but he would do so with extreme care and attention to shareholders' interests.[15] Three examples reveal this cautious approach and his canny business sense.

First, he hired R.W. (Ralph) Diamond, who later became a CM&S vice-president, to develop the differential flotation process for extracting zinc from ore shipped to the Trail smelter from the company's Sullivan Mine at Kimberley, BC. During the First World War, CM&S produced large quantities of lead for the Allies, but company scientists struggled to discover how to increase the production of zinc, the metal used in brass shell casings. The success of the Blaylock-Diamond process was widely recognized and would later win Blaylock the James Douglas Medal for Metallurgy from the American Institute of Mining and Metallurgy (AIMM).[16] His second innovation, described in more detail elsewhere, would earn shareholders substantial dividends into the 1930s when he resolved a pollution problem, resulting in a new profit centre.

Such masterstrokes gained him respect but also generated suspicion within the smelter workforce and its would-be union. A third example was of particular interest to Local 480. Long before becoming the company's third general manager, Blaylock had begun building a reputation for innovation in labour-management relations schemes, the centrepiece of which was cooperation in the form of workplace committees such as the WCC.

A few years before he received his AIMM medal, *Saturday Night* magazine in Toronto sang his and the company's praises by describing Trail as "a workingman's paradise" where there was "no talk of strikes" and where "no words of discontent or disloyalty to the Company is [*sic*] heard."[17] The cooperative scheme that Blaylock had advocated and supported financially nevertheless led to lengthy and heated arguments for and against unionization. By the mid-1930s, some smelter workers began to question the validity of calling Trail a paradise and with obvious justification.

They often worked twelve-hour shifts in the lead furnaces, the foundry, sintering plant, zinc processing plant, as well as smaller plants refining other metals and later fertilizers. Some men had trade skills, some were experienced machinists and equipment operators, but others worked on labour gangs shovelling and transporting heavy ore from boxcars to processing plants. They often endured record-breaking heat in summer and below-zero temperatures during West Kootenay winters. Each plant presented different hazards, depending on the metallurgical processes, some of which led to fatalities. While silicosis and lead poisoning were the most deadly workplace diseases, the men also suffered from exposure to intense heat, gasses, and dust.[18] Workers often complained that nothing was done to improve unsafe working conditions.

"There were hazards everywhere," former Local 480 President Al King recalled in describing the smelter workplace of the period. "There were hot metal burns and abrasions caused by furnace eruptions, and smoke and fumes from the furnaces that caused asthma and chest diseases."[19] Accident rates were high and getting higher, but there was no safety committee to question the company's handling of the workplace health and safety situation. In fact, management was often tone deaf. The *Times* once joked that an international conference studying the "menace of silicosis" should also examine the "dusty Kootenay roads" as contributing to the problem.[20] Such flippant remarks seemed a clumsy attempt to excuse the company of responsibility, but union supporters, and especially the Trail families that had endured workplace injuries and deaths, did not appreciate such callous efforts at humour.

Safety hazards and all-too-frequent workplace deaths and injuries only bolstered incentives to pursue unionization. Growing CM&S profits and increased dividends for its shareholders, even during the Depression years, could act as a catalyst for union organizing when workers learned of the company's five-year net profit average of $8.3 million for the late 1930s, $10.5 million over the war years, rising to $33.7 million in the post-war period.[21] Those high profit levels and persistent shortages of household staples might also have coaxed some Trail workers to seek ways to win a fair share of the profits in the form of improved wages and safer working conditions.

In 1938, as noted earlier, Slim Evans, representing Mine-Mill and the CIO, offered them what they were looking for, although not everyone saw it that way. Some workers would embrace the idea of a union, while others shunned it, having denounced the Communists among its leaders. Blaylock and the WCC represented the denouncers, and to some smelter families they offered what seemed a safer option.

Blaylock Stands Strong against the Union

Strictly enterprise-based schemes such as the WCC were thought to present real or imagined alternatives to adversarial trade unionism. WCC leaders were loyal, willing to accept Blaylock's benevolence regarding workers' welfare, and in some cases they were prepared to serve as his frontline anti-Communist agents. To assist them, Blaylock provided funding, paid time off work, meeting space on company property, and open access to the smelter workplace. In return, WCC leaders used anti-Communist rhetoric to discredit Mine-Mill organizers in company-supported publications and in the *Times*. Even before 1938, Blaylock, the WCC, and the *Times* had combined to dissuade workers from joining any union but least of all the CIO-backed, and allegedly Communist-led, Mine-Mill. Now, five years later, regardless of the ICA banning of company unions, the trio of allies were more determined than ever to undermine the still uncertified Local 480 as the smelter workers' legal bargaining agent.

Blaylock initially founded the WCC to ensure labour peace and to improve productivity at the CPR-owned CM&S smelter after what Stanley Scott called the calamitous 1917 strike. The strike failed partly because the parent union withdrew its support, but Blaylock was not taking any chances of a repeat work stoppage. Over the next twenty-five years, his quintessential company union stymied all challenges from discontented members of the smelter workforce. In fact, it was such a notable success that Blaylock boldly counselled other industrial leaders to "stop this warfare between capital and labor and substitute cooperation."[22] He had taken similar advice from other industrialists about how to control workforces, especially those likely to join unions. Though the WCC had his special stamp of approval, his idea shared similarities with schemes such as Britain's Whitley system and the one instituted at the Baltimore and Ohio Railroad Company. In fact, he referenced the Whitley system in a 1920 presidential address on cooperation to the Canadian Institute of Mining and Metallurgy annual meeting in Winnipeg.[23]

Although CM&S historians do not note it, the ideas of Sir Henry Thornton, president of Canadian National Railways (CNR) from 1922 to 1932, also influenced Blaylock. Thornton was the architect of a cooperative system at the publicly owned "People's Railway," and, as Allen Seager explains, the American-born Sir Henry was "a master of the inter-related arts of public and employee relations." He "had few peers" in cultivating such relations, even organizing a radio station to broadcast his ideas from coast to coast as "the hottest gospeller of cooperation."[24] And Blaylock most certainly borrowed from the Colorado Plan developed by future Prime Minister William Lyon Mackenzie King, author of the cooperation-espousing *Industry and Humanity*, a deceptively progressive sounding treatise with its stress on the importance of community spirit and cooperation among the parties to industry – labour, capital, management, and the community.[25] King had recommended the plan to industrialist John D. Rockefeller to mitigate the public relations disaster resulting from the bloody Ludlow Massacre in the coalfields of Colorado on 20 April 1914.[26] (Incidentally, the US National Guard turned a machine gun on Slim Evans while he was supporting the striking coal miners, further adding to his radical mystique.)[27]

Blaylock may also have studied labour relations as practised at the Pullman railway car company, where a much larger workforce of company-loyal African American porters and maids had embraced company unionism in the 1920s. There were similarities between the WCC and the Pullman Porters Benefit Association of America (PPBAA), including the company-controlled grievance process, financing PPBAA administrative costs, and sponsoring its annual conventions. As with WCC members, some Pullman workers saw the PPBAA as a way to be "part of one big family," engendering "a true cooperative spirit."[28] Blaylock also hoped to foster that spirit in his workforce, but like Pullman executives with the PPBAA he was unwilling to share power with his WCC.

The company union dovetailed exquisitely with Blaylock's other schemes to ensure workplace harmony and corporate prosperity in the 1920s and 1930s. These included "employee welfare plans[,] apprenticeships, a housing scheme, including life assurance, pensions, and various other schemes that brought the company prominently to the fore in industrial welfare," as described in local press reports.[29] So successful were the CM&S manager's efforts to maintain a modified company town that a *Saturday Night* magazine article asked why newspapers were not quoting Blaylock instead of the wealthy automaker Henry Ford regarding solutions to society's ills: "Could we not have a few more men like S.G. Blaylock helping to turn each industrial centre into a workingman's paradise?," the writer asked.[30] Within this paradise, Blaylock contended, the company had "established a friendship between the management and the workmen."[31] But there would be no room for a union, no place for friendly relations between organized labour and management, and no prospect of allowing the Red agitators at Mine-Mill to unionize Blaylock's smelter.

In addition to the welfare plans and the relative job security he assured them, Blaylock had earned the WCC's respect and that of many of the workers Local 480 hoped to win over. During the Depression especially, it was thought that CM&S employees were "passed over lightly." Wages were cut, "and working time, for single men, was halved," wrote company historian Lance Whittaker, but in cooperation with the WCC the president ensured that "practically none were laid off."[32] The men also came to respect "Mr. Blaylock," as Trailites still refer to him, for his business acumen. Since before the 1917 strike, smelter workers had observed the then CM&S assistant general manager as he help manoeuvre his company into increasingly profitable situations. Indeed, Blaylock seemed to be an industrialist with a Midas touch. A case in point in the late 1930s involved a charge that the smelter was polluting the environment around the farms of Stevens County near Northport, Washington, where a closed smelter had once been a CM&S competitor.

Company Fined for Polluting Washington Farmland

County farmers and other land owners along the Columbia River had long complained that sulphur dioxide fumes from the Trail smelter destroyed crops, rendered soil unusable, and caused substantial smoke damage. Eventually the International Joint Commission (IJC), formed in 1909 to investigate such cases, concluded that the CM&S owed the farmers $350,000 in damages. It also demanded that the pollution stop, creating concern for the Canadian economy should the smelter shut down. Enter Blaylock, who promised to "end pollution" as soon as proper abating devices were in place. Dissatisfied with the IJC's settlement proposal, the two national governments agreed to arbitration. The resulting tribunal filed its report in 1941, but by then Blaylock had turned "lemons into lemonade" through a process that recaptured the sulphur dioxide and converted it into profitable Elephant Brand fertilizer.[33] Keith A. Murray notes that the company was soon earning "more from the fertilizer and acid recovered from the wastes than it did from its depression-reduced smelting of zinc ores."[34] The case ultimately protected industry but failed to address serious pollution problems. As John Wirth argues, "Consolidated carried the spear for the industry, the managers of which knew each other and acted as a group when fundamental interests were at stake."[35] The ingenuity of Blaylock's solution could not help but impress WCC leaders and smelter workers in general.[36]

As the pollution tribunal's hearings proceeded in the early 1940s, smelter workers continued to hear arguments for and against forming a union, and it seemed that CM&S business successes such as the pollution abatement scheme could only add to the impediments facing union organizers. Why would the workers need a union with such a capable corporate leader at the helm? Were not the workers happy to find a small amount of the ever-growing profits appear in their pay cheques every month? As an early newspaper editor commented, "The descending smelter smoke will come to them as balm to the nostrils."[37] The Trail smelter dispute might also have inadvertently offered an argument in favour of unionization, for it revealed the hazards to which workers and the public were exposed by the failure to curb pollution in and outside the workplace. Communist unionists could point to the willingness of industrial employers to sacrifice workplace and environmental safety for excessive profits. They would also point to government complicity in favour of "protection of a vital economic resource" in spite of the pollution threat.[38]

The smelter fumes case shared headlines with the CIO, which was rapidly gathering support across North America in the late 1930s. The union's surge in popularity prompted the *Times* to redouble its efforts to stop the perceived Communist-inspired invasion of Trail. It launched a crusade against Local 480, regularly publishing articles hostile to the CIO, and warning smelter workers that Communists were behind the new labour organization. Al King scoffed at the *Times* for its "scathing editorials about 'Big Union Bosses'" and attempts to "inflame people against the very idea of the 'little guys' challenging the mighty citadel up the Hill." As far as the Communist King was concerned, and he did not hesitate to say so in his memoir, editor Bill Curran trucked in "real bottom line, capitalist dogma."[39] Other union leaders shared that view, insisting "the press was controlled by big business and deliberately unfair to organized labor."[40]

From the labour standpoint, Curran produced a toxic argument designed to strike the fear of unions into local smelter workers and their families. The number of stories about CIO-led strikes was rivalled only by the tally of anti-Communist articles about the CIO and about Communism in general. All but affirming the *Times*-Blaylock alliance, Elsie Turnbull noted that Curran was a "close friend" of Blaylock, "and as such supported Blay's many projects for community advancement." She added, "Blay saw it as his duty to shoulder responsibility by guiding both company and town through the hard years and he needed the support of competent and trustworthy individuals."[41] Apparently Curran had no qualms about his pro-company role and easily sided with the CM&S president in his use of the WCC to block Local 480. "It is obvious," wrote Curran in a *Times* editorial, "that in S.G. Blaylock ... Canada has one of its most able and socially-minded business executives." As evidence, he pointed to "the handsome benefits granted to laborers in the employ of the company through the forward-looking character of its labor policy."[42]

CM&S plant managers uniformly sided with Blaylock on the company union. His WCC system clearly awed them. It was "one of the most remarkable experiments in industrial labour organization on the North American continent," Lance Whittaker opined.[43] Howard W. Bayley, a forty-four-year veteran of the company, remarked, "There was not a shift lost by strikes and wages and fringe benefits at Cominco were comparable to any union organized company." He credited "Blaylock's strong personality and genuine sincere interest in his work force."[44] WCC leaders also revered Blaylock. "He was a powerful man," recalled William Campbell, the WCC's full-time, company-paid secretary from 1939 until its demise in 1943. "He had unlimited powers," Campbell insisted, and, during his time with the WCC, "we had no actually serious problems. They were all dealt with, as he [Blaylock] said, in a co-operative manner."[45]

Company Union Was "A Cozy Fellowship"

Local 480 activists did not share Campbell's view. They described the WCC as paternalistic, undemocratic, and corrupt. Former Local 480 executive member Les Walker recalled that a committee – there were several under Blaylock's system – was "composed of one man elected from each department on the Hill ... men appointed to the committee promptly quit work; that is, they came to work each day and punched in the clock but they never put their working clothes on." Walker added with chagrin that "they managed to get themselves on various sub-committees, such as fuel, gardening, fertilizer and all that sort of thing."[46] Al King called the WCC "a cozy fellowship" in which the committee members "were too scared to say boo." Blaylock "sat at the head of the table with a gavel and when that gavel came down, the decision was made – period."[47] The president's appointment as WCC chairman was "apparently divine in nature," King stated. "He was never elected.... Sometimes the men (they were all men in those days) would try and pass their own motions, but Blaylock just ignored them."[48]

Some Local 480 activists adopted a "work with them, work against them" philosophy reminiscent of the early Communist strategy of having members "bore from within" their unions to exert Communist influence. Ralph "Duke" Hyssop, who arrived from Alberta seeking work at the smelter in the mid-1930s, followed this approach with his WCC position. Hyssop was unhappy with Blaylock's favouritism toward loyal committee members, so "I got on the co-operative committee." As he recalled, "The main objective for myself and some others was that we would destroy [it]."[49] The WCC's weaknesses drew even those who were not passionate about joining the union. Some workers scoffed at its failure to negotiate a seniority system, while others complained that it was incapable of acting as a true workers' representative. "There was no such thing as a grievance," Local 480 member George Bishop remembered. "Just a friendly chat with the head man."[50] For fellow smelterman Pat Romaine, it "eventually reached the stage where nobody with any sincerity or conscience in them would run for the

committee." Romaine described the committee as a "hierarchy …
of very incompetent, lazy bums. They didn't have to do anything.
Just sit in the office."[51]

Local 480 complaints about the WCC were met with indifference, but naysayers clearly irritated Blaylock and his WCC loyalists. To nullify their impact, the company union established not
one but two publications with clandestine CM&S assistance. The
WCC first attacked the credibility of Local 480's *Commentator* in
the *Communicator*, a rival newsletter issued by a "group of bona
fide workers." The group claimed "the truth had been handled care-
lessly" by "deliberate and malicious liars."[52] They accused the *Commentator* of being run by "racketeers preying on honest workers"
that would lead the Trail workforce "into the hands of a communist group."[53] The *Communicator* ceased after a single edition, but
a second venture called the *Co-operator* ran slightly longer. Touted
as the "voice of the workmen" and not at all "inspired, reviewed,
'blue-pencilled' or censored" by Blaylock, the paper pledged to
"deal in absolute FACTS." The *Co-operator*, the editor stated, would
be "very much unlike the slanderous union sheets coming into
Trail and published by so-called 'leaders' and 'protectors' of labor
under the camouflage of the C.I.O."[54] The claim of independence
was a flat-out lie. CM&S personnel manager C.W. Guillaume later
told the RCMP that "we, through our paper, exposed the agitator
[Slim Evans] in his true colours and I am thankful to say I believe
it [the drive] is at last dead, if not buried."[55]

The *Commentator* denounced the *Co-operator*, arguing that it had
"descended to the lowest and most vulgar way of fighting, namely,
'red-baiting.'"[56] The WCC paper responded that "'Reds' Don't Like
the Co-op Committee System"[57] and that Local 480 Communists
were "agitating campaigners."[58] Apparently stung by the *Commentator*'s attacks on Blaylock and the WCC, the *Co-operator* editor
suggested that the CIO was made up of a pack of "foreign labor
parasites" led by "warped-minded bosses" who used "communistic inspired tactics." Moreover, it claimed that the CIO insinuated
that "we are ignorant human animals; that we lack the intelligence
and 'guts' to conduct our own affairs with the management of the
Company." The paper further chastised the union for suggesting

"we have allowed the Company to strip us of our rights and privileges, and that we have placed our bodies and souls and minds into the hands of an industrial Frankenstein." The editorial then praised Blaylock and condemned the CIO for its "rotten record of strikes and bloodshed and human suffering." Clearly, Local 480 had elicited a strong negative reaction from the company loyalists publishing the new organ. Purporting to speak for all CM&S workers, the *Co-operator* exclaimed, "We have a very distinct aversion to their particular shade of RED."[59]

What Was Good for the CM&S Was Good for the Workers

Roth agreed with Local 480's negative assessment of the WCC. What the union faced was a population that "had internalized company power to the point where they believed that what was good for the 'Company' was good for them." The WCC was only one aspect of the company's "web of paternalism." Its anti-union arsenal also included an array of schemes designed to ensure worker and general public support. Medical insurance and mortgage plans, funding of municipal improvement projects, sports events, and picnics were all evidence of the company's good intentions regarding the community. However, "these programs were not in any way philanthropic," Roth argued, but rather were "designed to protect company interests." He concluded that the CM&S "made the 'carrot' of paternalism also the 'stick' of coercion."[60]

Roth's account appropriately draws on research into corporate welfarism in Canada to examine Blaylock's WCC and his company programs. In his study of the Canadian steel industry, for example, Craig Heron notes, "The measures that promised some economic security probably worked more successfully at building workers' 'consent' to the company's undisputed control than most of the more transparently patronizing programs aimed at boosting loyalty and morale."[61] As Margaret McCallam emphatically adds, "Despite talk of profit-sharing, industrial democracy, or income security, employers continued to exercise their unilateral power to cut wages, speed up production, and dismiss union activists."[62]

Blaylock may have been sincere in his concern for workers' welfare, but his vision of welfare capitalism fit a pattern of business behaviour that privileged efficiency. The pattern, though, did not always achieve its desired results. As Gerald Zahavi notes, workers' loyalty was often contested; workers sometimes managed welfare capitalism to their advantage.[63] Lizabeth Cohen argues that welfare capitalism actually empowered workers and prepared them to join unions. She suggests that "by starting the process of bringing workers together in the workplace through mixing them ethnically and encouraging their collaboration in work groups, it helped equip them to challenge their employers several years later."[64] While Cohen and Roth seem to contradict each other, the result was the same in Trail: welfare capitalism, with its paternalistic underpinnings, and the failings of the company union, both exposed by Local 480, might have helped open the door to legitimate labour relations.

Blaylock hoped that the WCC, along with his version of welfare capitalism, would convince his workforce to refuse unionization and reject the Communists. As Andrew Parnaby explains, employers like Blaylock "hoped to nurture a sense of harmony on the job, gain greater control over the work process, and stave off the intervention of unions and the state." However, he adds, the "pursuit of welfare capitalism ... required more than the creation of a company union and promotion of a cooperative workplace."[65] In Trail, it also included questioning the real intentions behind the company's apparent good corporate citizenship. It was up to Local 480 leaders to reveal the capitalist motives behind Blaylock's plans and they willingly accepted the challenge.

Despite Local 480's early efforts to seed discontent about the WCC, workers endorsed the company union in April 1939 in what the *Times* called a "sweeping employee vote." For Local 480 organizers, the vote secured for Blaylock another year of what they considered a secretive system of worker control.[66] The *Times* also announced that it had learned of a union plot to "nominate and elect [CIO] sympathizers as departmental representatives" to the WCC. Editor Curran warned smelter workers "to beware of the insidious political machinations of a professional labor agitator."[67]

Meanwhile, Blaylock, now president, accelerated his behind-the-scenes efforts to stop Local 480. In a speech to the WCC's annual "smoker," for example, he made his long-held anti-union views clear: "Unionism is so easily converted into a racket," he stated. "It seems to thrive better on industrial strife than on industrial peace, consequently we frequently find its proponents distorting and magnifying everything that can be used to make dissatisfaction." He further criticized the union for "rarely ever giving credit where credit is due to a company, and where the giving of such credit would tend to increase the happiness of the worker."[68]

Blaylock gave the gathering of loyal workmen, which included foremen and shift bosses, an economics lecture replete with charts and graphs designed to show that the workers were getting their fair share of company profits and not simply forfeiting them to company shareholders. The *Commentator* repeatedly insisted that shareholders were reaping major benefits at union members' expense, pointing to BC Labour Department statistics to support its contention that smelter workers received below-average wages.[69] Then, referring to "the Utopia that the C.I.O. was headed for," Blaylock delivered a thinly disguised blow against Local 480's leaders, saying that recent community unrest "has undoubtedly been augmented by the poison-pen articles and teachings that have been distributed in our midst so industriously." He finished with an exhortation to WCC leaders: "Whether or not you decide to throw your lot in with international unions is mainly your own affair. It is hard for me to think that the Company would refuse you anything you could gain by striking [for] you have the comfort of knowing that your Company is your friend and that if trouble comes to you, it will do its utmost to help you as it has helped hundreds of your fellows in the past."[70] The smoker speech was a not-so-subtle indication that Local 480 had irritated the very top echelon of the company.

Gerald "Gerry" M. Thomson was among the WCC members in attendance at the smoker. A member of the smelter's labour gang, he enthusiastically supported local sports, especially the Trail Smoke Eaters hockey team. Thomson, who would soon be elected chair of the WCC, was an equally enthusiastic Blaylock defender.[71] However, his defence strategy would be complicated by the election to the WCC of Harry Drake, a charter member of Local 480 and a tireless Communist recruiter. Drake's election lent credence to the *Times*'s earlier charge that the enemy was nesting in the WCC camp.

Trail Meets the Reddest Rose in Labour's Garden

The WCC was reaching the end of its institutional life when Harvey Murphy, already a controversial figure nationally as the self-proclaimed "reddest rose in Labour's garden," first travelled to Trail from the Vancouver offices of Mine-Mill in March 1943.[72] After that he became a regular visitor to the smelter city, assuming his duties as Mine-Mill's western regional district director and Local 480's chief organizer. His spouse, Isobel, welcomed the new Mine-Mill post because money was tight for the Murphy family, which eventually included three children: eldest son Rae, Mary-Ann, and William (named after Wobbly leader Big Bill Haywood). The appointment also regenerated Murphy's reputation as a leading Red union organizer. He had been refused several mining positions in Alberta after his release from an internment camp in Hull, Quebec, on 9 September 1942.[73] He had been incarcerated for eleven months after a Defence of Canada Regulations advisory committee found him a national security risk.

As discussed earlier, the Communist Party had initially rejected Canadian participation in the war, then urged vigorous engagement after Hitler attacked the Soviet Union. Murphy, like all Communists, faced public anger over the political flip-flopping. When the party reversed its anti-war position, Murphy became a strong Allied booster throughout the rest of the world conflict. Meanwhile, the party, which the Canadian government had banned in 1940, was struggling to maintain a public presence. By 1941, the Soviet Union had joined the Allies, placing Murphy and other party stalwarts in a more favourable ideological light, at least in some political circles. The change might also have placed Local 480's Red leaders in a slightly better position to combat the anti-Communist CM&S president.

By most measures, Murphy was the right choice to finish the job that his fellow Communists Slim Evans and John McPeake had started years earlier. But Blaylock's West Kootenay industrial empire was well fortified, with the *Times* and WCC leaders providing a steady patter of anti-CIO name calling, economic fear mongering, and Red bashing. Trail may have been late in shaking off its company union chains, but now it was about to witness a seasoned and shrewd Communist union man in action. Some of the smelter workers would welcome Murphy's talk of gaining the freedom to decide for themselves once a "real" union represented them. Others would not so readily accept that Mine-Mill Local 480 was the best route to that freedom.

For Blaylock and his WCC leaders, Murphy was yet another outside labour agitator intent on invading the smelter and disrupting the big happy family that Elsie Turnbull and others lauded and that Blaylock pretended existed. A Communist union, the *Times* had warned, would disturb the relative tranquillity of their quiet company town. Murphy, well known to Trail Communists, if not the general population, had disturbed tranquillity in the past. Years of secret police surveillance records testified to it. Although his internment had removed him from the labour battlefronts that he had visited throughout the 1930s, he had vast experience at organizing miners, factory workers, and the unemployed.

Murphy had been involved in the CPC since close to its inception in the early 1920s and was tutored in left politics at the feet of Tim Buck, a Stalinist who would eventually become the CPC's general secretary. The young Murphy soon took to the streets as a militant political agitator and would appear on police watch lists wherever he went. Buck groomed him as a future party bureaucrat after seeing the young man follow the party line as he participated in strike actions throughout the late 1920s. In the early 1930s Murphy endeared himself to Alberta miners by advising the Mine Workers' Union of Canada, an affiliate of the Communist Workers' Unity League (WUL). When he married Isobel Rae, a Nova Scotia miner's daughter from Blairmore, Alberta, in 1934, it solidified a living link to his political romance with the Alberta miners. There he had gained much of the experience he would need to succeed in his new assignment. His experience during the Depression, assisting the unemployed workforce in Ontario in its fight for a decent living, would also be valuable in BC. Murphy's many clashes with anti-union industrial employers had equipped him to preside, if not over the collapse of the Blaylock regime, then at least to act as an exposer of CM&S flaws.

Now on 21 March 1943, Murphy was set to engage in his first smelter war. Would Blaylock, Trail's premier capitalist, disarm the life-long Communist challenger to his mountain domain? Would Murphy's long-held Communist beliefs and their unabashed public display prove a liability or an asset for Local 480? Would the anti-Red company union, now in the guise of the legal ISWU, try to use Murphy's Red past to undermine the local? Initially, it seemed that the answer to all three questions was yes.

"Underhanded Rumours and Gossip" Dissuade Workers

Soon after his arrival, a flurry of letters to the editor appeared in the *Times*, attacking Murphy and Local 480 Communists. Murphy joined the letter-writing spree, condemning the "underhanded rumours and gossip being spread in attempts to dissuade workers from joining the union."[74] He focused on those who told Trail's Italians that they would be interned if they became union members. He also criticized those who frightened smelter workers by saying they would lose their pensions if they joined. A. Oakey defended Murphy and "his splendid record as a fighter against relief cuts and those 20¢ a day slave camps."[75] It was a clear reference to his Depression-era work in Alberta and Ontario. "R.G.S.A." reminded smelter workers of the tough strikes of 1901 in Rossland and 1917 in Trail before charging the CIO "heels and lickspittals" with "ruthlessly leaving women and children in real want until the men crawled back to the owners for their jobs again." The letter writer told smelter workers that they did not need the help of professional labour leaders because they had "more security and privilege than any other workers."[76] Frederick Buckley contributed to the discussion through amateur poetry:

> For those of us who climb the hill,
> The most of us have had our fill
> Of letters written to the press,
> On "Kenny," "Murph" and Happiness.
> So let us form a union, gents.
> Let's unite some brains and common sense
> And go at things in moderation –
> All – labor, liquor and taxation.[77]

An anti-CIO "Smelterman" kept the debate lively with a warning: "Don't be so foolish as to sell your birthright to the CIO and pay them $1 a month or more for a promise. Don't do something that may result in the ghost town of Trail."[78] "Sincere" called the CIO organizers "enemies of our well being."[79] William L. Bell warned Italian workers in Trail to "beware of the fine smooth talk of the union," claiming he had witnessed police carting the Italian miners of Cape Breton, Nova Scotia, off to a camp in spite of them being union members.[80] Local 480 member Frank F. Meade would later refute the claim, pointing to their support of fascism as the real reason for their detention.[81] Meade also added a humorous assessment of the letter-writing squabble in a comment addressed to editor Curran. "We beg of you not to take our sunshine away by even cutting down your present ration of 10 anti-union to 3 pro-union 'letters to the editor,'" he pleaded sarcastically. "After all, we are but a tiny group of Local 480 members who have nothing much to live for. We are told that if our union takes over, Trail will be a ghost town ... men and women will starve by the thousands ... and our International representatives (who, they say, are really fugitives from Alcatraz) will milk us dry and then abscond with our dough."[82]

Editor Curran ended the letters barrage, announcing that the daily would stop publishing comments on the CIO-versus-WCC issue "unless such letter contains what the editor feels is some new contribution."[83] The letters debate had been a rare display of public participation in the pages of a newspaper seldom given to publishing political comments contrary to its own. Apparently, Curran considered that two further anti-CIO letters offered some "new contribution." M.A. Plumber questioned Murphy's claim that he was paid $200 a month. The letter writer wanted Murphy and the other "hot-headed agitators" from the CIO "sent back into oblivion so far as Trail is concerned until the big job [the war] is successfully completed."[84] Then "C.A.M." calculated that the CIO stood to gain $78,060 in union dues from Trail workers and asked, "Is our present peace of mind, our present independence and the many little 'unseen or unthought of bonuses' worth losing?"[85] Clearly, the WCC still had influence enough to ensure that Local 480 did not yet hold the winning hand against the company union. But Murphy was quickly manoeuvring into position to help them play it.

Often warned of the troubles that could arise with the coming of the allegedly strike-prone Red CIO, some Trailites considered Communists as bad as Nazis, or worse. Murphy, as much as he was a bona fide trade unionist, was also an old-line Communist who made no secret of the fact that he accepted the policies of Stalinist CPC leader Tim Buck. Of course, there would always be lingering doubts about how loyal Communists would be to the Allied cause. Some observers would later point to the CM&S's ultra-secret heavy water plant codenamed Project 9 in Warfield, BC, which began operations in 1943 to assist the Manhattan Project in building the atomic bomb.[86] Could a Communist union leader be trusted with such a vital state secret? It was just one of several critical reasons for Blaylock and the CM&S managers who followed him to get to know Comrade Murphy much better. And so it was for new ISWU leader Dave Kenneway.

Union Newspaper Attacks Company Union

The *Commentator* had incensed Kenneway in January 1943 with an article entitled "Fink Unions Show Hand," in which Local 480 leaders attacked him for preventing the collection of donations destined for a wartime Russian, i.e., Soviet, aid fund.[87] Women from the Rossland lodge of the Croatian Fraternal Union of America had initiated the fundraising effort, but Kenneway objected to it. The Soviets might now be Canada's allies, but that was not good enough for him. Trail Mayor Herbert Clark sided with the WCC leader in the controversy, while Local 480 defended the Croatian lodge's right to help Russia. One of the women Kenneway stopped from collecting money on Trail streets was Mrs. K.E. Dosen, spouse of Dan Dosen, a charter member of Local 480 and an avid Communist.[88] The local leadership saw that it had a duty to support the Croatian immigrants who were among its growing membership, but it also undoubtedly saw this as a chance to discredit the WCC. "This high-handed action on the part of these finks can serve no other cause but that of Hitler," the *Commentator* charged. "It is [an] indication of the depths to which they sink in carrying out their roll [*sic*] in a company union set-up."[89]

Kenneway may not have known it, but the Croatian lodge confrontation might have been the last anti-Communist act of the old WCC. The organization could and did apply for certification under the amended ICA, but was not accepted as a legitimate union. At the same time, Communists were angered that Mackenzie King had so far refused to legislate an end to a 1940 ban on most Communist activities, despite an all-party federal committee recommendation to lift it. The *Commentator* called it "a piece of class legislation directed against the working class" and criticized Justice Minister Louis St. Laurent for imposing the ban "on the grounds that he dislikes 'Communism' as a theory."[90] The union paper failed to mention that the delicate political balance that King struggled to maintain in Quebec might have influenced the decision to keep the ban in place. As Chris Frazer argues, "King intended to placate his Quebec power brokers who in no uncertain terms opposed legalizing the CPC."[91]

Also supporting Local 480 Communists was International Mine-Mill President Reid Robinson. Whether he was a Communist or not was openly debated for years. He had certainly surrounded himself with Reds, and his challengers used it against him. But Trail smelter workers' spirits were nevertheless lifted when he told a Mine-Mill convention, as reported in the *Commentator*, that "if the Communists believe that we should organize the unorganized to better the conditions of the workers of this country so that we can better prosecute the war effort – and you want to call anyone who supports such a program a Communist – you have that right to call me a Communist."[92]

Such international union support, coupled with the ICA changes, emboldened Murphy as he manoeuvred on Blaylock's far left flank. Letter writers were also primed for renewed battle. "Security" responded on the *Times* letters page in support of the union, noting that many smelter soldiers were members of Local 480 and they expected to find a union when they came home. "They would be our brothers if they were here now," the letter writer concluded, and they would return to their jobs well educated by other trade unionists fighting in Europe and Asia."[93] On the opposing side, "Strike-Shy" used poetry to outline the benefits that the company bestows on its employees:

Let's be reasonable and sensible,
Let's not chase rainbows,
Let's not be blinded by
High-sounding, impossible promises.
Let's not kill the goose
That lays the golden egg,
Let's not bite the hand that feeds us.[94]

As helpful as it was to Murphy, the amended ICA of 1943 did not ensure that Local 480 would finally win the hearts and minds of a majority of smelter workers. The end of the WCC was a definite blow to Blaylock's workplace hegemony, but he and his more conservative employees still posed a threat. Local 480, which had for so long been locked in public combat with the old WCC, had some important advantages, including an existing organization and political momentum. Now, however, it would have to engage in a smelter war against the ISWU, a newly constituted and legal organization. Its supporters, Trailites like the above letter writers, were set to hail the reinvented company union as it prepared for a BC Labour Relations Board vote that would determine whether

Mine-Mill or the ISWU would legally represent Trail's smelter workforce.

Independent Smelter Union Challenges Murphy

Preceding the vote, Local 480 issued a bulletin claiming that Sullivan Mine workers at Kimberley in the East Kootenay District had accepted Mine-Mill as their bargaining agent.[95] The ISWU refuted the claim, and that was followed by another plethora of letters in the *Times*, arguing for and against the increasing prospect of a Mine-Mill union being certified in Trail. "Contented" again led the charge, hailing the WCC-ISWU for ensuring that Trail workers "did not feel any effects of the depression." The writer charged Murphy with "collecting too much of the folding stuff" and postulated that no more than 5 per cent of smelter soldiers were members of Local 480.[96] Another letter from W.A. Plumber chastised smeltermen for "booing" ISWU Chair Kenneway at a meeting.[97] One from an "Anti-union Ex-Miner" counselled workers to remain members of the ISWU. "J.W.M." attacked Murphy for his "abuse of our hospitality and insults to our fellow citizens." He advised workers to "not be misled by the vague promises of these travelling organizers." In his view, and clearly echoing Blaylock's routine conflation of "Reds" and "Rackets" from south of the border, the CIO was "nothing but a streamlined racket that escaped the FBI." He added "any national tie-up with the CIO would soon find us governed not from Victoria or Ottawa but from Denver [the international union's Colorado headquarters]."[98] "Onlooker" from Rossland also took the ISWU's side. He wondered what CM&S employees overseas "will think when they come back and find they have to shell out $18.00 plus 'special assessments' every year to a bunch of large stomached gentlemen back in New York for which they don't get a darn bit more than they are getting now."[99]

When the LRB vote results were announced on 20 April 1943 the ISWU was the winner by a slim majority (1,977 to 1,888), making it the smelter workers' legal bargaining agent. The *Commentator* called it "pretty odiferous," questioned the arithmetical skills of the election scrutineers, and declared the vote a "boomerang" because more smelter workers joined the Mine-Mill local on voting day than the two previous days combined.[100]

In the midst of the letter-writing free-for-all, Blaylock purchased a full-page ad in the *Times* to counter "a decided increase in propaganda against big companies." He denied charges of war profiteering by displaying a complex array of figures showing that although the "company is making good profits," they were not excessive and much of it was reinvested in company operations. Blaylock provided a simplified balance sheet to show what the company actually owned, along with a chart of "interesting figures" to exhibit how much the company had spent. It was a sincere attempt to share knowledge of the business risks involved in running such a large corporation and the need to remain a lean operation during the war years.

Blaylock, the Allied forces booster, was clearly showing concern for his community's future, but it was also a comprehensive attempt to rebuff accusations of "profiteering and even of pilfering the public purse" that were often heard from Local 480 leaders and its letter-writing members.[101] The *Commentator* was succinct in its view that the "industrialists of Canada are organized to put over their freedom of exploitation program.... Coinciding with the slanderous smear campaign against the unions is the industrialists' attempt to organize company unions all across Canada."[102]

With Murphy at his front door and Local 480 gaining strength, Blaylock's public messages exerted more pressure for labour-management cooperation. "Labour relations are probably the most important single thing in the welfare of a nation," he wrote in a submission to a National War Labour Board (NWLB) inquiry.[103] "Unquestionably," he added, "the country's emergency is being used by some leaders of international labour to force international unionism over all industry." He also blamed the Wagner Act, President Franklin Roosevelt's New Deal labour law, named after US Senator Robert Wagner, for "a very large part of the labour unrest." And he attacked all labour acts in North America as "bound to create dissension between men and management rather than to create harmony and co-operation." Blaylock praised his record in establishing the "proper relationship between workmen and management" and openly criticized unions.

He further argued that his cooperative approach "tends to bring the workmen and the management into closer harmony, while the remote control bargaining agencies will tend to put them further apart." As evidence, he cited "the speeches of the international organizers, which consist almost entirely of abuse of management and industry, and frequently governments, in connection with high profits, poor wages, poor conditions and general profiteering." Continued wartime work stoppages might have prompted some readers to agree with him, including editor Curran, who pleaded with unions to follow the example of the British labour movement, which "postpones its class struggle until after the war."[104]

Smelter Poetry Added to the Union Arsenal

Congratulations seemed in order in mid-May when Local 480 announced that it had reached the majority required by BC law to once again apply for certification. Local 480 President Fred Henne immediately requested a meeting with Blaylock to commence negotiations for a first collective agreement.[105] As he did with Slim Evans years earlier, the company president refused the request and instructed the ISWU to "continue its battle against Mine-Mill under the auspices of a 'legitimate' union."[106] Little had changed, and why would it? Blaylock had installed much of the old WCC executive as the ISWU's officers. Also, attempts to challenge the ISWU through Local 480's new bid for certification led to a summer-long Labour Ministry investigation that decided against Mine-Mill. The decision would not be announced until later, but that did not prevent the *Commentator* from resuming its war with the company union. Among its now familiar weapons of choice was a poem:

We never speak of workers' rights,
We vote for the Company union.
They tell us that it leads to fights,
So I vote for the Company union.
The Company has always said
That men who talk like that are "Red,"

We listen to the boss instead
And vote for the Company union.[107]

Murphy's rhetorical flare seemed evident when the union paper also turned on Blaylock's fellow industrialists, charging that "corporation executives ... are skimming off gravy in salaries and bonuses with ladles that are from 50 to 200 per cent larger than they were in 1940."[108] The article listed the salaries of those executives and, while Blaylock's name was not among them, the union's implication was clear enough.

As living proof of his support for Local 480, Mine-Mill's Reid Robinson visited the smelter city as summer approached. More than 1,200 smelter workers and their families greeted him with a march through downtown streets to the strains of the Rossland City Band. Among other targets, he centred out Blaylock in his remarks to the crowd. "[A] man like Blaylock, who throughout the past years has been Monarch of all he surveys, will not give up this power easily," Robinson stated. He would "continue with phoney unions and any other power at his disposal to turn the workers away from their democratic union." He assured the crowd that Trail's smelter workers had "grown tired of Mr. Blaylock's despotic paternalism and wished a voice of their own."[109]

As if to counter Robinson's remarks about "phoney" unions, the ISWU reported that the National War Labour Board had accepted its request for a smelter worker pay increase of twenty-five cents. ISWU Chair Kenneway had requested the increase for tradesmen only, but the labour board initially rejected it.[110] Blaylock then appeared before the board in what might have been the final time that the creator of the WCC would publicly represent the employees. The NWLB subsequently reversed its decision and the *Commentator* grudgingly acknowledged the increase. "We say good for Mr. Blaylock and his representations," the paper remarked, "now let's get the increase for all the employees."[111] Kootenay West Conservative MP William K. Esling also entered the smelter war zone in fulsome praise of Blaylock and the ISWU. Although he did not use the term, he was indirectly warning workers in his constituency not to jeopardize their "paradise" by voting for Red Mine-Mill.[112]

Kimberley's Mine-Mill Local 651, which the LRB had certified a few months earlier, ratified a first collective agreement that November. The event encouraged the *Commentator* to assume that "company unionism will be no more."[113] Careful not to name Blaylock, the editorial further warned that "Hitler, darling of the German anti-union, anti-democratic big bosses, is being defeated and we want no little Hitlers to grow up at home."[114] When CPC leader Tim Buck visited the smelter city in mid-November, well briefed by his BC protégé Murphy, Local 480 extended "Tim a hearty welcome," describing him as "one of Canada's outstanding labor leaders."[115] The *Commentator* also republished two items from the Communist *Canadian Tribune* on the Amalgamated Union of Canada (AUC) to which the ISWU was affiliated.

At its November convention, AUC organizers had ejected the *Tribune's* scribe for calling the AUC a "new strike-breaking organization," the *Commentator* reported, adding that the AUC was "a den of finks."[116] Clearly, the AUC would get no sympathy from Local 480, for it wholeheartedly agreed with *Commentator* writer R.S. Gordon's claim that the AUC was "a fifth column among the workers" that is "part of the general offensive against labor" being pushed by social forces that included "a handful of renegades from the ranks of the workers."[117] Trolling for evidence of AUC meddling in smelter union affairs, the *Commentator* revealed that Charlie McLean of Trail was a first vice-president of "the new fink set-up."[118]

The ISWU scored another victory when the NWLB agreed that Trail smelter workers would get overtime pay for work performed on most statutory holidays.[119] The decision created yet another hurdle for Local 480 leaders, and more bad news would arrive soon when the Labour Department announced that there would be no representational vote at the smelter because the union did not have the required sign-ups.[120] Frustrated Local 480 organizers had been preparing for a possible vote, but even if it succeeded, the union's weaponry would not include the strike threat. Under urging from the Communists, many of whom saw their first allegiance to the survival of the Soviet Union, that right had been signed away when Mine-Mill's international office advised its locals to accept the CIO's controversial no-strike pledge in aid of the war effort. In Roth's view, "Mine-Mill's no strike pledge is a measure of Communist influence within the union."[121] However, as Laurel Sefton Mac-Dowell points out, other CIO unions refused to give up the strike weapon. Canadian labour leader Charles Millard, for example, "was supportive of the war effort but not at the expense of workers' rights."[122] Toward the end of the decade, Millard's name would become all too familiar to Local 480 when the leader of the United Steelworkers of America (USWA) presented the local with another challenge to its survival.

The federal Labour Ministry also seemed to play into the ISWU's hand when it announced that wage controls would be tightened and penalties increased on unions that strike in defiance of the law.[123] The ISWU could boast that it had at least won some wage gains for smelter workers and in principle it was against strikes. In the meantime, Blaylock continued to fight for his company union. In his year-end message in the *Times*, he stated that "a socialist state cannot succeed without ruthless dictatorship" and suggested that if unions were to get "undisputed power" Canada would "have a very unstable existence."[124] Murphy and Trail's Reds openly challenged that view, arguing that all those "attempting to create disunity and falsifying the real issues of socialism as related to post-war progress" represent the "conspiracy of big business against the people of our country."[125]

Wartime Anti-Communist Rhetoric Accelerates

As the smelter wars continued at home, Trailites read news of local smelter soldiers fighting in Europe. The *Times* hailed wounded tail-gunner Ken Burns as a hero for shooting down a Nazi night fighter.[126] They also learned that Squadron Leader Bill Strachan of Trail had been involved in a major air attack on Berlin.[127] Clearly, the war was not yet over but an end was in sight. As a further indication, "meatless Tuesdays" would soon be dropped completely in the smelter city, along with canned salmon rationing, but butter production was threatening to sink below the half-pound weekly ration. Buoyed by rumours of victory, Trail's three cinemas increased the number of war movies available. For example, Canadian-born Raymond Massey appeared at the Rio with *Action in the North Atlantic*, and Gale Sondergaard, spouse of future blacklisted Hollywood Ten member Herbert Biberman, starred in *The Strange Death of Adolf Hitler*. Even the cartoons could have a war theme, as in *Daffy the Commando*. Dancing opportunities included an evening with the Serenaders and their "medley of pepper-hot dance numbers" at the K.P. Hall. The Trail Junior Hockey Club was on its way to being the best team in Western Canada. The price of "socialist liquor" was on the *Times* editor's mind and he had *Vancouver Sun* columnist Bruce Hutchison illustrate how socialism doesn't work. "You may want to buy French champagne, but you'll drink CCF rye," Hutchison crowed.[128]

On the smelter war home front, Local 480 was getting closer to finishing its long struggle to form a Mine-Mill union, but several hurdles remained for Murphy and his team of local organizers. Another volley of anti-Communist rhetoric confronted Local 480 that winter when D.V. Mitchell, head of the AUC, told the *Times* that the labour movement should command no respect "so long as it broke its word by condoning strikes and walkouts."[129] The following day, Mitchell fenced with Murphy in a public debate that saw the two men slinging accusations at each other. It would not be the last time Trailites heard from Mitchell, for the AUC leader soon moved his national newspaper, the *Amalgamator*, to the smelter city from Hamilton, Ontario. Once in Trail, the monthly continued to publish as the voice of independent unionism. Vigorously anti-CIO, its primary purpose was to support and defend the notion of industrial cooperation. This appealed to some Canadian workers, including ISWU supporters in Trail, because it suggested an autonomous status instead of being tied to international unions like Mine-Mill. It also gave voice to the AUC's nationalist fervour. Although he did not publicly support the AUC, its penchant for cooperation appealed to the CM&S president.

As the new LRB certification vote neared in the spring of 1944, Blaylock devoted much of a forty-five-minute speech, aired on Trail's CJAT radio station, to extolling the virtues of free enterprise, dismissing the socialists, and chastising militant trade unionists.

"State ownership is fore-ordained to inefficient operation," he said of assumed CCF plans to nationalize industry. He hoped that his workers could become "full partners in the enterprise" because "the endeavours of the men would have been reflected in their pay cheques." He warned against the "dangerous views of many politicians," the *Times* reported, and advised rejection of the "propaganda put out by the apostles of gloom." Assuredly he was referring to Local 480 Communists. He then praised his company's wartime production levels and once again reminded workers that they "enjoy the highest wages paid in any similar industry in Canada." However, he was careful to avoid the issue of equal pay for women war workers who since mid-1942 had been working at the CM&S doing traditional male jobs for 80 per cent of the pay. Blaylock concluded his speech by ordering his listeners to "Snap out of our lethargy" and avoid developing a "defeatist attitude."[130]

The Blaylock broadcast grated on Local 480 Communist Harry Drake who won space in the *Times* to state that "while the C.M.&S. has built itself up to as Mr. Blaylock says, 'tops the world over,' C.M.&S. workers have received a very small portion of that in wages." He then refuted Blaylock's other claims, concluding that smelter workers have much to gain by joining Mine-Mill, for it promises to give them "a real share of the great wealth they have worked to create."[131] Murphy, too, appeared enraged by the Blaylock speech, commenting that "for Blaylock to assert that 'free enterprise' and the right of 'monopoly control' were things for which our boys are laying their lives down ... were [the] subversive utterances of a bigot." The company president "ridiculed the ability of the Canadian people to manage their own economic affairs and also expressed contempt for any government control of industry," Murphy railed. "Free enterprise, he [Blaylock] maintained, should have unbridled control of its operations."[132] If local Mine-Mill leaders were ever hopeful that Blaylock might eventually accept Local 480 as the smelter workers' bargaining agent, that speech made clear his adamantly negative views on unions and Communism.

In any event, it might have been the last such statement from the CM&S president, for in February the King government's long-awaited "Canadian Wagner Act" was introduced in the form of

Order-in-Council PC 1003. As the nation's labour law, it lacked teeth regarding unfair labour practices, the *Commentator* argued, but it would "greatly assist trade unions in avoiding difficult and expensive legal proceedings in which companies have been able to find refuge."[133] The new law made collective bargaining compulsory, called for mandatory grievance procedures, and superseded provincial labour legislation, including BC's ICA. Local 480 was poised to benefit from the new law and would do so, but not before yet another skirmish broke out with the ISWU.

Re-engaging in the Battle for Workers' Allegiance

One year after Murphy's arrival, the local again applied for certification and the ISWU re-engaged in the battle for members' allegiance. The *Commentator* countered this new offensive by dubbing the AUC's Mitchell "Canada's hopeful 'Labor Front Fuehrer'" [*sic*] and mocking him for pursuing a "career of company stooging started when he was made president of Sir Edward Beatty's flop C.P.R. company set-up."[134] Local 480's frustration over the ISWU's steady issuance of anti-Communist references spilled over to Blaylock for his "utter contempt for the rights of labor." Organizers warned smelter workers to pay no attention to his "rants" about industry not trying to take advantage of the war effort to reduce wages. The paper reminded readers that in 1943 a CM&S worker earned less money than in 1937. "Let us not be fooled by the glib phrases that he [Blaylock] uses to cover up the hidden wage cuts we have actually received during the war," the editorial stated. And let us not forget, the paper continued, that "the C.M.&S. Co. was a party to the sit down strike of industry against the 5% profit that our government was going to allow."[135]

With the LRB certification vote underway, for a few brief moments Local 480 could lay down its arms. Even though the LRB decision would not be announced for another month, the local announced with confidence that a victory was inevitable. So sure were they that a celebration was planned for 1 May, the Communist international worker holiday. In February, the *Commentator* had the sad task of publishing an obituary for Slim Evans, who had died from injuries sustained in a Vancouver traffic accident. Now with the vote being counted, Local 480 saluted the organizer who had started the march to victory.[136] His death was a symbolic emotional blow to the Local 480 Communists who had met him and been inspired by his tireless fight for industrial democracy, especially in Trail. Despite his initial failure, Local 480 was about to finish what Evans had begun.

Later that week an evening parade was attended by 1,300 Trailites who marched to "snappy march music," sang workers' songs, and carried banners "proclaiming 'Put Victory First,' 'Smash Fascism' and 'CIO Means Unity and Strength.'" As Roth described it, "The crowd was addressed by CCF MLA H.W. (Bert) Herridge, various Mine Mill officials and the Vice-President of the CIO Ladies Auxiliary. The guest speaker of the evening was IWA 'red bloc' leader, Harold Pritchett, who told those assembled that time was 'running out' for the 'Blaylock system.'"[137]

Then on 2 June, the cause for the celebration was confirmed. Mine-Mill organizers achieved the goal they had long been fighting for: the BC LRB finally recognized Local 480 as the legal bargaining agent for Trail's smelter workers. The local had persuaded recalcitrant immigrant workers, many of them with limited English skills, that the union was in their best interest. It had countered that portion of the community that had seen Mine-Mill as a foreign invader, demonstrating that the union's constitution ensured that local autonomy would be preserved. And it had overcome public concerns fomented by constant anti-Communist attacks from all sides since before Slim Evans arrived in 1938. After all that, it had won over the majority of smelter workers. The Red union had finally won.

The first set of union negotiations since the 1917 strike began soon after the announcement, and on 17 June 1944 a "working agreement" was signed, the *Commentator* reported. In it "CM&S agreed to recognize Local 480 and cancel all previous agreements thus terminating the ISWU bargaining agency status."[138] A grievance procedure was accepted at that time, but the local would have to wait for a wage settlement decision from the NWLB. The company acknowledged the union a few days after the LRB announcement as Local 480 named its bargaining committee. It was an amalgam of political persuasions from the left, including Reid Robinson, Mine-Mill international executive member Chase Powers, and Murphy. Added to the list were charter members of the local: Gar Belanger, Dick Gop, Dan Dosen, and George DeGroff – Communists all. Local labour politician Leo Nimsick, another charter member, was also on the committee.[139]

Forced by law to sign a contract with a union that he had so long opposed, Blaylock was not happy in his 1944 year-end message. As he put it in the *Times*, "Unquestionably there are revolutionary forces in the air. Let us keep them there as harmless as exhaust steam given off from a high-pressure engine doing good and useful work." Continuing the industrial metaphor, he advised his workforce to "not let yourselves be fooled. As with the engine, no constructive accomplishment results from these noises and vapours."[140] Soon afterwards, Blaylock promoted William S. Kirkpatrick to assistant general manager, a powerful position from which Kirkpatrick would serve as the CM&S's chief anti-Communist.[141] It was a bad omen for the smelter workers' new union, but more immediate concerns faced the Local 480 executive. Among them was the burgeoning number of female employees whom Blaylock had been hiring since mid-1942 to replace enlisted men in the smelter plants. Some of them would support the union, but others joined the anti-CIO crusade that remained determined to stop Local 480, regardless of its newly achieved legal status. Now the union would face new problems, but also acquire a new ally.

3

Women War Workers and Ladies Auxiliary Politics

Early in 1945, Local 480 and the CM&S announced that they had replaced the working agreement ratified the previous summer with a more official legal contract. A photograph on the back page of the *Commentator* showed the group signing the historic pact. Remembering the arrival of Slim Evans as the starting point of the Mine-Mill drive in 1938, the paper said simply the "agreement marks a big step forward for the workers on the Hill." The CM&S workforce would now enjoy a proper seniority provision, grievance procedure, shop steward system, health and safety improvements, and items agreed upon earlier like holiday and overtime pay.[1] The local indicated that there was more to negotiate when it gave notice that the one-year agreement would end as of 29 January 1946.[2] Blaylock had informed his shareholders of the new reality in his 1944 annual report. It was the final blow to his company union and his dream of a cooperative, union-free smelter. It also seemed that the Communists, among others on the Local 480 bargaining committee, had finally won a seemingly interminable struggle. But not everyone would be satisfied with the new collective agreement. Among the most dissatisfied was Blaylock.

The CM&S president had been forced by law to capitulate to the union. Even more grating was the fact that it was a Communist union. For Blaylock, the young McGill graduate who had dedicated his life to the smelter, the loss of control was a major blow. He had spent four decades ensuring that the company would flourish under his guidance. He could take much credit for building the city that had emerged from the rough mining camp he had first seen in 1899. Now, for him, the smelter wars would soon be over, for he stepped down that spring after a lengthy illness and in November he died at sixty-six years of age, marking the end of both a forty-six year career and the Blaylock era in the smelter city. R.E. Stavert, who, like Blaylock, was a McGill University graduate, replaced him.[3] His ascendency marked a brief pause in the smelter wars, but soon he, Bill Kirkpatrick, and other CM&S managers would continue the battle to unseat Local 480. In the renewed fighting between Local 480 Reds and Trail's anti-Communists, many new combatants would be introduced and some old company union members would rejoin the fray. Clearly, the anti-Communist spirit of Blaylock and his old Workmen's Co-operative Committee would continue to infuse the smelter workplace.

Also among the disappointed were some of the women smelter workers whom Blaylock had started to hire in July 1942. The women became members of Local 480 when the union was certified in mid-1944, but under Local 480's working agreement, their jobs went unprotected. In fact, the local leadership had agreed to "do everything in its power to help the company to carry out" its earlier promise to re-employ soldiers in their old jobs. This included "laying off all employees who have been engaged since the others enlisted," as reported in the *Times*.[4] When Murphy and the Local 480 bargaining team signed the agreement, it might have suggested to some that despite the principle of equality cited in the Mine-Mill constitution, the male breadwinner tradition remained paramount in the smelter city. That autumn, a debate occurred over who should be laid off first after the war – women or men. Clearly, Blaylock's agreement with the union would be honoured when the company announced that about 2,500 employees serving in the military would come home to their old jobs. Blaylock also told the *Times* he "hoped to continue in employment a large proportion of temporary men taken on during the war who are qualified to carry on."[5] He did not mention the women who had kept the plants running.

That first agreement was silent on any future prospects the Trail women might have envisaged when they began joining hundreds of thousands of Canadian women "streaming into the nation's industrial workplaces."[6] Their presence on traditionally male shop floors would soon test the sincerity of CIO claims to support equal pay for equal work. Trail women were as keen as any to sign up for work in wartime industries. When Blaylock advertised jobs on May Day 1942, "the firm's employment office was swamped" with about two hundred female applicants. The *Times* ad read simply "Help Wanted Female," and called for "applications for various types of plant work." The next day, a queue formed long before the office opened. But as David Michael Roth noted, what the ad did not say was that they would be "saddled with excessively long training periods or were designated 'helpers' rather than operators."[7]

The idea of women entering the smelter workforce led one company manager to query federal Labour Department officials on how best to apply the BC Factories Act to the employment of women. "Although it is not affirmatively stated in the Act, it is intimated that no woman shall be employed before the hour of 7:00 in the morning nor after the hour of 8:00 in the evening." He worried that "it will probably be found necessary to employ women on shift work, the same as the men."[8] *Times* editor Bill Curran shrugged off concerns about the Factories Act, seeing the influx of women applicants as "just another indication of the willingness of the women of Canada to buckle down and co-operate for an all-out war effort." Within the framework of total war, women backed men, "ready and willing to step into their shoes in war factories, on farms and in all necessary civilian services."[9]

A *Times* news photograph, picturing a young woman at work, was captioned, "Not long ago this attractive Canadian girl looked upon a file as something used solely to manicure her nails. Today, after joining thousands of other girls in war industries, she can handle a file as deftly as any man in turning out parts in an aircraft factory." The caption, which estimated that "between 50,000 and 75,000 women are now employed in industrial war work," seemed at once admiring but also amazed that they might be capable of performing male tasks.[10]

Trail Women Join Allied War Effort

Times cartoonist Glen Lehmann sketched front-page cartoon strips featuring the women smelter workers. In one he noted, "Men workers began to look to their laurels as women were called up to register for employment." The cartoonist then asked, "Who was it said, 'One women is as good as any two men?'"[11] Seventeen Trail women obviously thought the question applied to the armed forces as well when they joined the Royal Canadian Air Force, although positions open to them were still segregated from men's roles as pilots, gunners, and mechanics.[12] Like the *Times*, newspapers across the country heralded Canadian women for assisting the Allied war effort. In Britain, family responsibilities were the only barrier to women joining the wartime workforce. To assist them, hundreds of crèches and day nurseries were opened. Young unmarried women were advised to "enlist in industry with the same spirit of self-sacrifice as young men who have enlisted for fighting service."[13] That was the counsel of Mrs. Rex Eaton, assistant director of the women's division of Canada's National Selective Service program.

The smelter enthusiastically welcomed a female workforce, especially after the West Kootenay District returned a "Yes" vote of 10,364 to 3,653 in the plebiscite on conscription for overseas military service.[14] The positive response meant many more men would enlist, troubling their families with concerns for their safety. But it also meant more smelter jobs would be vacated for women. Earlier, the pro-conscription *Times* had warned that a "No" vote could lead to the Allies losing the war, and it reminded unions that "the very first acts of repression instituted by both Mussolini and Hitler upon their accession to power was the ruthless suppression of all labor organizations, the assassination of their leaders, and the theft of their funds."[15]

Trail women needed no similar warnings about what losing the war might mean. Across all age groups they willingly entered the smelter workforce, "proving they could do anything a man could," according to Elsie Turnbull. They did do traditional office work in all departments, but they also worked in the assay office, metal refineries, leaching plant, and ammonia and hydrogen plants. "Dressed in coveralls, rubber boots and leather gloves, they acted as a clean-up gang. They shovelled sand for concrete shell covers; they scrubbed dirty cathode plates and did light work in tank rooms."[16] Takaia Larsen compiled an even more comprehensive list, revealing that women were also employed at carpentry, industrial painting, and welding, "as well as various jobs in the coke ammonia, nitrate, and sulphuric acid plants and the rubber shop." Women were often assigned to janitorial duties, she added, "but more often than not they did much the same jobs men did."[17]

"The women, by golly, are breaking the chains that have bound them for hundreds of years," enthused Graham Dolan, editor of International Mine-Mill's *Union*. He encouraged locals to support equality for women war workers with the rallying cry "More Power to 'Em."[18] It was a fresh outlook on gender equality that not all CIO unions would appreciate once the war ended. While equal pay appealed to some Trail workers, women elsewhere were also concerned about the fate of BC men as they saw the mounting casualties published in the *Times*. The daily focused on immediate matters of war – the listed dead and missing in action after the Battle of Dieppe and other events in Europe. It was disinterested in the new social order Local 480 leaders and others on the left sought.

So pleased was the CM&S with its women war workers that the new company magazine, *Cominco*, noted, "Women today are making one of their most direct and most important contributions to the war effort in industry." *Cominco* columnist Jean Thomson added, "Here in our own plant as elsewhere the women are taking over the jobs heretofore carried on by men. They are doing a good job; some are even showing how to do a better job." She applauded "the women power that is complementing manpower," even if many smelter jobs were dirty, boring, and tedious. Nevertheless, she wrote, "There's something very exciting and romantic about millions of women marching to their war jobs every day and swarming home at night. Eager, busy, they are piling up material force behind the greatest armies in history." Her glowing account painted the women as "girls who never dreamed of a job outside a department store or an office." Now they "are getting grease on their hands and liking it."[19]

Thomson may have been right, but as Larsen points out, in the double bind of gender duties, women were still expected to "continue their labour at home" as the wives, mothers, and daughters of soldiers. Despite such demands, media propaganda glamourized their role. Norman Rockwell famously created the American feminist icon Rosie the Riveter as a cover illustration for the *Saturday Evening Post*, widely read by English Canadians, including Trail subscribers. Canadian propagandists had already coined Ronnie the Bren Gun Girl and other symbols for the same purpose two years earlier.

Local 480 Leaders Address Calls for Women's Equality

On 5 May 1945, the war ended for Trail's smeltermen-soldiers fighting in Europe. Seventy-four of them had died and five were missing in action, according to company records.[20] They had helped liberate Fortress Holland and the rest of Nazi-dominated Europe. Now soldiers in bivouacs talked of "home, demobilization and that unfinished war in the Pacific," noted the *Times*.[21] Trail's wounded, like twenty-one-year-old Private Alex B. Connell of the CM&S's phosphate plant and Private Ray Scott, were returning home for good.[22] So was future Trail mayor F.E. "Buddy" DeVito, a radio technician with the RCAF who would take over his father's shoe repair business. He would soon become a stalwart supporter of Local 480, taking a job as a temporary Mine-Mill representative.[23] Also returning was Gunner Warren H. Watt of the CM&S blacksmith's shop.[24] And there would be many more.

On 7 May, the *Times* announced that the "Greatest Conflict Is Now Ended" and Trailites were planning their victory parade for the following day. Thousands would gather in Butler Park to watch a parade weave through the smelter city.[25] Citizens took the news that the war was finally over "quietly, almost docilely," the *Times* reported. "No sirens wailed, no whistles sounded as officials waited for the government announcement proclaiming the day VE-day,

but for the man on the street it was VE-day with or without proc-
lamation. The most usual question was 'Do we go to work?'"[26] The
possibility that the smelter wars might also be at an end could only
enhance the euphoric atmosphere.

Many of Trail's women had been highly praised smelter workers
who were among a quarter of a million women in Canada who
worked in war industries.[27] But their presence in the smelter plants
posed new problems for Mine-Mill, especially if the local intended
to adhere to the Mine-Mill constitution, with its insistence on gender equality. Tensions in the workplace would mount as women
occupied a larger space in the male-dominated union. Thus, even
as Mine-Mill began to prevail in Trail, gender revealed further
fault lines in the workplace and at home.

While many unions paid only lip service to women's equality,
Joan Sangster has argued that Mine-Mill and other Communist
unions "tried to highlight women's union and class consciousness."[28] In the early 1930s, for example, Harvey Murphy, then working with miners in the Crowsnest Pass area of Alberta, recognized
that "a negative attitude on the part of the miners' wives ... would
prove fatal to union solidarity." As Allen Seager noted, Murphy saw
the women "not only involved themselves tirelessly in the more
mundane aspects of relief work, but proved their determination
to win a better way of life for their children, on the picket line and
during the marches and demonstrations which became an almost
daily occurrence."[29]

In Trail, though, some women doubted whether Local 480 leaders shared these attitudes, and this complicated the local's bargaining and political agenda. If local leaders did subscribe to a rigid
Marxist class analysis, they may not have fully acknowledged the
role of gender at that time. However, had the union seen the advantages of linking class with gender, perhaps Trail's women might
have played a different role in what Ruth Frager calls the "adaptation and resistance not only to class inequality but also to other fundamental aspects of domination and subordination" that the CM&S
represented.[30] As it was, the local seemed content to avoid the issue.

Although Mine-Mill's constitution demanded support for wom-
en's equality, it was not obvious that the Trail local would uphold

those values. There were in fact numerous signs that it would favour the traditional views of many of its rank-and-file male members. Although local union leaders were willing to include women, it was only if male members benefitted as wage earners and only within their limited understanding of women's role in the union. In effect, it was union patriarchy. Nevertheless, the women brought important gender considerations into play. Local 480 leaders knew, for example, that they needed women war workers to bolster sagging membership figures during the organizing drive.

In the late 1930s and early 1940s, membership lagged in the double digits (a mere seventy-three in 1941). As the war gained momentum, Roth noted that "conditions set up a vicious cycle that devastated union growth." High wartime turnover required constant recruitment in a fluctuating workforce. As "membership bottomed out and recruitment stagnated," signing up the new female workforce was imperative. But this meant a change in tone and emphasis.[31] To attract female workers would require an organizing strategy that promised unionization would have a positive impact for women. One tactic of persuasion was to show that female workers would enjoy increased wages, as had occurred at some wartime workplaces organized by the CIO. As early as the spring of 1941, the *Commentator* reported CIO-bargained increases that "mean clothes, entertainment, and freedom from worry for the worker and his wife; it will enable some to marry. These dollars won by the CIO will buy education and food for millions of workingmen's children."[32] Elsewhere it noted, "Women are the biggest winners in the new pact between the Steel Workers' Organizing Committee and the U.S. Steel Company." The base wage would rise to 72.5 cents an hour from the previous 56 cents, "the same as the minimum rate for male workers."[33]

Women Quickly and Effectively Filled Male Jobs

This was an enticing prospect for Trail women, and as they entered the previously male-only plants on the Hill, the local might have been expected to support the CIO demand for equal pay for equal work. Instead, local leaders subordinated women's pay equality to

protect male members from post-war losses. Larsen, who interviewed eleven women war workers for an oral history study,
argues that the union leaders "took the stance that they were only
temporary workers."[34] *The Commentator* signalled what women
could expect when it released a gossip item in the paper's popular
"I Heard on the Hill" column. The piece noted that the company
was "toying with the idea of filling some smeltermen's jobs with
women." Treating the rumour as a joke, the writer asked "whether
it is to be in the melting room, sheet-casting, tank-pulling, lead
sheet or Tadanac police," all traditionally male roles.[35] If it was
meant in good humour, however, the joke was on the men. Women
quickly and effectively filled these jobs.

Understandably, then, as the organizing drive continued, support for the as-yet-uncertified local was mixed among women war
workers filling vacancies left by the 2,359 enlisted men destined for
overseas duty. In 1944, the CM&S workforce totalled 6,437, which
included employees at Sullivan Mine in Kimberley and other surrounding CM&S properties where women were also working in
non-traditional jobs.[36] Using a BC Labour Department determination that 7.7 per cent of workers in five BC smelters, the largest
being CM&S, were women, we could estimate that as many as 500
women were employed at the smelter at the peak of wartime production.[37] It is an imperfect indicator; at best a calculated guess.
There is no government or company record to verify how many
women were employed from 1942 to 1945.[38] However, Larsen suggests that "almost 2,000 women workers" may have been doing
traditionally male jobs during the war.[39] CM&S President Blaylock did not specify in his annual reports how many women were
hired, merely noting that they were used "extensively" and provided "splendid services" alongside "old employees [retained] after
normal pensionable age."[40]

Regardless of the exact number, the women were now a fact of
smelter life with shared common concerns different from the men
they replaced. The first was unequal wages. Women earned only
80 per cent of the rate enjoyed by the departing soldiers for largely
the same work. As Larsen notes, "Women's wages never reached
the level of men's." Even so, the CM&S ceiling was "far above" the

prevailing minimum for women. She also notes, "Many women across Canada were paid as low as 65 percent the wage of men."[41] Nonetheless, the wage rate was a sore point, one that Local 480 addressed partly through a *Commentator* poem:

Ladies, we invite you, now you're
Working on the hill,
Come join your union brothers,
Make this union stronger still;
Accept no lower wages, no matter what they say,
If you replace a man, you're entitled to his pay.[42]

In the same edition an article expanded on the poem's main point, urging women to join the union "for a greater production effort for sure protection of your rights to equality." The paper added, "Without complete equality there cannot be complete unity of purpose in [the] winning of the war."[43] The writer reminded the company that paying lower wages to students the year before had caused production to suffer, and that the same could happen with women. Despite the magnanimity of the poem and article, women posed a continuing problem for the male leadership of Local 480. Beyond lip service, poetic or otherwise, the union was not prepared to address the obvious wage disparities, even if the issue reached the bargaining table.

Underlying all these tensions was a strong dedication to a male breadwinner model within the smelter ranks. While Local 480's Red organizers might have agreed theoretically with the ideal of female equality, they were not about to challenge the bedrock working-class values of many of their members. Going too far might, of course, have undermined men's support for Red leadership in the context of certification votes or local union elections. Much effort had already been expended to convince the remaining male workforce to join the union. In addition, as Roth notes, "While this assurance of equal rights may have stemmed from a strong egalitarian impulse among Local 480's membership it also reflected a fear that women might undermine the union."[44]

Women Fully Engaged in Fighting Fascism

Another women's concern was the perceived need to postpone efforts to foster women's equality while the war carried on. Local 480 Communists, once unsupportive of the Allies, had been fully engaged in the fight against fascism since mid-1941 when Hitler invaded the Soviet Union. Women's equality, it seemed, would have to wait until that fight was won. For Trail Communists, the war became a convenient excuse: women's wage parity had to be set aside for the sake of total war. Ironically, wartime propaganda, whether left wing or simply pro-British, painted an unambiguously enthusiastic portrait of women war workers, showing them as integral players in the battle for increased production and in their role overseas. In an article entitled "British Compliment the Work of Canadian Girls," for example, Trailites learned that some of the forty-five Canadian women working at the Mechanized Transport Corps in London, England, were "driving lorries, ambulances, government cars, mobile canteens and libraries." One woman from Victoria "[is] a full-fledged mechanic and overhauls vehicles," the article declared.[45] In the United States, a University of Chicago "experiment in training women for war industries" had attracted 1,200 applicants for initial openings. Sixty women eventually attended the ten-week course to be trained for wartime roles as administrators and supervisors in "five major fields ... office supervision, personnel problems, accounting and statistical techniques, secretarial practice, and business organization."[46] Such reports encouraged Trail women to serve the war effort by doing traditional male jobs in the smelter. However, the articles did not specify they would be doing them for discriminatory wages.

In spite of the proud portraits of women smelter workers, men in the Trail plants maintained control of all supervisory positions while women in varied ways were identified as temporary presences. Despite their more than satisfactory work, their labour remained desired only so long as men were unavailable, and increased employment opportunities exacerbated high turnover rates at the smelter. Blaylock reported that the average pre-war turnover was about 10 per cent. "The labour shortage during 1945 was more acute than in any of the former war years," he added. "The situation was dealt with by giving preference to productive operations, by continuing to use women extensively, and by retaining older employees after normal pensionable age. The splendid services of the women and these older men are gratefully acknowledged."[47] It was a rare public acknowledgment.

Blaylock cheered the women, but it was clear to progressive unions like Mine-Mill that there was potential for exploitation. Still, the union response was hardly adequate to the task of ensuring gender equality in the workplace. The CIO was committed to a policy of equal pay for equal work, as Wendy Cuthbertson explains, noting that "it was wartime conditions that had encouraged CIO unions to take up the cause of women's equality." She further notes that "the most frequently used argument for equal pay was women's right to equality." However, the unions also "argued the merits of equal pay in terms of boosting the war effort and supporting male wages."[48] Local 480 was no different. "If women are employed at the smelter," argued the *Commentator*, "it is partly the responsibility of the men to see that these women are paid at the going rate, and not used as a means of job competition." In a further indication that the local was less than committed to gender equality, the union paper bluntly proposed hiring the unemployed "before any stampede for women is created."[49]

Local 480 leaders were caught betwixt their union's emancipatory rhetoric and the political and cultural realities of their male breadwinner values. In that regard, Larsen is pointedly critical, noting that President Al King's account of Local 480's wartime role was "devoid" of women workers' voices. As King stated in his memoir, "When the war was over ... and the veterans came back to work at the Trail smelter, the women had to leave.... They went willingly, I think, because they knew when they took the jobs that they were just taking our places while we were away."[50] Larsen counters that "there is no first-hand evidence that all female workers were happy to leave their jobs," and she asks, "What voice did they have to protest?"[51] She concludes that Local 480 never accepted women as equal members of the workforce.

The *Times* and other analysts of the situation argued that this absence of support was a sign of the times and that everyone understood that women would have to leave their wartime jobs when the men returned home. But as Dorothy Sue Cobble argues, in the United States "most hoped to keep these plum jobs at war's end."[52] Trail women may have shared that view, but Local 480's male members and its Communist leaders never supported such a possibility. Researcher Joanne Pepper's oral history interviews with male smelter workers in BC revealed that the men generally viewed women workers as temporary. As one interview subject put it, "My wife went to work in the hydrogen plant because she had to have something to live on while I was away." When she was laid off, she never worked outside the home again.[53] Indeed, they were following masculine traditions that harkened back to the earliest days of the mining and smelting industry in the province. Clearly, patriarchy was central here, but even for some women equality was a threat to the nuclear household ideal. Hence, many conservative women continued to oppose equal rights and sexual liberation.

Male Breadwinner Attitudes Clash with Women's Equality

Judging from Pepper's interviews and Larsen's conclusions, the Communist leadership's dedication to class-based solutions and male breadwinner considerations ruled the day as women were forced out of higher-paying jobs at the end of the war. When they left their smelter jobs, at least some women, possibly the majority, stopped earning a living wage. They fell back on lower-paying work as domestics, hospitality workers, and office clerks. Many returned to unpaid work as housewives or, as King put it, as "unpaid employees of the goddamned company."[54]

Cobble argues that in the 1930s, when women joined union ranks in droves, "unions neither made special efforts to organize jobs in which women worked nor did they adjust their ideology to embrace the differing perspective of women."[55] In the 1940s some women did take "to the picket lines and to shop-floor leadership," but few did so in Trail.[56] Local 480 leaders gave women scant support for self-advocacy. Some of the more doctrinaire CPC members might have argued that class came foremost in the struggle against capitalism, but none seemed to consider gender or ethnicity as factors of analysis. The possibility that gender-related concerns might merge with class interests to further worker solidarity apparently did not occur to them. Instead, King and other Communist union leaders viewed women's equality as subordinate to the real enemy, which was the capitalist class and its system. As a result, women went back to the home and returning soldiers went back to their old jobs. The male traditions were maintained, but the challenges to it would continue to stretch the limits of Mine-Mill as an advocate of gender equality.

For those women war workers who did join Local 480, some fully embraced the union. During the war, for example, Irene Vetere became a union trustee and a shop steward in the sulphate plant in Warfield. Betty Mar and Peggy Ball were also elected as trustees.[57] Local 480's male members nevertheless expected the union to represent male interests first. Mine-Mill was "proud of its 'rank and file democracy' within which 'women members are guaranteed equal rights,'" King stated in his memoir.[58] In Larsen's view, however, "Mine Mill regarded women more as wives than workers. At this time they were more important to the union as auxiliaries than full-fledged members."[59] Serving the war effort at home was also seen by male smelter workers as more traditional women's work: sewing, knitting, organizing drives of one type or another, and volunteering for Red Cross duties. Even women who enlisted in the military were given a choice of mostly traditional roles. Only in the factories did women move beyond "women's work," and much to some people's surprise, women worked well.

Jean Stainton, who served in the smelter's oxide leaching plant from 1942 to 1945 at a daily wage of $4.35, remembered enjoying the job despite male condescension. "Management realized that we were turning out to be better than they thought," she recalled. At first, though, they "just thought we were silly women not realizing that women are very good at multi-tasking." Stainton did not support the union. When she learned that Local 480 leaders planned to eliminate performance bonuses in favour of a more equitable wage system, she turned against them. "We told them, 'Why don't you leave it this way? We're getting the bonus,'" she recalled. "Now if they make it that we get X number during the day we're going to lose the bonus. We could tell that this is what would happen, but they didn't listen to us. Then they were crying afterwards."[60]

Other women shared Stainton's view that smelter jobs paid well and were a way to help soldiers overseas. They also shared her anti-union sentiments. "Smelterwoman," for example, wrote to the *Times* to complain that a CIO organizer had "requested that I join the union or threatened I would lose my job."[61] In a second letter, she called Murphy a liar and charged that he "doesn't believe us women can do a man's job and stay in the fighting line." She advised women to "be brave and keep in line with an honest and desirable heart and soul to fight Hitlerism."[62] "Laborer's Wife" chastised these letter writers for not identifying themselves. Isabelle Piper instead asked women to "lend a helping hand to the cause of Labor."[63] In the anti-union *Times*, such letters of union support were aberrations.

Male Attitudes Couched in Patriotic Terms

Whether or not they supported the union, wartime jobs gave some Trail women a glimpse of what might be possible. CIO support for gender equality, however uncertain, "contributed to their expanded sense of their rights and their proper due," Cuthbertson argues.[64] Larsen agrees that women's "horizons and opportunities did expand," but "stereotypes and generalizations persisted." Men's comments about women war workers illustrated "the dominance of a male breadwinner ideal as female competency was consistently described in male terms."[65] Men's predominant view, that a woman's place was in the home, was often couched in patriotic terms. An article in the *Rossland Miner*, for example, argued that "while other nations seek to destroy our way of life, claiming womanhood and her great gift of motherhood, for the nation, we still believe, and are fighting for, the sanctity of our homes and the family life." The writer concluded, "The strength of the nation still lies, we believe, in the home."[66] Even "A Rossland Union Woman," writing in the *Trail Ad-News*, a *Times* rival, expressed her "women's appeal" in similar terms. She argued that women were "letting our boys down by not fighting together in an organization such as a trade union through which you can get equal rights with men, better jobs and better conditions." But she also advised that "when you have done this you will be able to proudly welcome them home and truthfully admit that you have done a good job while they've been gone and have made things easier for them to take over."[67]

Such home-front loyalty did not preclude a critical debate in Canada that would encourage Trailites to at least consider whether it was socially acceptable in post-war North America for women to join the traditionally male workforce and to challenge the breadwinner concept. In the short run, however, and like elsewhere in Canada, Trail women faced what has been called "the prevailing twentieth-century pattern of privileging men in the workforce." As Joy Parr further observes, men maintained their breadwinner status under a capitalist "system run by and mainly to benefit some men."[68] A study of mining women reiterated the point, using Mine-Mill as an example. "Mine Mill's commitment to social unionism ensured that women's activities, although separate from those of the male union members, were regarded as legitimate (at least by the leadership)," wrote Laurie Mercier and Jaclyn Gier. "Yet the space the women were able to claim within the Canadian Mine Mill still reaffirmed the male breadwinner's role and limited women's activism to the cultural prescriptions of domesticity."[69] Regardless of that assumed legitimacy, it was clear that Local 480 was going to follow what Ruth Milkman described as a "family-wage ideology [that] relied heavily on the male's right to an improved standard of living as the family breadwinner, and implied a fundamental difference between the rights of male and female workers."[70]

By the end of the war some of those women would question why their union had not devoted itself more to resolving women's workplace issues, but for the moment duty called. As Cuthbertson explains, women would be "urged to leave what was assumed to be their home-centred private life and take up the masculine public duty of aiding the war effort." For the women, the war had opened up a vision of "a larger world they could inhabit, one with more vocational choice, greater financial security and independence, the chance to work outside the home after marriage, and the opportunity to lead."[71] Larsen found that Trail women war workers depicted the war as "a time of change and mobility and the post war period as one of stagnancy and restriction," yet wartime experiences had given them new ways to perceive themselves and their capabilities. "They carried these changes with them for the rest of their lives, influencing their marriages and families."[72]

Even before the war ended, then, demands for equal opportunities for women were being postponed, and any widespread effort to support such demands would not surface with any collective force until Second Wave feminism arrived in the 1960s. Still, as the Allies advanced towards decisive victory, and women workers prepared to resume their lives as homemakers or in more traditional female jobs, CCF MLA Laura Jamieson of Vancouver called for a twenty-five-cent raise. The wage hike was secondary to her desire to allow women the choice to remain in the male workforce. In the *Times* article, she claimed that the "cycles of depression" among female workers "are characteristic of the capitalistic system with security of income denied the family." She also blamed capitalism for its failure to "provide for low cost housing," adding that its "refusal to provide health insurance led to a high maternal and infant mortality rate."[73]

Local 480's Communists agreed, but they did not see the benefit of connecting the fight against capitalism to women workers at the smelter. Instead, they sponsored a Smelter Queen contest "in recognition of women's rights."[74] It was billed as part of the 1945 May Day celebrations and would be a way to "commemorate the great influx of women into industry and organized labor." The *Commentator* considered it a fitting event.[75]

Harvey Murphy's *B.C. District Union News* reminded Trail readers that for women war workers, so much heralded, peace began with mass layoffs. As small compensation, Local 480 had asked the company to give laid-off women the annual Christmas bonus. The company complied and sent each woman $37.50, representing "half the Christmas bonus."[76] It was a stinging reminder that, although they did equal work, women never received equal pay.

A sarcastic *Times* letter writer would later call upon Trail women to join her "International Union of Down-Trodden Housewives of Trail, Rossland, and Kimberley." She signed the letter "Aw. Turnitoffsky," a pun referring to Murphy's original Polish surname Chernikofsky.[77] Some women likely found it humorous, but the loss of jobs and the union's disregard of it were no laughing matter.

Women Workers Return to Traditional Roles

Although most of Trail's women war workers returned to traditional roles, they had helped precipitate what Claudia Goldin called a "quiet revolution" in which ever more women entered the workforce in the ensuing decades. "These working-class women," Mercier suggests, "sought more fundamental change, both in their relationships with male unions and in the world. They struggled for women's equal rights and universal child care, world peace, and inter-racial solidarity, and in general a more progressive post-war society."[78] Regrettably, change came slowly. With the war in Europe won, few if any women found non-traditional work at the smelter.[79] Instead, the CM&S and Local 480 welcomed soldiers home to promised jobs.

Ruth Roach Pierson summarized the situation: "The war's slight yet disquieting reconstruction of womanhood in the direction of equality with men was scrapped for a full-skirted and re-domesticated post-war model, and for more than a decade feminism was once again sacrificed to femininity."[80] Trail women's wartime work experience was no exception. Women working in the retail sector at department stores like Eaton's and Simpson's, for example, faced similar employer discrimination. "Drawing on the widespread assumption that women were transient wage earners," writes Donna Belisle, "department stores deliberately kept women at entry-level salaries."[81] Susanne Klausen cites Pierson's argument in examining the Port Alberni plywood plant on Vancouver Island. The factory opened in January 1942 and began hiring women workers several months before the Trail smelter did so. "The Canadian government's National Selective Service's strategy of channelling single (and eventually married) women into war industries was motivated purely by desperation for female labour power and not out of commitment to women's right to well-paid employment."[82]

Considering the actions of Murphy and Local 480 Communists regarding women war workers, gender analysis reveals that Trail women experienced material inequality after the war. Concerns for returning veterans ensured that most women would not realize a continuation of their wartime earnings and status. Some did praise women, even advocating that they remain in smelter jobs, but the prospect of former employees returning home after risking all for country and freedom created an immense political and ethical problem for those who wished to maintain the wartime status quo. Meanwhile, another group of Trail women was preparing to enter the debate about conflicting gender roles and breadwinner traditions.

As the war persisted into the mid-1940s, letters to the *Times* revealed that inside workers' homes, many smelter spouses were also among those dissatisfied with Local 480. Since the union drive began, they frequently worried that Mine-Mill would breed strikes and thus undermine household income. Early on, a *Times* letter writer accused the union of starving strikers' children and urged the editor to "keep on rubbing it into the C.I.O."[83] Another, calling herself "A Smelterman's Wife," chastised union organizers for wasting workers' precious time. "When our evenings work is over, and the bucket is filled," she wrote, "we take one last look at the big stacks and pray God for the safety of our men."[84] Still another "Smelterman's Wife" wrote about a young man who had died when the union refused to assist his family after he had scabbed. "Last night there were six women in my home," she added, "and all were against the C.I.O. idea."[85] "Company Man's Wife" argued, "If we allow a few injustices to blind us to good things, we make it very hard for our husbands. Each day they are up against the arguments meant to foment trouble [by] the agitators scattered through the plant." She asked smelter spouses to "stop for a minute to consider how contemptible is this element of disruption in our midst under the guise of bettering our lot." She warned smelter men that union leaders "will disappear fast after they have led you into trouble."[86]

Some of the union's female critics subscribed to the Catholic Church's view that the union was to be avoided, for it would "dictate to us in the best Hitler style."[87] Some of them would volunteer for the Red Cross or join other service groups to assist the war effort. Some, for example, were members of the Imperial Order Daughters of the Empire and among their roles was a silence campaign to prevent the enemy from learning of Allied troop movements or the position of war plants like the smelter.[88] Other spouses joined religious-based organizations, but several Trail women also opted to join Mine-Mill Ladies Auxiliary Local 131, chartered on 27 June 1944. It was the same year American singer-songwriter Woodie Guthrie sang about ladies auxiliaries being the "the best auxiliary that you ever did see."[89] No doubt this champion of working people meant auxiliaries like those in Mine-Mill.

"The ladies have shown great interest in the struggle of Local 480," Mine-Mill representative Don Guise, another Communist, told the *B.C. District Union News*. Thirty women signed the charter application. Edith Woytella was the first president, A. Littley was secretary-treasurer, and Leona Pollack was recording secretary.[90] The executive included Edna Henne, wife of Local 480 President Fred Henne, and Kay Dosen, wife of Dan Dosen, a Communist charter member of the local. He had worked closely with CIO organizer Slim Evans in the late 1930s. Communist Tillie Belanger, wife of Local 480's first president, Gar Belanger, was among the founding members, and she and Kay Dosen added political action to the auxiliary agenda.

Mine-Mill Auxiliary Shows Independent Spirit

Larsen's study discounts the possibility of an effective political role for the auxiliary, arguing that in the post-war period Local 480 leaders relegated women to a support role. "Although much progress and many changes had indeed occurred during the war regarding ideas about gender," she commented, "after the war it was simpler to regress back to those 'old ideas' and circumvent those changes even within a union which claimed to recognize 'the rights of all women to free independence, the right to be treated as equals with men in all dealings such as wages, working conditions and grievances."[91]

As other scholars have recognized, such organizations had separate constitutions and the political will to act in women's as well as men's interests at the smelter. Trail's auxiliary was a prime example of how "auxiliaries offered a way for them to participate in class politics and work for their economic interests and communities outside the home." Mercier explains that Mine-Mill, unlike many international unions, "recognized the broader political and economic value of women's participation and actively encouraged women's auxiliary membership, often arguing that 'A union without the women is only half organized.'"[92]

The presence of Communists on the auxiliary executive might have created a sense of complacency amidst Local 480's Red leaders. After all, even before Ladies Auxiliary Local 131 was chartered there were healthy signs of an independent spirit. A few months earlier, the *Commentator* reported that Henne addressed a meeting of future auxiliary women, where he suggested their function was to "be a follow-up of Local 480." Lucia Sigfried, a visiting International Mine-Mill Ladies Auxiliary vice-president from Idaho, countered that the auxiliary did not "just follow" but worked alongside the local.[93] She won the point and got a round of applause from the gathering. Once chartered, the auxiliary immediately showed its support for the Communist-led local, yet it maintained its independence of the union. Belanger and Dosen subscribed as much to the Mine-Mill constitution as their spouses. They were not interested in playing the wartime role of other Trail spouses, such as participating in knitting circles, and some refused to be known solely as the wife of someone, an identifier that even Mary Biner, the *Times* women's page editor, rejected as inadequate to describe women's role. As she saw it, "All in all, Mrs. Trail is rapidly becoming an important cog in Canada's war machine."[94]

It stood to reason, then, that ladies auxiliary members would not see themselves as a mere adjunct of the male-dominated union, providing meals, organizing bake sales, and supporting husbands at home. Contrary to male expectations, they planned to actively defend the union against outside attacks. Years later, spouses of prominent Local 480 activists broadcast a message of support entitled "How Disruption of Our Union Affects the Womenfolk."[95] Tillie Belanger occasionally used Mine-Mill's *Union* to warn that Local 480's enemies "are nothing more than vultures out to destroy you and Mine-Mill." Her politics were clearly stated in one article where she argued against union action that "tends to disunite the working class but strengthens the ruling class to the point where it can further exploit and destroy the Trade Union Movement and the freedom of the working class."[96] As Local 480 President Henne had learned, Local 131 members could often be fiercely independent but remain ideologically in agreement with him and other local left-wing leaders.

One *Commentator* writer, perhaps recalling Sigfried, reflected on how "brothers and sisters of the surrounding communities" had worked side by side to establish "a broader democracy in the feudal empire of the Consolidated."[97] Murphy sometimes overlooked the strong support of women, but with nudging from spouse Isobel he would publicly recognize their importance. During mine workers' battles in the Crow's Nest area of Alberta in the 1930s, for example, he acknowledged, "Lots of women participated in the strike and we relied on them."[98] But he, as with Henne and other Local 480 leaders, usually viewed the auxiliaries as being behind rather than alongside the union. Al King, for example, claimed that they recognized the importance of auxiliaries, but Larsen challenged the claim. "His statement about the function of these Auxiliaries illustrates the attitudes towards women that the union held," she argued, and those attitudes did not recognize a role that was not subordinate to men.[99] In King's view, "Their purpose, as set out in our Constitution, was to see to 'education and training of women in the labour movement and to assist their Local Union in time of need and labour disputes, to support the Union in its legislative efforts and to provide educational and cultural activities for our members and their children.'"[100] Larsen added that King, while proud of his union's "rank and file democracy" and its putative guarantee of women's rights, "regarded women more as wives than workers."[101] Like Henne, the men of Local 480 seemed to envisage a typical auxiliary member as a "good union girl" who "worked to support her family, used makeup moderately, kept her stocking seams straight, and went out on the picket line with her man because having 'girls come on the line ... puts more pep in the gas.'"[102]

Not Just Whist Parties and Tea Dances

Contrary to that image, auxiliary members were far from mere sponsors of social activities like whist parties and tea dances. In fact, the mandate of Mine-Mill's Canadian auxiliary constitution included the education and training of women in the labour movement, assistance to their local unions in times of need and labour disputes, support for the union in legislative work, and the provision of educational and cultural activities for union children. Elizabeth and Andrea Quinlan argue that Trail's Local 131 and other Canadian auxiliaries applied themselves to achieving their political ends through the execution of their constitutional obligations. Through their study of newsletters from twenty-five auxiliary locals in Canada in the late 1940s, the Quinlans conclude, "Traditional forms of 'women's' work were crucial to maintaining the social fabric of the union and provided a local system supporting the health and welfare of the community." They further conclude that auxiliaries were "more than a 'reserve army' of emotional and supportive labourers. They acted as independent organizations." They add, "In practice, their fund-raising activities provided them with some financial autonomy, which they used to support their own political agenda including women's emancipation."[103]

Mercier adds that auxiliary members "took advantage of strikes to station themselves publicly on picket lines, they utilized assumptions about their roles in the feminized space of the kitchen to insert themselves into union affairs."[104] At auxiliaries like Local 131, "the male unionists' attention to the kitchen space, to the women's delight, represented some acknowledgement of the women's value to the union's cause and an accession to at least one of their requests." But the process of being acknowledged as political activists was frustrating. A Cobalt, Idaho, auxiliary president urged her members to continue offering their help to the local union, but

Mercier notes that she also pressed them to insist that "women can do more than cook a good dinner, put on a banquet or help with that dance or picnic."[105]

Although Mine-Mill auxiliaries worked primarily to support the development and preservation of a democratic union movement, police officers saw them as potentially subversive organizations. Mercedes Steedman elaborates: "During the post-war period, whenever an auxiliary in Rossland, British Columbia, or Port Colborne, Ontario, held a tea party," she reveals that "local RCMP officers would report the event to the Security and Intelligence Branch in Ottawa." Even Christmas raffles, bazaars, and charity draws were documented.[106] In the case of Communists Belanger and Dosen of Local 131, police interest was piqued even further. Like other progressive auxiliary members, they "worked for the cessation of weapons testing, for full disarmament, and for the creation of conditions that 'would enable women to fulfill their roles in society, as mothers, workers, and citizens which includes the right to work, the protection of motherhood, equal rights with regards to marriage, children and property.'" Mine-Mill women like those in the Trail auxiliary "held a different vision of postwar economic and social recovery, and in the immediate postwar years, week after week, year after year, they continued to organize around that vision and build on it, despite constant RCMP intimidation and surveillance."[107]

The Trail auxiliary's organizational skills were recognized at the international level with some US auxiliary leaders crediting Local 131 as an innovator. In fact, International Mine-Mill promoted the local's display of leadership as a way to increase auxiliary involvement, including an essay contest. Women needed to join men in "upholding our International Constitution," argued the winning essay, which was published in the *Union*. And they needed to "'preserve the democratic rights of all workers' including 'freedom to choose one's own religion, or politics.'"[108] The writer was Rachel Wood, a former war worker at the Trail smelter and Local 131's financial secretary.

Perhaps the Trail auxiliary's boldest organizational effort was a defensive action in 1947 when Belanger and Dosen, among others, took issue with Butte, Montana, miner's spouse Mary Orlich, president of Mine-Mill's international auxiliaries. During the 1946 Butte miners' strike, Orlich had "invoked the language of class in urging others to 'war on these big bosses,'" but she "quickly diverted her wrath away from corporations and onto Mine Mill."[109] "Commies are a common enemy," she declared in the *Saturday Evening Post*, pledging to "organize all housewives in America to fight this scourge."[110] Perhaps the change of heart came partly from home: Orlich was married to one-time Butte Local 1 President Dan Orlich, a vocal anti-Communist. Canadian Auxiliary President Kay Carlin of Sudbury, Ontario, warned Orlich that she was "playing right into the hands of reaction."[111] Auxiliary Local 77 at Kirkland Lake, Ontario, demanded Orlich's "immediate expulsion from the ranks of honest working women" – a call Kimberley's auxiliary Local 137 supported.[112]

The Trail auxiliary even more fiercely opposed Orlich, accusing her of "pandering to the capitalist press." "You say it is the Commies who are disrupting the unions," wrote Local 131 Recording Secretary E.M. Busquet in the *B.C. District Union News*, but "it is people like yourself, who are the stooges of Big Business by playing right along with them in the labor-splitting tactics, who are the true disruptors." Her next statement might have come directly from Belanger and Dosen, the two leading Reds in the Trail auxiliary group: "You are in the same category as the Hitlerites in Germany and the Mussolinis in Italy who first disunited the unions through rotten propaganda and then were able to build Nazism and Fascism," she lambasted Orlich. "Do you want this to happen in America? We believe that you have made a terrible error in attacking a minority group in the Union and that you [must] resign immediately."[113] Other Canadian auxiliary members called Carlin the real troublemaker. The *Times* fanned these ideological differences, promoting dissension among Canadian auxiliaries. It predictably saluted Orlich for her stand against Communists in the union movement. Relying heavily on the *Post* article, editor Curran agreed with Orlich that "when the commies are in the picture, nobody wins."[114]

Red Baiting Revealed at International Auxiliary

The affair led International Mine-Mill to disband the auxiliary and organize a new one after charging Orlich with "deliberately neglecting Canadian locals 'for disruptive reasons.'" Orlich continued to battle the Communists, but she was marginalized within the union. Mine-Mill men also condemned Orlich's Red baiting but, as Mercier notes, they did so through gender stereotyping, dismissing her as "a particular gender rather than [a] political weakness." The Tired Mucker, Murphy's star columnist at the B.C. District Union News, characterized her as "just a simple little housewife" duped by the "Great Dog" of capitalism.[115] The BC paper also reported that a Butte Mine-Mill Local 1 executive member accused Orlich of "meddling in men's union affairs" and dubbed the Post article "the usual run of anti-union hokum."[116] Auxiliary members like Belanger and Dosen rejected such sexist attitudes and, with the Orlich battle concluded, they turned to other initiatives, including support for Local 480 in its confrontations with the CM&S.

Although Trail's auxiliary continued to fight anti-Communist union adversaries, the Local 480 leadership's view of its role was not one of equal partnership such as Idaho Auxiliary President Sigfried had described to President Henne. Instead it was to be a mere appendage in the male union's class war in Trail. Mercier argues that this "inability to embrace the potential of working-class solidarity across gender lines, union rhetoric to the contrary, diminished labor internationalism's clout to match global capital."[117] Belanger and Dosen would themselves be irritated by their own party's view that women merited only secondary status. As Joan Sangster points out, "by failing to question the ideal of the male breadwinner, socialists obscured a full exploration of women's economic exploitation" well into the future.[118]

Still more internal political contradictions loomed ahead with regard to Mine-Mill auxiliaries, but Murphy ultimately acknowledged that a successful auxiliary could help overcome the idea that a trade union "is only for the men and women have no interest…. [The] whole family is affected." If not for women's organizing, he claimed, "strikes in mining towns would not be effective."

Therefore, the labour movement "is as important to bring home to the women as it is to the men." Murphy highlighted women's "power" in the home and in reaching other women in the community. He also admitted that the "main trouble there is still the attitude of the men towards the Auxiliary." His spouse, Isobel, an active auxiliary member of Britannia Ladies Auxiliary Local 133 in Vancouver, had likely encouraged this more enlightened view, but by then the moment for achieving effective class solidarity, combining gender with class, was fast disappearing.[119]

When Trail's auxiliary women welcomed home their smelter soldiers, they were confronted with another social contradiction. They knew men were suffering from disillusionment different from their own. They learned that veterans who were forced to congregate in hobo jungles before the war were now seemingly resigned again to similar camps. In the aftermath of the bloody world conflict, women heard those men ask themselves whether anything had changed. While they were abroad, their smelter colleagues, male and female, had engaged in an internal war that involved repeated attacks on Local 480 leaders because they were Communists. The *Commentator* told them that Mine-Mill leaders were being "persecuted, jailed, beaten, hunted by police, and killed" for activities in militant trade unions. It blamed the "Red Bogey" for undermining "organized labor, its leaders or supporters, who with justice in their hearts, fought to better the lot of the common man." These "Red Bogey men" who use "this Red issue" were "despicable." They "fall into the Hitler category in attempting to divert the attention of people away from the real issues so that these reactionaries can become the ruling force." Such tactics, the paper warned, would "cause division and return us to the road to Fascism."[120] Auxiliary women like Belanger and Dosen likely would have agreed with that assessment.

With women war workers returning to traditional roles, the notion of a future free of gender bias was postponed in the smelter city. Women continued to support men, and men continued to foreground the male breadwinner ideal. The auxiliary maintained its independent stance and, as internal workplace conflict intensified between Mine-Mill, the ISWU, and later the raiding

Steelworkers union, Local 131 members found themselves filling more pressing political support roles while continuing to function as food providers and social conveners.

War-weary Trailites may have been forgiven for feeling indifference to the fast-paced political developments being set in motion by a federal election call in mid-1945. Their weariness soon increased after learning in the *Times* that smelter workers had been secretly producing "heavy water which is used to control the release of energy in the [atomic] bomb."[121] Coupled with those worries, the men and women of Trail would once again have to choose sides regarding Local 480. The end of the war transitioned to another kind of war, and the union again found itself at the centre of the conflict. It would be a war of ideologies, with the Catholic Church playing a key role within the smelter city's immigrant enclave and on the anti-Red front lines. Italian workers and their families would be at the centre of the drive, some advocating for the union and others rejecting it.

4

Mine-Mill Courts Trail's Immigrant Enclave

Officially the Second World War did not end until Japan surrendered on 2 September 1945, but with the fighting finally over, social relations were forever altered both globally and in remote corners such as Trail. Local servicemen began to return to their old jobs, supplanting women at the smelter. Some soldiers welcomed their new status as Local 480 members, others continued to balk at its Communist leadership. There were mixed memories of the "good old days" when Blaylock's Workmen's Co-operative Committee (WCC) reigned in Trail, and some of its remnants remained opposed to the new Red union. When the opportunity arose, they would again work to oust Local 480, emphasizing even fiercer anti-Communist arguments than before. Indeed, post-war battles involved nativist attitudes, ethnic traditions, cultural differences, Old World politics, and religious affiliations. The Catholic Church and Protestant denominations emerged as key opponents of Local 480. Their priests, ministers, and lay elders influenced congregations with spiritually based critiques of Communism, but nowhere did religious-based anti-Communist arguments resonate more deeply than within Trail's immigrant enclave.

Although the Allies had been victorious, home front households were still dealing with the meat rationing that had remained in force during the year and restaurants pondered what to serve patrons on meatless Tuesdays and Fridays. The continuation of beer rationing presented an even greater challenge, but potato shortages would soon end. Laid-off women war workers welcomed the arrival of Mackenzie King's famous "baby bonuses," prompting the *Times* editor to complain that the city's banks were being inundated with new clients uneducated about banking practices. The cheques were sent directly to the mothers. In this way, the women could preserve some money for the household rather than see it in some cases flow directly into the beer parlour.[1] Some of the bonus money might even be set aside to enjoy a light-hearted movie like *Two Girls and a Sailor* or a musical like *Meet Me in St. Louis.* Staying at home, they might tune in to a CJAT broadcast like *The Man Who Dreamed Too Much.* The Italian Maple Leaf Band entertained patrons at the Colombo Lodge, and the Rossland Ramblers Orchestra played at some Local 480 social functions.

That autumn the *Times* had reported the role the smelter had played in developing the atomic bombs that had been exploded over Japan, decisively ending the conflict in the Pacific and sending a warning to the Communist Soviet Union. The world had entered the nuclear age and the Cold War. Incongruously, given what we know today about the impossibility of surviving a nuclear holocaust, the *Times* advised Trailites on how to cope with possible future bombings. This further fuelled post-war fears, especially among immigrants whose families in Europe had been directly affected by the war. Synchronized with church intentions, the daily also resumed its crusade against socialism and Communism. Following the *Vancouver Sun*'s lead, the *Times* declared Marxist intellectual Harold Laski that "high priest of the left" who "shouts from every stump in England that the new age of communism is dawning and that capitalism will soon be only a memory."[2] Although local church leaders from the three major denominations held different shades of opinion, they largely backed the *Times*'s opposition to Communist-led dissent.

Trail's clergy frequently advised immigrant parishioners, especially Catholics from Italy, Croatia, and other Slavic communities, who made up 30 per cent of the population, according to the 1941 Canada Census.[3] They warned them to avoid unions, especially "those Godless Communists" at Local 480, Al King recalled.[4] A similar message reached Protestant congregations. Now they redoubled their efforts, with members of the clergy who had earlier supported unionization also coming under attack. Always critical of Red sympathizers, the *Times* was unrelenting in its excoriation of Dr. Hewlett Johnson, the dean of Canterbury. Christened the "Red Dean" by the national media, senior figures in the Church of England criticized him for his Christian Marxism and for preaching cooperation with the Soviet Union.[5] Johnson was among only a few church leaders to sustain support for unions, but his political views were scarcely binding on Canadian prelates. The November 1947 Synod of the Ontario church, for example, heard a thundering denunciation of "Russia and Communism" from senior bishop C.A. Seager.[6] In fact, most counselled their working-class congregations to beware Red outsiders such as Mine-Mill Western Regional Director Harvey Murphy. Interestingly, one of Murphy's early experiences with the church helped the union during the Crowsnest Pass miners' strike of 1932. Reverend M.A. Harrington, who later became the Roman Catholic bishop of Kamloops, BC, refused to join an anti-union campaign in Blairmore, Alberta. Murphy publicly denounced Protestant ministers in the town's "Red Square" but exempted "the Catholic priest who has remained neutral."[7]

Trail smelter workers heard and read about church elders touting a pro-employer ideology, and such religiously sanctioned political views carried influence in the workplace and at home. In Trail's pioneer years there was also "a culture or subculture in which non-belief was an acceptable option," explains Lynne Marks. And in West Kootenay mining and smelting communities "this culture was grounded in labour radicalism and socialism."[8] Even so, many Local 480 members rejected the atheism of Communist labour leaders such as Murphy, Al King, Gar Belanger, and Harry Drake. In fact, King was a kind of object lesson regarding the link between Marxism and godlessness. A former altar boy, the former Local 480 president once remarked, "I'd never heard of good people not believing in God." Yet his reading of Karl Marx's *Capital* and *The Communist Manifesto* led him to reject the church.[9] Not all union members followed this path, but in Trail some understood the Communist-led union to be irreligious, if not anti-Christian.

This was no small matter in the smelter city or in other parts of the Kootenays where church leaders believed workers were susceptible to spiritual teachings. In the spring of 1909, for example, many towns were part of a two-month-long evangelistic campaign of religious revival and moral reform. The committee guiding the campaign was "concerned about the region's reputation for vice and labour radicalism," wrote Norman Knowles, noting that the *Nelson Daily News* lauded the evangelists as preaching "a man's religion with power and vigour."[10] The revivalists were uncomfortable with the labour movement's "emphasis upon class conflict," but they shared the labour leaders' language and rhetorical style. Knowles added that they appealed to workers' notions of manhood and insisted that "Jesus was a worker who proclaimed a message of 'brotherhood and co-operation' rather than competition."[11]

The Religious and Secular Mixed Freely

Such messages were delivered at sermons in at least some of Trail's thirteen churches where parishioners, especially immigrant families, worshipped regularly. The book *Trail of Memories* describes the various denominations including Mormons, Baptists, Lutherans, and Seventh Day Adventists.[12] Canada Census figures for 1941 show that in addition to almost a third being Catholic, about 21 per cent of the population was Anglican (Church of England).[13] In the management village of Tadanac 12 per cent were Catholic and 30 per cent were Anglican, including CM&S President S.G. Blaylock.[14] Moreover, religious life was never merely local. The politics of Ontario, Quebec, and the Old Country circulated within the clergy and laity. The religious and the secular mixed freely in the local smelter workforce, and on the surface this could seem irrelevant to Local 480.

Church attendance was not an official concern of the union, and smelter workers were free to worship as they pleased. Indeed, prominent labour leaders encouraged this. CIO President Philip Murray and Canadian Steelworker President Charles Millard, for example, both came from strong Christian backgrounds.[15] Their religious motivations and the preaching of CCF leader J.S. Woodsworth, Methodist Marxist Albert E. Smith, and Toronto-based social gospeller Salem Bland influenced many. Richard Allen explains that this "call for men to find the meaning of their lives in seeking to realize the Kingdom of God in the very fabric of society" could in the minds of many labourers seem like a call to embrace socialism as a radical form of Christianity.[16] A.E. Smith spoke of the "essentially religious spirit of Labour" and founded several labour churches in Western Canada before abandoning Christianity in favour of Communism.[17]

A short time after the war ended, however, church attitudes in Trail rapidly turned towards rabid anti-Communism. A *Times* reprint from the *Canadian Churchman* illustrated that attitude when it stated, "Communism is a creed of nihilistic revolution for the attainment of which all cruelties and all betrayals of normal human values are justified."[18] Nevertheless, union leaders concluded that a key challenge was persuading first- and second-generation immigrant families to accept the union as religiously tolerant. The challenge included accepting that most immigrants retained some of the Old World values that their forefathers and foremothers had brought with them when they migrated from Europe in the late nineteenth century.

Among the first to arrive in Trail in 1895 were the Italians, some of whom travelled north from Montana copper magnate F. Augustus Heinze's Butte smelter.[19] Many of them had been lured by the New World promises of shipping agents who were paid for delivering cheap and docile labourers to companies such as the Canadian Pacific Railway (CPR) and its CM&S operations in Trail. By 1910, more than half the smelter workforce in Trail was Italian.[20] By 1939, however, 75 per cent of the workforce was native to Canada or other parts of the British Empire, suggesting that some second-generation eastern and southern Europeans had begun to assimilate.[21] This made both social and economic sense. Immigrant children were on average better educated, had possibly learned a trade, and were more likely to be promoted to shift boss and foremen roles. Also, during the war many immigrant women filled the positions of their soldier spouses and other male relatives, perhaps opening more doors to social acceptance in the community.

Anti-union Messages Flowed from Local Pulpits

To win labour board certification in 1944, and to retain its membership over the next decade, Local 480 leaders understood they had to appeal to immigrant workers and their families. This meant accepting, or at least tolerating, workers' strong religious ties and the anti-union propaganda coming from the pulpit. The union's efforts to engage non-Anglo labourers, though, fuelled nativist and racist complaints that "foreigners" had brought the Communist union to Trail. It was a view that politicians and governments reinforced with dark pronouncements about outside agitators, often assumed to be foreigners. Thus, while in principle the union was committed to the fight for racial equality, the social and cultural geography of Trail imposed practical constraints on what the union could fight for without alienating a majority of Trailites.

The term "racial" applied primarily to African Americans in the United States, although Asians increasingly battled for similar rights on the West Coast in the twentieth century. Notably, Mine-Mill's constitution reflected that usage. However, as David Roediger and others have argued, "The equation of blackness with the ethnicity of new immigrant groups" within the labour movement lessened the status of the "other." The concept of "whiteness," he adds, allowed Anglo-Saxon workers to make themselves the default standard of racial acceptance.[22] By contrast, Italians in Trail or any person with a swarthy complexion faced discrimination based on a peculiarly northern European metric of whiteness.

Such views must have concerned some within Trail's immigrant enclave, particularly those who fled to Canada to escape economic depression, war, and discrimination in Europe. Many had come from Catholic countries with strong antipathies to leftist ideology. Parents conveyed Old Country convictions to their sons and daughters, but there is no clear evidence that the second generation adopted those parental views. Conversely, Local 480's long struggle to gain support, and local churches' anti-union views, suggest that cultural factors did influence union acceptance before the war. Such values remained prominent in Trail's immigrant enclave after 1945. This played a significant role as Cold War anti-Communism surged. Thus, even after Local 480 became the legal representative of smelter workers, Catholic and Protestant clerics remained opposed to Communism. Using religion to build opposition to unions might have seemed a new tactic to Trail's unionists, but in fact it was as old as the labour movement itself.

In the formative days of North American unionism, the "Protestant religious press was bloodthirsty in its reaction" to workers in general, noted Richard Hofstadter. "The laborers were described as 'wild beasts' and 'reckless desperadoes'" who, "if they could not be clubbed into submission," should be "mowed down with cannon and Gatling guns."[23] Fortunately, organized religion tempered its anti-proletarian views in the 1930s. Mainstream Protestant churches, perhaps sensing they were losing working-class support, noticeably softened their views, even for a time embracing the CIO's industrial unionism. The Catholic Church also encouraged clergymen to work with unions, depending on the circumstances.

Ironically, Local 480 leaders found themselves citing excerpts from the sermons of several American religious leaders, including a member of the Central Conference of American Rabbis. "Religious leaders of all faiths have gone on record many times in support of collective bargaining through union organization," noted the *Commentator*, adding, "They realize that genuine social justice, a fundamental principle of all religious teachings, must be put into action in our world today. They recognize the only possible way of putting this principle into action; by means of collective bargaining by the workers through a union of their own choice."[24] In the same article, the Local 480 organ argued that the "company-dominated Union, the so-called independent Union, labor spies, the discharge and the blacklist, are still too frequently the American industrialist's answer to man's fundamental fight to organize."[25]

Father Charles Owen Rice was among the clergymen Local 480 lauded for their opposition to company unions such as Blaylock's WCC. "No matter what happens," Rice remarked in the *Commentator*, "the companies win and the workers lose."[26] Richard L.G. Deverall, editor of the *Christian Front*, opined that Pope Leo XIII believed Catholic unions were "most appropriate" and that the CIO was an organization that "took in all the workers, including

Negroes and the unskilled." Many of Trail's Italians and other southern and eastern Europeans often fit the latter category. "Not only is it every Catholic's privilege to join the CIO," Deverall said, "but it is every Catholic's duty to join this union."[27] Methodist Bishop Francis J. McConnell also appeared in the *Commentator*, stating that the "non-union man eats the fruit planted and cultivated by the unionist."[28] Reverend John P. Monaghan's pro-union message on the American network radio program *Catholic Hour*, produced by the National Council of Catholic Men, was also meant to appeal to Trail's Catholic workers. A published author, Father Monaghan urged them "to join Unions so that labor can become, as it should be[,] 'one of the most vital organs in a democratic social order.'"[29]

Labour Priests Turned on Red Unions

It was the priests who "actively supported trade-union struggles – almost entirely CIO – through public speaking, picket-line involvement, and a multitude of other activities," noted Steve Rosswurm. They "played a particularly significant role in legitimizing CIO organizing drives and refuting charges of communism."[30] But as anti-Communism became a dominant preoccupation for leaders of national labour organizations and Canadian and American government officials, most if not all the churches turned against Communist-led unions. As Rosswurm explains, "Purely negative anticommunism became all consuming to Catholic labourites," and "radicalism of any sort became increasingly suspect." He concluded that "procapitalism became a political and religious litmus test. Working-class Catholics … were left to cope with the vagaries of American capitalism on their own."[31] Catholic clergy eagerly supported the purging of Communists from unions such as Mine-Mill.

As Robert Asher further notes, even pro-union priests were "very worried about the emergence of communist-led unions." This led "to many Catholics, not just priests,… forming various kinds of organizations that are dedicated to trying to identify and expel those who are considered communists from labour unions."[32] Numerous Catholic clergymen preached anti-Communism in the

United States. Among them were Father Peter Deitz, "a veteran laborite," Paul Weber, "the nation's most important and intellectually innovative ACTU [Association of Catholic Trade Unions] activist," Father Philip Carey, "director of the Xavier Labor School," and Father Eugene F. Marshall, who "attacked two Catholics" in his Massachusetts parish for voting in favour of a Communist union president.[33] But none was more effective than Canadian-born Charles Coughlin, whose weekly radio broadcasts were syndicated on American radio and heard by many Canadian listeners.

Coughlin rallied opposition to union organizing in both countries, and his rants were widely influential in the late 1930s among Catholics and other faiths. Father Rice, notwithstanding his earlier statements against company unions, also led the fight against the CIO, inserting himself into union affairs wherever Catholics were in large numbers. "One outstanding characteristic of Rice's anti-communist efforts," Rosswurm notes, "was its sheer opportunism – his acceptance of aid from virtually anyone." Rice "received a car from Chevrolet's central office for 'important work for the welfare of … [the] country and sane industrial relations.'"[34] CIO president Murray assisted him.

A staunch Catholic, Murray pursued his campaign against Communist leaders in CIO unions from early on. He saw his CIO work as tantamount to enforcing papal encyclicals, particularly Pope Leo XIII's "Rerum Novarum." The 1891 encyclical supported the right of workers to organize and join unions while also condemning Communism. In 1931, the pope issued "Quadragessmo Anno," also called "On the Reconstruction of the Social Order." In keeping with Murray's personal mandate, the document warned Catholics "against the tenets of Socialism." The CIO leader strongly supported the anti-Communist work of the ACTU, had his national office subvert left-wing unions, and quietly sanctioned union raids. Murray even "bankrolled Father Rice's anticommunist activities," Rosswurm noted.[35]

Mine-Mill was a specific target of Catholic anti-Communism. When two anti-Communist activists approached Father Joseph E. Donnelly in 1942, this fully committed anti-Communist focused on the brass-making factories around Waterbury, Connecticut.

Mine-Mill locals in the state's Brass Valley were a key concern. Donnelly established the Westbury Catholic Labor Council (later the Diocesan Labor Institute) as the base for his long struggle. He recruited more than twelve labour priests, warning "dangerous outsiders preaching unhealthy ... un-American political theories and social teachings were trying to take over the local union."[36]

It is not clear whether Trail's religious leaders held a similar collective position, but the presence of so many practising Catholic and Protestant smelter workers signalled the need for Local 480 leaders to redouble efforts to counter strident anti-union religious messages if they were to gain and retain a majority of Trail's smelter workers. Such was part of the intent of special meetings that the local organized for Italian workers.[37] But as Father Donnelly and others turned against Mine-Mill, publishing and broadcasting their anti-Communist messages, no matter how much Local 480 Communists tried, a change of heart was doubtful. So critical were the public views of religious ideologues such as Donnelly, Rice, and Coughlin that many union publications, including Mine-Mill's, took pains to publish any pro-union comment from men of the cloth.

In one *CIO News* item, for example, Father Michael Mulcaire of Portland, Oregon, praised the CIO for preaching "the doctrine of Charity and Justice which Christ himself preached almost 2,000 years ago."[38] Despite the pro-labour stance of some labour priests, however, clergy escalated their war on the CIO, its Communist unions, and anyone who worked with them.[39] Constantly trying to allay fears about the CIO's alleged Communist ties, the *Commentator* published the views of sympathetic religious leaders. Catholic Archbishop Victor Sanabria of Costa Rica was but one example. "Reactionaries all call me a Communist because I open my arms to the poor," he stated. "For these people, Christ would be a Communist too."[40]

Despite attempts to reform the union image, many smelter workers and their spouses remained sceptical of Local 480. In a typical response early in the union organizing drive, "An Observant Woman" told the *Times*, "The Catholic Church is not against unions but prefers the WCC in Trail."[41] She was probably right that most clergy preferred company unions or no unions at all. They remained adamantly anti-union, especially regarding the CIO, and assuredly anti-Communist. Their views seemed bound to dampen the Local 480 message among Italians and other immigrant families without whose support there could be no union.

Faith-based values help explain resistance to Mine-Mill among immigrants. When that resistance softened, immigrant men began to assume elected roles within Local 480. Slavic immigrant Dan Dosen, for example, was repeatedly elected as a union officer. Italian immigrant's son Remo Morandini, who served his apprenticeship on the Hill in the 1940s, became the local's secretary-treasurer in the early 1950s. But the church never ceased to be a source of influence in the immigrant enclave. Its warnings against joining unions, coming from a revered institution, remained persuasive among Italian and other immigrant groups. As Richard Polenberg explains, "Nationality communities within each city might center on the church." The war had heightened "ethnic self-awareness" and churches were pillars of their communities.[42] Those from the former Austro-Hungarian Empire, for example, tended to be stalwart Catholics who felt pressure from local clergymen who remonstrated against any sign of union support. Some parishioners, however, did reject the dictates of the local clergy.

Donald Avery notes that churches faced "some degree of indifference and hostility which went beyond what they had known in the conservative world of the European village." Some parishioners regarded clergy "as agents of an exploitative landholding class in Europe – in short[,] men whose talents could be easily adapted to the needs of North American capitalists."[43] Avery's observation applies to Trail as well, where "all of the churches" supported the CM&S, according to Al King.[44] Moreover, company managers reciprocated by supporting religious leaders. King complained that most supervisors were "staunch Presbyterians who surrounded themselves with an array of largely Scottish subordinates who had many things in common – they loved Scotch whisky, haggis, and the company, and they hated unions and anyone from the inferior (i.e., Non-British) races."[45]

Pioneer Preachers Brought Word of God to Trail

Unsurprisingly, religion influenced the smelter city even during its pioneer mining days, when prospectors and future smelter workers received the ministrations of missionary-minded clergymen. Among the earliest was the Anglican Reverend Henry Irwin, affectionately known as Father Pat.[46] Others followed, but while the early churches and clergymen brought the Word of God to pioneer mining communities, it was not until the Reverend A.E. Smith arrived in Nelson in 1911 that a pro-socialist fervour reached Canada's mining West. As noted earlier, Pastor Smith was a radical proponent of the social gospel. As he remembered in his posthumously published autobiography, he did not limit himself to the pulpit of Nelson's Trinity Methodist Church on Sundays, but brought the Word and an acute sense of social justice to surrounding mining camps. Years later Smith joined the CPC and became the tireless director of the Communist-aligned Canadian Labour Defence League (CLDL), which came to the aid of jailed union leaders and often defended persecuted immigrant radicals.[47] In the early 1930s Smith toured widely to secure the release of eight imprisoned national Communist Party leaders, including General Secretary Tim Buck. Smith's adventures regularly made the news and were generally known among the Canadian left. Local 480 Communists were well aware of the legend of the "Red Reverend."

The CLDL excelled at "skillfully intertwining communism with the defense of civil liberties in Canada," J. Petryshyn explains.[48] They launched protest campaigns, bringing a substantial following but also influencing the country's political leaders. Those efforts came at a cost. Like the CCF's Woodsworth, Smith lost standing among Methodists after the Great War, and after the Second World War the only pro-Communist Methodists were connected to Chinese missions. This was also the case with Dr. James G. Endicott, a Methodist missionary whose father had been moderator of the United Church of Canada.[49]

A founder of the Canadian Peace Congress, Endicott brought his views to Trail in 1950. His visit probably came at the request of his cousin, Dr. William James Endicott, a prominent medical practitioner respectfully known to Trailites as "Dr. Jim." The visit coincided with the formation of the Trail Peace Council endorsed by Local 480, whose members helped collect signatures for the Stockholm Peace Petition, a document the *Times* and other media called "a piece of Communist trickery."[50] The daily quoted Endicott as fearing "the Christians more than the communists because too many Christians worshipped Mammon."[51] Dr. Jim and his family were notable exceptions, actively participating in the council and the collection of names on the peace petition.

For many reasons, then, Local 480 leaders eventually concluded that courting West Kootenay churches was a mug's game. Indeed, the *Times* later reported that the Vatican instructed Catholics worldwide not to vote for Communists.[52] The Trail church adhered to the policy, and other denominations counselled their congregations similarly. Such views resonated with Blaylock, the son of a British-born Anglican minister named Thomas Blaylock. Local 480 leader Gar Belanger recalls that the Catholic Church circulated a leaflet to Trail Italians urging them to oppose the union. In a 1983 interview, he questioned whether the church had acted alone, implying that Blaylock may have helped draft the anti-Red document.[53]

Regardless of alleged company-clergy complicity, anti-union scolding from the pulpit, and nativist attitudes, Trail's immigrants were never the docile workers that shipping agents and other labour recruiters had portrayed to employers. Many were unaware of the pressures they and their families would encounter in North American industries such as CM&S and in company towns like Trail. But neither were they devoid of political opinions and employer expectations. Although some early Italian and Austro-Hungarian immigrant workers may have been "ignorant of the political ideologies of the union," Blaylock and other CM&S managers feared that they were "probably conspiring radicals."[54] They had some justification. Many eastern Europeans were cognizant of the socialist, Communist, and anarchist debates rippling through workplaces back home. Some may have tried to escape political persecution during the social and economic turbulence of the late nineteenth and early twentieth centuries. As Laurie Mercier and Jaclyn Gier note of mining women, it helped that "although the immigrant populations sought new opportunities, they also brought with them the traditions of labor from their home countries, traditions that often led to even more radical responses to the exploitation they encountered in their adoptive or temporary homelands."[55]

Old Country Leftists Supported the Union

Still, it remained for Local 480 to convince immigrant smelter workers, especially the numerous Italians, that it made sense to stick with the Communist-led union. Thus Local 480 leaders sought out union sympathizers inside the immigrant enclave. Italians retained pride in their native political heritage and nineteenth-century revolutionary leaders such as Giuseppe Garibaldi and Giuseppe Mazzini. Some were also aware of the anarchist movement supported by Errico Malatesta, a friend of anarchist visionary Mikhail Bakunin, and of Malatesta's promotion of the union movement. Although they might have been discreet, some Trail immigrants were likely Old Country leftists who encouraged fellow smelter workers to support the union. George Pozzetta notes, for example, that North America had become home to "a variety of leftist radicals, who sought very different cultural and political goals." He argues that syndicalists such as Carlo Tresca and Arturo Giovannitti "considered Italian Americans as part of the world proletariat."[56] They encouraged mass strikes and radical-led worker demonstrations.

Indeed, Avery argues that many European immigrants, especially from Italy and the former Austro-Hungarian states, hailed from societies "where collective action against economic and social exploitation was an established fact."[57] Many had been exposed to social protest movements back home, and many "were prepared to resist forcibly the demands of exploitative capitalism in Canada."[58] Contrary to religious doctrine, this included joining unions and embracing socialist ideas. Immigrant workers were willing to mount working-class protests of their own, and Avery reports that work slowdowns occurred often. In Trail, most immigrants were likely "more attuned to rural peasant than to urban industrial values," yet such immigrants still contained the "suitable raw material for a militant working class."[59]

In shaping that militant consciousness, many immigrants joined radical union organizations such as the Industrial Workers of the World (Wobblies) and the One Big Union, an organization that shared some of the same principles as the IWW. It was active in the West Kootenay after the First World War. In fact, smelter workers Local 105, still struggling after losing the 1917 strike, was courted as an affiliate of the radical OBU.[60] These were the social forces they believed were seeking social change through revolutionary action.[61] The earliest immigrants would have been aware of the Western Federation of Miners, Mine-Mill's original name, and its radical history. Some would have heard stories from old-timers recalling the 1901 Rossland miners' strike, the 1912 labour unrest in BC mining camps, and the 1917 smelter strike. Yet in Trail and elsewhere Old World peasant cultures and North American identities "helped transmit a sense of cultural uniqueness," argues Polenberg.[62] Local 480 had to navigate all these cultural counter-currents to survive.

Trail's immigrant workers hoped to create a new life in the smelter city, but they met the same racism and exploitation others had faced from nativists and those who owned and controlled industrial North America. Al King, reflecting on the many nationalities employed at the CM&S smelter in the early years, recalled "the Welsh and the Danes in particular were outstanding for their union militancy."[63] Later he regularly witnessed discrimination against workers from eastern and southern Europe, as well as a high degree of chauvinism. "The longer I worked at CM&S, the more injustice I saw," he recalled. "Apart from the well-known health hazards,... the company was highly organized into a 'pecking order' that delivered blatant discrimination at its lower end." He describes the trap that awaited the immigrant worker: "If you had good connections, or were WASP [white Anglo-Saxon Protestant], you had an edge. On the other hand, the workers who got some of the dirtiest, crappiest jobs were the Italians. They called them 'wops.' There were others who were also treated badly."[64]

Local 480, if it were to adhere to the Mine-Mill constitution, had to protect its immigrant membership from ill treatment. To that end, the *Commentator* tried to assure immigrant workers of the union's value by publishing articles and letters that addressed issues of specific concern to them. As noted, these included positive comments from Catholic leaders, but they could also read about improved workplace health and safety, news from the Old Country, union demands for sickness and funeral benefits, workers' compensation, and other labour legislation. The local even tried to use the courts to counter corporate and Catholic Church anti-union messages in its appeal to immigrant families.

In one early case involving the well-known D'Andrea family, CIO organizer Slim Evans filed a legal charge of "intimidation" against CM&S President Blaylock. Invoking British Columbia's newly minted labour law (ICA, 1937) the charge was laid after Louis D'Andrea claimed he was intimidated by an article in *Liberty*, a popular American magazine that Blaylock had circulated to employees. The anti-union article featured a Frankenstein-like figure stomping on buildings and destroying everything in his wake. Across his bare chest was stamped the word "Lawlessness."[65] D'Andrea said it turned him against the union. Five days later, D'Andrea told a Trail police court that "I was yellow" in explaining that he had been threatened by other workers for his support of the union and was afraid they would ostracize him or worse.[66] The trial was big local news, with *Times* reporters treating D'Andrea as a farcical dupe. This damning image helped discredit the union's assertion that Blaylock was guilty. D'Andrea, "Harassed by Conflicting Emotions, Hoists a Few for Moral Support," reported the *Times* in its typically dismissive style.[67]

Intimidation Charges against Blaylock Dropped

Mine-Mill lost the case, despite the best efforts of lawyer John Stanton, who suggested that Blaylock had used the company union to undermine Mine-Mill. Stanton noted that Tim Buscombe, the WCC chair, had suggested the article would be "a good one to distribute to CM&S employees."[68] The WCC revelation, coupled with

D'Andrea's stumbling testimony, led Judge Donald MacDonald to declare Blaylock innocent. The *Times* reported him calling the case "a crown of thorns pressed down on the brow of labor," adding that "some great advances have been made in the cause of labor. Some great mistakes have been made in the cause of labor, and I think this is one of them." The daily reduced the trial to "a day of light humour."[69] The conservative *Labour Truth* was equally unimpressed, noting even the CPC had criticized Local 480 Communists for using such a "foolish charge."[70] Church leaders now had another example of why Catholics should avoid Local 480.

The court case heightened scepticism about whether the Communist-led union could guarantee immigrant equality, but Harvey Levenstein argues that in International Mine-Mill's commitment to equality and non-discrimination, Communist unionists "distinguished themselves from many non-Communists through the sacrifices they were willing to make for racial equality." Mine-Mill Reds played key roles in combatting discrimination "in both shops and union affairs," yet regional leaders such as Murphy knew they had to walk a fine line in upholding the union constitution.[71] Even as memories of D'Andrea faded, immigrant workers remained uncertain. When Murphy opposed a mine employers' scheme to bring to Canada "displaced persons from Europe on ten-month contracts," there were lingering doubts. The issue involved hiring 2,300 foreign workers, an action Murphy dubbed "post-war adventurism in labor importation." He decried the program's explicit anti-Communist stipulations, complaining that it might lead to the unfair treatment of Canadian workers.

On the one hand, he supported workers "suspected of communist leanings" or trade union sympathies. As he put it in his *B.C. District Union News*, "No man was or will be selected by the bosses' team who has ever evinced the slightest inclination towards becoming a trade unionist in his native country." Moreover, "He must not be a thinker, his back alone is wanted, and if his head were not needed for muscular control, he could just as well leave it behind in Europe. It's not required by the bosses." On the other hand, "If a pool of unemployed, competing for jobs, is established in the industry then wages can be kept to the lowest standards."

Murphy did not oppose immigration but criticized the selection of "unskilled workmen" who would be "under contract to pay back their debt" and could be "liable to arrest and imprisonment for breach of contract if they" sought other employment. He labelled it "a dastardly scheme."[72]

It was fine-sounding rhetoric that echoed how Murphy and Local 480 had dealt with women smelter workers after the war. As we've seen, Local 480 leaders said they wanted fair treatment for the female workers who replaced soldiers, but they feared that women's lower wages would suppress male wages as well. This and the foreign workers case forced Murphy to devise arguments that would both support Mine-Mill members and show concern for the plight of imported labourers. Immigrant workers in Trail had to sort through considerable contradictory evidence to determine whether the union would actually protect them from discrimination.

Local 480 leaders had to address ethnic differences and religious beliefs within the immigrant enclave below the Hill, but they may not have realized that the religious values of workers were part of the "complicated nature of working-class identities" that shaped their politics.[73] Like other industrial workers, Trail's smelter workers were a complex mix of "competing hierarchies and overlapping identities."[74] Communist leaders were aware of the importance of those factors, but they never fully grasped the nature of immigrant working-class culture. As Rosswurm observes, "It was the working class and its rock-solid commitment to a set of values that the communists and their allies – past and present – could not understand and respect, but could only caricature or condemn. Some of these were spiritual, some political; many praise-worthy, others mean, prejudiced, and reactionary. All were deeply held."[75] With such a large immigrant workforce, allegiance to local clerics and to the immigrant enclave might have trumped union allegiance. However, this was not the case in Trail.

Twenty-Six Nationalities Worked at the Smelter

Clearly, Local 480 faced an immensely diverse cultural tableau. The 1941 Canada Census listed twenty different European and Asian immigrant groups in Trail.[76] But a handwritten registry of CM&S severances from 1928 to 1932 reveals that twenty-six nationalities, not including British subjects and Americans, worked at the smelter.[77] Croatians, though not as populous as Italians, also contributed to a diverse Kootenay cultural landscape. By 1914, that population had swelled to between six and ten thousand mostly young males in Canada.[78] Like other immigrants, often-unscrupulous labour recruiters tended to misguide them. Many were sojourners seeking money to return to their homelands. Some found prosperity. Others, as Ervin Dubrovic notes, found "poverty, illness, maiming, frequent alcoholism and madness."[79] Most men worked in mines "filled with noxious gases." Their "health deteriorates quickly; they live in small, smelly and crammed accommodations." They were "uneducated and spiritually neglected, [and took] to alcoholism [and] debauchery."[80]

Many immigrants worked in steel mills, mines, and smelters in Ontario and BC, Anthony W. Rasporich explains. They "were among the first in Canada to accept ... the United Mine Workers of America" and to join the Croatian Fraternal Union, a branch of which was established in Rossland.[81] Those who settled in Trail built a small community among the Italians in the Gulch, and they founded St. Cyril and Methodius Lodge 281, with a membership ranging from twenty to thirty miners.[82] Rasporich notes that "Drahomanov populist social democrats" – followers of Mykhailo Drahomanov, a Bulgarian-born socialist scholar who supported the liberation of the southern Slavs from the Turks – were among the first of three waves of Croatian migrants to Canada.[83] Human and labour rights advocates such as the Slovenian author Louis Adami and Croatian Communist Stjepan Lojen shared their brand of politics with fellow immigrants.[84] Croatians were scattered around the BC interior. Some worked at the Granby mine at Copper Mountain, others in Princeton. Both towns had notable CIO and Mine-Mill presences. Croatians in Trail were "more firmly established" according to Rasporich, with more of them married and supporting Canadian-born children. Management regarded these longer-term residents as "conservative Austrians," while a newcomer such as Kootenay Croatian Petar "Pio" Fucek participated in several miners' strikes, promoted "radical ideas and organization among the mining fraternity," and was interned as an enemy alien during the First World War.[85]

Small as it was, Trail's Croatian and Slavic population might also have been influenced by radical Ukrainian and Finnish immigrant workers, especially in mining communities elsewhere in BC and Alberta. Each ethnic group formed its own association, published a news organ, and promoted its own, often-radical political views to other ethnic communities around the country. Polenberg argues that immigrant newspapers and radio stations "bound immigrants to their native cultures," but they were on the wane after the Second World War as governments more closely monitored their content.[86] Ukrainians and Finns supported the CPC "because of its emphasis on industrial organization and the unemployed," and "the party's advocacy and at times use of violence strongly appealed to many European immigrant workers."[87] Communists offered a bridge between their former and current homelands, Avery also argues, and "enterprising European 'comrades' were given an opportunity to become involved in trade union and political activity" inside the CPC.[88]

Doukhobors Rarely Participated in Union Affairs

Like other immigrant groups, Doukhobors also endured nativist pressures. Persecuted by the Russian Orthodox Church and the czars, members of this peasant religious sect migrated to Canada from southern Russia in 1899 and to the Kootenays in 1908. Kootenay historian Greg Nesteroff notes that some of his Doukhobor ancestors worked for the CM&S and "were integral in building the Brilliant dam for Cominco in the 1940s."[89] But Blaylock made no attempt to embroil his company in Doukhobor conflicts, and they played little role in CM&S smelter affairs. Company documents record a handful of Russian employees in the early 1930s, but it is not clear whether they were members of the sect.[90] Moreover, given the views of future CM&S Vice-President R.D. Perry, it is doubtful that sect adherents would have found employment at the smelter. In the early 1960s, when Doukhobor violence was at its peak, Perry remarked in the *Times* that "an outside enemy couldn't get away with these depredations but a fanatical group, pampered over the years as a quaint, religious sect, can terrorize Canadians and destroy their property because of a lack of protection."[91] President Blaylock made no attempt to embroil his company in Doukhobor conflicts – to do so might have stirred hostility from other immigrants and stockholders.

There is no evidence that Doukhobors were heavily involved with the union, and an incident at a later date illustrated the group's estrangement from it and the CM&S.[92] The Sons of Freedom subsect's bombing of the CM&S-owned West Kootenay Power and Light Company transmission lines brought local animosity to a head.[93] Frequent coverage of Doukhobor troubles in the *Times*, much of it focused on violent activities, turned Anglo-Saxon nativists even further against them. Some smelter workers and CM&S managers saw a vast, unbridgeable difference between the sect and Canadian society. The BC branch of the Canadian Legion called the military exemption extended to religious groups because of their pacifism "a gross injustice," which forced "British speaking people ... to take up arms to help defend people who are unwilling to do their part." The *Times* reported that the Trail Legion branch, which had long objected to the exemption, concurred with the "resolution of protest."[94]

The Trail-Rossland area was also home to a small Asian population, but census records reveal no employment at the Trail smelter until the 1930s when company records include a few Chinese cooks.[95] Ronald A. Shearer notes that some Chinese found employment in Rossland doing "menial tasks in low social status" jobs. They were relegated to "the bottom of the social hierarchy, a social underclass perhaps one step up from the prostitutes who shared Chinatown with them."[96] During the Second World War, Japanese families were even less visible while being interned in the Slocan Valley near Nelson, prompting authorities to speculate that someone could escape from the camp and provide information to the Japanese military. The Trail Board of Trade, of which Blaylock was a prominent member, strongly endorsed keeping the Japanese out of the smelter city, when the possibility of employing coastal internees reared its head. As Patricia Roy explains, "Although recognizing that the Japanese were 'industrious, frugal, and generally speaking good citizens' who had generously contributed to war savings drives, to avoid giving 'any Japanese sympathizers an opportunity to aid the enemy', the Trail Board of Trade recommended moving all Japanese east of the Rockies and closely supervising them."[97]

Local 480 leaders paid scant attention to the Japanese camps, but they were aware of local internment camps of another type. One of them had once helped build union solidarity. During the Depression, jobless men were placed in relief camps on the outskirts of Salmo, China Creek, and Shoreacres. In April 1935, some men joined a province-wide strike called by the Relief Camp Workers' Union, led incidentally by Local 480 organizer Slim Evans, to protest low pay and poor conditions. About 64 out of 100 Kootenay strikers were arrested and "close to 60 were of foreign extraction."[98] The *Times* blamed "communist agitators" who sought only "to make trouble."[99] Although not organized at that time, Trail smelter workers witnessed the strike action and read about the Vancouver demonstrations, both of which possibly increased fear of unions but also may have heightened interest. Whatever their views, or those of the Blaylock-friendly WCC, when Evans appeared in Trail three years later as a CIO union organizer, there was some awareness of his capacity to lead.

Italians Assert Patriotism, Are Assured Jobs Are Safe

Throughout the organizing drive and into the post-war period, Local 480 leaders knew they needed to find ways to capture and hold immigrant interest. To that end the *Commentator* built solidarity with Red immigrant workers by complimenting the Russian people as neighbours to, and liberating heroes of, Slavic people during the war. "In the smoking, corpse-littered streets of Stalingrad," the paper argued in 1943, "the safety of British and Canadian cities has been won. The Russian people are defending not Russia alone, but humanity."[100] During the war it was normal to hear pro-Soviet sentiments, but the *Commentator*'s passion for the Soviet Union was aimed particularly at immigrants who might share Local 480's politics. Different tactics were used to appeal to Italians.

Amid increasing hostility within the Trail community, Italians' sense of ostracism only grew after Mussolini extended his military adventurism from Libya and Ethiopia into British territory, including Egypt. As a result, the *Times* announced that Colombo Lodge leaders pledged the "complete loyalty of every Canadian citizen of Italian origin in Trail."[101] Lodge leaders also reported, "Every wage earner in the Italian community has arranged to give $1 or more a month to the Red Cross fund throughout the war." In a telegram to Prime Minister Mackenzie King, they dissociated themselves "absolutely from the policy being followed by the Italian government in declaring war on Britain and France."[102]

Lodge leaders understood that Mussolini's collusion with Hitler threatened the status of Italo-Canadians in the mining West, so, as Patricia K. Wood notes, the lodge "formed an 'anti-Fifth column organization' and, with $450 collected from Italian workers[,] pledged to establish their own Red Cross unit."[103] There were "several arrests in Trail," she added, "and some pressure to 'check up on' the Italian employees of Cominco." Wood cites a letter from "'an old veteran'" questioning "how much of their money was being sent to family in Italy and thus 'financing Mussolini's war effort.'" Blaylock denied there were any problems. "They are working peacefully," he said. "As long as they continue to do so they can do just as much good toward Canada's cause as anyone else."[104]

Reporting on Blaylock's reassurances, the *Times* described a meeting with the Italians as "an emphatic demonstration of patriotism on the part of Trail Italians to their new allegiance." The daily added that the Italians – about four hundred at the meeting chaired by Colombo Lodge President Oliver D'Andrea – "felt sure that the arrangements being made will take care of any eventuality in a satisfactory manner." Blaylock was prepared to allow the Italians to continue their work with the Consolidated, "provided they took over the responsibility for all their nationals," the *Times* further reported. "If they could do so they would remain in good standing, but on the other hand as the country was at war failure on their part to prevent sabotage of any kind by their nationals would be fatal to Italian interests in the company.... Mr. Blaylock warned they might be subjected to much unpleasantness if Italy declared war, but advised them to keep their tempers."[105]

The *Commentator* responded angrily, claiming Blaylock had but one goal: "to suppress one section of the workers, to divide them from their fellows and ultimately to make exploitation of both Italians and non-Italians that much easier." From Local 480's perspective, "Mr. Blaylock told Italians that they must spy on each other and report to the CM&S if they wished to remain in good standing with the company."[106] This might have appealed to some immigrants who supported the union, but ethnic tensions inside the smelter bared more complex issues. Some anti-Local 480 nativists cautioned, "'You've got so damn many wops and so many of these Scotchmen, you'll never get them all together,'" Local 480's Gar Belanger recalled hearing. The leadership had "to ignore this propaganda that was seeping underground all the time saying 'you can't do it.'" Belanger saw company manipulation at work. "I think the company actually utilized it through some people on the job." The union executive nevertheless stood firm. As Belanger further noted, "This was all a bunch of crap because it doesn't make a difference who people are, they have the same hopes and desires for a decent life. So we go to a few Italian fellas, people that we knew. They started to come around. We had meetings with them on a pretty regular basis.... We just ignored the so-called racial thing. We went ahead as if they were just men, that's all. We were correct in that analysis."[107] That policy perfectly embodied the Mine-Mill constitution's anti-discrimination clause.

Some Immigrants Sided with the Company

Clearly, though, there was a need to recognize tension building among immigrant workers and to understand that some families viewed the union as contrary to church teachings. The union's pro-Soviet stance must also have worn thin on immigrants who were victims of Soviet expansionist actions. Perhaps they viewed the union option as a pointless socio-economic strategy. After all, thanks to Blaylock, they could order cheap coal through the company, buy groceries at the company store, and grow vegetables in the company gardens, where everything from water to tools was supplied. Thus some immigrant workers saw more advantages in the CM&S than in Local 480. Blaylock's philosophy, as noted earlier, was one of friendly cooperation between workers and employers rather than collective bargaining. This was acceptable to some immigrant workers.

Fred Tenisci, an Italian smelter worker and businessman, was among those who supported the company. Local 480 leaders knew that Tenisci and others disparaged the union, but they were uncertain how to combat them. Virginio Tesolin, a pro-union farmer of Italian descent from Grand Forks, BC, about sixty-five kilometres west of Trail, offered one solution. In a letter written in Italian and addressed to the *Commentator*, he criticized Tenisci for siding with the company and for discouraging Italians from joining the union. "Tenisci says that workers are satisfied [with] these conditions of working and also of payroll, and sings … thanksgiving and praise to CM&S." The likes of "Tenisci are for big companies, are licking the feet of CM&S," Tesolin raged. Then, praising the CIO, he argued that the union "is strength and we are determined to join despite CM&S and all Tenisci." Referring to anti-union smelter workers as "saboteurs," he concluded, "When you're not organized, you are at the mercy of the Industrial Company."[108]

Tesolin's animosity was sparked in part by Tenisci's support for Mussolini's fascist party, but he was also motivated by his belief in unions.[109] By publishing his letter in Italian, Local 480 leaders hoped to garner union support among Italians. Tesolin's willingness to come forward also revealed that not all Italians were beholden to Blaylock; some were willing to give the CIO a chance. Perhaps they hoped the Tesolin letter would convince other Italian workers to join the union, but it did not stop other Trailites from trying to dissuade their fellow immigrants from supporting Mine-Mill.

The *Commentator* noted, for example, that an Italian businessman "is using his influence to intimidate workers of Italian descent from joining the union." It advised readers to "note that the only two Italians ever to damn the union publicly in Trail are now spending their time in a concentration camp." It was a reference to two men who "were very loud-mouthed in praise of the CM&S and spent considerable time in collecting guns, from Italians for the CM&S," as Blaylock specified. The union paper called them out for "advising members to quit the union, and in trying to keep other Italians from joining." In continuing the scolding, it said, "They thought they were smart enough to cover their Fascist activities with a cloak of approval of their anti-unionism from the CM&S. They weren't." The union paper then assured readers, "No worker of Italian descent need be afraid to join the union no matter how much the CM&S is displeased."[110] One of those businessmen was Tenisci, whose pro-Mussolini comments eventually landed him in the Hull, Quebec, internment camp. Ironically, Harvey Murphy was incarcerated in the same camp for at least part of Tenisci's stay, but there is no evidence the two ever met.

Churches Step Up an Anti-Red Crusade

Vocal opposition to the union continued within the immigrant enclave, but like for all Trailites, regardless of their national origin, the post-war period brought hopes of receiving some of the spoils from the long, costly conflict. Some saw that a Mine-Mill union could help win those spoils in the form of better wages. Enough workers voted to support Local 480 the year before the war ended that new CM&S President R.E. Stavert had to be as vigilant as his predecessor, the legendary Mr. Blaylock. Some of the enlisted men and women were back at work and some had supported Mine-Mill even from the battlefield.[111] Immigrant enlistees had joined the military roll, and some had returned viewing the union as their best opportunity for a better post-war Trail.

The coming Cold War would put new political pressures on the immigrant community, especially with the passage in the United States of the McCarran Internal Security Act and Walter-McCarran Act. Both laws were designed to curtail perceived subversive elements among immigrants. Both fuelled the Red Scare that was gathering force, and it would be felt in Trail. The result was a "nationwide roundup of foreign-born workers and political activists."[112] Churches agreed with the anti-Communist laws, and they continued to influence the immigrant enclave. By then, clergy had refined their anti-unionism and anti-Communism strategies.

For local churchmen, war's end might have signalled an end to the fight against Communism. Perhaps now their fears of immigrant parishioners siding with the Red union would subside. Perhaps Sundays could return to the pre-Murphy days when people still remembered the gentle Father Pat. Perhaps now, finally, the warnings of church elders would be heeded and Trailites would see that Mine-Mill and its Red leadership were bad for the smelter city. But such prayers would go unanswered and their parishioners would not always behave as counselled. Still, early cold warriors, some from local churches, continued to condemn Local 480 and support anti-Communist efforts to lure immigrant workers from the Mine-Mill fold.

A continent-wide post-war surge of strikes preoccupied national labour leaders, but some continued to embrace religious teachings. The Canadian Congress of Labour (CCL) signified its own commitment to religious-based activism when, at an assembly for Moral Re-Armament in Mackinac Island, Michigan, it endorsed a quasi-religious movement seeking cooperation between labour and management. The assembly, attended by seven hundred delegates from the United States and Canada, drafted a "manifesto on the future of industry and of democracy." It claimed that "Labor's destiny," in part, was "to find again the fire and conviction of labor's pioneers, that labor led by God can remake the world." Signatories included Canadian Steelworker leader Charles Millard, Steelworker international representative John V. Riffe, and Elroy Robson, assistant to CCL President Aaron Mosher.[113]

For some older Local 480 members, the MRA's manifesto surely rekindled memories of the company unionism that Blaylock so cherished. And though perhaps not yet well known in Trail, Millard's signature on the manifesto was also significant. For some Catholic immigrant smelter workers, the MRA might have seemed promising. After all, Pope Pius XII would soon give it his blessing for its efforts to "abolish Communism."[114] But despite the endorsement of Millard and others, Trades and Labor Congress (TLC) President Percy Bengough would later call it a threat to organized labour. The *Times* called him "irresponsible." In the editor's view, the TLC leader's comments "detract from the real efforts MRA adherents are making in labor-management affairs."[115]

The Mine-Mill local continued to hear from local clergy, including the Right Reverend F.P. Clark, Anglican bishop of Kootenay, who supported the anti-Red crusade, citing local church doctrine that called Communism "the greatest threat in the world today."[116] There was a "communistic fear of organized Christianity," the *Times* sermonized after the war, condemning the "red persecution of churchmen" who "practice a genuine religion which fundamentally rebukes and destroys the false 'religion' of Marxism."[117] Such views gained currency when the US Congress later pressured the immigrant community, placing Mine-Mill squarely in their crosshairs. Much later, for example, in the Northern Ontario Mine-Mill stronghold of Sudbury, Bishop Alexander Carter assigned Father Alexandre J. Boudreau to establish a labour school. His sole aim was that "Mine, Mill must be destroyed, and disappear from the map of Canada."[119] Boudreau trained Sudbury workers in the anti-Communist tactics that eventually fuelled a major Steelworker raid that divided the workforce in the Nickel Belt town. It was redolent of the labour priests who had turned on Communist unions in the 1940s.

As time distanced them from the war, some immigrants would still listen to the clergy, but enough smelter workers rejected advice from the pulpit to sustain the union, at least for the moment. Now, however, Local 480 was about to face another hurdle, one steeped in anti-Communist ideology. A political battle was on the horizon in the next phase of the smelter wars.

5

A Clash of Ideologies in the Kootenays

Although the shooting war had ended, Trail's smelter war was shifting into a higher gear in 1946. Local 480 had earned the right to represent all smelter workers, and its Communist leadership had won the loyalty of enough immigrant workers to win the support of a majority. But opponents of Mine-Mill and other leftist unions did not surrender. South of the border serious threats to unions were emerging. Closer to home, smelter families were re-articulating church-centred and media-fostered concerns about militant unions such as Mine-Mill. Canadian labour reporter Jack Williams noted in the *Times* that a rash of post-war strikes exemplified the "clouds gathering on the Canadian labour horizon." He further observed that 1945 strike patterns paralleled those leading up to the 1919 Winnipeg General Strike.[1] Although Local 480 avoided joining the 1946 strike trend, having successfully negotiated a new contract, media rumblings exerted more pressure on Trail Communists and accelerated attempts to dislodge it. This time the struggle for survival would involve repeated clashes between the Communist Party of Canada and the socialist Co-operative Commonwealth Federation. Whether its members liked it or not, Local 480 would be fully engaged on the coming ideological war front.

Meanwhile, Trail households continued to adjust to post-war reality. Wage and price controls would be lifted at the end of January and Canada could boast that it sold more than a billion dollars' worth of war supplies to the Americans, some of it produced in Trail.[2] Heavy snowfall in the Kootenays sent some smelter families to the ski slopes of Red Mountain near Rossland. Some Trailites sought the distractions offered by local cinema proprietors who happily capitalized on the situation, taking their share of the last pay cheques of women war workers now being laid off to make way for the bulge of returning military men. Humphrey Bogart starred in Ernest Hemingway's *To Have and to Have Not* at the Rio, while Bing Crosby and Ingrid Bergman got acquainted in *The Bells of St. Mary's* at the Strand. Trailites could still dance to the big band sounds, but orchestras led by Tommy Dorsey, Benny Goodman, Glenn Miller, Canadian-born Guy Lombardo, and others were giving way to solo vocalists with accompanying small bands. In fact, after an American Federation of Musicians' strike from 1942 to 1944, all but the vocalists had been locked out of recording studios. When the strike ended, Frank Sinatra and Perry Como, along with the venerable Crosby, were the dominant musical sounds heard on Local 480 members' radios.

By early 1946, the defection of Russian cipher clerk Igor Gouzenko the previous September led Ottawa to initiate a spy probe. Gouzenko gave Ottawa authorities names of several alleged Soviet spies. In March, Montreal Communist MP Fred Rose was charged with espionage under the Official Secrets Act. Communist organizer Sam Carr was suspected of being a Soviet spy recruiter and would soon be on trial. Updates to both stories appeared regularly on the *Times* front page.[3] Interestingly, the daily seemed to miss a story that was relevant to the West Kootenay Doukhobor population. Emma Woikin, a Saskatchewan member of the persecuted religious sect, was also convicted of spying and imprisoned.[4] Harvey Murphy later told his *B.C. District Union News* readers that Rose's trial was like trying the Soviet Union with "dime thriller dramatics calculated to impress and thrill the ignorant." Still, it did help heighten smelter workers' wariness of the Communist-led Mine-Mill.[5] The media frenzy also empowered anti-Communist Claire Billingsley, who had resigned from the Mine-Mill representative's job Murphy had arranged for him the previous year. Dissatisfied with his role as Murphy's Kootenay appointee, and witnessing growing public expressions of anti-Communism, he had decided to campaign for the Local 480 presidency.

By the summer of 1946, perhaps energized by Gouzenko's Russian spy revelations, police in the Kootenays were attempting to build a case to deport Murphy, "the well known Communist," himself an immigrant who had come to Canada from Poland as a boy. In September they noted his strike-supporting speech to a Mine-Mill District Union meeting in Vancouver. "In his usual manner, he flayed capitalism, the government, Liberals, etc.," wrote an unnamed police officer.[6] "Responsible labor leaders are convinced that Communists in Canada and the United States are aiming at nothing short of a general strike," the *Times* warned.[7] The next day it reprinted a *Financial Post* article accusing "rabble-rousing, balding Harvey Murphy" and other Communists of exerting "a powerful influence in ten major Canadian unions."[8] It was all considered respectable and necessary Red bashing for CCL President Aaron Mosher as he conceived his plan for the future purging of rebellious Red affiliates like Mine-Mill.

In October, a Mine-Mill hard-rock miners' strike at thirteen BC locations ended and miners "emerged as the highest paid in North America," according to Local 480's Al King, and there was no visible damage to employment prospects.[9] Trail's smelter workers, having avoided the strike thanks to their 1946 collective agreement, supported the miners during their long struggle. Nevertheless, the Trail Communist club and Local 480 were in disarray as the West Kootenay region entered labour's cold war, with Billingsley soon to lead the way. When Mine-Mill hired him on Murphy's recommendation in 1945, Billingslcy stated that "to build a Union worthy of the support of all the C.M.&S. employees, I'm sure we must have truth, trust, understanding and co-operation."[10] The *Commentator* hailed him for his wartime role in encouraging workers to make substantial Victory Loan investments and for his leadership on the employees' medical committee. Billingsley had initially embraced the union because he saw "so much favouritism up the hill" and believed that "stronger representation" than Blaylock's WCC was needed.[11] Within two years, however, Murphy and the Local 480 Communists concluded that the Saskatchewan-born Billingsley had no intention of living up to the *Commentator's* initial praise, at least not in the way Murphy had hoped.

Few knew it then, but Billingsley would later reveal himself to be a determined anti-Communist at the head of an anti-Mine-Mill group within Local 480. Al King would later describe its members as "opportunists." It was a label King and other leftists bandied about in Communist circles during the 1940s, especially concerning spurned BC CPC leader Fergus McKean.[12] Joining Billingsley were carryovers from the WCC and its legal successor, the Independent Smelter Workers' Union (ISWU). As he prepared to replace former bomber pilot Don Berry as president, Billingsley campaigned on the issue of leadership: who would best represent smelter workers? He played heavily on their anti-Communist feelings and consistently fomented those sentiments as he tried to lay the groundwork for what would later devolve into a plan for the total demolition of Red Local 480.[13]

Loyalties Seesaw between Union and Company

After consuming forty tons of CM&S-supplied turkey over the Christmas period, the smelter city's denizens rang in 1947 "with no undue rowdiness," as the *Times* put it. Soon after, Local 480 began its annual round of bargaining.[14] Tea and coffee prices were on the rise, as were bread prices, and meat rations might be instituted if a meat packers' strike continued. All of it gave Local 480 negotiators good reason to seek a pay raise. Before January ended, they had called for a conciliator to reach an agreement with CM&S. The *Times* published a roundup of strikes in 1946 and claimed that unions, with a record 205 work stoppages, had set an "all-time high in Canadian industrial history."[15] A secret police report agreed, dubbing it "the second round in Labour's post-war battle for increased wages and better living conditions."[16] Trail Knights of Columbus heard from Father Wilfrid Brazeau on the occasion of the Catholic service club's tenth anniversary. He echoed the views of FBI Director J. Edgar Hoover in stressing in the *Times* that "our society is threatened by the deadly evil" of Communism.[17] Stories about the atomic bomb circulated unabated, but the world "had a feeling that 1947 – no matter what it has in store – is bound to be an improvement over 1946," or so the *Times* editor guessed.[18]

Several events that spring influenced smelter workers whose loyalties continued to seesaw between company unionism and Local 480's Reds. First, there was the contentious re-election of International Mine-Mill President Reid Robinson, which triggered a hail of accusations and suggested to the *Northern Miner* in mid-February that his leadership had a "Moscow smell."[19] Despite the hubbub, Vernon Jensen, who explored the question of Robinson's political affiliation, was unable to conclude that he was a Communist.[20] Second, and perhaps more influential, were the revelations of Pat Sullivan, the Communist secretary-treasurer of the TLC since 1943 and leader of the Canadian Seaman's Union (CSU). Sullivan disavowed the CPC and levelled allegations against several Communist union leaders, including Murphy. After reading Sullivan's claims, the Mine-Mill western director used his *B.C. District Union News* column to call him a "Judas" and a "sell out" who, like others, "betray their fellow men." Murphy also noted that the ISWU, Trail's affiliate to the Amalgamated Union of Canada (AUC), had distributed Sullivan's comments to the smelter workforce in hopes of further undermining the Mine-Mill Communists.[21] Meanwhile, the *Times* contended that Sullivan's statements had thrown organized labour into the "throes of a convulsion" involving a struggle between "the rank and file of many unions and a powerful handful of Communists."[22] To the general public, this might have rekindled memories of the Gouzenko revelations. To CCL leaders, Sullivan's statements were more ammunition for ousting their left-led affiliates.

Following a summer of more anti-Communist attacks, Murphy sensed that the Trail local was in trouble. He knew that several "right-wing" CCF members had taken control, and the CPC club had been "totally ineffective" in wresting it away. He responded by hiring Jack Scott, a war hero and veteran Communist, to "get the Party in shape" and to resolve the festering political mess at Local 480. It was a "terrible situation," Scott recalled. "Several good people were there but they just did not know how to go about things. Some were fairly heavy drinkers and women-chasers, and they spent most of their spare time at that occupation rather than politics."[23] Scott applied himself to the task, much appreciating that "Murphy wasn't underfoot."[24] The district director had been busy elsewhere in his vast western territory, acting, in Scott's view, as "lord of all he surveyed," leaving Scott unfettered by a man who had "nobody to say nay to him."[25]

Scott clearly did not like Murphy, but their paths to Red unionism followed a similar trajectory. Both joined the CPC early, Murphy in his youth in the 1920s and Scott in 1931. Both had been organizers in the unemployed workers' movement in Ontario. Scott may have met Murphy when they organized for the Workers' Unity League (WUL) on the Prairies in the early 1930s. When the CPC dismantled the WUL in 1935, ordering Communists to merge with CIO unions, Scott joined the 1935 On to Ottawa Trek led by Slim Evans, the original CIO organizer in Trail. But in spite of their similar political affiliations, Scott considered Murphy a "thorough bureaucrat."[26]

Taft-Hartley Act in United States Poses New Problems

Scott's efforts in Trail paid off. Soon he had persuaded about thirty party members to start attending CPC club meetings. Having re-established a local political base, Scott then turned his attention to Local 480. First he got himself elected zinc plant shop steward and then chief steward. He quickly learned that smelter conditions were "really terrible": long hours, restrictive workplace rules (no talking, no smoking, no coffee breaks), hazardous workspaces, prejudice against immigrants, and disrespectful supervisors.[27] It was also clear that rectifying these problems required a long and taxing struggle. In Scott's view, Murphy's dictatorial behaviour made things worse, so he challenged him. "Murphy was used to throwing his weight around," he recalled in his memoir, and Scott had vowed to stop taking orders when he returned from Europe as a decorated war hero.[28] Their differences sharpened as the two men vehemently debated bargaining and ideological issues.

As Scott pursued his assignment, *Times* readers were warned to beware "the menace of the cancer of communism which is rampaging through the vitals of our society."[29] Sullivan's revelations received full play with the editor, who predicted that Sullivan would "Release Bigger Expose of Reds."[30] Anti-Red stories were always prominent, but they began to increase when the US Congress passed the Taft-Hartley Act in June 1947. Among other things, the new labour law required American labour leaders to sign affidavits swearing they were not Communists. Failure to do so would bar their unions from using federal Labour Department services. As David Caute explains, big business in the United States had "spent several million dollars each year on stimulating the belief that the Wagner Act, the union shop and the repeal of 'right to work' laws were all products of Moscow's machinations."[31] Other historians, such as Robert W. Cherny, argue that Taft-Hartley was ostensibly intended to avoid a repeat of the 1946 rash of strikes.[32] For Murphy and Local 480 Communists, however, it created a new mood of fear and intimidation, and it gave new impetus to enemies such as the AUC, which stepped up its anti-Mine-Mill campaign with the *Amalgamator*. Billingsley compounded Scott's problems by deciding he no longer wanted to be part of a "Communist-dominated union."[33] Instead, he drew closer to the AUC, an independent union advocate and enemy of international unions like Mine-Mill. The *Commentator* called it a "scab 'federation'" with strong links to employers.[34]

That fall, Billingsley was elected local president, replacing Berry, and *Times* editor Bill Curran magnanimously congratulated Local 480 members on "having the courage to cast aside its Communist president."[35] Fred Henne, who had been elected president in 1944, had opened the door for Billingsley by taking a Mine-Mill representative position in the far north. Berry replaced Henne briefly and in October, Billingsley handily won the local election. Soon "paranoia and fear infected everyone," Al King recalled. It was hardly surprising that the Billingsley group, exploiting "the popular 'anti-red' phobia," was in the ascendency.[36] King was puzzled that "some of the guys on the Hill honestly believed that we, the more left-leaning members of Mine Mill, were dangerous to them."[37] Billingsley then set to work. He received unexpected assistance in November from an article by former Communist John Hladun in *Maclean's* magazine. Under the heading "They Taught Me Treason," Hladun, who had attended the International Lenin School in Moscow, tagged Murphy as a fellow graduate and alleged they had been trained in espionage techniques and military action.[38] Murphy told the *Times* it was "poppycock," but later admitted that he had attended the school in the early 1930s, a potentially damning admission at a politically charged time.[39]

Second Red Scare Infiltrates Trail

Early 1948 was filled with an odd assortment of news. For example, Trial city council had ordered prostitutes operating out of the Victoria Annex on Bay Avenue run out of town. High food prices had forced government action to set price ceilings. The pope urged that atomic energy be used only for peace. Columbia River floods created a state of emergency in downtown Trail later that summer and would soon be remembered as the Great Flood of 1948. Henry Wallace became the ill-fated presidential candidate for the Progressive Party in the United States. India's Mahatma Mohandas K. Gandhi was assassinated. CM&S was under investigation for accepting unfair freight rates. The company also offered to build a new arena and seek cheaper housing loans for its employees.

At the Strand's Saturday matinees, the kids could see Daffy, Donald, Goofy, Bugs, Popeye, and Porky. Adult viewers could see Cary Grant and Myrna Loy in *The Bachelor and the Bobby-Soxer* or Maureen O'Hara in *Miracle on 34th Street*. Laurence Olivier was *Hamlet* at the Odeon. *Gone with the Wind* was still in demand. But the Cold War was about to ensure that Charlie Chaplin in *Monsieur Verdoux* was probably the last Trailites would see of the popular comic actor. He would soon be blacklisted as an alleged Communist. Country singing star Hank Snow and his Singing Rangers appeared at the Playmor in nearby South Slocan, Bobby Roberts and his orchestra regularly played at the K.P. Hall, and the Kootenay Boys Orchestra kept couples dancing at the Legion Hall. Local 480 Communists, however, had little spare time for such amusements, for their struggle for survival was promising to get even tougher.

The union bargaining team had successfully negotiated collective agreements annually since 1944, but years of infighting over the local's Communist links took a toll. Across Canada, from the founding of the CCF in 1932 to the creation of the CCL in 1940, a negative reaction to Communism was also building and about to explode with the purging of Communists, heightened vilification of the CPC, and expulsion of Red affiliates from national and international labour bodies. CCL President Mosher supported the travel restrictions the American government was already practising, and he told the *Times* that the "dominion must be on guard against subversive elements" as well.[40] Closer to home, the CM&S was preparing a more aggressive strategy in its opposition to the Reds.

CM&S Vice-President R.W. (Ralph) Diamond, the gifted metallurgical engineer whom Blaylock had hired decades earlier, had launched the first prong of the new strategy the previous September, telling an engineers' meeting and subsequently *Times* readers that Communism was "a destructive subversive force" with which "there must be no compromise."[41] Bill Kirkpatrick, the man Blaylock had appointed as CM&S assistant general manager, followed in February with a CJAT radio address to smelter families adapted from a pamphlet innocuously entitled "Your Union and You." His target was Communism and local Reds. "Very skilfully and highly organized efforts are being made," he said, to "bring your locals under communistic domination." They were supposedly "working vigorously and continuously to destroy our freedom." Communists would take away "your freedom to bargain collectively." Al King quoted the broadcast, calling it "a blatant management attempt to urge union members to get rid of any suspected Communists."[42] A *Times* editorial supported Kirkpatrick, who later became president of the Canadian Chamber of Commerce, claiming the CM&S manager only wanted to "strengthen, not weaken, your union."[43]

The editorial triggered a full page of *Times* letters. R. Adamache, a Local 480 member, accused Kirkpatrick of "trying to split Labor!"[44] "Worker and Democrat" suggested that Adamache was a Communist, but even if not, "the Murphys and Cherinikoffskys

[Murphy's real surname misspelled] would appreciate your mode of communistic attack."[45] "A Businessman" also called Adamache a Communist for praising the Soviet Union, adding, "I have fired a red hot machine gun on hoards [sic] of misguided Germans who like the present communists had been sold on the idea that their dream of world conquest was righteous."[46] Adamache urged *Times* readers not to listen to "the propaganda of the capitalists."[47] Al King accused the *Times* of using pro-Kirkpatrick claims to "inflame people against the very idea of 'little guys' challenging the mighty citadel up on the Hill."[48]

With Billingsley presiding over Local 480, anti-Communism ruled at the union office and on the Hill. ISWU Secretary J.A. Saunders announced the dissolution of the company union, but its disappearance did nothing to quell the animosity directed at King, Murphy, and others. Hladun, a one-time West Kootenay resident, Ukrainian nationalist, and a man thoroughly disillusioned with the Soviet Union, renewed his attack on local Communists and Murphy. The *Times* reported on his "brilliant exposé of communism" to a Nelson audience.[49] The anti-Red crusade was further emboldened when the *Times* announced in mid-March that Justice Minister Louis St. Laurent was "cracking down on labour-union communists fleeing from the anti-communist Taft-Hartley labor law of the U.S."[50] Both the TLC and the CCL wholeheartedly supported a government ban on Reds. They also refused a Mine-Mill request for assistance on a cross-border travel issue. That paved the way for the second deportation of Reid Robinson, recently demoted to Mine-Mill international vice-president, as a subversive labour union official. Maurice Travis, unlike Robinson a vocal and unrepentant Communist, replaced him. Then an unexpected incident further alarmed the largely non-ideological rank-and-file smelter workers who were already sceptical of Murphy as their chief negotiator because of his openly leftist politics. Any increased Red baiting only exacerbated worker confidence in Murphy and Local 480's leadership. It also presented the anti-Communist CCL leadership with more pretexts to rid the labour movement of Murphy and the other Communists that

Sullivan and Hladun had identified. What happened next took the anti-Red cause to a new level.

Murphy's Underpants Speech Creates New Setbacks

The incident took place on 8 April at a banquet in the BC capital of Victoria. Murphy gave an impromptu speech in which he scolded eighty-two labour leaders attending an annual labour lobby of provincial politicians. Fifteen offended delegates promptly walked out of the meeting when Murphy refused to withdraw his remarks. Irving Abella recounts the event, which began with "a good deal of drinking and carousing." Murphy, who apparently had had too much of his favourite whiskey, made "some highly distasteful remarks about the private lives of some labour leaders." One of his "less lurid" statements was that "the Congress officials were 'phonies' and 'red-baiting floozies.'"[51] The next day, Murphy's drunken remarks appeared on the front page of the *Vancouver Sun* in a story written by an enterprising reporter named Jack Webster. Webster, like the CCL leaders Murphy criticized in his speech, was no friend to Communists. "They had taken over the labour movement and I believed they had to be evicted," he stated in his memoir. "I hounded them."[52]

According to Webster, who some believed had helped orchestrate the event, Murphy was angry that the CCL did not support Robinson after the Canadian government arrested and deported him. Murphy "denied that Robinson advocated [the] overthrow of the Canadian government," Webster wrote. "'It's a lie,' he [Murphy] said, 'and they can't prove it. It shows up our red-baiters including CCL officials.'"[53] The Canadian Press news service soon reported that CCL Western Director William Mahoney, later to play a key role in Trail, called Murphy's remarks "unsubstantiated, improperly presented and despicable charges." Mahoney said the speech "destroyed the prestige labor needs to do its job and give bread and butter to the people."[54] Perhaps more hurtful, Malcolm Bruce, a former colleague of Murphy known for his own caustic political outbursts, told the *Times* his one-time comrade's comments were "wholly indecent and inexcusable."[55]

Al King remembered the speech vividly and in graphic detail in his memoir. Murphy "told the full meeting that if Mosher was going to kiss the boss's ass, he better be sure to pull his pants down first."[56] Scott recalled that the speech was "funny no doubt, but not exactly tactful."[57] Vancouver shipyard union leader Bill White, also a Communist, added a gritty personal touch. Puzzling about the fuss, he remarked, "You hear people blame the downfall of the Communist Party on Murphy's Underwear Speech, but Christ, they were just waiting for any phoney goddamned excuse and that happened to be it."[58] White later claimed the CCL's actions against Murphy and ongoing internal party bickering led to the demise of the CPC as "the dominant force on the B.C. labour scene, and the end of any widespread militancy in B.C. labour."[59] This accorded the speech too much importance, but Stephen Gray drew a similar conclusion when he argued, "The Marxist tradition in British Columbia was left gradually to wither on the thin vines of political sectarianism and academic discourse."[60] What is undeniable is that Murphy's speech handed anti-Communists a ripe opportunity. Their first move was to suspend the Mine-Mill director for two years.

The suspension hardly diminished Murphy's power in Trail. He was still an effective union organizer and negotiator. As Mine-Mill lawyer John Stanton recalled, "He related well to working people, who enjoyed his gravelly-voiced exposés of the greed and stupidity of certain employers and politicians." He described Murphy as "cat-like," always able to land on his feet, adding, "His more than generous ego and a certain foxiness were so noticeable that one could never be quite sure where one stood with Murphy."[61] Regardless of such views, he was not foxy enough to escape the CCL Red hunters.

The underpants speech opened a new phase of the Cold War in Trail. They had been cursing radicals for decades, but now the CCL and TLC, following the lead of their American counterparts, had the perfect excuse, as White said, to escalate their anti-Red attacks.

The incident in Victoria renewed talk of expulsions and may have legitimized the purging of Reds from the CCF. After all, the CCL's national leadership, spurred by future National Party Leader David Lewis, had already endorsed the CCF as labour's party and in so doing fostered hopes of gaining a stronger foothold for the party in Trail.

Cold War Political Allegiances Fray

In the late 1940s, the union movement entered a period of "[political] violence seldom witnessed in the history of Canadian labour," argues Bryan D. Palmer.[62] It was a period marked by escalating confrontations between the CCF and the CPC. Activists within the CPC, who had been tireless union organizers in the 1930s, were now seen as evildoers dominating the movement. Some depicted the CCF as purveyors of "heroic democratic socialism" versus the "dark forces" of Communism and, in Palmer's opinion, the CPC lent credibility to this depiction by its willingness to "alternatively encourage and discourage class struggle as evidence of its disregard for the workers' true needs."[63] Despite the CPC's shifting labour policies and some "shady dealings" by Communist labour leaders, Palmer argues that Communists, including some in Trail, still believed they could sense "the mood and needs of their membership."[64] Calling Communism in Trail a "dark force" was hardly accurate, nor was the suggestion that Local 480 Communists disregarded workers' needs. As Reg Whitaker and Gary Marcuse note, they were part of a tradition of "visible agitators" that called for "radical changes in Canadian society." In so doing they attracted "the enmity of business leaders, conservative politicians, and union rivals."[65] They knew which side they were on, but would they be able to defend themselves in this climate of building hatred?

In retracing the history of labour socialism in Canada, political scientist Gad Horowitz argues that the "extreme left varieties" in BC originated in the American tradition of radical unionism represented by Mine-Mill's predecessor, the Western Federation of Miners.[66] Horowitz suggests Americans adopted the Marxism of European immigrants, whereas Canadians accepted the milder

Fabian socialism espoused by a largely British immigrant popula-tion.[67] Considering that early waves of immigrants were British, this theory may be true, but Horowitz seems to deny a role for politically savvy groups of Marxist thinkers who arrived later from eastern and southern Europe, as discussed earlier. These radicals had an influence on workers, even in remote settings such as Trail.

Those immigrants, among others, had elected non-Communist Daniel O'Brien as president of the British Columbia Federation of Labour (BCFL) in 1944, but also placed three top Communists on his executive board, including Harvey Murphy as first vice-pres-ident. Horowitz argues that the provincial coalition government cooperated with the Communist-led BCFL "in diverting the labour vote from the CCF."[68] This arrangement led to an ideological war between the CPC and the CCF as the two parties engaged in a con-tinuous battle for electoral supremacy. The ensuing struggle was as contentious and divisive in the Kootenays as anywhere, and Local 480 was on its front lines, but the local's Communist leadership was caught in a dilemma.[69]

While some Local 480 members still maintained CPC member-ships, many were also CCF activists. They may have been loyal to their Communist chief negotiator and to the Local 480 Reds within the leadership, but they chose to seek political solutions from both parties. During their long struggle for survival in the 1940s and early 1950s, Local 480 members did not consistently follow a sin-gle ideology. Political pragmatism made sense, but it led CCF anti-Communists and CPC local members to continually subject each other to public opprobrium, thus confusing and frustrating voters. Whenever possible, some smelter workers had voted for left alternatives ranging from the old Socialist Party of Canada (SPC) to the CPC and the CCF. Yet early voting records for the federal riding of Kootenay West suggest that the majority of Trailites more often than not opted for Conservative candidates at the ballot box. From 1903 to 1915, for example, they elected Conservative Rich-ard McBride as BC premier.[70] From 1921 to 1945, Trail helped elect Conservative William K. Esling first to the provincial legislature in Victoria and then to the federal Parliament in Ottawa. Esling, born and educated in Philadelphia, was a pioneer newspaperman who once owned several newspapers in the region, including the *Rossland Miner* and the *Trail Creek News*, the city's first newspaper and predecessor to the *Trail Daily Times*. Like his fellow Tories, Esling was a vocal anti-Communist and an inveterate supporter of local business, especially the CM&S.[71] Few labour-friendly candidates won in BC until 1933, when the CCF gained several seats on the strength of about 30 per cent of the provincial vote.[72]

No left candidate succeeded in the Trail-Rossland riding that year, but the party's success heightened local awareness of the left-wing movement and gave impetus to worker-friendly regional politicians such as Local 480 member Leo Nimsick, who garnered a modest 891 votes in 1937. Nimsick was eventually elected as a labour candidate, but leftward politics had its limits. CPC candidates never won the Trail-Rossland riding, nor were they even viable contenders. Federally, Esling held the Kootenay West seat until he retired. In 1945, H.W. "Bert" Herridge won it for the independent "People's CCF" and continued to hold it as a CCF member throughout the 1950s and beyond.[73] Federal Communist candidate Matilda "Tillie" Belanger ran against him in the 1953 election, but garnered only 347 votes, a mere 1.9 per cent of the vote.[74]

However marginal at times, the local left-wing vote had always alarmed the CM&S. The *Commentator* and the Communist *Pacific Tribune* were particularly vexing when they highlighted the company's record profits during the war years. Local 480 used such data to curry favour with politicians who agreed with their views, but they encountered significant barriers, including company union advocates, corporate paternalism, and internal dissension among workers who self-identified differently. As well, the local leadership had to cultivate a greater sense of class solidarity among the workers. Meanwhile, the CM&S was busy undermining all such agency.

Times Calls Local 480 Leaders "Parlor-Pinks"

Trail's workers were certainly aware of their working-class status and the class distinctions within the smelter city. Labour-friendly politicians had fuelled this consciousness since the late 1930s with bold statements about the smelter management class's dominance over workers' lives and the need to challenge capitalism as epitomized by the CM&S. Colin Cameron, a left-wing CCFer who represented Comox, BC, in the provincial legislature from 1937 to 1952, established a loyal following in the West Kootenay District as far back as 1939 when he wrote an article for the CCF's *Federationist* entitled "Why a Union Is Needed in Trail." The smelter, he said, embodied the "evolution of Capitalism" and the "class struggle."[75] The "venomous attack" from an outsider, in this case a Vancouver Island Scot, incensed *Times* editor Curran, who called on city council to demand a formal apology. Cameron's remarks were calculated to boost the local union drive, but his radicalism could hardly have helped the public image of Local 480 Communists. Nevertheless, this did not seem to slow the energetic Reds who, as we have seen, went on to win the support of smelter workers.

The wartime banning of the CPC as a subversive organization blocked Trail workers from participating in the electoral process as CPC supporters, but by 1943, the Communists were laying plans to continue their political work under the Labor-Progressive Party (LPP), with Murphy on its national planning committee. In Trail, Local 480's Harry Drake, with help from LPP National Leader Tim Buck, formed an LPP branch in hopes of securing support from smelter workers.[76] But such aspirations came to nothing. Soon after Labour Day that year, the CCL and the CCF announced a political partnership that had major implications for the political ambitions of Local 480 Reds. The *Times* may have unwittingly come to the LPP's aid, warning that it "is impossible for the CCF to be the representative of labor and still represent other classes."[77] Apparently believing that the new alliance could lead to a mass revolt, editor Curran warned, "Revolution can never be the ... permanent solution to any problem, political or economic."[78]

That autumn, Curran charged the CCF with "promising everything to everybody."[79] He later concluded, "The CCF brand of socialism is outmoded utopianism" tantamount to "totalitarianism."[80] The *Times* had been baiting Reds since the early 1930s, when it became a daily. It never missed an opportunity to attack the "parlor-pinks and the rabble-rousers" of the labour movement.[81] Now Curran warned workers not to embrace "a system, which, under some vast bureaucracy, would control and regiment their whole future."[82] This poorly described Local 480's Communist leaders, and the parent union, but it served well as part of Curran's well-worn and relentless pro-CM&S mantra.

Also serving to undermine Drake's hopes for the LPP, Local 480 was embroiled in a local political controversy when it claimed publicly that the CCF had agreed to join forces with the LPP as the Rossland civic elections neared in late 1943. The CCF denied the claim in a *Times* report. Then the daily hinted that the LPP and CIO had collaborated to allow Communists to enter into local municipal politics. When the ballots were counted, the *Times* trumpeted the defeat of labour candidates, saying they were "backed by both the CIO" and the LPP, and that "Rossland electors obviously do not want politics brought into their civic affairs."[83] Drake responded to the CCF's rejection of the LPP's proposal of unity, stating it constituted a "great threat against a united labor movement." The Local 480 Red, who had long faced the brunt of anti-Communist and anti-union criticism in Trail, concluded that "red-baiting of this sort, attacking the left wing of the labor movement[,] confuses the real issues facing the people and will allow reactionary forces to return to the pre-war times of so-called free enterprise and monopoly."[84] It was not the last time the CCF and LPP would lock horns or that Local 480 would find itself embroiled in political controversy.

When Herridge was nominated in 1945 as the CCF candidate for the federal riding of Kootenay West, the *Commentator* dutifully rallied Local 480 members around the Kaslo, BC, farmer. "Are we going to sit idly by twiddling our thumbs," the paper chided members, "saying it doesn't matter who gets in, our vote wouldn't influence the outcome anyway?" It warned that a loss in this federal election could take them back to "the cutthroat days of keen competition, forcing the wages and living conditions of other people down, developing another descending spiral of human welfare." Local 480 should not be a "free riding 'maverick' in our Canadian commonwealth, but a more determined 'active citizen,' one that would vote against ever returning to the 20¢ day relief camps, and the spectacle of disillusioned youth asking for a job and getting tear gas and clubs."[85] Presenting a class analysis of the "industrialists of the world," it insisted that if the management class could manoeuvre for their class interest, then the working class should do similarly. "Are we to sit idly by and allow the Blaylocks and Mitchells [federal Labour Minister Humphrey Mitchell] to rant about the Pinks and the Reds and to castigate the international unions?"[86]

In supporting Herridge, Local 480 unwittingly spiked his prospects. CCF "chieftains in Vancouver" (the CCF's BC Council) nixed the nomination, viewing Herridge as too closely associated with the union's Communist leaders. The *Times* exploited the divided left, remarking that it "appears that freedom of choice of CCF candidates is curtailed and that the wish of the electors of any riding can be overruled by a supreme council of some kind in Vancouver."[87] The CCF leadership's rejection of Herridge's nomination spurred additional criticism from the *Commentator*. It advised CCF leaders not to "interfere with the free, progressive flow of the logics of life and retard the movement of the people in their united march onward."[88] Drake encouraged Kootenay progressives to weld "themselves into a common bond." The Liberal-Conservative coalition, he insisted, "stands threatened by CCF policy, and as a result of the considerable swing to the left of the masses in the last few years." Herridge had the support of Local 480 members and "his policies on the war, and for [political] unity, have been supported by the LPP," but the *Times* warned that there were "malicious attempts being made to represent Mr. Herridge's nomination as purely LPP-influenced, deliberately [to] confuse people and act as a cover for anti-unity forces in the CCF leadership today."[89]

CCF's Herridge Accused of Communist Sympathies

During the following spring, the *Times* again criticized the CCF executive for opposing Herridge, declaring that by shunning the popular candidate the party has "destroyed its own organization in this riding for many years to come." To "those whose ideals do not include socialism and who look towards the continuation of our way of life under the system of free enterprise," the CCF had bared a "major weakness in party ideology."[90] A week later, the daily reported that the LPP had endorsed Herridge as the "People's CCF" candidate in the June Dominion of Canada election.[91] The CCF leadership then replaced Herridge with Frank Tracy, also from Kaslo. CCF BC President A.T. (Thomas) Alsbury, who would later become mayor of Vancouver, explained in the *Times* that Herridge "will masquerade as a federal candidate" but "he will be the actual spokesman of the Communist Party."[92] That was as good as it got for the *Times* in its untiring crusade against the left. The next day the editor called Herridge an unreconstructed Communist, "whatever title he may assume," and "those who want him to run" supported LPP policies.[93] This included Local 480, which had circulated a petition urging the CCF executive to accept Herridge's candidacy.

CCF Avoids Association with Communist Party

In late May, the CCF placed an advertisement in the *Times* noting that CCF MP Angus MacInnis, an ardent anti-Communist, would address Kootenay voters. The son-in-law of the late CCF leader J.S. Woodsworth, MacInnis would speak against Local 480's support of Herridge. MacInnis was unequivocally aligned with the party's national leadership on the question of collaborating with the CPC. As James Naylor and others have shown, the CCF had adopted a policy of "avoiding any public association with the Communist Party," yet rejecting "knee-jerk anti-Communism."[94] The ad warned that a "great national movement is being attacked by the most unscrupulous campaign in Canada's history." It also tried to debunk some of the anti-CCF arguments, insisting "every possible lie, distortion and slander is being used by Big Business and its political parties against the thousands of Canadians who form the CCF."[95]

The distance between the CCF leadership and local sentiment erupted at a public meeting a few days later. MacInnis tried to justify the CCF rejection of Herridge to a Trail audience by explaining that "Herridge got too big for the party." This brought a volley of accusations of CCF hypocrisy. When confronted with the issue of how long Frank Tracy had been a party member, MacInnis was unable to answer. The meeting degenerated into accusations against smelter workers who had "belonged to the 'Maple Leaf' union [a reference to the ISWU] or to the CIO."[96] War veterans in attendance might have shared these concerns, but for many, politics, regardless of its colour, was secondary to getting resettled at home and resuming work at the smelter.

The ensuing election exposed the weakness of the CCF position, and Herridge rode Local 480's unwavering support to victory in Kootenay West and a seat in Ottawa. He polled more than a thousand votes ahead of the Conservative candidate. Meanwhile, the official CCF candidate lost his legal deposit, winning only 8 per cent of the popular vote. CCF federal leader M.J. Coldwell, touted in certain quarters as the "next prime minister," emerged with only three British Columbia seats – four, counting the rebellious Herridge. The *Times* was unhappy with the Herridge win, calling him "an orphan in a strange land" and declaring that the new MP was tainted by his Communist support.[97]

In reality, Herridge's victory was less about his supposed Communist sympathies than a power struggle with the CCF. Indeed, his commitment to Communism was never clear. Local 480 supported Herridge because he backed smelter workers' right to a fair deal from the employer and perhaps because he was the only electable leftist in the West Kootenay. With its electoral losses, CCF support dipped in BC and federal elections, and the Social Credit Party soon took over many of these CCF ridings behind future Premier W.A.C. Bennett, a popular right-wing leader who promised prosperity. CCF stalwarts nevertheless blamed Communist influence for the losses, and, as Benjamin Isitt explains, "powerful forces in the national CCF and B.C. section turned against dissidents in their own ranks." Ironically, Herridge, once expelled from the CCF "for advocating cooperation with the communists," was readmitted to the party.[98] The *Times* noted that Local 480 eventually withdrew its endorsement of the CCF as "the political voice of Trail's Local 480."[99]

The political fallout from the 1945 election continued to interest Trailites, ample evidence of which could be found in the anti-CCF *Times*. Voters across BC, Ontario, and the nation pondered its significance. A royal commission investigated charges by Ontario CCF leader E.B. "Ted" Jolliffe that, among other things, Ontario Premier George Drew had organized a political "Gestapo," spying on CCF and other left politicians. Journalist Walter Stewart described a "hate campaign" in which Drew set up a political police force in 1943 using tax money. Captain William J. Osbourne-Dempster, code named D.208, was a "political spy" assigned to setting up files on "anyone who levelled any criticism against the government, free enterprise, or international finance," Stewart reported.[100]

Meanwhile, the CCF's provincial council punished the Kootenay West riding for its defiance during the Herridge nomination squabble by severing ties to the People's CCF. It withdrew the Trail CCF club's charter and suspended neighbouring Warfield's charter. The Trail club fought back. "We had hoped that the decisive expression of the people's will in Kootenay West would cause the provincial executive to realize that a very serious mistake had been made," a member of Herridge's campaign committee wrote to the *Times*. Instead, the party leadership assigned an organizer to build "a movement purged of all those democratic elements who insist upon the fundamental right of the rank and file to choose the members who will represent them in the parliaments of this country."[101]

A week after the expulsion and suspension, two Herridge supporters wrote to the *Times* to say that the local clubs "believe in the democratic rights of the people to choose their own candidate and we also believe in the principles of the Regina manifesto," notably its call to nationalize the banks and other private institutions.[102] By that point it was clear that not everyone in the CCF leadership shared those beliefs. The party was moving toward the centre of the political spectrum. There would be less room for revolutionary platforms such as those contained in the famed manifesto. The *Times* noted a comment in the CCF-supporting *Canadian Forum* advising party leaders to shift the CCF program from "all-out socialism to some socialism." The *Times* interpreted the magazine to say, "What our society needs in order to win the peace is enterprise, both public and private."[103]

"People's CCF" Causes Short-Lived Political Rebellion

Such ideas departed significantly from the beliefs of the "People's CCF" in the Kootenays, and although the political rebellion was short-lived, it strongly suggested that the majority of Trail's smelter workers were more interested in bread-and-butter results than in winning any ideological battle. For CCF leaders, cultivating a less radical image held out the promise of electing more CCF candidates. For leftists like those at Local 480, who adhered to a "revolutionary stance" and radical social change, the CCF was decreasingly a political home. In Naylor's view, radical ideals had been cast aside. "Labour socialists, had seen themselves, by their essence, as outsiders" and "Labour's position gave workers a unique ability to understand capitalism, develop an ethical critique of capitalist social relations, and organize themselves, as a class, to replace it."[104] Anti-capitalism was fading in the CCF, and the demands of its manifesto were giving way to a strategy of parliamentary reformism. Local 480's Communists had no place at the national table, and their role within the provincial CCF was diminishing as well.

The purging continued in late July as the CCF executive expelled three Kootenay members for supporting Herridge. Harry Drake was among them. Payback came during the 25 October BC election, when the CCF, while winning fourteen seats elsewhere in the province, lost the Trail-Rossland riding formerly held by Herridge to a Liberal-Conservative coalition candidate. The coalition easily secured a majority in Victoria. Social Credit did not win in any of the sixteen ridings it contested, but the right-wing party ran strongly, revealing things to come. Tim Buck's Communists ran twenty-one candidates, but won no seats. The *Times* crowed that the LPP had achieved its purpose of dividing the left and punishing the CCF for its failure to "co-operate."[105] Murphy's *B.C. District Union News* supported former Local 480 organizer and war veteran Sgt. Gordon Martin's bid as a Communist and Local 480's Bill Cunningham as a "People's CCF" candidate for Rossland-Trail. Neither won.

By the late 1940s, Herridge had long earned the respect of Local 480 members as their representative in both provincial and federal jurisdictions. He had his detractors as well. He was a "fence-sitter" in the eyes of former Local 480 Secretary-Treasurer Remo Morandini.[106] But along with CCF leftists Colin Cameron and rebel CCFer Rod Young, a one-term MP from Vancouver, Herridge represented labour. The BC CCF also found working-class voters gravitating in their direction instead of the national party, and the provincial CCF council even supported the CPC on some issues. In one of his frequent attacks on the CCF and the CPC, Curran placed a pox on both parties. "To what extent the Communists are using the cloak of the CCF to further their aims, it is, of course, impossible even to guess," he opined, "but both are devoted to the weakening and elimination of many of our institutions."[107]

Such editorials, coupled with the Herridge affair and the open criticisms voiced by CCF rebels, contributed to the vacillation of Trail smelter workers as the Cold War intensified. As Isitt notes, CCF leaders were "desperate to distance themselves from Soviet Communism." They opposed "unity with Communist and non-Communist workers against a common enemy."[108] Al Warrington, a Communist Local 480 executive member, recalled that the local CCF group "wouldn't take in anyone who they suspected of being a Mine-Mill guy."[109] Despite the bad blood, Leo Nimsick, a member of the bargaining team that negotiated the first Local 480 collective agreement in 1944, was eventually elected to the provincial legislature on a CCF ticket in the Cranbrook District. The East Kootenay also sent Thomas Uphill to Victoria as MLA for the Fernie riding where he served coal miners' interests for forty years. A Boer War veteran and a future Fernie mayor, Uphill ran as a candidate of the Fernie and District Labour Party. He "was friendly with the Communists," Tom Langford and Chris Frazer stipulated, which "infuriated the anti-communist leadership of the BC CCF."[110]

By 1948, animosity between left and right within the CCF and between it and the CPC was set to explode. Although the CCF opposed anti-labour legislation, its leaders were also responsible for some of the most vicious anti-Communist commentaries. In its ongoing war with local anti-Communists, Local 480 was caught between rival parties with competing left-wing ideologies. Some members supported both, favouring the CPC in ideological debates at clandestine club meetings, but voted for the CCF at the ballot box, as in the Herridge case. About half the founding executive of Local 480 were CPC members and advocates of the Communist-inspired Popular Front movement in the 1930s and early 1940s. Seven of the fifteen founding members of the local were Communists. Several held executive positions after the war and would remain loyal Mine-Mill members into the late 1940s.[111] From the end of the war on, their ties became ever more frayed. Their political loyalties were regularly tested as some members adhered to the CPC's class analysis of the workplace and society, while others backed the CCF's democratic socialism and still others its evolving social democratic posture.

Murphy Stoked the Anti-CCF Machine

The CCF and the CPC shared some policy views and both tried to exploit their commonalities in appeals to members, but Trail's Communists and CCF adherents had been intra-class enemies since the socialist party's inception. In spite of the CCF's anti-capitalist stance, CPC members viewed the CCFers as sell-outs. Always a strong supporter of Stalinist CPC Leader Tim Buck, Murphy stoked the anti-CCF machine with hardline condemnations of the socialist party, seizing every opportunity to denigrate the CCF. By the mid-1940s, the angry denunciations that characterized the "social fascist" name-calling of the Comintern's Third Period gave way to less strident battle cries. When, for example, the party tried to encourage local unions to affiliate, Murphy replied, "The CCF has challenged the right [of labour] ... to fight for legislative gains except through their party."[112] (In Stalinist analysis, the Third Period was to witness capitalist economic collapse and a rise in worldwide worker solidarity.)

As Isitt notes, "Throughout its history, foreign policy and cooperation with the Communist Party were persistent sources of conflict in the BC CCF."[113] Some CCF leaders insisted the party could advance only if it shunned Communists. To that end it tried to purge all its Reds. Much of this "Red War" revolved around the International Woodworkers of America (IWA), with Murphy acting as a key adviser to the largest BC union and a bastion of labour Communism in the province. From 1946 through 1948, Murphy played a feature role in IWA District One President Harold Pritchett's struggle against an anti-Communist group within his union known as the "white bloc." The group, characterized by some as business unionists, had existed since 1940 and had split the union along left-right lines.[114] The split focused attention on several controversial issues, including the Marshall Plan for the reconstruction of Europe (which the white bloc supported and Pritchett opposed), support for the CCF as labour's political voice, and the IWA's supposed subservience to the Soviet Union. The division was exacerbated by the passage of the Taft-Hartley Act, sanctifying white bloc anti-Communism.

Central to the split was Pritchett's fight against amendments to BC's Industrial Conciliation and Arbitration Act in 1947 and 1948. He argued that the Canadian Manufacturers' Association (CMA) had assisted in drafting the amendments to bring the province's labour laws into closer alignment with the US Taft-Hartley Act. Murphy helped shape the IWA's opposition and was partially responsible for the split, Stephen Gray argues. For Pritchett's supporters, "the traditions and struggles of the 1930s still echoed" and Murphy played on those memories.[115] Similar to some of the Trail smelter unionists, "many of these men were noted for their inattention to broader ideological and party work," Gray remarks.[116] But, as Isitt notes, those days had passed and the Red Wars of 1948 ultimately "curbed communist power in B.C. unions."[117] The split precipitated the BC IWA's break from the international to form the Woodworkers Industrial Union of Canada, which was a disaster for IWA Communists. Like Mine-Mill, they were ousted from the Canadian labour movement. Murphy, concluded Gray, "had a large say in the decision" to break away, describing it as "one of the worst mistakes the [Communist] party ever made."[118]

The CCF remained in ideological turmoil for years to come, eventually suspending maverick MP Rod Young, a Trotskyist. Elaine Bernard attributes this to Cold War anti-Communism. The

CCF's drift to the right "was vehemently opposed by many party members who fought to reaffirm the socialist character of the organization." But as Bernard put it, "Rod Young became the stick with which the right successfully beat the left."[119] Local 480 was among those caught in this fight. Some members identified with the old SPC, a founding organization of the CCF whose BC section adamantly supported political education and Marxian-guided political action. Unsympathetic CCF leaders blocked "two Trail CCF Club delegates" from discussing their more radical views at a Vancouver convention.[120] In the midst of this political scrum, the local was battling to hold to its Mine-Mill roots against a growing opposition of anti-Communists. Trailites were made well aware of the affair surrounding the "controversial CCF'er" in the *Times*.[121]

At first glance, the BC section of the CCF was a Marxist-leaning thorn for federal party leaders such as National Secretary David Lewis. Indeed, as Isitt writes, CCF members such as Ernest Winch and son Harold Winch saw themselves as further left than the CPC. They even called themselves "comrade," much to the chagrin of Lewis and others. In his autobiography, Lewis recalled his animosity towards the Reds in the 1940s. He was "a strong opponent of communist activity in the labour movement," seeing CCF stalwarts as naive for not realizing that the CPC was "one of Stalin's puppet instruments for the defence of the Soviet Union and of his brand of communism around the world."[122] Yet years later Lewis still rued the political rivalry between himself and Murphy because of how it undermined their joint fight against capitalism: "No one in the CCF or in the labour movement enjoyed the factional struggles which lasted for some years; they consumed time and energy which could have been put to more productive use." The bitterness of the split always remained close to the surface, but Lewis regarded the differences as "unavoidable for the sake of both the unions and the CCF."[123]

Left-Leaning Smelter Workers Demoralized

Others describe the CCF-CPC wars as a drag on the union movement that watered down the CCF promise to represent workers and their families in the legislatures of the land. Political scientists Leo Panitch and Donald Swartz argue that the ideological warfare of the 1940s led the CCF to align with "the most conservative and opportunistic elements of the union leadership, who, upon winning this internecine struggle, placed their own indelible stamp on the labour movement." They further argue that the "crusade" to oust Communists after the war "was directed against the tradition of socialist ideas and militant rank-and-file struggle, as much as at members of the Communist Party."[124] CCF leaders' motives were undoubtedly also influenced by global developments and shifting allegiances. Lingering animosities about the CPC's shifting policies before and after the Hitler-Stalin non-aggression pact also mattered, and as a result the party never fully recovered its credibility.

In the next decade, Trail's left-leaning smelter workers were demoralized by repeated revelations about the Communist world. Some renounced their membership during the civil war in China, others withdrew when the Stalin-era atrocities were exposed, and still others followed upon learning of the further suppression of democracy in Eastern Europe. Disillusionment bred more and more hostility towards full-blown Communists in the ranks. Discussions about the negative aspects of world Communism brought cheers for the CCF's victory over labour's Communist left. Lewis, MacInnis, Coldwell, and other CCF leaders proudly pointed to the removal of a perceived impediment to electoral success. Eliminating radicals also curtailed opposition to the party's rightward policy thrust. However, for members still wishing to fight capitalism, the party leadership's hardening views represented a closing of that possibility. Naylor notes that while many CCF Marxist socialists rejected the CPC, they nevertheless had much in common. He adds that other CCF members, especially those from the old SPC, disregarded "CCF prohibitions on political alliances with Communists."[125]

Disagreements intensified as the Cold War legitimized the purging of leftists from the labour movement and the CCF, and changes at the national level destabilized relations between the CCF and Local 480 leaders. In Trail, Mine-Mill Reds faced off against an energized right. The CCF shuffled further right in endorsing the United Nations decision to enter the Korean War and rejecting of the Stockholm peace petition. In response, Local 480 members established the Trail Peace Council and collected petition signatures. When Nimsick signed the document, he made himself even more of a pariah in the CCF leadership's eyes, yet CCF MLA Ernest Winch's name was also on the list. Party moderates regarded the petition as a Communist-inspired measure and refused to endorse it. As Isitt states, they "viewed the [Peace] Congress as an LPP (Communist) front and would have nothing to do with it."[126]

CCL and the CCF executives viewed Murphy's 1948 suspension from the BCFL as good for both organizations. They hoped to eliminate an obnoxious radical, but they could not end his union's "class struggle." (Mine-Mill was one of the few Red unions to leave intact its constitution's Marxist language. It read in part, "The class struggle will continue until the producer is recognized as the sole master of his product ... [and] that the working class, and it alone, can and must achieve its own emancipation."[127]) Murphy simply moved to a conciliation board and spoke out against logging companies on behalf of the IWA.[128] He also returned to the Crowsnest Pass area of Alberta to support Communist Ben Swankey's election campaign.[129] It was familiar and friendly territory, a reminder of his role in forming one of the nation's first socialist city halls at Blairmore, but others could not escape his indiscretions.

In August 1948, the *Times* praised the CCL for suspending Mine-Mill, resulting in 5,000 Local 480 members being "removed from the CCL fold."[130] Murphy told the daily that "reinstatement should not be too difficult," but there were obstacles.[131] The furore surrounding Murphy enabled Billingsley to retain the Local 480 presidency in the July 1948 elections, beating out Harry Drake, the skilled mechanic who had introduced Al King to Communism. Jim Quinn, a one-time member of the provincial legislature and fierce anti-Communist, was also elected. Billingsley consolidated control of the executive committee by barring Mine-Mill representative John Gordon, "a nice fella [but with] socialist ideas."[132]

In September, Murphy won a vote of confidence from Mine-Mill, but it was a local victory. Hostility remained entrenched elsewhere. A few weeks later the *Times* reprinted a *Vancouver Province* article claiming Murphy had outlived his usefulness as "a communist tool," with the CCL's Mahoney quoted as saying, "Murphy's petty and childish defiance might make more difficult the task of the miners' union to have itself reinstated with the CCL." The daily concluded that "as an exposed Red and recognized trouble-maker," Murphy has shown that "he is more interested in raising Cain than in raising wages and working conditions."[133]

Stage Set for Further Anti-Red Manoeuvres

The left lost more ground at the CCF's 1948 national convention when a resolution opposing the Marshall Plan, seen by some as anti-Soviet and anti-union, was defeated, but the ideological squabbling was hindering the CCF quest to win over trade unions. Even so, it did not prevent party leadership from moving against its left wing. Indeed, it headed full-speed into the Cold War allied with the CCL in eliminating Red affiliates in what the *Times* dubbed a "roaring battle over communism."[134] Murphy's suspension, a headline-grabbing ejection of Jack Scott at the US border that autumn, and continuing developments on the international Communist scene, especially in China, set the stage for further anti-Red manoeuvres.[135]

Late in 1948, a Canadian Press article noted that Reds "absorbed a sound trouncing in Canada's two big labor congresses, and by the end of the year they were pretty well on the run on all Canadian fronts." The TLC's Percy Bengough and CCL's Aaron Mosher assured affiliated anti-Communist unions that Red purges would intensify in the 1950s.[136] As a result, Trail workers faced a ferocious political storm. Billingsley's anti-Communists further threatened Local 480 from the inside, tempering hopes of recruiting smelter workers as members to the CPC. Indeed, no broad effort followed, but that may have allowed smelter workers to continue supporting their Red leadership, raising anew the question of just how Communist Mine-Mill's leaders were. It is a question for which few historians provide a clear answer.

Vernon Jensen, in his US study of Mine-Mill's Communist connections, focuses mainly on the international union, arguing that the Reds worked to destroy democracy and "concentrated on persuading the organization to espouse their policies." What those policies were he never clearly states, but "they were always careful not to challenge the concept of collective bargaining." They "usually created the impression of being militant bargainers and staunch defenders of the workers' interests," Jensen continued. "They were astute enough to know that they could not accomplish their real purposes if they could not make a positive showing to the rank and file." For Jensen, examples of good trade union practice were merely "camouflage for gaining freedom to pursue other objectives as it suited them." He frets that Communists proffered "left-wing policies and programs," but he fails to explain how this "convenient camouflage" harmed union membership.[137] The Red-led Local 480 is a particularly problematic example with which to test his theories.

Murphy and Local 480 leaders knew the Red baiting would only worsen in the Cold War 1950s. Indeed, the *Times* foreshadowed these troubled times when it advised unions to "remain aloof from political parties ... because world revolution has no part in labor's legitimate progress."[138] The *Commentator* replied that this must be "very appealing to the Times' sponsors (Big Business)," but workers had as much right as big business and industry to participate in politics.[139] Still, the union's survival depended more and more on the leaders focusing on bread-and-butter issues. Some observers view this as a failure to convert Trail into a Red bastion, but the pragmatism of Murphy and Local 480 leaders solidified local Mine-Mill support.

Solidarity took precedence because the Communist leadership was about to face its greatest threat yet. It came in the form of an adversary that had emerged from the ranks of organized labour itself to lead the labour movement's anti-Communist campaign across North America. Maddeningly for local Red leaders, it would be led by one of their own members, a smelter worker pledged to purify the union's pink-tinged image who would ally himself with local clerics, CM&S management, and those immigrant workers who remained reluctant participants in Communist-led Mine-Mill. Once again Local 480 was about to face a challenge to its legal right to represent smelter workers, and this time the challenger was the formidable Steelworkers union.

6

Steel's Cold Warriors Raid
Trail's Red Union

Four years had passed since the war ended, and in 1949 Local 480 members continued to be buffeted by competing leftist ideologies within the union and anti-Communist elements within the community. As discussed elsewhere, both the CPC and the CCF were eager to establish a strong voting base. Now, as that fight continued, all signs pointed to a new phase of union disruption that would push local Red leaders to their limits. Harvey Murphy's ill-advised underpants speech the previous spring became a pretext for more anti-Communist purges that ostracized radical locals from the labour movement. As part of the anti-Red campaign, the CIO-affiliated Steelworkers would soon be sanctioned to raid Mine-Mill locals across North America. The presumed victory would relieve the CCL of its troublemakers and empower CCF factions aligned with Big Labour. Trail's Communists seemed doomed to lose control of Local 480, yet nothing would transpire quite as the combined opposition had hoped.

As in previous years, 1949 saw new attacks on left-wing unionists, and Mine-Mill remained a key target. The attackers were bolstered by the political phenomenon of McCarthyism, and the Trail local, despite its relative geographic obscurity, was vulnerable to this continental anti-left siege. Some dynamics of the attack were as present in the smelter city as in other Mine-Mill locations in the United States. Some tactical responses were also similar, but Local

480 had its own resources with which to resist the rightward tilt of the CCL and the more centrist elements of the CCF.

In examining the motivations of the Steelworkers' raiding strategy, the Local 480 story reveals nuances that historians may have overlooked, but on the matter of Mine-Mill, historians often cross swords along ideological lines, with the union becoming a political punching bag for both the right and the left. However, the personalities, adversarial situations, and blend of left politics in the West Kootenay shows that there was no monolithic political machine at work in Trail or, for that matter, anywhere else. Although smelter workers did not sympathize with all the views of Local 480's Communists, nor remain uncritical of Harvey Murphy's Marxism, neither did Murphy impose his Communist Party doctrine upon them. Trail Communists acted pragmatically with an eye on rank-and-file interests. This mattered greatly when they came under fire from enemies old and new as Cold War hysteria swept across the United States and Canada. Yet while this was a continental story, it also mattered that in Trail the battle began slowly and clandestinely from within.

Times Backs Raiders, Questions Local 480's Legitimacy

Trailites may not have known it yet, but a new kind of war was about to be unleashed in the smelter city. Those who did know were as preoccupied as everyone else in the quest for post-war normalcy and security. That included adapting to household changes. Margarine, for example, was starting to appear more often on Trail dinner tables, and it was promising to drive down the price of butter.[1] The CM&S Company Store continued to provide coffee at fifty-eight cents a pound, dog food at two tins for twenty-nine cents, and "camping and hot weather specials" like sandwich spread at forty-three cents for a sixteen-ounce jar. At the Odeon, Richard Widmark appeared in *The Street with No Name*. Ingrid Bergman was Joan of Arc at the Strand. Elizabeth Taylor and Janet Leigh were *Little Women*. CM&S (soon to be Cominco) premiered its

Technicolor film *No Man Is an Island*, about the company and its employees.[2] With so many of Trail's veterans having fought in the air force, the RCAF band from Edmonton was heartily welcomed when it played the Trail high school auditorium. Dick Ballou and his orchestra were at the Playmor in South Slocan. CJAT broadcast pop concerts by the Toronto Symphony Orchestra. Even with the new normal, however, labour peace in the smelter city remained elusive.

Early in the year, while the Steelworker leadership was still eyeing the right moment to launch what some Local 480 leaders later characterized as an invasion, the anti-Red *Times* was readying itself for renewed political sorties into Mine-Mill territory. The resulting back-and-forth gave some indication of what would follow. In an editorial, "Do Reds Run Local 480?" editor Curran suggested that Murphy "is busy these days telling the boys 'on the hill' that this communist stuff is a lot of hooey." He then likened Murphy to revolutionary Soviet leader Vladimir Lenin. "Communism, to hear Murphy talk, is no insidious, rotten scheme to control the minds and bodies and souls of the whole world," Curran crowed. "It is a 'sweetness-and-light' campaign to elevate and make princes out of the poor downtrodden peoples of the world."[3]

Readers quickly responded. F.J. Warne wrote, "I am not a communist and I am sure that my firm and unshakeable belief in God and Christianity would not be compatible with membership in the communist party," but he would "defend Murphy's right to believe what he pleases, as long as his beliefs do not conflict with his union obligations."[4] Ernie Weed scolded Curran, saying he had "fooled very few people with your red-baiting and union splitting attempts." He then accused the editor of supporting the CM&S in its efforts to "break the union at any cost!"[5] Other letter writers, though, shared the *Times*'s concerns. One letter titled "Is Local 480 Commie Tool?" counselled smelter workers to think of their wives, children, and country. "Men like Harvey Murphy," the author cautioned, "are out to destroy our Canadian way of life, and sell our country to the Kremlin."[6] Weed again retorted, "I would much rather wear the communist mask than the Fascist one which has been stuck on you."[7] One of Local 480's few female activists, Irene

Vetere, also spoke out: "You all yell 'communism,' hoping to build up such a hysteria within the union that the members will be so busy fighting amongst themselves or searching through that smoke of yours [that] they'll miss the real issue at stake, namely, their bread and butter."[8] Curran was unapologetic, reminding readers that the daily was "unalterably opposed to communist infiltration into labor unions." His objective was to "drive that insidious and unwholesome little group of communists into ... obscurity."[9]

In mid-March, Communist *Pacific Tribune* writer Bruce Mickleburgh reignited a long-standing local controversy when he published accusations about deceased CM&S President S.G. Blaylock. Mickleburgh accused the industrialist of combining "terrorism and paternalism" so that "scores of thousands of workers cursed the name Blaylock." "To them his company unionism meant miserable pay, stretchout, speedup, industrial illness, accident, and – above all – fear."[10] CM&S General Manager R.W. Diamond was similarly criticized for anti-Communist statements that were "a package of poison for the mind" and for promoting a "'good' union with 'responsible leaders,' not 'Communists' like Murphy." This riled Trail's anti-Communists, but there was more to come. Four smelter workers – Gar Belanger, Ernie Weeks, Lloyd Noakes, and Jack Scott – further antagonized relations by distributing the Mickleburgh articles to Local 480 members at plant gates. The *Times* said the articles were "verbal sewage" by "philosophers of snarl" who hoped to "completely paralyze" the local metal industry.[11]

On 1 April, the day annual contract negotiations began, the *Times* reported that the four employees had been "sacked" for distributing "maliciously untrue statements" about the company.[12] As Al King saw it, CM&S management had brought its "full vengeance ... down on [former Local 480 President] Gar Belanger's head, along with those of the three co-workers."[13] Local 480 President Billingsley distanced himself from the affair, telling the *Times* that the articles were part of a "smear campaign."[14] He nevertheless succumbed to membership pressure and filed a grievance that went to arbitration, with Murphy representing the union. The majority report upheld the dismissals, but Murphy's minority report stressed the ideological reasons behind the firings, arguing that the plant-gate distribution of the articles was retaliation for "pamphlets delivered with pay envelopes by the company over past weeks." Those pamphlets included "attacks on district union officers [that were] maliciously anti-labour in their content." The *B.C. District Union News* claimed the company's response was "slanderous and malicious to a far greater extent than the leaflet complained about."[15] Belanger's firing was nevertheless upheld. The Mine-Mill paper said board lawyers quoted the British Masters and Servants Act to support the company's "right to fire employees for holding opinions contrary to their own concerning policies of the company."[16] Al King said the arbitration panel's decision epitomized the company's "full vengeance" against Mine-Mill.

Local 480 Encouraged to "Decapitate Itself"

The controversy generated by Mickleburgh hastened Billingsley to support a Steelworker raid on Mine-Mill. In Al King's view they were using it to foster "a spirit of division inside the union, encouraging it to decapitate itself."[17] For Billingsley, Communism was the real enemy. He remembered how Harry Drake, Fred Henne, and Richard Gop had "tried desperately to get me into the Communist Party," promising they would get him elected local president. For Billingsley, Local 480 was a Red hotbed; CPC members controlled the union. There were no more than 125 Communists in the Trail area, he estimated, but their influence was outsized. "If you're hungry, and you can't feed your kids," Billingsley argued, "you're going to join any organization that promises your kids are going to be fed."[18] As King saw it, however, Billingsley was leading a hugely destructive force against Local 480 and he had an abundance of help.

Beyond Trail, Billingsley posed a threat to Murphy's authority over the union's western region. When Billingsley was elected president of the BC District Union in the spring of 1949, Murphy declared in the *B.C. District Union News* that the results were null and void, citing irregularities involving the Mine-Mill constitution.[19] The *Times* editor, heavily betting on Billingsley to win, had forecast Murphy's "ouster," but Murphy's action threw a wrench into Curran's hopes.[20] New elections would not occur until October, but Murphy was unapologetic. He admitted that the cancellation was "disappointing," but he insisted it showed "how seriously we treat the upholding of the constitution."[21] This time, though, most observers saw only a political ploy that confirmed a habit of manipulation and underhanded politics that the CCF and CCL had criticized for more than a decade.

With a Local 480 election scheduled for that May, Al King tried to re-energize his campaign for the presidency, but his defeat in July and that of other Red candidates prompted the *Times* to boast that "not one red was elected."[22] Given another term as president, King warned, Billingsley would "subvert the union ·from within as a leader of a group of unionists eager to leave Mine-Mill for the Steelworkers Union."[23] In reality Mine-Mill's problems were internal as well. Murphy's high-handed actions led delegates at the CCL convention to expel Mine-Mill in early October. The *Times* declared the "communist heyday in Canadian unions is about over," but it warned that "communists will not relinquish their stranglehold on Mine-Mill." Murphy, the "communist mastermind of western Canada[,] will continue on his nefarious course."[24] The same month, Murphy announced the results of the District Union election re-run: Communist Ken Smith had defeated Billingsley by about one hundred votes. It was hardly a surprise.

The Mine-Mill election was but one front in a many-sided war. The Smith victory was tempered by the news that the CIO had dropped six affiliates from good standing, including Mine-Mill. In all, ten affiliates were under investigation for being "too 'left wing.'"[25] The investigation was a reminder that while the Canadian Manufacturers' Association (CMA) had failed to insert a Taft-Hartley-inspired anti-Communist affidavit into BC's 1948 amendment to the province's labour law, the ICA, Big Labour had decided that leftist unions were no longer an asset. Adding insult to injury, the *Times*'s year-end news roundup portrayed 1949 as a "spectacular" year because "Canadian labor tightened the screws on communists."[26] Perhaps the only good news for Local 480 was that Bill Curran had accepted a new job managing the *Nelson Daily News*, but his replacement was no better for the union.[27] King feared the British-born Dennis Williams would bring "a more sophisticated and … a more dangerous editorial expertise toward combating organized labour in Trail." Instead of the "blatant anti-union pro-employer fulminations of past Trail Times writers," the new editor would turn up the Cold War heat.[28] The daily would feature even more Red baiting as Murphy and the Local 480 leadership prepared to face another major struggle, perhaps its biggest to date.

Labour Movement Turns on Red Affiliates

While Local 480 waited for the next anti-Communist salvo in early 1950, the year brought fresh threats to peace. Revolutionary leader Mao Tse-tung was moving quickly to repaint China Red after his victory in the long civil war against Chiang Kai-shek, but another war was brewing in nearby Korea. Further increasing the threat to peace, the *Times* reported that US President Harry Truman had approved the development of a "super hydrogen bomb … far surpassing even the latest atomic weapons."[29] Truman, who had earlier dismissed rumours that he might drop the "most fearful weapon in the world" on Korea, now stated that he might do so.[30] Perhaps it was political posturing in the wake of Republican gains in the recent US mid-term elections. Perhaps it was a smokescreen to cover the negative economic impact of the eleven-month-long recession of 1948–9. Meanwhile, the Russians, who had detonated their first atomic bomb the previous year, were building an atomic arsenal in an arms race to match those the Americans were stockpiling.

Closer to home, the House Un-American Activities Committee (HUAC) was investigating an "atomic mystery man." HUAC had pegged Boris J. Pregel in connection with the discovery that Canadian uranium had been sold to the Soviet Union during the war.[31] *Times* readers were also told they could "live through an A-bomb raid" as instructed in a thirty-two-page US government booklet selling for a dime.[32] Whether or not Trailites found this information useful, it was hardly reassuring, with Canada doing some sabre rattling of its own in announcing that Canadian troops might soon be fighting alongside Americans in Korea. The reality of Canuck boots hitting Asian ground registered quickly when Defence Minister Brooke Claxton later announced that soldiers in Princess Patricia's Canadian Light Infantry, where smelter soldiers had once served, would soon be bound for Korea.

On the Cold War political front, Trailites were informed that an ambitious young lawyer named Richard Nixon was shaping his future career with the conviction of alleged Soviet spy Alger Hiss for perjury in the ongoing HUAC hearings. Senate investigations were also gaining momentum under Senator Joseph McCarthy, America's Number One Communist witch-hunter. His anti-Red speeches would resonate across the continent and would eventually reach the smelter city, where another kind of smelter war was about to begin for Local 480's Reds.

Murphy and other left labour leaders were also increasingly threatened as CCL leaders continued to feed their long-nurtured hatred of Communist unionists. They shared a personal dread of the Red leaders like Murphy and many other Reds who had been schooled in parliamentary procedure. These radicals regularly challenged conservative leaders at union meetings and conventions with points of order and other constitutional tactics seen as disruptive and often embarrassing to the leadership. The CCL leaders held them in contempt, and they were not alone. Persistent anti-Red propaganda in papers like the *Times* stoked anti-Communist sentiment across society.

The threat turned real for Local 480 when the *Times* reported that CCL President Aaron Mosher had sanctioned the Steelworkers "to organize the workers in Canada's metal mines and smelters."[33] The long-threatened raid was soon unleashed on Mine-Mill locals across North America when Mosher deemed them legitimate targets for the well-heeled million-member international union. At first the objective in Canada was to hit smaller locals in the gold-mining regions of Northern Ontario and Quebec. Raid architects initially ignored the CM&S and Inco Limited, the world's largest producer of nickel at the time. Both were seen as "impregnable," argued Ontario Mine-Mill activists Mike Solski and John Smaller. But soon Steelworkers began to raid larger locals such as Local 480, Local 637 in Port Colborne, and eventually Local 598, Mine-Mill's largest Canadian affiliate with 13,000 members in Sudbury.[34]

Canada's labour movement had been upgrading its fight against Communist unions since the founding of the Communist Workers' Unity League (WUL) in 1929, but they had not eliminated them. By 1950, however, all the essential anti-Red purge requirements were in place. In "its battle against communism," Irving Abella notes, "everything was fair to the CCL leadership."[35] Yet "unquestionably, very few members of the expelled unions were Communists…. Their sole crime was simply their insistence on electing leaders to whom the Congress objected."[36] The decision to purge grew from "the anti-Communist hysteria which hallmarked the late 1940s and early 1950s," Abella continues. "The Congress patriotically decided to rid itself of its left-wing membership. This was accomplished without too much difficulty or even much soul-searching. The Communists had to go and ways were found to expel them. That these ways were brutal and perhaps even unconstitutional was irrelevant."[37] The CCL effectively emulated its craft-union counterpart, the TLC, which, as Mine-Mill lawyer John Stanton documents, had already ruthlessly purged itself of the Communist-led Canadian Seaman's Union (CSU).[38] Like the TLC, CCL leaders devoted more time, energy, and money to the Red purges than perhaps any other task, and perhaps with some justification since the radical changes the Communists desired were not goals the CCL and TLC leadership shared.

USWA an "Oligarchy of Staunchly Conservative Men"

Organizationally, the Steelworkers were a very different union from Mine-Mill. The USWA was bureaucratic and centralized in its decision-making, and leaders departed substantially from rank-and-file wage levels and class associations. It was "an oligarchy of staunchly conservative men," notes Judith Stepan-Norris, and it contrasted sharply with Communist leaders, whose salaries stayed close to those of the rank-and-file. Her analysis also showed that the higher the pay for a union leader, the less likely he (and it was a mostly male leadership) tolerated dissent. Thus the Steelworkers were an "enduring and powerful bastion of anti-Communism within the CIO."[39] Other labour historians agree that the USWA was probably the most predatory of the CIO-CCL unions, and its leadership was probably the most doctrinally anti-Communist. Its attack on Murphy and Local 480 was certainly among the most notorious examples of Red baiting in Canadian labour history. Canadian Steelworker leader Charlie Millard judged that it was worth it. A win in Trail would be a precious jewel in the crown for the raiding Steelworkers.

For Millard and others, battles with Mine-Mill were inherently ideological. For example, when Mine-Mill representatives criticized the Marshall Plan, a hugely popular post-war stimulus program seen by some as benefitting multinational corporations, their opponents would argue that the Communist objectors' unstated problem was that the Marshall Plan was anti-Soviet. Mine-Mill also attacked American foreign policy on convention floors, openly and ceaselessly criticizing the CCL's anti-Communist views and its failure to organize the unorganized. In short, Communist leaders wanted the labour movement to assault post-war capitalism, not collaborate with it, and it was easy work for critics to link Red positions with Soviet designs. Some would pay for their pro-Soviet views with their jobs and the loss of a sense of personal security. Marginalization of Communist leaders also undermined the credibility of the 1930s view of Trail's labour socialists and Communists that a working-class revolution was possible even in post-war North America.

For Stanton, the union purges revealed the "harmful things that working people can be induced to do to one another" when guided by "an aggressive, power-hungry group of union leaders."[40] Solski and Smaller argue that Claire Billingsley and his pro-Steelworker Local 480 executive adopted "the 'boring from within' tactic in the strategy to destroy Mine Mill." They in fact seemed to follow a kind of raid playbook. "First, executive boards purporting to act on behalf of Mine Mill members created issues of dissent with International convention and conference decisions," noted Solski and Smaller. Then "they withheld per capita payments; and, finally, they withdrew from Mine Mill, attempting to take the local membership either into the CCL or directly into the Steelworkers."[41] John Lang argues that because this involved persuading local leaders to switch allegiances, the Steelworkers' "huge patronage system" could have a "corrupting influence on local labour leaders."[42] Local 480's Al King saw it the same way.

For loyalists to the Red leadership, Billingsley was a Quisling determined to destroy the union by concocting a "damned devil's brew" that the Mine-Mill local would have to contend with.[43] The Billingsley group stopped payments to the strike fund and death benefit plan, and they "emptied the bank account by paying each other full wages."[44] Billingsley, self-described as the "Number One Bad Boy in the union split," had earlier said that the local's "money was channelled into Communist front organizations."[45] Thus for him draining the treasury was necessary to erase the local's Red taint. He was what the Steelworker raiders needed to oust Mine-Mill's Red guard, but he was also a godsend for the CCF, which was collaborating with the Steelworkers. With Billingsley on the inside, the CCF and Steel had only to wait to be led through the smelter gates. As the leading cold warrior union, the USWA was an obvious ally against the Red menace. Now it was time to formally invite the raiders to town.

Murphy, King, and other Communists viewed CCF-CCL-Steelworker anti-Red politics with considerable alarm. King knew that Billingsley "and his bunch of githorns" had been working hard to convince Local 480 members that the USWA was their best option. Indeed, as King remembered, with the aid of the CCF-CCL alliance against the Reds, the plan was "to exclude all active Mine-Millers ... from all union business." His frustration was in part proprietary: "It was the Communists who built the goddamned union."[46] The CCF, CCL, and Steelworkers had all developed anti-Red positions in the 1930s that they then nurtured throughout the 1940s. This was a golden opportunity for Millard, a former CCF member of the Ontario legislature, and Billingsley. To take advantage of it, Millard assigned Herbert Gargrave, a former BC CCF MLA (Mackenzie), to coordinate the smelter raid with Millard overseeing the operation from afar.

A former Mine-Mill man now aligned with the Steelworkers and a top CCL leader, Millard also assigned CCL Western Director William Mahoney and CCF organizer Murray Cotterill, both Steelworkers, and CCL Public Relations Director Jack Williams, a former Canadian Press reporter, to keep close watch over the raid zone. Billingsley meshed with most of the crew. Cotterill, Mahoney, and Williams were in his words "good guys," but Gargrave came off as self-aggrandizing because winning was part of his personal strategy to be re-elected to the provincial legislature. Clearly, the raid was linked to politics. In Sudbury, for example, the Ontario CCF "performed the classic exercise of self-immolation," refusing to endorse its candidate Bob Carlin in Ontario's 1948 election unless he supported the CCL position on the Mine-Mill raids. As Solski and Smaller note, the seat went to the Conservatives, and a CCF stronghold was "destroyed for many years to come."[47] Now, two years later, BC's Trail-Rossland riding was on the table.

Insiders Aid Raid with Anti-Red Propaganda

On 9 February 1950, the very day US Senator Joseph McCarthy gave his speech in Wheeling, West Virginia, inciting what became known as McCarthyism, the Steelworker raiders attacked Trail. Armed with Billingsley's endorsement, an ample supply of anti-Communist literature, and a war chest big enough to buy regular advertisements in the *Times*, the "blitz" began. A full-page ad warned Mine-Mill members that to remain in the Canadian labour movement, they had to accept the USWA as their new bargaining agent. Given the CCL expulsion of Mine-Mill, this was technically true. The ad advised shop stewards to abandon Local 480. Billingsley, his executive, and all stewards and chief stewards except Communist charter member Dan Dosen resigned en masse. Local 480 Reds regarded the ad as tantamount to a request for the local to commit suicide, and the gambit seemed likely to succeed. Instead of the Number One bad boy, Billingsley now saw himself "branded all across Canada as being a traitor" by Mine-Mill and other Communist-led unions.

Billingsley explained his role in the raid strategy: "I just turned all these cards loose up the hill and in about two days we had,

I guess, a couple of thousand signed up."[48] King depicted Billingsley diligently visiting all the plants, "telling people that Mine
Mill was no longer in existence," and signing them to the USWA.
The company was fully complicit, blessing Steelworker efforts. As
King saw it, management allowed these "traitors to their union"
to sign up members on company time.[49] "When Billingsley and
the Steel raiders signed up our members, they asked them to sign
two things. One was to the company, revoking their dues checkoff
to Local 480." The second was a Steel membership card, "but no
money changed hands [even though the] law required that a minimum one dollar be paid whenever anyone signed an application
card as a union member."[50] That oversight and USWA's failure to
administer an oath on signing a union card were fatal mistakes that
would later affect the raid.

In the meantime, a week after the first Steelworkers ad appeared,
the CIO formally expelled Mine-Mill. Billingsley was elated. As
the "provisional president," he told the *Times* the expulsion confirmed his own actions. Mine-Mill was "an utterly powerless
instrument for collective bargaining or local union service."[51] Others demurred. Kitch Bannatyne compared the Billingsley group's
walkout to Japan's attack on Pearl Harbor and asked, "What kind
of blood flows through the veins of the ones who are responsible for this split in the working men?"[52] His comment triggered
another letter war. Murphy, meanwhile, helped mount a counter-
action to keep the smelter local in the Mine-Mill fold. Calling the
raid "a most disgusting exhibition of treachery," he accused the
Steelworkers in a *Times* report of paying the CCL $50,000 for
the Trail jurisdiction.[53] He also appointed John Gordon, a future
Rossland mayor, as Local 480 administrator. Gordon convened a
meeting on 10 February attended by hundreds of confused members. Murphy assured them that Local 480 was far from dead.
Gordon called for nominations to fill executive positions, and Jack
Scott nominated King for president. King remembered Gordon
sending those nominated to the big washroom at the back of the
hall: "You eighteen go back into the toilet and when you come out
of there, whoever you decided on among yourselves will be the
new president."[54]

As a result, King was named president and the new Local 480 leadership, dubbed the "Shithouse Executive," was charged with mounting the counterattack. Their first concern was an empty bank account. King appealed for help from other Mine-Mill locals and worked to win back the support of the membership. Bargaining would begin on 1 April, and if the union did not have a majority signed up by the end of January, the company could file to decertify it. The Steel raiders could at the same time apply to the BC LRB for certification. In the Mine-Mill camp, King recalled that "it seemed the entire world including the church, the press, the company, the leadership of the CCF and too many other unions all wanted to see the end of Mine Mill."[55] Adding to the confusion, the Steelworkers announced in the *Times* that they had named the raiding group the Trail and District Smelterworkers Union Local 4281.

Local 480's defenders took to the airwaves and print media. Gordon blamed hangovers from Blaylock's old company union and the ISWU, its legal reincarnation after the war, for splitting the union. As he put it in the *B.C. District Union News*, they were doing so through "deliberate falsehoods and misrepresentation."[56] Former Local 480 President Percy Berry called the raid a "dastardly act." Adopting a Shakespearean tone in his *B.C. District Union News* comment, he praised the Local 480 loyalists as "men who balk at condoning treachery, deceit, men who know full well there is an honorable and decent way to settle all differences, without turning worker against worker, wife against husband, brother against sister and home against home." He then charged the raiders with "setting a whole community aflame to satisfy the greedy ambitions of a few."[57]

"Cheerful Cynic" Mocks Steelworker Raiders

Writing as "The Cheerful Cynic," Chuck Kenny used his *B.C. District Union News* column to amuse loyal Local 480 members and mock Steelworker raid leaders. Murphy preferred the rhetoric of betrayal, portraying the Billingsley "clique" as "traitors," "seceders," and "ratting shop stewards" from "the old company union gang."[58] The CCL was "guilty of 'treachery unknown to decent labor organizations." He then rallied Mine-Mill members to remember "our martyred dead [as] we fight to see these traditions live."[59] New to the executive, Communist Al Warrington chided those who discredited Mine-Mill as "Communist" and advised union members not to follow "these Iscariots."[60] Mine-Mill defenders also bought ads in the *Times*, one of which included a report condemning raids and pledging to protect Local 480 from the Steel raiders.[61]

Demonization characterized the actions of both Mine-Mill and the USWA. Addressing a mass meeting in Trail on 19 February, International Mine-Mill President John Clark told the crowd that the CIO-CCL raiders were "worse than 'Pinkertons and paid stool pigeons and union busters of early labor history in North America.'" Ontario's Bob Carlin "compared the CIO-CCL tactics with those of Hitler" and urged Trail women to "stand behind their husbands." Chase Powers, a Communist on the international executive, called the Steelworker tactics "those of 'cannibals'" and similar to "Mussolini's telling the Ethiopians he was going to 'liberate' them." Murphy compared the Billingsley group to "the executive of the Knights of Columbus walking out and joining the Orange Lodge."[62] In response, the USWA bought another full-page *Times* ad on 21 February that explained "Why the C.I.O. Expelled Mine, Mill," pointing to the union's legacy of "devotion to the Communist Party."[63]

Throughout this internecine union struggle, a crew of police officers kept the raid "under close but discreet surveillance" and recorded many comments as it gathered evidence of the assumed "subversive activities" of Mine-Mill. Police Constable J.G.E. Murray of the Grand Forks, BC, detachment submitted frequent and detailed reports on Murphy and other Communists involved in the events in Trail. There was much evidence to sort through. On 20–22 February, Mine-Mill convened a national convention in Trail attended by International Mine-Mill leaders and other union dignitaries. Two Tacoma, Washington, Mine-Mill convention guests were refused entry to Canada at the Paterson, Washington, border crossing near Rossland. Authorities said they lacked proper credentials. Secret police reports said the two were a "diversionary action" meant to deflect attention from International Mine-Mill Secretary-Treasurer Maurice Travis, a leading Mine-Mill

Communist who had been banned from Canada. Travis had travelled north to attend the conference and secretly to assist the fight against the raiders. His stay was short-lived. Billingsley had guided police enthusiastically to where he was staying and cheered when Travis was delivered to border guards, saying, "They should have thrown the book at him."[64] Watching it all, Constable Murray reported that "the battle for supremacy is close" and the situation "generally tense." He also noted "both unions are indulging in 'exposees' [sic]."[65]

The union-against-union confrontation escalated in March with each organization purchasing half a dozen ads. The Steelworkers alluded to the smelter's atomic bomb–related heavy water plant, secretly codenamed Project 9, arguing that "operations in Trail are vital to the national security of Canada." The *Times* speculated that the Communists were "waging such a desperate battle here" that they could stoop to passing secrets to the Soviet Union.[66] Mine-Mill gave as good as it got, but as the month wore on, tempers flared. In one incident at the Legion Hall, King was charged with assault after Charles Bradbury, a member of the newly formed rival USWA local, told the *Times* he was "kneed in the groin" when he allegedly "shouted profanities" at Murphy. Bradbury had recommended "shooting the likes" of Local 480 Communists, just as he had the Japanese enemy during the war.[67] King, a Second World War veteran, was arrested, convicted, and given a suspended sentence. While the incident could have bolstered Mine-Mill's fortunes among members who respected King for his toughness, an image that resonated with the male breadwinner culture of Trail, it could also have further blackened Local 480's name by substantiating suspicions among USWA backers that Communists were insensitive and violent.

The Legion infraction was relatively minor compared to Labour's Cold War violence south of the border, and it certainly did not lead to an abatement of hostilities. In early March, the USWA applied for certification to the BC LRB. Late in the month Local 480 announced its plan to negotiate a seventeen-cent raise for smelter workers when collective bargaining began. The demand seemed reasonable, given that the CM&S (soon to be Cominco) had announced a \$41.5 million profit for 1949 in its annual report.[68] But the Steelworkers responded on 1 April with another ad warning smelter workers not to "be fooled" or "used by the Communists behind Mine-Mill." Mine-Mill retaliated five days later in an ad decrying the USWA's "despicable underhanded methods."[69]

Woman Rumoured to Be Local 480 Mastermind

During a lull in the "union war" in mid-April, Constable Murray heard rumours of a woman in Trail "'master-minding' [the] Mine Mill campaign." The woman in question was Communist militant extraordinaire Becky Buhay, long remembered in Red circles for her leadership of the CPC's women's department and for being what Steven Endicott called a "pioneer socialist feminist in Canada."[70] Buhay, a well-known CPC leader, never visited Trail during the raid, but she was not the only female that worried Murray. The Steelworker raid also attracted Ladies Auxiliary Local 131, which broadcast anti-Steel warnings over radio station CJAT.

The broadcasts and other pro-Mine-Mill actions confirmed to Constable Murray that the auxiliary local had been reorganized and that the "background of the individuals is significant." He noted that four of the auxiliary members, Mrs. L.E. Walker, Mrs. G.L. Woods, Mrs. V. Nelson, and Mrs. L. Bogie, were spouses of prominent Local 480 activists. Local 131 came under further suspicion for broadcasting a message of support for the union on 27 February entitled "How Disruption of Our Union Affects the Womenfolk."[71] In it they advised the Steelworkers "to keep away from Mine Mill especially where they have an active Auxiliary." They added a punchline in the *B.C. District Union News*: "The female is deadlier than the male every time."[72]

Constable Murray also noted that Local 480's defences against the Steel raiders were strengthened by three other developments that spring. First, Murphy hired F.E. "Buddy" DeVito, an RCAF veteran, as a temporary International Mine-Mill representative. It was another smart move on Murphy's part, since DeVito was a fiercely proud member of Trail's Italo-Canadian community. In addition, Constable Murray noted that DeVito "takes the stand

that I.U.M.M. & S.W. is right in this dispute and that it has benefitted the City of Trail."[73] Second, Father Clarence Duffy spoke at a
10 March meeting as a representative of the Canadian Peace Congress, a national advocacy group that some saw as a Communist
front organization. Father Duffy advised Local 480 members to
"'stand fast' against the inroads of 'raiding' so-called labour organizations and that 'the good would win out in the end.'" He then
"gave his blessing" to Local 480.[74] The third development involved
Liberal MP Jim Byrne, who also took Local 480's side in the Trail
raid. The Kootenay East member turned on CCF MP Angus Mac-
Innis, a founder of the CCF and a devoted Red battler. Byrne, a
proud Mine-Mill Local 651 executive officer at Sullivan Mine in
Kimberley, BC, told MacInnis in the House of Commons, "My
union steadfastly refused to become a part of or join the political
machine of the CCF Socialist party." The allusion to a CCF-CCL
cabal operating against workers' interests in Trail and Kimberley
could not have been made more clear to MacInnis, who count-
er-charged that Byrne was "parroting Harvey Murphy" and that he
"should state clearly where he stands, with Harvey Murphy or with
[CCL Secretary-Treasurer] Pat Conroy."[75] At least that is how the
Communist *Pacific Tribune* saw it.

The Steelworkers ad campaign and Mine-Mill's responses continued into May, with Steel boasting in the *Times* that they had
won the "greatest wage increase gained in Canada this year" after
a thirteen-cent-an-hour wage hike was achieved at its Hamilton
local.[76] *Times* editor Dennis Williams mostly kept clear of the raid
battles, but he did publish an editorial comparing Communism's
hammer and sickle to "Hitler's crooked cross."[77] Also in May and
much to the chagrin of the CCF and the CCL, the LRB rejected the
USWA certification bid on grounds that some card signers were
not in good standing because the USWA had waived their initia-
tion fees. Raid coordinator Gargrave announced that the raiding
union would appeal the decision, but the *Times* called it a "major
victory" for Murphy.[78] The ruling, a significant setback for Gargrave and the Steel raiders, was met with jubilation at Local 480.

Millard and other USWA leaders were stunned. They decried
the rejection under the "not in good standing" rule as a mere

technicality and accused the LRB of ruling out of fear of the industry and the CPC. They also seemed to pivot immediately back into war mode, calling the decision "short-sighted" and pledging in the *Times* that "this key defence plant [the Project 9 tower in Warfield] will be wrenched from the grip of the communist machine." Steelworker leaders also accused some employers of "dealing with the communist unions in order to save a few cents an hour."[79] Murphy rubbed salt in their wounds when he editorialized in the *B.C. District Union News* that the CCL had "somehow confused this court action and the developments in Korea." He added that the raiders and their CCL allies "have branded the government's Labor Relations Board as supporting 'communists'.... What simpletons they must think the workers are."[80] At a USWA Local 4281 meeting, the *Times* reported that the uncertified union aspirants nevertheless resolved to "carry on the fight" to "purge a communist-controlled organization."[81]

On 23 May, Local 480's leaders signed a new collective agreement, and two weeks later they filed a civil suit against Billingsley and two collaborators "for breaking their oaths and deserting their posts."[82] The action, reported in the *B.C. District Union News*, may have helped Mine-Mill lawyer Stanton delay the LRB vote. Meanwhile, with the LRB denying the Steelworker application, Ladies Auxiliary Secretary Tillie Belanger announced a "giant victory celebration" in the *Times* that would acknowledge that "in spite of all the lies, red-baiting and general disruption Steel has indulged in, our workers ... have shown their true desire for democracy and honest trade unionism, not dictatorship of Millard and his raiders."[83]

Local 480 Celebrates "Giant Victory" with a Ball

When the celebration took place that July, Murphy praised the local, noting, "It was the first time in the history of Trail ... that a ball was held to honor the smeltermen." Later he reported "thousands dancing on the huge arena floor" to the music of a band from Spokane, Washington, several hours' drive from the smelter city. In his *B.C. District Union News* column he also noted with pride that the event had raised $300 for Manitoba flood relief, with each participant paying a "nominal charge of one dollar."[84] Victory was short-lived, however, and the labour peace was soon being threatened again.

By autumn 1950, Local 480 leaders faced more Red baiting, partly due to their outspoken opposition to Canada's participation in the Korean War. Miraculously, Murphy and the others escaped purging, even though the labour movement was in full Red-cleansing mode. In September, the USWA won a reprieve from the Supreme Court, which overturned the LRB decision against it. Having won that court battle, the Steelworkers still had to win the membership vote. At the same time, the TLC spent a week "thrashing the red fringe of its 500,000 members," then ordered its affiliates to "rid themselves of communistic officers." The *Times* described it as a labour convention that will go "down in Canadian labor history as one of the roughest on communists."[85] The CCL felt more impetus to continue its own purge when past Canadian Seaman's Union Leader and former Communist T.G. "Gerry" McManus told *Maclean's* readers, "The reds are ready to wage war inside Canada." The *Times* reprinted his statement and his list of ten top Canadian Communist unionists. McManus added that many Reds are also "operating under cover in the armed forces."[86] Citing these allegations, the *Times* characteristically urged that "no guard must be dropped, no word let slip, no action left unreported which can aid these persons in their avowed intention of sabotaging the Canadian way of life."[87] Even though he was among McManus's top Reds, Murphy negotiated a 7.5-cent raise for smelter workers that November to cover the rise in the cost of living associated with the Korean War. The *Times* was opposed to the raise.[88]

Elsewhere, Mine-Mill pushed back on several raiding fronts. In Idaho, Mine-Mill Local 18 at the Bunker Hill Company in Kellogg fought a Steelworker raid that shared some circumstances with Local 480. Katherine G. Aiken points out that they faced the disadvantage of a company union, Taft-Hartley-inspired harassment of Mine-Mill's Communist leadership, an anti-Communist movement, and an inside instigator.[89] In Montana, "ingrained radicalism" may have led to anti-raid militancy. Vernon Jensen argues that the raid failed in Butte because Local 1 had a radical left-wing contingent, a strong company influence, and an intense local dislike of outsiders. Unlike in Trail, where Billingsley played a key role in ushering in the raiders, the Steelworkers failed to court local leadership in Butte. Nor did Butte businesses, especially the primary mine employer, appreciate Steel taking Mine-Mill's place and perhaps compromising company control more effectively than the smaller Mine-Mill had done.[90] A Steelworker victory in Montana "might have marked a turning point" in mining and smelting unionism, Jensen further argues, but he does not address the potential influence of the success in Trail during this period, even though its anti-raid effort was at least as notable and well publicized in the *Union*, the international's newspaper.[91]

David Saposs asks of the Butte raid, "Why did a rank and file, which is basically non-Communist, decisively support a Communist-line leadership?" The answer for him was that "the residue of class-consciousness ... made the Butte miners deaf to the charge of Red."[92] Laurie Mercier's account of the Steel raid on nearby Anaconda's Local 117 partially agrees, explaining that "Montanan workers may have been anticommunist, but they clung to the ideals espoused by their independent, western-based union." Some workers in Trail were anti-Communist, but a critical factor distinguishing the Canadian context was that many Trail workers also belonged to the left-wing CCF and were adept at using it to win support for their local issues. Back in Montana, Mercier argues that the Steelworkers' anti-Communism did not convince a majority of Local 117 members at Anaconda to abandon Mine-Mill. Instead, regional allegiances undermined the Steelworker venture. The USWA complained that Mine-Mill "had an advantage in extolling their union's historic presence in the West."[93] The same could be argued for Trail, but Red baiting was an undeniable assist for the raiding union. Critics suggest that the Anaconda local's eventual capitulation to the Steelworkers "assured the rapid demise of Mine-Mill," but nothing was foregone with the Canadian locals, including Local 480.[94]

Emboldened by the Butte and Anaconda victories, Utah workers also managed to beat back a Steelworker raid. "Under the deft control of Al Skinner," Mine-Mill thwarted the big union, wrote Jensen.[95] Connecticut's Brass Valley copper workers also retained Mine-Mill, as did miners in Arizona. In fact, soon after its expulsion from the CIO, Mine-Mill won thirty-eight of forty-seven National Labour Relations Board elections in the United States. As Robert Keitel argues, the Steelworkers' attempt to "lure the miner away from his union" through Red baiting backfired. Instead of inciting "rank-and-file resentment against their leadership, [it] possibly added to the solidarity of the union to withstand external attacks."[96]

Trail, among many other Mine-Mill locals, "resisted raids by the right wing and survived, and, unlike the UE [United Electrical workers], the IFLWU [International Fur and Leather Workers], and the UPW [United Public Workers of America] ... [Trail] also evaded disaster at the hands of the Communist Party's foremost leaders." They would later call from the underground for "a return of the left wing to the mainstream of American labor," noted Communist activist Joseph Robert Starobin.[97] Local 480's political independence also defied the party dictate as the local girded for a new round of USWA raiding.

"Cheerful Cynic" Attacks *Maclean's* Pierre Berton

With Trailites facing another frigid winter in 1951, Canadian troops were still not engaged in the Korean War, but the Princess Pats soldiers were awaiting orders to do battle with the Reds. Meanwhile, Murphy praised the Soviet ambassador to the United Nations for proposing a ceasefire in Korea and called on Canada to support it.[98] That spring Local 480 leftists were stunned by news that Ethel and Julius Rosenberg had been convicted of passing atomic secrets to the Soviets. Also disturbing to Local 480 activists, who had felt the sting of *Times* editorials for years, was news that the daily was planning a $100,000 expansion, thanks in part to the advertising revenue generated by the Steelworker raid. Later in the summer, the smelter city would celebrate its golden jubilee, and the CM&S would announce it was selling the Company Store to the Hudson's Bay Company, another sign that perhaps the long years of paternalism that existed while Blaylock was alive were waning. A national "buying power survey" rated Trail as "51 percent better than the Canadian national average," quoting annual family income at $3,789 compared to the national average of $3,492.[99]

Though there was hope that the smelter wars were finally over, the threat of a renewed Steelworker raid haunted the Mine-Mill union hall. As The Cheerful Cynic told his *B.C. District Union News* readers, the New Year was starting out more or less where 1950 left off. "Local 480 gets ready for bargaining, the steel workers get ready for disrupting, the CMS gets ready for a big laugh (seeing their employees split), the local radio station gets ready for a big boom, the Trail Times gets the red ink out of moth balls, the RahRah gang of last February 9 gets free radio time (paid by honest workers) to practice elocution over the ether waves, and the citizens of Trail and district are entertained for a few weeks by watching a minority group of wage earners trying to cut their own throats with a red herring."[100] Some of the *Times's* "red ink" warned Trailites of the evils of Communism, pointing to Korea as "conclusive proof [of] what communism means to ordinary, decent people."[101]

In early March, the battle over the right to represent Trail's smelter workers took a new turn partly favourable to Local 480 Reds but also a boost for Steelworker raiders. The BC Supreme Court agreed to hear Local 480's civil suit against Billingsley and his confederates. Two weeks later the Court granted the USWA's request for a representational vote. The legal table thus seemed even, but the Steelworkers found ways to keep the focus on Mine-Mill's Communists. Addressing the problem of rising costs of living, raid coordinator Gargrave argued against price controls. "Wages are not holding their own against the rising living costs," he wrote in the *Times*, and consequently to freeze or control wages under such conditions is to freeze injustice.[102] Despite such pro-worker views, The Cheerful Cynic dubbed Gargrave "Hustling Herbie" and pictured him "prancing down the street on a snow white charger with a bucket of red paint under each arm." In his usual strident fashion, Local 480's Chuck Kenny suggested, "Everybody was red or riding pink elephants, including the company and the government conciliation board."[103] He might have included a writer from *Maclean's* who was about to become the Steelworkers' new ally.

On 1 April 1951, six years after the *Times* had told its readers about the role of the Trail smelter in the production of the atomic bomb, Pierre Berton retold the story, this time emphasizing how a Communist-led union controlled workers at a secret plant that supplied the US Manhattan Project. Berton would later become one of Canada's most respected journalists, a television celebrity, and a popular historian. In 1951, however, his article, crackling with sinister reminders of the 1945 Gouzenko spy revelations, had delivered Cold War paranoia to the doorsteps of Trail residents.

Long aware that Murphy was a proud and unrepentant Communist, Trail's unionized smelter workforce might not have been shocked by Berton's talk of Reds running the Mine-Mill local. Few residents, though, fully realized the role heavy water, produced secretly from the US Army-financed plant in nearby Warfield, might have played in developing the atomic bomb. Berton flagged how "the reds are still on top in a fight that could involve our security."[104] He described the "hush-hush" wartime plant, arguing, "There is good reason to doubt that Project 9 has been wholly isolated from the Communists who run the Mine-Mill union." Trailites may not have realized the plant's vulnerability to sabotage and the ease of converting nearby fertilizer plants "to munitions-making." Berton warned readers that the "significance of the atomic developments at Trail has not escaped the Communist Party." As proof, he quoted the Communist *Pacific Tribune*: "The atomic products of Chalk River and Trail can be made to serve the interests of humanity, but only if the jackals of big business within the labor movement are decisively ousted." Berton also took personal shots at Murphy, who was "paunchy," "husky-voiced," and "one of the top Party members in Canada" who ran Mine-Mill's western Canadian district "as a one-man show." For Berton, there was no separation between Murphy and the party line in his *B.C. District Union News*, and he appointed representatives "who are almost always Party members or Party followers." To Berton, there was something fundamentally odd about Murphy, with whom "his henchmen dislike going to movies or hockey games ... because he's apt to take his eyes off the screen or blueline at crucial moments to talk shop."[105]

Wielding Patriotism to Stigmatize Mine-Mill

The article neatly conformed to the aims of the Steelworker raiders. Berton tied Mine-Mill to Communist firebrand Beckie Buhay, who he claimed was clandestinely present to assist the Mine-Mill local, a suspicion Constable Murray had shared but was unable to substantiate. Berton also warned of the presence in Trail of International Mine-Mill leader Maurice Travis, whom Berton described as a "huge man" with "a patch over one eye which was kicked out in a fight with Steelworkers." Berton concluded by noting the darkly mounting support for "the Communist-controlled union." Like other mainstream journalists, as well as the Steelworker raid leaders, Berton wielded patriotism to stigmatize Mine-Mill. Morris Wright, the long-time editor of Mine-Mill's *Union*, argued that such claims degraded the labour movement and "brought the raiders into ever closer collaboration with employers and their stoolpigeons, antiunion politicians, vigilantes, the antilabor press, and backward workers who identified their interests with the employer."[106] Accusations of a lack of patriotism, coupled with years of Red bashing, rankled those Local 480 members who had served in the Second World War.

It fell to the *B.C. District News* to rebut Berton's well-timed attack seemingly designed to undermine the union's 1951 bargaining program and bolster the Steelworker raid. The Cheerful Cynic claimed *Maclean's* had "issued scarlet-colored glasses to one of their writers and turned him loose on Trail."[107] Columnist Chuck Kenny satirized Berton, noting that he had indeed visited the Local 480 offices and was apparently "a bit taken aback when he saw the fresh blood dripping from the sickle and hammer…. We poured him a flagon of vodka with Joe Stalin's compliments" and he "was soon leading us all singing the 'Red Flag.'" Kenny wondered whether "the Steel Workers were paying his [Berton's] expenses." In a final slight, he quipped that the local gave the journalist "a few samples of our A bombs and H bombs and he promised to come again next year around bargaining time and give us some more publicity." Thus the union tried to laugh it off, but the Berton piece offered additional ammunition to the anti-Red contingent in Trail.

In early May, Local 480 got some long-awaited good news when the provincial LRB rejected the Steelworkers' reapplication for certification, again confirming Local 480 as the legal bargaining agent for Trail's smelter workers. Refusing both the order of Supreme Court Justice John V. Clyne and the advice of the *Times*, the board noted, "The applicant has failed to prove that a majority of employees in the bargaining unit applied for are members in good standing of the applicant union."[108] Amazingly, the board also rejected the USWA's allegation that Local 480 was "communist dominated," reporting that it could find no evidence to support that Steelworker claim. CCL President Mosher called the decision a "denial of basic democratic rights." Murphy replied that it "comes with ill grace ... from a man who ... voted to decertify the Canadian Seaman's Union" and to expel Mine-Mill without a membership vote.[109] The *B.C. District Union News* predictably reported that the decision "completely demolished" the Steelworkers' case and damned the union and its allies for "using blackmail" on Local 480. "Their own stock-in-trade, red baiting, reached the most ridiculous depths" when "their red smear" enveloped the LRB and CM&S.[110]

Although bargaining had already concluded, and BC Appeal Court Chief Justice Gordon Sloan awarded the local a mandatory union dues checkoff system, Gargrave continued his Red baiting. Advertisements in two June editions of the *Times* criticized Local 480 for its slow negotiations, low wage demand, and the so-named "Murphy-Sloan Formula" as a means to "force every worker – Mine-Mill supporter or not – to pay into their treasury."[111] By month's end, however, the automatic dues checkoff issue was losing traction and Local 480 had settled for a 17.5-cent raise.[112] Gargrave remarked in a letter to the *Times* that the company "got off very lightly with Mine-Mill," implying that the Steelworkers would have wrung a larger raise, but he refrained from further anti-Communist comments.[113]

The contentious LRB ruling faded more slowly. At the CCL's autumn conference, Secretary Pat Conroy told delegates the LRB should be condemned for refusing to certify the Steelworkers. He accused the board of acting "in collusion with a communist union [Mine-Mill] to break a CCL union."[114] During hearings in September over changes to BC's ICA, Gargrave returned to the LRB's refusal to certify the USWA local, arguing it should have allowed certification based on the union's acceptance of the members-in-good-standing rule. Murphy called Gargave a "liar," and the Steelworker raid coordinator replied in kind.[115] Not wishing to refight the ruling, though, Local 480 focused on changes to the act that would modernize trade unionism: faster certification, the right to strike after negotiations break down, and the right to discuss union business in the workplace.

A "Reign of Suspicion, Fear, and Thought Control"

The company also waded in, recommending that the act be "amended to prohibit communists from holding office in a labor organization or representing any labor groups in collective bargaining."[116] The *Times* applauded this as a "masterpiece" that "struck a necessary blow" at Communist union leaders.[117] Murphy attacked the company's main proposals, particularly the one insisting that union leaders sign affidavits, as an attempt to create a "reign of suspicion, fear, and thought control."[118] Gargrave added that the Sloan formula would "voluntarily grant approximately $14,000 a month to a suspect communist controlled union one month, and the next month propose a ban on [Communists]." He called the proposal "ludicrous," then added sarcastically that "the company should be well satisfied with Mr. Murphy."[119]

Throughout autumn of 1951 the CCL was besieged by top-executive resignations during a power struggle between the USWA's Millard and the CCL's Conroy. The internal acrimony, which eventually ended with Conroy's resignation, relieved some pressure from Mine-Mill. Instead of continuing to raid Local 480, Millard had to focus on consolidating his CCL power base. Murphy took advantage of the pause to produce a facsimile of a cheque as proof of his previous claim that Millard had purchased the right to raid

Mine-Mill, paying $50,000 to the CCL.[120] The raid, he argued, "was part of a miserable sell-out by the CCL big shots, secretly conniving with Millard – a cash sale – selling the workers in the metal mining industry."[121] Through it all the CCL leadership continued to purge Communist-led affiliates, expelling the International Fur and Leather Workers Union (IFLWU) after a "clamorous uproar from left-wingers" at its annual meeting. Far from cowing Mine-Mill, the IFLWU expulsion simply raised its ire. As Joan Sangster notes, the AFL's Amalgamated Meat Cutters and Butcher Workmen Union (AMCBW) took a similar approach to the Steelworker raiders in that it "tried to entice workers away from the IFLWU by stressing two issues: it claimed to be far superior at bargaining ... and it relentlessly pressed home a patriotic [anti-Communist] appeal."[122] Mine-Mill repeatedly rejected both claims, but that did not stop Conroy from supporting the Steelworkers' tactics.

Surprisingly, in October, USWA Local 4281 announced a new, two-month drive for Local 480 members. The raid was on again. Soon Gargrave told the *Times* of a "healthy" membership in Trail and "surprising success."[123] Murphy complained that the Steelworkers' James "Shakey" Robertson was helping to "maintain the disruption which has already cost the United Steelworkers over half a million dollars of the workers' money." Robertson was a former miners' union secretary from Cumberland, BC, the Vancouver Island town where labour martyr Ginger Goodwin is buried. He was "doing a Hladun," Murphy charged, "his stock-in-trade being that he is a turn-coat Communist."[124] (John Hladun, as discussed earlier, had previously visited Trail to discredit Murphy because he was a Communist.)

The CM&S piled on with an advertisement in early November extolling the virtues of free enterprise, and a week later the company laid off three shop stewards for leading a wildcat strike in the lead smelter. A thousand Mine-Mill members protested at the plant gates, as reported in the *Pacific Tribune*, with Ladies Auxiliary Local 131 distributing leaflets demanding, "Put the stewards back to work!" and "No more unjust firing of our union brothers."[125] After a Local 480 member attacked a Local 4281 member for passing out raid literature, the USWA's Robertson claimed that

Murphy "organizes with violence." Murphy replied that he would "sue Steel for libel if they don't retract that statement."[126] The threat may have had a positive effect, for the USWA ceased to distribute the raid materials until the issue of the fired stewards was resolved.

Both unions were back in court near the end of November. The same week, the *Times* took issue with the LRB, charging that its actions regarding the ongoing question of the Steelworkers' certification application were "cloaked in secrecy."[127] As the year ended, the arbitration board ruled against Local 480 in two of the three steward layoff cases. Year-end news round-ups said labour unity had been tested in 1951. Nowhere had that been truer than in the smelter city, where yet another raid attempt was rumoured for the New Year.

Company Takes Aggressive New Anti-Red Tone

At the start of 1952, the weather only slightly hindered attendance for *The Day the Earth Stood Still* showing at Rossland's Capitol Theatre. The Smoke Eaters were showing renewed enthusiasm for their chances to win the Allan Cup, Canada's senior amateur hockey crown. Later in the year, local baseball fans cheered or booed as the Yankees beat the Dodgers to win the World Series with a homer by young slugger Mickey Mantle. A major new pulp and paper and sawmill operation was about to begin construction in Castlegar, a satellite community where many smelter workers chose to live away from the smelly smokestacks of Tadanac. Some smelter workers might even move to the newly created northern town of Kitimat to find work in the huge aluminium plant being built there. The new mills would bring new jobs along with new unions. The cost of living index hit a new high, prompting the *Times* to assert that it had risen 90 per cent since 1939. It was bad news for consumers but would provide a slight advantage to Local 480 at the bargaining table later that spring. Trailites anxiously awaited the crowning of Queen Elizabeth as the first female British monarch since Queen Victoria. They were less anxious about the coming BC election.

Fulgencio Batista led a coup in Cuba; the Doukhobors, pressed by local politicians to find a home elsewhere, were considering relocation to Guatemala; and Albert Einstein had renewed his plea, and it was noted in the *Times*, to "protect mankind against the atom bomb."[128] Trailites welcomed a visit from Prime Minister Louis St. Laurent on Labour Day, the first ever for a Canadian prime minister. Richard Nixon made his famous "Checkers" speech, playing on public sympathies for his donated pet dog to cinch his spot as the running mate of Republican presidential candidate Dwight D. "Ike" Eisenhower. The presidential race was heating up, with Democrat Adlai Stevenson claiming he would repeal the labour-unfriendly Taft-Hartley Act. And as proof that the FBI and the US Justice Department were continuing a vigilant hunt for Reds, eighteen more Communist Party of the USA (CPUSA) leaders were arrested.

Early in the year, perhaps judging that its recommendations about the proposed ICA amendments were not sufficiently heeded, the CM&S published a full-page ad in the *Times*. In vintage Cold War style, it was headlined "Communism." It was an aggressive new tone from a company that had remained relatively silent during the bitter union rivalry between Mine-Mill and the Steelworkers. Since 1944, the final full year of Blaylock's presidency, the company had been forced by law to accept Local 480 as the smelter workers' bargaining agent. Now, sensing an opportunity to eliminate the union, it unleashed a stronger-than-usual anti-Red message. The amendments committee was unlikely to disallow Communist union leaders, so CM&S instead took its case to the people via the *Times*, insisting on its "right to refuse to accept for permanent employment Communists or other subversive characters."[129] The CPC was "highly disciplined," and its members "slavishly" obeyed party dictates, which included supporting the revolutionary policies of the Soviet Union. The company, along with the CCF and CCL, were drawing an ever-tightening circle around Local 480. The *Times* seconded the CM&S's call to refuse anyone who "would follow the dictates of the Kremlin."[130]

Local 480 still had allies, of course, most notably Local 651 at Sullivan Mine, which in January purchased an ad in the *Times* urging Trail workers to "cast forth the disruptive elements who labour at the task of publishing disruptive bulletins and who spend the dues of other Union men to create and foster ill feeling and trouble amongst the workers."[131] Later, the daily reported that Local 649 at Copper Mountain, BC, condemned "the tactics used by the anti-labor Steel organizers in Trail," daring Gargrave and Shakey Robertson "to come to Copper Mountain and try these same union-busting tactics." They would find a "hot welcome."[132]

Local 480 Rebels Found Not Guilty in Conspiracy Case

In February, BC Supreme Court Justice J.O. Wilson found against Mine-Mill in its conspiracy case against Billingsley, Laurie Hamilton, and L.R. Bailey, and ordered the local to pay all damages. Gargrave hailed the LRB rejection of the conspiracy suit, and rumours soon circulated that the raiders might redouble their efforts to convince smelter workers to switch unions. In the midst of this turmoil, the union tried to sustain its normal functions. During the hiatus between the initial raid and threatened new ones, Local 480 leaders turned to the annual round of negotiations. The problem was that the inter-union smelter war had become normality. At a pre-bargaining meeting, for example, the *Times* reported that Local 480 representatives criticized the USWA, which had re-applied for certification two days earlier, for "'continued disruption' on the eve of bargaining."[133] The USWA, meanwhile, advertised that it had again signed a majority of the smelter workers and was offering them a chance to join a union that was not "unduly dominated by members and supporters of the world Communist movement."[134] Murphy again called the raiders liars for claiming to have signed a majority of workers and accused them of splitting the bargaining unit. The *Times* suggested that labour-supporting MLA Leo Nimsick had "compromised" the CCF by siding with Mine-Mill over the Steelworkers.[135]

Finally, in mid-May, an LRB vote determined that Local 480 had won the right to represent about five thousand workers in Trail. Earlier the board had granted the local joint bargaining rights with Local 651 in Kimberley, strengthening its negotiating power. The struggle for union supremacy in the smelter city seemed at an end, but the vote was worryingly close, with fewer than three hundred votes separating the two contestants. Still, it was decisive enough that even the *Times* called on Steelworker Local 4281 members to desist and rejoin Local 480 so as to present "a united bargaining front."[136] Seeming to cede the high ground to Local 480, the daily added, "Labor's hand is strengthened by this decisive result and the good of the community is served by the elimination, which it is hoped will result [in an end] of the constant bickering in the jurisdictional dispute which has flared in Trail for two years."[137]

It had been longer than two years. Since the late 1940s, the Steelworkers had been methodically preparing to raid Local 480, clandestinely at first and then in greater openness, starting in February 1950. Now this latest smelter war was finally coming to an end. "Red-Tinged Union Triumphs at Trail," read the *Vancouver Sun*'s headline on 15 May. The vote "ended the biggest, longest and most bitter jurisdictional fight in B.C. labor history," the daily added.[138] When the victory celebrations subsided, Murphy ordained that any of the eleven raid conspirators who had steered Local 480 members to the Steelworkers in the late 1940s would have to stand trial if they wanted to rejoin Mine-Mill. But others would be welcomed back into the fold.

At the close of May, the USWA dropped its certification application at the LRB. With the long battle behind them, Local 480 was ready to run USWA leader Millard out of town when he visited Trail on 1 June. Earlier the *Times* confirmed that Gargrave was also leaving and "expected to be given a new organizing assignment elsewhere." The USWA would, however, keep its office until the three-year lease ran out. A Mine-Mill bulletin quipped that it meant "three more years of disruption."[139]

Local 480 Shuns Canadian McCarthyism

Like other union raids in North America during the 1950s, Trail's monumental struggle pitted two unions against each other in a way that strengthened the company. Deception and secret collaborations marked the contest. The LRB hearings exposed unscrupulous actions by both unions. The board's decisions nevertheless held, bringing anti-Communist criticism from as far away as the *Vancouver Province*. Al King credited Murphy for orchestrating the victory over the Steelworkers. He was "brilliant, tactically," King wrote, but most of the established labour leadership did not share this view.[140] Contempt was the more consensual sentiment. The business press stopped at nothing to discredit Murphy and Mine-Mill. Even Mine-Mill lawyer John Stanton agreed with the business press's depiction of Murphy as an opportunist.

Stanton had attended the court proceedings and LRB hearings to add legal weight to the Mine-Mill arguments being presented. Trail experienced "the full fury of a Steel raid backed by the leaders of the Co-operative Commonwealth Federation and the CCL," he wrote.[141] Noting that the CCF would gain electoral support from a Steel win, Stanton argued that the CCL "made Mine Mill a punching bag by suspending it."[142] For Stanton, the USWA lived up to its cold warrior reputation. He observed that being "unable to attack Mine-Mill's record as a good, fighting union which represented its members well, Steel resorted to innuendo and to anti-communist ploys."[143] Yet he noted, "Failure at Trail caused no change in policy for Steel. To that union it was only a small tactical loss. The main strategy of raiding went on." In May 1950 at the USWA's international convention the union had pledged to organize workers like those in Trail. Stanton concluded, "To speak of 'organizing' workers who were already well organized may sound irrational, but in the crazy logic of the Cold War, 'anything goes.'"[144]

In July 1952, a fifty-three-day strike for better wages in the American steel industry monopolized the attention of Millard and other Canadian Steelworker leaders, rendering the Trail smelter raid ancient history.[145] By year's end, the US Senate issued a report urging rank-and-file Mine-Mill members to revolt against their Red leadership. After reading it, Murphy stated in the *Vancouver Sun* that BC Mine-Mill members would have "nothing but contempt" for it, because they "are solidly behind the leadership, regardless of politics, because we do a job as union leaders."[146] And he was correct, despite the view that good bargaining was somehow a "blind," as Jensen called it, for Communist infiltration.

This is not to say the smelter war had no effect. The failed raid did indeed disrupt the grand plan to reshape the North American labour movement by purging radical Reds. Trail was a small bulwark against that agenda, but the battle seemed to turn less on ideology than on insider-outsider dynamics. In H. Keith Ralston's view, "Neither the minuscule Communist group in Trail nor Harvey Murphy himself could have rallied the Trail workers without the affront to their regionalism from the Steel raid." Murphy was, of course an outsider, but he had been Local 480's chief bargainer for many years. Gargrave, though, "was completely 'from the coast,'" argued Ralston. "Once again local people rallied against interference from 'outside.'"[147]

Yes, Billingsley's group were locals, but they undermined themselves by willingly handing Local 480 to a mega-union with little allegiance to Trail. Like the Communists in the small Montana farming community that Gerald Zahavi studied, Trail Communists fought for "alternate social, intellectual, and psychological spaces within the greater society around them."[148] In so doing, they posed no threat to the community. In fact, Local 480 was an exemplary practitioner of homegrown social unionism or what Mercier called community unionism. The leaders were part of the local political culture and able to lend support to social causes, often by sidestepping unwanted CPC policy based on what made sense locally.

Murphy, King, and others may have been consummate Red foot soldiers, but they were disinclined to march in lockstep with any political party. The Communist-led local's continued support for CCF MP Bert Herridge, who had backed them in the raids, was partial proof of their willingness to travel whatever political path proved most advantageous to the local union and its rank-and-file members, regardless of party politics. In 1953, however, in an apparent change of heart, the local supported Communist Mathilda "Tillie" Belanger as its federal nominee. A registered nurse and spouse of Gar Belanger, the local's first president, Tillie had been secretary of Mine-Mill Ladies Auxiliary Local 131.[149] As noted earlier, she supported Local 480 and advocated a larger role for the auxiliary in the politics of smelter workers. Herridge handily won the seat and Belanger came in last with 347 votes, losing her legal deposit.[150] Despite the loss, however, her candidacy signalled the Local 480 leadership's renewed eagerness to officially support the CPC over the CCF. But it also signified the unwillingness of Local

480 members to follow their Communist leaders. Moreover, it may have presaged the fear that would accelerate as the McCarthyites and the broader base of cold warriors pursued their anti-Communist mission.

The Mine-Mill propaganda campaign instilled the view that the Steelworkers, CCL, and CCF were interlopers. Although some were sincere in their belief that the Red purges were best for the movement, these outsiders were portrayed as primarily interested in the union dues and votes of smelter workers. They were willing to join with the local array of anti-Communists to ostracize workers because of their beliefs. This was not unlike the response of hundreds of other industrial workforces that found themselves invaded by the Steelworkers in the 1950s. But Trail succeeded. Similarly, many locals had the support of ladies auxiliaries, but none were stronger in their political support for the Communist leadership and against the raiders than Trail's auxiliary Local 131. That the USWA raiders disregarded that support diminished their chances of success.

On that broader international stage, as with its willingness to fight for peace, the Trail local revealed a strength that the Cold War had already subdued in other Mine-Mill locals. Trail Communists did not face the same intensity of McCarthyism that US locals did. Nevertheless, as secret police reports show, they were still confronted with the threat of public disgrace powered by the state. Despite this vulnerability, however, they did not fully succumb to those negative social forces. Instead, they developed an anti-raiding strategy that included creative cultural tactics redolent of the Communist-inspired Popular Front in the 1930s. Perhaps its physical isolation helped protect it from a full McCarthyite onslaught, but the Canadian government's silent complicity with US authorities suggests that it was as vulnerable as anywhere else. Indeed, Murphy had been an ideal target for the anti-Communists, but he would continue to be a wily adversary. In that role, as we will see now, he would devise two ingenious strategies to deflect critics and win public favour.

7

Resisting Canadian McCarthyism in British Columbia

Local 480 may have survived the alliance of Kootenay anti-Communists and the raiding Steelworkers in Trail, but national public opinion was turning against the left, and Communist union leaders were being purged and persecuted. Nevertheless, the local did have allies in its struggle against Canadian McCarthyism. H.W. "Bert" Herridge, the Kootenay West MP first elected in 1945 on a wave of Popular Front support, continued to use his *Commentator* column "Jottings from Ottawa" to decry the right-wing movement creeping across the international boundary. Herridge asked whether Canada was "going to allow U.S. congressional committees to put the finger on any Canadian" and whether the government would force Canadians to "submit to a witch-hunting cross-examination."[1] The *Commentator* noted that Stanley Knowles, the young North Winnipeg CCFer who held the seat of the late founding leader J.S. Woodsworth, had also publicly opposed "all efforts to establish McCarthyism in Canada."[2] Beyond Parliament Hill, embattled unions such as Local 480 led the resistance to this growing menace to civil society, but Mine-Mill also sought new strategies as North America moved deeper into the Cold War maelstrom.

Trailites, like all Canadians, desired a lasting peace, and by 1953 prosperity seemed within sight for smelter workers and their families. Cominco had purchased the largest zinc furnace in the world, an investment that suggested the company had bright prospects. Eaton's, the mail-order giant, purchased two new stores in the Trail area, indicating expectations of rising sales as Local 480 continued to negotiate annual wage increases and better benefits, including the possibility of a superior pension plan. In fact, the Dominion Bureau of Statistics reported that Trail had the highest per capita income in Canada.[3] The first television set soon arrived in Trail with the promise that sets would be available for everyone within the year. Some smelter families would make the extravagant purchase, but many families were still living on a budget. Super-Valu was selling two loaves of bread for twenty-five cents and pork chops at fifty-five cents a pound. Oddly, the statistics bureau reported that Trail held the record for the largest percentage of "roll your own" smokers, adding that the smelter city ranked fifth in Canada for number of women smokers. On the broader social scene, *Half-Breed* with Robert Young was playing at the Capitol in Rossland. Cecil B. DeMille's *The Greatest Show on Earth* won the Oscar for best picture. Crowds in Butler Park cheered the crowning of Queen Elizabeth II. They also marked the success of Edmund Hillary and Tenzing Norgay in scaling Mount Everest. And Smoke Eater fans were in agreement with the Canadian Press's naming hockey great Maurice "Rocket" Richard Canada's top athlete.

There were strikes that year, of course, almost as many as in the watershed year 1946, and layoffs were looming at Cominco, making people wonder what Communist-led Local 480 could do.[4] BC politics were rapidly shifting right with the conservative Social Credit Party gaining control of the provincial government. Down south, Republicans Dwight D. "Ike" Eisenhower and HUAC witch-hunter Richard Nixon replaced Harry Truman's Democratic administration. Soviet leader Joseph Stalin's death might have offered a chance to end the Cold War, but detente seemed more elusive than ever. Canada sent a thousand troops to Korea, and the United States detonated the world's first hydrogen bomb in the Pacific Ocean. Trail civil defence teams took atomic bomb emergency courses. Hucksters played on public anxieties, offering "a big fat pill costing about $4 [that] probably would save you from radiation sickness or death from an A-bomb."[5] Perhaps the desire for peace spurred churchgoers to follow American evangelist Billy Graham's globetrotting Christian crusade.

In the midst of all this, Quebec labour organizer Patrick Walsh, an alleged Communist, stepped forward to condemn Ethel and Julius Rosenberg, the couple charged with Soviet spying in the United States. Like Pat Sullivan, John Hladun, and Gerry McManus before him, Walsh also exposed Communist unionists, accusing them in the *Times* and elsewhere of spreading "communist propaganda and caus[ing] discontent and strikes."[6] Walsh was the research director of the anti-Semitic Canadian League of Rights (CLR), a contributor to Canadian fascist Adrien Arcand's Unité National, and was associated with the anti-Communist L'Action catholique.[7] He was also a police informer who praised Quebec's repressive Padlock Law of 1937 that attempted to suppress communism and bolshevism, and he testified against alleged Communists before HUAC in Washington, DC.[8] As with the earlier cases, the *Times* devoted its front page to Walsh's claims, while hailing the TLC for easing out "the last stronghold of communism" by suspending the United Fishermen and Allied Workers Union.[9]

The free enterprise system was on the rise, Communism was in retreat, and Local 480 needed a new political strategy. Partly it needed to remove the Red taint, but it also needed to retain its hard-won dignity as an affiliate of one of the continent's great trade unions. Two continental events presented possibilities for accomplishing these goals. The first involved a famed singer, the other a blacklisted movie. There was an easy way and a hard way to survive politically in the Kootenays during the 1950s Cold War. In one direction lay reunification with the Canadian Congress of Labour and a safer political home inside the Co-operative Commonwealth Federation. The other route led to continued pariah status.

Local 480 President Al King and his Communist executive members chose the more socially progressive and harder way, risking the further disapproval of local churches, media, and conservative social and ethnic organizations. Conversely, the harder way also promised to revitalize its reputation as an independent-minded union that stayed true to its constitution and, at the same time, distanced itself from the spectre of Stalinism. The local had little to lose in light of its victory over the Steelworkers as the raiding subsided. Indeed, it had become the undisputed leader of labour in the Kootenays.

Famed Singer Banned from Mine-Mill Conference

The local's new political strategy was associated with rapidly unfolding events in Vancouver at the end of January 1952. Harvey Murphy was busy managing the setting up of the fourth annual national conference of the Canadian wing of Mine-Mill as well as the ninth annual meeting of Mine-Mill's Western Regional District. The combined event presented the regional director with a new opportunity to place Mine-Mill in a more sympathetic light. But he needed a hook. He found it in Paul Robeson. Murphy invited Robeson, an acquaintance and world-famous opera singer, actor, and civil rights activist, to address the joint meeting and sing for the two thousand or more delegates.

On the day of Robeson's scheduled arrival, Mine-Mill District President Ken Smith, Secretary-Treasurer Les Walker, a long-time Local 480 member, and Murphy drove the forty-eight kilometres to Blaine, Washington, to escort Robeson across the Canada-US border. However, they returned empty handed. Robeson had had his passport seized and was told he was barred from leaving the United States. The singer returned to Seattle with his travelling companion, Vincent William Hallinan, a left-wing lawyer from San Francisco. Hallinan, who had also been invited to address the meeting, was legal counsel for Harry Bridges, the Australian-born leader of the International Longshore and Warehouse Union (ILWU), whom government officials had long harassed for his suspected Communist activities. (*Commentator* readers had been following Bridges's battle with US authorities since 1939.[10]) Hallinan called the border incident "typically Nazi" in the *Commentator*.[11] He had been banned as well.

What happened next exemplified Murphy's ingenuity as a union organizer and political operator. To salvage the situation, he arranged for Robeson to call the Vancouver convention from Seattle's Marine Cooks and Stewards Union hall (the singer was an honorary member). When the call went through, one of the world's great bass-baritones entertained the throng of trade unionists for fifteen minutes. Robeson received an enthusiastic response when his voice came through the phone lines, as well as concern when the audience learned of how his passport had been confiscated. Tension ran high in the Denman Auditorium, as the gathering transformed into a protest meeting.[12] Mine-Mill and Communist Party presses dwelled on the crowd's emotional response to Robeson. Murphy's *B.C. District Union News* called the Robeson affair "a slap at freedom" and printed a resolution passed by the meeting urging delegates "to vigorously protest against this action of the U.S. Department of State."[13] International Mine-Mill's *Union* devoted only slightly less space to the event, and the Communist *Pacific Tribune* filled a full page.

The mainstream media was decidedly less sympathetic. The *Vancouver Sun* wrote only that "leftist trade unionists" were foiled and paid cursory attention to Robeson's telephone concert.[14] The daily noted that the singer would offer a concert at Blaine's Peace Arch Park in the spring, as per a promise Murphy had made to the joint meeting. The *Sun* did not report Murphy's suggestion that the whole border incident was part of a broad policy of thought control. But with that notion in mind, the conference agreed that public resistance was, and the promised Peace Arch concerts were an excellent starting point. If American authorities would not allow Robeson to come to Vancouver, Murphy reasoned, then Mine-Mill would bring its members and thousands of Canadians to Robeson.

Had the authorities needed to defend the suspension of the singer's constitutional right to free passage, they might have said it was a matter of national security; they were protecting the nation from the threat of Communist infiltration. But they needed no such defence. After all, it was the McCarthy era and Communist sympathizers and radical labour leaders were fair game. For the singer-activist's adoring Canadian fans, Robeson's ban defied logic. He had earned worldwide recognition for his art, intellect (he was a lawyer said to speak several languages), and athleticism (he had played college football and for a short time went professional with the National Football League). How could his own government turn on him? The answer was partly to be found in his visit to the Soviet Union, during which he called the "workers' state" inspiring. Such behaviour was enough to justify the US action, which to some Canadians seemed undemocratic at best and fascistic at worst, to borrow Hallinan's terminology. Nevertheless, the action against Robeson had enjoyed the secret complicity and approval of the Canadian government.

Despite the singer's popularity, the lead-up to the first Peace Arch concert was beset with problems. First, although Robeson garnered accolades abroad, his popularity at home had plummeted, partly because he defiantly continued to publicly laud the accomplishments of the Soviets, lambaste President Truman for his Korean War decisions and his failure to support anti-lynching legislation, and celebrate Stalin's birthday.[15] Robeson had openly criticized American policy since the 1940s, and that alone ensured a battle line was drawn between him and the State Department. His caustic remarks about American corporate exploitation added to American excuses for withdrawing his passport, and arch-anti-Communist FBI Director J. Edgar Hoover authorized relentless spying operations. By the 1952 concert, Robeson had been roundly condemned as a "fellow traveller" and Kremlin stooge by everyone from world-champion boxer Sugar Ray Robinson to Robeson's fellow entertainer Josh White.[16]

Murphy had thus chosen an ally who made the US and Canadian governments equally jittery. Despite denials by Canadian authorities, Mark Kristmanson traces Canadian government concern about Robeson to at least 1940, when officials were advised to bar his entry under the War Measures Act. Police informants watched Robeson more closely after that, and the Mounties stepped up surveillance when he appeared on Canadian stages. His political statements had long made authorities want to ban him from Canadian soil.

Canadian Authorities Secretly Support Banning Robeson

By the 1952 concert, Canadian authorities had thoroughly documented Robeson's views, and they had sufficient information to support the State Department's contention that the American singer should be barred. In fact, there had been a decade of data gathered by cold warriors on both sides of the international boundary. Canadian officials were no more tolerant than American ones. Murphy and other Mine-Mill Communists might have suspected that Prime Minister Louis St. Laurent had "authorized the ban," but because the Americans acted first, St. Laurent's official action, or lack of it, remained secret.[17] Canadian authorities were nevertheless complicit in banning Robeson, with police reports suggesting that the popular singer had used his concerts as a cover for Communist activities.

As political scientist Reg Whitaker notes, Robeson's "quest for equality led him over the years towards definite sympathy for the philosophy of Communism, and to support struggles that were also supported by the Communists," but for ordinary Canadians he was more likely known and honoured for singing "Ol' Man River" in Hollywood's version of *Show Boat*.[18] Meanwhile, the Canadian government saw him simply as a Red and worked to ensure Robeson's songs and speeches did not reach Canadian ears. As early as 1947 and as late as 1956, the federal Cabinet recommended banning the singer. St. Laurent even insisted that Robeson's Canadian concert earnings be subject to income tax. This action might have seemed a further intrusion, but it was a legal requirement applied to any foreign worker.

Fans See Singer's Ban as Overreaction

The 1952 concert, then, would have been a serious, albeit legal, defiance of official views in both nations. But despite clandestine government measures, Robeson's ban must have struck his admirers as an over-reaction, for nowhere were fans more captivated by Robeson than in Canada. But these were not normal times. The ultra-paranoid Communist witch-hunts in the United States were shadowed by a less noisy yet pervasive repression in Canada. Robeson and other members of the entertainment industry, especially those working in Hollywood, were prime targets for cold warriors. Murphy, other lower-profile Communists, and Local 480 leaders were also targets. But Robeson, along with other internationally known musicians and film stars, endured a special enmity. Marian Anderson, for example, was well known as a classical opera singer. But people the world over, including Trailites, also knew her as a quiet but forceful voice for social justice after her famous 1939 Washington concert at the Lincoln Memorial. It was considered a pivotal moment in the Civil Rights movement.[19] Though Trail families did not get a chance to see Anderson perform live, they were treated to the music of various entertainers. The FBI suspected many of them of having Communist sympathies, but Robeson presented an even more appealing target for the FBI's Hoover.[20]

The singer faced angry criticism that he was a member of the Communist Party, a charge he always denied. Nevertheless, Robeson defended the rights of Communists during the anti-Communist witch-hunts. And like all African Americans, he also contended with the social barriers of racial segregation.[21] His outspoken criticism of the 1947 Taft-Hartley Act, a sure sign that he supported Red unions, must also have irked the federal authorities, along with the compliant AFL and CIO leaderships that had generally accepted the regressive legislation. The goal was to marginalize leftist voices, yet their actions, as Laurel Sefton MacDowell argues, actually cemented bonds. That radical left minority in the labour movement "remained loyal to Robeson and maintained contact with him, even as he came under FBI surveillance, his phone calls were tapped, and his rooms bugged."[22]

In addition to Taft-Hartley, authorities used the Smith Act (1940) to authorize the indictment of Communist Party leaders, and the McCarran Act in 1950, permitting the stifling of dissent and the creation of internment camps for subversives.[23] Robeson spoke out vehemently against both laws, and Mine-Mill leaders, Local 480 Communists among them, echoed such critiques of US domestic and foreign policy. Now Mine-Mill was about to benefit from its association with, and championing of, Robeson's rights. Their support of him provided a world stage for speaking out against repressive state controls, the fragility of human freedoms in a capitalist state, and the racism that permeated the US labour movement. In the past, few Black workers had crossed the Canada-US border to work at Cominco and subsequently join Local 480. Nevertheless, the union fought discrimination where it could. When Vancouver longshore worker Clarence Clemons, an African American, was beaten to death in December 1952, local members joined "thirty-three residents from Trail [who] sent a petition to the Vancouver mayor and the police commission" demanding justice after an inquiry ruled the death an accident.[24]

When Mine-Mill Alabama Regional Director Asbury Howard, another African American, was turned away at the border while attempting to attend a Local 480 meeting, Al King and local CCF politicians mounted a similar protest.[25] This was all in keeping with Mine-Mill's history of "invariably" taking "the most uncompromising stand against racism."[26] For example, when the CIO's Operation Dixie, a post-war organizing drive of African American workers in the Jim Crow South, collapsed under anti-Communism, Mine-Mill continued to back the civil rights movement, even as anti-Red CIO unions such as the Steelworkers abandoned all pretence of organizing African American workers. In fact, the Ku Klux Klan was said to control the Steelworker local in Birmingham, Alabama.[27]

A Perfect Ally in Mine-Mill's Anti-war Activities

The Korean War also complicated the situation surrounding the Robeson Peace Arch concerts. The concerts – there were four – came as the war entered its second year. Communist parties and "progressive" unions in Canada and the United States had strongly opposed Allied or US-led United Nations participation in the war. They had also called for a ceasefire, regardless of ideological differences. With Robeson's pre-existing reputation for fighting for peace and freedom around the world, he was a perfect ally in Mine-Mill's anti-war activities. Murphy, meanwhile, was poised to reap a public relations boon from the concerts. However, other events would soon intervene. As described in the previous chapter, as the concerts were to begin, the Steelworkers again claimed to have signed a majority of the smelter workers. A new battle for control of the Trail smelter workforce was unleashed, making Local 480's much-needed participation in concert planning an added burden but one with potentially positive consequences. The concert went ahead as planned on Sunday, 18 May 1952.

Writers for Communist and Mine-Mill publications attending the concert reported an impressive audience. Some, including Murphy, guessed that 40,000 people were there. The *B.C. District Union News* reporter exhausted his bank of superlatives, declaring, "The numbers participating and the degree of enthusiasm attained, exceeded even the wildest dreams of the District Union sponsors." He called it "a victory second only ... in the annals of the district" to Local 480's defeat of the Steelworker raiders.[28] The *Pacific Tribune* noted, "Neither obscure threats of 'trouble,' the studied smears of the daily press nor all the subtler intimidations could deter people who felt a sense of personal outrage" over the travel ban.[29] The *Union* said "the unprecedented turnout was a new triumph for the union fresh from its victory over CIO Steel at Trail."[30]

By all union accounts it was a heart-warming occasion, a veritable Woodstock of its time. Families picnicked and listened to Robeson sing and speak. Children asked for his autograph. Men and women sought to shake his hand. Robeson addressed the largely Canadian audience graciously and in statesmanlike fashion. By the time the crowds departed, Mine-Mill felt it had a major victory to celebrate, but not everyone agreed. The Vancouver dailies highlighted traffic jams and the presence of the border patrol. The *Times* limited its coverage to a paragraph from the Canadian Press wire service. It estimated a mere six thousand had come to hear the "Negro baritone."[31] This was a far cry from how Local 480 member Elmer Pontius remembered the event. He experienced a sense of rapture at being in the huge crowd. He had risked the long journey by car from Trail with other union members and fellow Kootenay Communists. On the drive home, they were "elated in the wee hours of the next morning."[32]

Flush with success, Murphy and Local 480 immediately planned a second concert for the following summer. At the same time, a recording of the 18 May concert went into production as a three-disk set under the title *I Came to Sing*, a title borrowed from a poem by Chilean Communist Pablo Neruda.[33] The record "sold out," according to Mine-Mill District President Ken Smith, and the proceeds helped to defray the cost of the concerts.[34] Mine-Mill milked the public relations benefits of the concert as much as possible. And who could blame it? Its leadership had been ostracized from the main labour movement, hunted by Cold War authorities, and hounded by police spies in both countries. The McCarthy Senate hearings and those of the House Un-American Activities Committee (HUAC) dampened any public sympathy for Red unions from the early days of the CIO. Public opinion, shaped by fear, had shifted substantially away from unions. All of this made the success of the concerts all the more imperative for Mine-Mill and the Communists.

The *Commentator* promoted future concerts with a photo of Robeson and reprinted reportage from the *B.C. District Union News*. "We protested then and we are still protesting," one article proclaimed, "and with Paul, we will keep on fighting for those things we all hold in common 'so long as there is a drop of blood in our bodies.'" The newspaper noted with irony the hinged gates of the Peace Arch and the inscription, "May these gates never be closed." Given Robeson's denial of passage, this was not the reality, for "those gates are closed." The paper urged Trail readers to "get to the Peace Arch on the appointed day, by car, by train, by thumb or by God." The gathered forces would "by sheer weight of numbers, counted in the thousands, force those gates open again, so that not only the continental canned generals, the Skywanis and the rotund Rotarians may pass freely back and forth, but also you and I, Paul Robeson, Vince Hallinan and a score of others may also enjoy the privilege of visiting freely with our friends and neighbours, at will."[35]

It is not clear whether many Trail smelter workers or mine workers at Cominco's operations in Riondel and Kimberley heeded the call. It was a 650-kilometre drive to the coastal border, and while Kootenay residents such as Pontius were among the throng at all the concerts, how many others followed was not recorded. However, Local 480 had taken major ownership in the Robeson concerts. The *Commentator* later explained the local leadership's rationale for supporting the musical events. As the paper saw it,

Local 480 had played a leading role "in a fight, which not only involves civil liberties but also our rights as Canadians to determine whom we wish to hear sing and speak. It is our answer to the McCarth[y]ites who seek to dictate to Canadians their particular brand of thought control."[36] Such sentiments did not impress anti-Communist labour leaders in Canada and the United States, who had quickly fallen into line with Cold War thinking. Supporting a Communist-led union's publicity concerts, no matter how pure the larger cause, was not appealing to CIO unions, given the anti-Communist views that dominated the political landscape.

Peace Arch Concerts Sweetened the Victory

Mine-Mill was also vexed by an ongoing struggle for the soul of the left, as discussed in a previous chapter. Would it be Communist or social democratic? This was the political backdrop to how labour leaders viewed the concerts. The Steelworkers union had tried to add to its ranks another 5,000 dues-paying members at Trail, and it hoped to strengthen its status in the CCF by delivering those workers' votes. Coming on the heels of the LRB decision against the USWA, the concerts sweetened the Mine-Mill victory, but they also might have given the union a false sense of security.

The Mine-Mill of the 1950s was a pale image of its former self. When the Western Federation of Miners became Mine-Mill in 1916 to distance itself from its former radical image, Mine-Mill began a long evolution towards a less imposing political force. The union continued to take progressive stances, including its anti-racist, anti-war, anti-capitalist, and pro-women's rights positions, but the CCF and CCL purges ensured its pariah status in the post-war world. Mine-Mill had enemies everywhere. The RCMP, CIA, FBI, and other agencies tasked with rooting out Communists constantly harassed its leaders. In Trail, as elsewhere, members were regularly pressured to abandon their union.

Mine-Mill saw the concerts as a multifaceted way to engage in the political moment, but the kudos it won from some quarters for fighting for Robeson's constitutional rights was also a fight for its own survival against the radical right. As MacDowell argues,

"Mine Mill's rhetoric about civil liberties, while genuine, also reflected its interest in broader civil liberties for its leaders, so that they could work politically without constraints, and create a better climate for their views." They paralleled the tactics of the CPC's early campaigns, in which the rhetoric of freedom and democracy was used to protect its leaders. Certainly self-interest drove the CPC's activists, "but it inadvertently helped protect the civil liberties of others as well. The larger audience attracted to Robeson's concerts wanted to see him, undoubtedly, but many were also concerned about guarding civil liberties in a period when policymakers determinedly escalated security measures."[37]

Benjamin Isitt characterizes the concerts as symbolic of the defiance that marked the BC Communists and the BC Mine-Mill leadership. It was an "unlikely series" that the Cold War era tried to purge from the historical record. This amnesia also abetted the historical purging of Mine-Mill itself.[38] At the time, though, the first Peace Arch concert, starting as it did in the Cold War spring of 1952, must have seemed as if the stars were aligning for Robeson and Murphy. From one viewpoint, their collaboration was a chance for the union to build public support for its many causes. With the singer as a willing partner, the Red union leaders could make a much broader statement about the things they believed in and that made them militant trade unionists. It allowed Mine-Mill, and indirectly the Communist Labor-Progressive Party (LPP), to thumb their noses at the governments that had harassed their leaders for years. For once the movement had commanded an audience far greater than was customary. People listened when Robeson came to sing, and Murphy, Local 480, Mine-Mill, trade unionism, and the left were the beneficiaries of a moment that is largely forgotten today.

From another viewpoint, however, the concerts could seem a hopeless effort in a political environment in which the union movement was at war with itself. From that perspective, the concerts were waving a large Red flag in the face of non-Communist unions, especially the Steelworkers. Under the CIO's Philip Murray in the United States and the CCL's Aaron Mosher in Canada, both conservatives, the concerts were provocations that reinforced their determination to eliminate the Communist-run unions that threatened a post-war compromise with labour being sought by both national governments.[39] With Murphy and the Red leaders at Local 480 among the most militant elements of the Canadian labour movement, the concerts signalled their defiance of McCarthy-influenced administrations in Washington and Ottawa, and the House of Labour itself.

Murphy, always wily when it came to political manoeuvring, orchestrated one of the most enduring cultural events in labour history. But as a defence strategy, if that is what they were, the concerts failed to buttress Mine-Mill. They did, however, accomplish something less measurable. Many concert-goers, including Trailites, gained awareness of multiple issues of world significance, including peace, racism, and the negative impacts of the Cold War. The smelter community's population was exposed to debates from afar, partly in the pages of the revived *Commentator* and, as always, in the *Times*. Citizens who cherished Robeson's voice heard progressive views and witnessed the arbitrary power of the state in trying to control public opinion. Murphy, though, remained keenly aware that Local 480 was as vulnerable as ever. In an interview with broadcaster Jack Webster, the Mine-Mill district director said he feared the raids might return, and less than a week later Charlie Millard issued a "declaration of war" against Mine-Mill in the *Vancouver Province*. The Steelworkers were "preparing the groundwork for a general 'liberating' raid by Steel on Mine-Mill locals across Canada."[40] With the second Peace Arch concert fresh in people's minds, a third was planned for the summer of 1954 and a fourth was held in 1955. Regardless, it seemed Mine-Mill's cultural front had no deleterious effect on the Steelworkers' raiding spirit as it roamed the continent in search of other targets.

Left-Wing Film Opens a Hornet's Nest

McCarthyism seemed slightly diminished, with a senator calling for McCarthy's budget to be "slashed," but it was not yet dead in early 1954.[41] *Times* readers got their daily fill of news about more US hydrogen bomb tests in the Pacific, an outbreak of hostilities between the Communist Viet Minh and French colonial forces in Southeast Asia, and renewed concerns about the shaky Korean truce. All increased the horrifying prospect of another world war. Snuggled beside such reports were predictions of an industrial boom in Canada, the continued government kidnapping of Doukhobor children to force them to attend residential schools, the refusal of entry to another Mine-Mill official at the border, and as always there was more Red baiting. Along with grievance handling, shop steward recruiting, and spring bargaining concerns, raid readiness continued to subsume Local 480's energies, with Millard promising renewed union warfare.[42] The smelter wars, it seemed, were not quite over. As Trailites awaited the next battle, life in the smelter city pulsated with escape options.

Jazz great Duke Ellington entertained a thousand Trailites at the Trail Memorial Centre, playing "Squeeze Me But Please Don't Tease Me" and other hits. The Serenaders and the Rhythm Kings were still a main attraction at local dances, and citizens with more highbrow tastes could also enjoy the Royal Winnipeg Ballet. War hero Audie Murphy blazed across the Wild West at the Odeon. Gregory Peck starred in Ernest Hemingway's *The Snows of Kilimanjaro*, and the Three Stooges shared the screen with the Ma and Pa Kettle and Bowery Boys movies. The Trail Little Theatre won top amateur honours provincially and nationally for its performance of *For Love or Money*. The *Times* warned that "TV-fatigue" was affecting students who spent too much time watching the little screen. Sports fans took a moment away from watching the Smoke Eaters to hail Britain's Roger Bannister for cracking the four-minute mile and cheer young Ontario distance swimmer Marilyn Bell for being the first person to swim across Lake Ontario.

Continued criticism from local anti-Communists seemed to render the security of Local 480's Communist leaders as precarious as ever. Then International Mine-Mill opened up a hornet's nest by agreeing to sponsor *Salt of the Earth*. The film's director and producer were suspected of being Communists. As a result, they had been blacklisted in 1947 ostensibly for refusing to testify before HUAC; they subsequently became known as members of the Hollywood Ten. *Salt* was soon labelled subversive. Thus the fight to produce and distribute the film became a frighteningly intense and at times violent Cold War undertaking. By early 1954, *Salt* drew a phalanx of critics determined to ban it from North American theatres.[43] Observers considered the threats against the film an affront to freedom of expression and an indirect attack on its sponsor: Mine-Mill. Along with the Robeson concerts, suppression of the controversial film placed Murphy and Local 480 under heavy scrutiny, but that very attention was also another chance to challenge the repressive Cold War atmosphere. The local responded by sponsoring a public showing in the Kootenays of the only American film ever blacklisted in the United States.[44]

To cold warriors and anti-unionists, *Salt*'s fictionalization of a 1951 strike against the Empire Zinc Company in Grant County, New Mexico, was a blow against the capitalist system and anti-union hegemony. For them, *Salt* threatened free enterprise and the American way of life. Communist members of Local 480 considered it a fair critique of what they had been fighting, but other members might have perceived it as a harmless Hollywood love story in a faraway Mexican-American community. Whatever the local views, Trailites' interest was piqued when Mexican-American trade unionist Anita Torres visited the smelter city in January 1954 on a promotional tour and recounted the events that led to the making and possible unmaking of *Salt*.

Torres and her husband, Lorenzo, had been involved in a violent, fifteen-month strike at the Empire Zinc mine in Bayard, New Mexico. Trail audiences were moved by her recollection of company and police harassment, the use of scabs, and the public campaign to discredit their union. She explained how the men and women of Mine-Mill Local 890 faced down "machine guns and police goons" and even went to jail.[45] Torres depicted a struggle against the heart of Cold War political intolerance, including the fight against the anti-Communist Taft-Hartley Act and other repressive laws. She also touched on the case of Clinton Jencks, the Mine-Mill representative who was arrested and jailed under Taft-Hartley, and the personal ordeal to make *Salt*. Local 480 audiences listened attentively to this "heroine of Mine-Mill," and Ladies Auxiliary Local 131 presented her with two blankets (an appreciative gift as the young Torres experienced her first Canadian winter). Local 480 treated her to a Smoke Eaters hockey game, a sport she mistakenly assumed was played on horseback.[46]

Torres's tale of overcoming reactionary forces added a touch of optimism to lingering post-war concerns. Like everywhere else, Trailites feared the possibility of renewed world war, the atomic bomb, economic instability, and political intimidation. For a small contingent of Communist trade unionists, those fears seemed increasingly real. As Gary Marcuse and Reg Whitaker note, by the time of the Korean War, "the focus of the anti-Communist campaign had shifted from the ideological threat posed by Communists to the threat of industrial sabotage by individual Communists."[47] Trail's Mine-Mill membership was an obvious target. RCMP surveillance teams were ferreting out subversive elements in a "meticulously organized, extensive, and explicitly ideological" manner, writes Larry Hannant.[48] This was a time when, as historian David MacKenzie argues, "many Canadians were suspected of so much disloyalty and subversion based on so little evidence of any wrong doing."[49] It was even worse in the United States during what David Caute calls "the great fear."[50]

Salt Arrived in an "Era of State-Induced Paranoia"

Produced at the height of an era of state-induced paranoia, *Salt* departed from the rules of censorship that Hollywood studios had been operating under since the Production Code Administration – or the Hays Code named after Will H. Hays – was introduced in the 1930s "to protect the masses from the evil influence of the movies."[51] Hays was president of the Motion Picture Producers and Distributors of America from 1922 to 1945. During the Progressive era, when filmmaking was coming of age, "the cinema championed the cause of labor, lobbied against political 'bosses,' and often gave dignity to the struggles of the urban poor," Kay Solan explains.[52] But the Hays Code aimed to regulate such political inclusions along with its moralistic mission to curb sexual and violent content. *Salt* producers defied the Hays rules, borrowing on earlier filmmakers' attempts to depict class struggle and worker solidarity.

Famous directors such as John Ford, Billy Wilder, and Frank Capra strived for a more sympathetic image of working people, sometimes portraying industrial unions in a positive light. However, other filmmakers characterized workers as victims, union organizers as thugs, and, of course, union leaders as sneaky Communists. Such images easily passed favourably through Hays censor Joseph I. Breen.[53]

Salt producers sought to escape such negative Hollywood characterizations by portraying a real-life event that included "the related themes of sexual and ethnic repression."[54] By interrogating the Cold War era's political sensibilities, *Salt* invited what Ellen Schrecker calls the "injustice of McCarthyism."[55] Mining industry employers similar to the CM&S objected to its overt glorification of working-class unity as well as its emphasis on racial and gender equality. *Salt* exposed the underbelly of capitalism's inherent inequality, and conservatives responded by blacklisting the film as a social and cultural threat.

In his study of the suppression of *Salt*, James J. Lorence shows how influential conservatives in the film industry, including Hollywood unions such as the International Association of Theater and Stage Employees (IATSE), worked to undermine the film's production and distribution. Lorence contends that *Salt* "provides a mirror of Cold War America that reflects not only the intense fear that gripped Americans in this period, but also the dark side of corporatist settlement that locked business unionism and corporate power in a firm embrace in the 1950s."[56] Ellen Baker argues that the suppression of *Salt* meant the loss of a "vibrant alternative popular culture" and "a generation of committed organizers and a critical perspective on American political economy."[57] Paul Buhle and Dave Wagner concur, placing *Salt* among a rich legacy of ostracized films.[58]

The year 1954 was another tough one for leftists in North America. Even institutions unrelated to trade unionism, such as the Canadian Broadcasting Corporation (CBC) and the National Film Board of Canada (NFB), endured harsh political scrutiny. Given this level of state and corporate surveillance, Local 480's plan to show the film in Trail was risky business. Some local leaders and long-time Communists such as president Al King and Harvey Murphy had already faced official anti-Communism, yet Torres's account about the Local 890 strike, Jencks's jailing, and the making of *Salt* emboldened Local 480. Resisting censorship was a chance to live up to Mine-Mill's reputation for fighting discrimination, which included its locally unpopular support for the Doukhobor community when local unionized railway workers threatened the Sons of Freedom sub-sect with "vigilante action."[59] Torres's description of the vigilante scene in New Mexico echoed Local 480's willingness to oppose discrimination on principle.

On 14 March 1954, just two months after Torres's visit, following several glowing reviews of *Salt* in the labour press, and after attempts to suppress the release of this "celluloid document of socially conscious unionism," *Salt* premiered at New York's Grande Theater.[60] The *Union's* Morris Wright noted the "overflow audiences" and raved that "many have called it 'the best picture I ever saw.'" The *New York Post* called it "solid picture making" and "not subversive in actual content," making the *Post* writer wonder why "so many people have worked so hard to keep it from being made or shown at all." The *World-Telegram* actually thought *Salt* downplayed the violence, saying it showed "much less of repression, discrimination and violence than actually happened."[61]

In spite of a boycott orchestrated by IATSE on orders from its New York office, the Canadian premiere took place at the Variety Theatre in Toronto on 9 August 1954. *Salt* director Herbert Biberman remembered that they were "relegated to a miserable theatre ... with equipment so poor that it was almost impossible to understand the dialogue."[62] The Toronto public broke the IATSE boycott, reported the *Union*, but the paper admitted the showing had been "greatly hindered by opposition from the projectionists' union." CBC film critic Nathan Cohen called *Salt* "an exciting experience, a deeply human drama in the documentary manner perfected by the Italians in such masterpieces as *Open City*, *The Bicycle Thief*, and *Shoe Shine*."[63] However, much of the mainstream US media dismissed the film as Soviet propaganda and avoided reviewing it. The *Times*, despite its years of anti-Communist editorializing, failed to review the film. However, it had done its best to undermine it by publishing articles with headlines like "Mine, Mill Movie Said New Weapon for Russ[ia]," and "Mine, Mill Filming Hit from All Sides."

Local 480 Promotes *Salt of the Earth*

Local 480's promotion of *Salt* stalled during the bargaining period that spring, but it accelerated after ratification of the collective agreement in June. Promoting the film was difficult. Virulent media and political attacks on *Salt* mounted throughout the summer. The *Commentator* countered by urging members to ask their politicians to help get the film into Canadian theatres. "The fight is still on to bring [the film] before the Canadian people for the first time," the union paper noted, but "Big Business opened up its guns on this story, even as it started to be filmed, in a brazen attempt to smash and sabotage its production."[64] Interestingly, while cold warriors were focused on suppressing *Salt*, another blacklisted Hollywood filmmaker, Carl Forman, saw his masterwork *High Noon* succeed at the box office. Like the Hollywood Ten, Foreman had faced HUAC's questioning and eventually left the United States to make films in Britain. *High Noon* has been called a left-wing western because Foreman moulded his script to expose right-wing hysteria.[65] But it escaped the kind of wrath that *Salt* experienced.

Toronto unions continued to rave about *Salt* at the largest Labour Day parade in the city's history. More than seventy unions joined Frigidaire Local 303 of the United Automobile Workers, which used its float to salute *Salt* as "the most exciting motion picture union workers ever made." Fronted by a Canadian Legion band, the float stressed "the entertainment value of the picture with its humor, human emotions, love and tenderness." Praise from union papers was listed on the float. "Ranks with Grapes of Wrath," effused the *Bindery News*. "A great film," noted *Ford Facts*. "A motion picture of, by and for workers," opined *Hotel and Club Voice*.[66] Beyond the parade, though, the assault continued.

Murphy railed at critics, accusing the big theatre chains of "sabotaging it and denying to the movie goers the opportunity" to see it.[67] His *B.C. District Union News* also published testimonials about the film, including one from Ernest Winch. The outspoken CCF MLA from Burnaby, BC, declared that *Salt* was "an excellent film, and faithful in the slightest respect to life." He laughed at charges that the film was propaganda, arguing that "anything is propaganda to the bosses when they are revealed in all their nakedness, and this film doesn't exaggerate their tactics in the least. They are and have always been much more ruthless than they are shown in the film."[68]

The problem for supporters and critics alike, however, was that each group largely preached to its own choir. This bifurcation of audiences resulted in a failure to break down the barriers erected by both camps. Indeed, from the moment *Salt* was conceived, it was in trouble that only deepened over time, and the problems only increased when screenwriter Michael Wilson, brother-in-law of *Salt* producer Paul Jarrico, joined the film crew. Wilson had won an Oscar for *A Place in the Sun*, the 1951 film adaptation of American novelist Theodore Dreiser's *An American Tragedy*. He went on to write two more Oscar winners, *The Bridge on the River Kwai* and *Lawrence of Arabia*. He had also been blacklisted after HUAC declared him an unfriendly witness.

Like many Hollywood film workers, Wilson and Jarrico had been in the Popular Front, a broad coalition of activists that Michael Denning notes "increased influence on the participation of working-class Americans in the world of culture and the arts."[69] As the Great Depression deepened, director Biberman, Jarrico, and Wilson joined the Communist party and became more active in Hollywood unions as they gained strength and challenged work rules at the big studios. After they were blacklisted in 1947, the ostracized filmmakers turned their talents to making a film that would exhibit all the progressive traits that they felt were missing from traditional Hollywood screen offerings. They eventually found what they were searching for in the New Mexico strike and wrote the script in cooperation with its main subjects. Such writing by committee was contrary to the top-down studio system. So was the egalitarian ethos that marked the film's production style.

Billed as "an honest movie about American working people," *Salt* recounted a real-life story that highlighted the powerful role of women in winning the strike.[70] From Carl Weinberg's perspective they succeeded by carefully constructing three scenes that highlighted the film's main themes. In the first, Ladies Auxiliary Local 209 proposes that the women staff the picket line. Next, they are shown on the picket line and being arrested. As Weinberg notes "Not only did women ... maintain their lines; they also jumped on cars, threw rocks at strikebreakers, and deployed various 'domestic' items as weapons."[71] Both scenes illustrate a militant feminist group enacting their convictions as politically aware women. At a time when many Mine-Mill men were uncomfortable with the leading role played by females, the filmmakers highlighted this agency, thus challenging filmgoers with a depiction of women as more than supporters of a male-dominated union. Given their own demand for independence, members of Ladies Auxiliary Local 131 in Trail supported the independent stance taken by the New Mexico auxiliary. The fact that they hosted Torres and would attend a showing of the banned *Salt* was tangible evidence of that support. The last scene shows men hanging laundry. Weinberg calls it "the most striking in the whole film" and far in advance of Second Wave feminism's emphasis on "job discrimination, the politics of housework, and the sexual double standard."[72] Thus *Salt* was not simply a class-based critique of post-war capitalism but also a direct challenge to the male breadwinner tradition seen in wartime Trail.

Portrayal of Female Strike Supporters Inspires Trail Women

For Weinberg and others, class, gender, and ethnic relations form the heart of *Salt*. Through that prism, Ellen Baker suggests, we see "the interplay of historical contingency, individual action and larger historical dynamics." *Salt*'s micro-history offers a "nuanced understanding of the texture of local society and of the relationship of local society to larger historical forces."[73] That description applied to the smelter workers and the smelter women of Trail in the 1950s, a factor that clearly resonated with them during the film. Other analysts focus on *Salt*'s efforts to counter the right-wing propaganda that flowed so freely in the North American media.

It was an example of how filmmakers could exercise the principles of cooperation, collaboration, and communalism to create a film that would stand as an artefact of what could be done when filmmakers were allowed to express their political vision rather than be restricted by the studio rules created by Hays with the compliance of movie moguls.

Torres had recounted to Local 480 members how *Salt*'s filmmakers and their novice cast encountered hoodlum violence and vigilante actions. Trailites also learned of the US government's refusal to allow *Salt* star Rosaura Revueltes to re-enter the United States to complete filming after visiting her home in Mexico. It seemed the authorities would stop at nothing to oppose the showing of *Salt*, leading International Mine-Mill's Denver office to comment on the intensity of the Red Scare tactics against the film.[74] It also puzzled Rossland's George B. Casey, who saw it while a guest delegate at the International Mine-Mill convention in Louisville, Kentucky. In his view it was "a class conscious movie that will be a dividend payer wherever practiced."[75] Casey was a founding member of Local 38, the WFM local that had once represented Rossland miners. Trail's Mine-Mill leaders also contended with anti-Red forces as best they could, but as Local 480's Al King observed, "Because of anti-red hysteria, a lot of people didn't want a pro-union movie ... to be made."[76]

With such angry opposition, both internationally and locally, it seemed increasingly unlikely that Local 480 could show the film. Finally, the November edition of the *B.C. District Union News* announced that the "celluloid curtain" had risen.[77] *Salt of the Earth* would be shown in the Kootenays. The local first thought it had secured a Trail theatre in September, either the Strand or the Odeon, but the "top brass put their foot down." The Vancouver-based cinema owners had joined the Cold War–inspired blacklist crusade. The *Commentator* complained, "We as free Canadians (?) are not to be exposed to a film that portrays the life and love story of a Mexican-American miner and his wife by the veto of these high movie magnates."[78] The local almost abandoned the search for a venue in Trail, but then a break came. The Castle Theatre in nearby Castlegar, where many smelter workers lived, agreed to show *Salt*. The union paper advertised five screenings on 15 and

16 December, and it reprinted a positive review that had appeared in the *New York Times*.[79] Bosley Crowther noted that *Salt* depicts a "conflict that broadly embraces the love of struggling parents for their young."[80] This hardly sounded like the evil Red menace that many newspapers had described.

Despite the many attempts to suppress *Salt*, local movie-goers seemed anxious to see it. Smelter poet E.M. Nobes, a Local 480 office secretary, joined about nine hundred residents at the Castle Theatre, many travelling the forty kilometres of gravel road from the larger centres of Trail and Rossland.[81] Like others in the audience, Nobes was deeply touched:

> It made me feel with each new reel
> Unprecedented pride
> To know Mine, Mill has brought this thrill,
> To warm your heart inside.[82]

Pride and warm feelings came at a cost to the international union, however. The film and its union sponsor suffered repeated salvos from cold warriors such as future American president Ronald Reagan, then head of the Screen Actors Guild. Joining him was the anti-Communist IATSE leader Roy Brewer and numerous friendly HUAC witnesses. The New York–based labour columnist Victor Riesel worked closely with Brewer, FBI Director Hoover, and others to ensure that *Salt* stayed blacklisted.[83] Reisel saw *Salt* as a "potential danger to the Korean War effort."[84] Meantime, former colleagues of the Hollywood Ten were revealing to HUAC the names of anyone they thought might be a Communist. Even former Hollywood Ten member Edward Dmytryk, born in Grand Forks, BC, turned on his colleagues.[85]

Police Accuse Murphy of Fostering "Subversive Element"

For Murphy and the film's Local 480 boosters, *Salt* was a cultural way to resist, but it was at best a minor triumph. The film was never widely distributed, and the Red baiting did not abate. As hockey and ski season approached, the *Commentator* noted, "Our membership all throughout Canada are subjected to big scare headlines and all the intimidation and hysteria against our Union that the big boss and the paid press can muster."[86] Police continued to track the movements of local Reds. Constable J.J.E.R. Boissonneault of Nelson Special Branch, for example, provided detailed assessments of the situation, noting that while the local was under the "control and guidance" of "a strong subversive element," a "movement has been afoot in local 480 to oust Al King." The constable also observed that Murphy "had spent considerable time in Trail prior to the elections in an effort to boost King's stock," but "the rank and file were not impressed." King won the election with 570 votes that December, only 170 votes more than challenger Pete Jensen, suggesting to the constable that King was in for a "precarious year."[87]

Other police reports seemed to confirm that the Steelworkers were about to renew their raids on the "red-tinged" union, but it was unlikely that Charlie Millard and his big CCL union would mount a new attempt at Trail despite a prediction in the *Vancouver Province*.[88] The spirit of resistance that had been on display at the Castlegar showing of *Salt* still prevailed in Trail. When the smoke settled, as much as it ever did in the smelter city, what remained was an intact local union despite an increasingly hysterical anti-Communist world.

At the start of 1955, Robeson was still fighting to regain his passport and *Salt* producers were battling in the courts with the movie establishment. Speculation about atomic weaponry continued apace, with several high-ranking military personnel arguing that a nuclear war could be won. Among them was Admiral Arthur W. Radford, chair of the US Joint Chiefs of Staff.[89] Meanwhile, US scientists would soon be pleading with the UN to conduct a study of how many nuclear bomb tests "the human race can stand without grave danger."[90] McCarthy still made the headlines but far less frequently after Congress censured him, and the earlier intensity of the Cold War evolved from the highly public spy probes and alleged traitors' trials to the more secretive espionage later depicted in John le Carré novels. The *Times*, celebrating its sixtieth anniversary (it had been a weekly until 23 April 1928, when it became a daily), was still fighting its private war against Communism by reprinting the views of other anti-Reds, one of which slammed "the new communism," noting that it "retains all the evil that makes it a menace to mankind."[91] In other ways, too, Trailites carried on much as they had done since the post-war period began.

Smoke Eaters fans were momentarily jarred from their seats to follow the fate of Maurice "Rocket" Richard after spectators rioted at the Montreal Forum to protest his suspension from the National Hockey League. The twenty-second annual Kootenay Music Festival would see record numbers exhibit their talents that spring. Trailites of Italian descent celebrated the fiftieth anniversary of the Cristoforo Colombo Lodge. Some residents would make the all-day drive to Spokane, Washington, to see popular variety show host Ed Sullivan and his "Toast of the Town Revue." Local youth got involved in "Teen Town," and some would compete for one of four new scholarships established by Local 480. Abbott and Costello were at the Odeon. *The Caine Mutiny* and *Shane* were showing at the Auto-Vue Drive-In. Local merchants were enjoying extra public attention due to "Trail Days," a weekly invitation to shop downtown. TV watchers could now peruse a *Times* insert listing their favourite shows. Among them were the *Mickey Mouse Club*, *Howdy Doody*, *Rin Tin Tin*, and the ill-fated *$64,000 Question*.

As 1955 progressed, there was more talk of founding a Canadian Mine-Mill union after Local 480 proposed to partition Canada's Mine-Mill locals from the international at the twelfth annual BC District Union convention. Well into the year, Murphy continued to rail against local theatres for refusing to screen *Salt*. He even charged Cominco with censoring it in Tulsequah, a northern BC mining community.[92] But he was now preoccupied with founding the autonomous union. Concerned like many Canadian Mine-Mill locals that the anti-union spirit of laws such as the Taft-Hartley Act and the Communist Control Act of 1954 were undermining the labour movement north of the border, Murphy suggested that quasi-independent status "may mark a new epoch in unionism on this continent." It would underscore Mine-Mill's dedication to democratic unionism, rejecting "stricter and more bureaucratic control and domination" and ending the "expulsions, suspensions, and threats" that had plagued the locals for so long.[93]

Finally in July, with the blessing of the fiftieth international convention in Spokane that spring, seventy delegates from across Canada formed an all-Canadian Mine-Mill union, placing it among the ten largest labour organizations in the country at that time.[94] The meeting was held in the old Rossland Miners' Union Hall, where so much of local labour history had occurred since WFM Local 38 members built it in 1898. As Murphy noted in the *B.C. District Union News*, it was "a fitting place" for the realization of "the dream of the original founders of our great International Union in Canada." Stressing unity, Murphy concluded that Mine-Mill members, "those of the present, and the hardy old-timers of the past, were as one in voice and deed and the labor movement of this continent, whose eyes were on Rossland for those days, witnessed events of great importance."[95] Among the resolutions adopted was one encouraging locals to purchase ten copies of *False Witness*, the telling confession of Harvey Matusow, the FBI informant who had put Clinton Jencks of *Salt* fame and many others behind bars.[96] Schrecker chronicles Matusow's career as an informant, noting that even his confession did not sway a judge in El Paso, Texas, to exonerate Jencks. He believed that Matusow's about-face was part of a Communist plot. Another resolution reported in the *Commentator* urged them to "endeavour to further the distribution of the Mine, Mill film 'Salt of the Earth.'"[97]

The promotion of cultural events such as the Peace Arch concerts and the showing of *Salt of the Earth* did not lift the Red taint from Local 480. Nor did Local 480's participation in organizing the events lead dissenting smelter workers to be more accepting of the Communists at the helm. By 1955 McCarthy was finished and Murphy was deeply involved in Canadian Mine-Mill, but Mine-Mill's international leaders still faced years of court battles. For Al King and the others at Local 480, the goal of supporting the larger social causes endorsed by their union had been achieved only momentarily, for the two events passed quickly into a murky Cold War history almost as ostracized as Mine-Mill itself. Conversely, those who had once supported the company union assaults and

Steelworker raids finally seemed to accept Al King as their president. Communist haters continued to reside in Trail, and the local Cold War carried on for a time. But for Trail's smelter workers, Mine-Mill continued to bargain good contracts and act as a watchdog on company behaviour, especially health and safety concerns. If it ever did matter to the majority, their Red leadership, albeit watered down by the Cold War, would carry on for years to come.

Conclusion: The Complicated History of Local 480

The smelter wars seemed well and truly over as 1955 slowly edged the world away from McCarthyism. The US State Department eventually returned singer-activist Paul Robeson's passport, but right-wing political lobbying would sustain the blacklisting of *Salt of the Earth*. Mine-Mill leaders would spend the rest of the decade and into the 1960s fighting in the courts against accusations that they were Communists. Local 480 would continue organizing mine workers in the west, with the able Al King, who held the local presidency throughout the decade, now assigned to the task. No stranger to workplace action, King saw several of those locals strike in the mid-1960s. The Trail local would also maintain the battle lines whenever the Steelworkers raided, a practice that continued unabated until the two unions merged in 1967.

In mid-1955, Mine-Mill locals in Canada had decided that affiliation with the international union no longer served it. At a conference at the Rossland Miners' Union Hall, Canada's Mine-Mill locals voted for full autonomy. It marked a milestone for host Local 480, which was then the largest Mine-Mill affiliate in Western Canada. Indeed, the conference vote for autonomy signalled the start of a new era for Canadian Mine-Mill locals, but gaining autonomy was politically fraught. Under the new arrangement, Canadian Mine-Mill locals agreed to maintain fraternal ties with their American parent union, but the break might have gone another way. When right-wing US Senator Barry Goldwater, eventually a presidential hopeful, joined with a big zinc corporation to press for an embargo on zinc, US Mine-Mill agreed with it, recalled Al King.[1] Mine-Mill in Canada told Prime Minister Louis St. Laurent that they were against the embargo idea, which was eventually dropped. But the leadership dispute helped pave the way to leaving the international body.

For the Trail local in particular, the conference spelled the end of a bitter contest for survival that had lasted since the late 1930s, when a Communist union organizer named Arthur "Slim" Evans brought the CIO to the smelter city. Communist-led affiliates like Local 480 hoped that by creating a new organization they could at least dull if not eradicate the US-influenced Red baiting that had long afflicted their union. Local 480 might also have hoped that it would signal the denouement of the local anti-Communist campaigns that had plagued it from its earliest days.

The July conference also marked the end of Murphy's role as Mine-Mill western regional director, and his job as chief negotiator for Local 480 would be complicated by his role as vice-president of the new national union. His departure also brought an abrupt halt to the publication of the *B.C. District Union News*, leaving the revived *Commentator* to serve as the lone voice of the local. There was speculation that the CPC would appoint a new editor to replace Murphy, suggesting the party had been in control of the biweekly *News* for the past decade, but the paper permanently ceased publication. Murphy would continue to visit Trail, although his presence in the smelter city would steadily diminish. As editor of the new national *Mine-Mill Herald* he ensured that the activities of Local 480's Communists were well reported, including their continuing resistance to McCarthyism and other attempts to impose political repression.

A year after the founding of the Canadian Mine-Mill organization, the Communist community was shaken to its roots by Soviet Premier Nikita Khrushchev's exposé of Stalin-era atrocities. Revelations about the Great Terror of the late 1930s and other destructive Soviet policies drove many members to abandon the party. There is no way to calculate how many Local 480 Reds joined the exodus, but we do know that Al King was among them. Later in the decade, Murphy, the man who called himself the "reddest rose in the garden of labour," resigned from the party after an Ontario Labour Relations Board member suggested that doing so would help Mine-Mill to fully participate in the new Canadian Labour Congress (CLC).[2] "But it didn't matter a hang," quipped Murphy.[3]

Communist memberships fell again in 1956 when Soviet tanks rattled into Budapest to crush a Hungarian revolt. That fall at the CCF conference, delegates adopted a new guiding document called the Winnipeg Declaration to replace the Regina Manifesto. Influenced partly by the party's rise to power in Saskatchewan, some believed a moderation of its socialist policies was the path to federal power through social democracy. Others, however, viewed the new document as softening the quest for a socialist economic strategy for Canada, replacing it with a proposal for a mixed economy within the capitalist system. For the left wing of the party, among them some Local 480 activists, it might have seemed the demise of a real commitment to working-class revolution.

Old and new labour historians have long understood that the events of the 1950s, including those recounted here, represented a turning point in leftist history. The merger of the CCL and the TLC to form the CLC in 1956 marked a shift to the right. Murphy's efforts to restore labour unity in BC through cultural events and peace activism did not halt the deterioration of revolutionary fervour, and anti-Communists assisted that decline by framing calls for peace and unity as Red ploys. Vernon Jensen himself called unity "mostly a blind behind which the left-wing forces were building for the future."[4] Allen Seager notes, however, that Murphy "refused to recant his political beliefs, or 'bend the knee' to the 'socialist' witch hunters."[5] In the end, it was Murphy's bargaining skills and his life-long promotion of trade unions, not party membership recruitment or revolutionary rhetoric, that made him a resilient union figure and helped the Trail union survive.

Similarly, for some members of Local 480, seen as a left bulwark in the Kootenays, the CCF's policy shift and the CPC's precipitous fall from grace seemed to spell the abandonment of ideals that the Communist union leadership had long espoused. But these endings did not signal a final defeat for the small group of Reds who had fought and largely won the smelter wars. They could claim victory in many instances, including struggles against a CCF leadership and local conservatives set on annihilating Mine-Mill. They held their own against the powerful CM&S, an employer that had endeared itself to the community once erroneously described as a workingman's paradise. They defeated the company union, turned back the Cold War–inspired Steel raiders and their smelter collaborators, and resisted the destructive tendencies of the CIO, the CCL, and the Catholic Church. Indeed, as the new, autonomous Mine-Mill began, Local 480 Reds had much to celebrate, even though the fight for survival was hardly at an end.

Why Did Trail Support Local 480?

Given the continental and global forces working against the survival of a Red union, *Smelter Wars* has asked why Trailites accepted and then defended a union vilified by the right and the CCF left alike. The most straightforward answer is that Local 480 sustained the respect and support of Trail's smelter workers because, regardless of the infighting, it defended workers' interests. What complicates this assessment is the anti-Communism that otherwise gripped Trail from the earliest days of what has been called the "Age of the CIO."[6] Smelter workers did want better wages and working conditions, which Murphy obtained for them, but did they also want the kind of radical social change that Murphy and Mine-Mill Reds advocated? There were divided loyalties in Trail, but the majority of Trail's smelter families accepted the local, in spite of its Communist history, because it was an effective defender of their class interests.

Sympathy for a local underdog against a corporate giant – the workers' David versus the company Goliath – might also have mattered. That Local 480's leaders were from Trail, and thus insiders, also had an influence. Such acceptance would have grown from an appreciation of Local 480's interminable struggle to survive. Unlike many North American smelting towns, for instance, Trail saw little violence during the 1940s and 1950s. Confrontations did occur at the plant gates, and fist-fights did break out in local beer parlours – the Arlington and Trail Hotel were favourites – but the union did not embrace sabotage or other violent measures to fight an employer that engaged in anti-Communist rhetoric. Instead, Local 480 deployed reasoned, if at times bombastic, arguments in newspapers, radio broadcasts, and speeches. They mixed fact, opinion, and amateur poetry to deliver blows of rhetoric and sarcasm.

The union used these weapons to criticize a paternalistic style of management that had cowed workers into submission for more than two decades. It deftly exposed the fallacious claim that a company union could truly represent workers while being funded by the company. With the founding of the *Commentator*, Local 480 also showed it could challenge the anti-Red, anti-union *Trail Daily Times*, often exposing the latter as a tool of the smelter owners and a shill of free-enterprise capitalism. The *Times* continually escalated its attacks against the union and its Communist leaders through syndicated articles, editorials, and letters to the editor. It tried especially to leverage gender differences in the community, encouraging smelter spouses to write anti-union diatribes, but the *Commentator* stood its ground, working to foreground class differences over other categories of identity.

What further complicates matters is how history itself played a role in Local 480's acceptance among smelter workers. In Trail's early years, we can observe what British social historian E.P. Thompson described as the making of a working class over a long gestation period marked by strikes, protests, and other forms of resistance.[7] The evolution of that consciousness was manifested in the 1901 Rossland miners' strike and the 1917 smelter strike that Ginger Goodwin led. Both events were ingrained in the memories of old-timers who regularly recounted them to later generations of smelter workers. Others recalled the early political influences in the Kootenays as left-wing parties struggled to co-exist. This lived and embodied past supports the contention that Trail's working class matured over a long period and that Local 480 found support among some Trailites to develop as a left-wing union. This gradual process also shaped labour-management behaviour and future social relations between the union and the CM&S. The lengthy battle against company unionism also influenced attitudes about the Red union. Anti-Communist supporters of Blaylock's Workmen's Co-operative Committee regularly confronted Local 480, yet the majority of workers rejected its arguments and those of its legal clone, the Independent Smelter Workers' Union.

The impact of the union on Trail's women also complicates explanations of why Local 480 survived. Although many eventually supported Local 480, some women embraced it reluctantly. Many homemakers, for example, disavowed interest in the Red-tinged local because they feared it could become a drain on family income, especially during strikes. Some women provided moral and material support, but others saw little benefit. Female war workers also threatened to undermine support for the Communist leadership when they demanded stronger adherence to the Mine-Mill constitution on gender equality and a reconsideration of its support for the male breadwinner model. Ladies Auxiliary Local 131 also challenged male attitudes towards women, even as it supported Local 480's Reds. A post-war opportunity might have been lost when the union agreed to mass layoffs of women at war's end. The debate certainly helped map the political terrain for a later feminist movement, and it set an example for other North American auxiliaries for how to remain independent from male unions and exert pressure for progressive initiatives.

In short, Local 480's survival elicits a series of contingent and qualified historical responses. Immigrant workers slowly gravitated toward the union, but ethnic loyalties and religious beliefs pushed and pulled them in idiosyncratic ways. Local churches did encourage congregations, many filled with immigrant families, to reject Local 480 as a pack of godless Communists. Many took that advice. The local leadership had few defences against church pronouncements, and their efforts to win the church-going smelter workforce by providing comments from pro-union priests and other progressive members of the clergy were ultimately futile. Spouses of smelter workers were prime targets for anti-union and anti-Communist messages from the churches, and letters to the *Times* by mothers, wives, sisters, and daughters attested to the success of those messages. It was no different inside the union.

A Labour-Socialist Tradition Lingered in Trail

In the struggle for ideological acceptance, Local 480 members debated political preferences, and most did not blindly adhere to any one party. Some were card-carrying Communists, but supporting the CCF was an option that many members exercised at election time. There was a lingering labour-socialist tradition, and the local had its share of autodidact street Marxists, men like Murphy, Bill Pritchard, Ernest Winch, Harold Pritchett, Jack Kavanagh, and others. The local's defence of Bert Herridge and his People's CCF also showed a willingness to reject party policy when it did not suit local needs. As further evidence, Cedric Cox, another charter member of Local 480 who worked as a pattern maker at the smelter, won Ernest Winch's Burnaby CCF seat after Winch's death in 1956. The Rossland-born Cox served in the Royal Canadian Navy during the war, and upon his return he married Winch's daughter Eileen.[8] After moving to BC's Lower Mainland, he supported such left-wing causes as the "Fair Play for Cuba" campaign. Like Herridge before him, his election blurred the lines between Communist and social democratic activism, though only Herridge brought the matter to a full boil.

Only a handful of smelter workers signed CPC membership cards, but many more incorporated Communist views into their home-grown beliefs. Trail's fellow travellers ultimately sided with Local 480 leadership on bargaining strategies, and they accepted the local's views on many social and economic issues of the day. However, there is no historiographical consensus about this. CIO historian Robert Zieger has noted that industrial workers did not have "much stomach for the kinds of root-and-branch confrontation" that Communists often promoted, but members in Trail did trust Murphy and the local's Communist leadership to act in their collective and class interests.[9] Mine-Mill in Trail, as with Laurie Mercier's local in Anaconda, Montana, saw itself as part of a broader leftist community and acted accordingly. For example, it joined the Allied war effort with other Communists, as Chris Frazer has described, but some enlistees had to reject the party's anti-war stance in the late 1930s. Local 480 supported strikes, community improvements, and fundraising for the less fortunate, and it fought racial and political injustices across Canada and the United States. It was in the vanguard of the 1950s peace movement.[10] But these actions, however radical for the McCarthy era, were not evidence of a seething hotbed of Communism, as repeatedly claimed by journalists, police agents, church leaders, company managers, and others in the smelter city.

Nothing underscores the complexity of this story like trying to figure out just how Communist the Local 480 Communists were. If we define a Communist as someone who advocates the violent overthrow of an elected government, there is no evidence that Local 480 Reds served as Soviet-controlled spies or that they were guided to sabotage the then-largest lead and zinc production facility in the British Empire. Certainly Communist smelter workers were at times rabble-rousers in defending their political views at local pubs and at political meetings. They also circulated Communist Bruce Mickleburgh's highly critical *Pacific Tribune* articles about Blaylock and the CM&S. In concrete terms, though, there were no work stoppages while Communists served on the Local 480 executive. Indeed, thanks to Murphy, Mine-Mill adhered to the CIO no-strike pledge throughout the war. This could be construed as Local 480 Reds supporting the Soviet Union and world Communism, but a no-strike pledge was surely meant to aid the war effort. Mine-Mill's rigorous acceptance of that pledge after Hitler invaded the Soviet Union was seen as a self-aggrandizing move. War had created a much-enlarged potential membership in the mining and smelting industry, and a show of patriotism could have softened the public view of Communist union leaders. Yet when Local 480 Reds might have had a chance to pass nuclear secrets to the Soviets after Blaylock decided to aid the US Army in building the heavy water plant in Warfield, no such effort emerged, in spite of the suspicion author Pierre Berton expressed in *Maclean's*. In fact, Communist influence was mostly limited to articles in union newspapers such as the *Commentator* that borrowed Marxist language to express political opinions.

Conversely, if a Communist is defined as someone who clandestinely seeks to control unions by manipulating a political process with the intent of influencing policy and daily union activities, then there is definitely evidence at Mine-Mill. Jensen, for example, has documented a political "machine" at International Mine-Mill headquarters, describing International President Reid Robinson as a "willing tool" that "left-wingers" used to "gain great influence at the top of the organization."[11] The resulting clamour from adversaries distracted the union leadership from its task of representing the rank-and-file. For all the ballyhoo at union meetings, however, the only impact on members' well-being was the waste of funds and energy that would otherwise have been dedicated to organizing, bargaining, and grievance appeals.

A minority of Local 480 smelter workers did complain about being ill served by the Communist leaders, and they used anti-Communist rhetoric to discredit the union. The problem, however, was that despite the rumours, there was little evidence of any radical subversives in Trail. Randi Storch argues that local Communists in the American Midwest did not always follow the dictates of the party.[12] Bert Cochrane explains that unionists often took issue with national and international party positions, believing that these would not work in their communities. Each community had its own unique circumstances, employers, and working-class dynamics.[13] Harvey Levenstein finds the same elements at work in the auto industry, where Communists "ignored or defied the party line."[14] In Canada, historians of the left such as Ian Angus, Ivan Avakumovic, Norman Penner, William Rodney, and others point to a similar defiance.[15] Even in Trail, with the maverick Stalinist Murphy leading the way, we spy the complexity of leftist unions' social and cultural politics on a continental scale.

Murphy Was Respected and yet Vilified

The politics of personality are crucial to this interpretation. Smelter families did not always like Murphy, nor did all Local 480 Communists like his politics, but his reputation among Trailites as a

fearless and successful organizer and negotiator against the powerful and profitable CM&S mattered greatly. There were instances
in which he was not guided by the interests of all Trail workers,
and detractors such as Mine-Mill lawyer John Stanton and Communist labour leader Bill White seized on such moments.[16] What
seemed to save Murphy, though, was an unwavering intent. His
blend of western-based labour socialism and a freewheeling form
of local Communism revealed a desire to advance goals that Local
480's Red leaders considered progressive, despite CPC views to the
contrary. This path was set in the earliest days of Local 480's Communist leadership. As we have seen, Communist Slim Evans led
the initial charge in the late 1930s as part of the movement toward
industrial democracy that the CIO symbolized. Communist John
McPeake carried the CIO banner when Evans was Red baited out
of town. Communist Murphy advanced the work of Evans and
McPeake to see the local certified. And Communist Al King's small
cohort of local Communist trade unionists defended that legacy
during the peak of post-war anti-Communism.

This did not mean the local's Communist leaders did not make
mistakes. Rather than advocate solidarity with the CCF, for example, they dissipated much of their energy in fruitless attacks. In the
1930s, Murphy and other Communists accepted the instructions
of the Soviet Comintern's Third Period, calling the CCF "social fascists." Trail Communists Harry Drake and Gar Belanger tried to
coax the already circumspect CCF to embrace unity, but this too
was seen as a manipulative gesture. Elections for the Mine-Mill
District Council were another misstep. When Communist candidates appeared to lose, Murphy arbitrarily voided the results and
held a new election seeking a more favourable outcome. Put simply, there were some reasons to mistrust Trail's Communists, and
national CPC leaders also earned this distrust.

For Lita-Rose Betcherman, for example, Tim Buck and Tom
McEwen were "cynical and opportunistic," more interested in the
"advantages of martyrdom" and willing to play the "politics of prov-
ocation." She roundly criticized them for failing to recognize when
authorities acted humanely. "Instead of welcoming such actions
the Communists tried to find ulterior motives. They maligned and

undermined other groups who were seeking ways to alleviate the suffering of the jobless. The party leaders deceived themselves and their followers about Stalin's Russia. Only by comparison with a stony-hearted Establishment might they seem like ... heroes."[17] Murphy was guilty of practising a similar brand of take-no-prisoners ideological warfare, as fellow Communist Jack Scott observed, and Murphy seems vulnerable to accusations of using the bargaining table to "camouflage" his aim to aid the Communist cause.[18] What critics must contend with, however, are Local 480's excellent collective agreements with no apparent left-wing political motives.

The bread-and-butter thesis for why smelter workers accepted a Communist union is also complicated by the twists and turns of the Steelworker raids. These conflicts revealed both strong support for Local 480 Reds and the tentativeness of that loyalty. The election of Claire Billingsley as Local 480 president in 1947 revealed smelter workers' contingent faith in Mine-Mill. Billingsley campaigned to lure members to the Steelworkers, and many joined his revolt, blindsiding Local 480 leaders. The outcome, though, was not as over-determined as the David-and-Goliath billing suggests. This was a tremendously intimate battle, pitting workers and families against each other. In the case of Labour Relations Board hearings and those dealing with changes to the labour laws, it also pitted lawyer and legislator against each other. The resulting bad blood seemingly benefitted the employer, yet for nearly three years Local 480 repulsed the raiders. The very resilience of the local inspired Trail supporters, as well as unions across North America, to resist Cold War enemies. The Steelworkers' anti-Communist strategy worked in other smelter towns, but in Trail it made Local 480 members defiant. Support for Red leaders ultimately repelled the much larger union and sustained the local for another fifteen years.

That Local 480 Communists were mostly home-grown smelter workers, not the "outside agitators" Trail's anti-Communists claimed, was another factor in sustaining local support. Men and women who came home as decorated veterans helped parry the rising tide of anti-Communism, and the remaining leaders who declared themselves Communists faced the ostracism that unfolded elsewhere. But they "were very much upfront about resisting McCarthyism," recalled Bill King, Al King's brother and a former labour minister in the BC NDP government of Dave Barrett. "They didn't shrink away from their beliefs and their radicalism at all."[19]

Although job seekers poured in from other parts of Canada and the United States, union leaders who worked at the smelter were supported by other Trailites when they were fired or harassed out of jobs by smelter foremen and managers. Members interpreted such pogroms as blows against the community as a whole. This homegrown factor also emboldened Red leaders to challenge the employer. They could argue with some credibility that they were managing a union in the best interests of a community built not only by the company through its largesse but also by the workers through their toil. All this buttressed Communists as they struggled against the strident anti-Communism threatening to stifle Local 480.

Trail's experience, along with that of some other Mine-Mill locals, thus stands in contrast to continental patterns. The Red purges drastically reduced the number of members with "a much wider social vision than most other American unionists of the 1950s."[20] This process left many battle scars that undermine trade union power to this day. Indeed, in ejecting Reds such as Murphy and the Local 480 Communists, who were widely acknowledged as effective trade union leaders, the movement lost its chance to effectively challenge capitalism's hegemonic grip on the postwar economy. Further changes in federal labour law and labour-management relations also curbed any possibility of 1930s-style shop-floor revolts. Mine-Mill's tradition of fighting employers and its Communist baggage did not fare well in this new era. Compromise at times hog-tied Trail workers in ways that privileged anti-Communists, but it did not silence Local 480's radical stances to the degree that it curtailed the will of other unions to confront employers and to challenge capitalism.[21] The victory over the Steelworkers, though significant, also thrust Local 480 to the periphery of the union movement, a holdout against the post-war legal compromise that most CCL unions had accepted.

1 Mine-Mill organizer Arthur "Slim" Evans (middle) arrives in Trail in 1938 to begin organizing smelter workers. Fellow Communist union organizer Tom Forkin is on right. The man on left is unknown. Credit: Courtesy Pacific Tribune Archives.

2 Albert "Ginger" Goodwin organized the 1917 smelter strike that led to the creation of the Workmen's Co-operative Committee, a company union. Goodwin was shot in 1918 while evading military service. BC workers organized a one-day general strike over the killing. Credit: Cumberland Museum and Archives.

3 Workers at the Trail smelter, including many immigrants, pour metal ingots by hand in the 1930s and 1940s. Credit: Courtesy USW Local 480.

4 S.G. Blaylock, a McGill University graduate, arrived in Trail in 1899 to begin his forty-four-year career. Credit: Courtesy Trail Historical Society.

5 *The Commentator*, Local 480's newspaper, often used cartoons in its fight to organize smelter workers. This is one of a series about the union drive that mocked company president Selwyn G. Blaylock. It appeared on 23 January 1939. Credit: Courtesy USW Local 480.

6 S.G. Blaylock created his Workmen's Co-operative Committee to limit the possibility of another strike after the 1917 battle. At this meeting in 1942, he confers with WCC president Dave Kenneway (reaching for cigarette). Others pictured are unknown. Credit: Courtesy Trail Historical Society.

7 Local 131 of the Mine-Mill ladies auxiliary supported Local 480 as it battled anti-communists. Credit: Courtesy Laurentian University Archives.

8 Trail's Cristoforo Colombo Lodge, established in 1905, houses one of the oldest ethnic associations in Canada. This detail of a mural at the entrance to the lodge depicts the various activities that involved Italian immigrants, including a strike (upper left corner). Credit: Courtesy Maureen Travers.

9 Immigrant workers were among the rabid Trail Smoke Eaters hockey fans. The team won the world amateur hockey cup in 1939 and again in 1961. Credit: Courtesy City of Trail.

10 Al King served as president of Local 480 from 1950 to 1960. He was an avid communist with a strong loyalty to the Trail community. Credit: Courtesy USW Local 480.

11 Bill Curran served as editor of the *Trail Daily Times* from the early 1930s to the early 1950s. He was a vocal anti-communist who used the newspaper to advocate against the union. Credit: Courtesy Trail Historical Society.

How a Red Union Bosses Atom Workers At Trail, B.C.

Openly controlled by Communists, the Mine-Mill Union doggedly holds its grip on one of Canada's most vital industries. Its domain includes a carefully guarded heavy-water plant in the B.C. mountains. An anti-Communist rival claims a majority of the workers, but the Reds are still on top in a fight that could involve our security

By PIERRE BERTON

Communist Harvey Murphy runs the Mine-Mill Union which controls 4,000 workers at Trail, including some in secret Project 9 — an atomic plant.

IN THE SMOKY little smelter town of Trail, huddled deep in the gnarled recesses of B. C.'s Kootenay mountains, one of the most significant union struggles in modern labor history is being fought out against a backdrop of atomic secrecy, Communist infiltration and charges of political opportunism.

Here, the United Steelworkers of America, the continent's most powerful industrial union, is challenging the right of the 57-year-old International Union of Mine, Mill and Smelter Workers to bargain for the men who work for one of Canada's richest corporations, the Consolidated Mining & Smelting Co., a subsidiary of the Canadian Pacific Railway.

The contest at Trail is something more than just another union squabble. In the first place, the Mine-Mill union has, for more than a decade, been run by the Communist Party for its own purposes. In the second, Canada's first atomic plant is at Trail. CM&S has been producing heavy water for U. S. atomic research — perhaps for a hydrogen bomb — for almost eight years.

So far the Steelworkers have failed to uproot the Communist-led union. They were given the job in January, 1950, when the Mine-Mill union was expelled by the Canadian Congress of Labor. But, after a year of B. C. Labor Board hearings, court cases, appeals and counter-suits, the Mine-Mill union and its Communist-dominated executive is still legal bargaining agent for Trail's 4,000 workers — even though only 1,700 of them actually belong to it.

Although the Steelworkers, in a whirlwind campaign, were able to win 2,300 smeltermen to their cause, the government-appointed Labor Relations Board of B. C. has declined to certify them. And the Trail employees themselves have as yet been given no opportunity to vote on which union they want to represent them.

Some strange things have been going on in B. C. since the union struggle at Trail began. A Liberal M.P. has come out publicly in favor of the Red-run union. A leading American Communist with a black patch over one eye, barred from Canada, has managed to stay at large four days in Trail. And the Canadian Congress of Labor has hotly charged that CM&S has given aid and comfort to the Communist union for the sake of a "bargain-basement contract" — a charge vigorously denied by the company.

In the background looms the grey square tower of the company's hush-hush "Project 9" which has been producing heavy water for the U. S. since 1943. Project 9 and the great hydrogen plant with which it is linked, is set apart from the sprawling fertilizer plant and smelter works by a high picket fence, a sign that says "No Admittance Without Authority," several uniformed guards, the RCMP, and an elaborate screening process and pass system — part of which is under FBI surveillance. But there is good reason to doubt that Project 9 has been wholly isolated from the Communists who run the Mine-Mill union.

The key men in the Trail local are Communist Party members or Party liners. One of them works as an oiler in the heavy water plant itself. He was identified to this writer as a member of the Labor Progressive Party in 1945 and was recently on the executive of his union.

Another works in the adjacent hydrogen plant as maintenance man. He is not known to be a Party member but has consistently followed the Party line and has distributed copies of the Stockholm Peace Petition within the plant itself.

The plant is vulnerable to sabotage because of the great squat storage tank close by which holds 200,000 cubic feet of highly inflammable hydrogen. Nearby is an ammonium nitrate plant, producing thousands of tons of fertilizer. It can easily be converted to munitions-making. (It was a shipload of ammonium nitrate that blew up in Texas City in 1947 destroying much of the town.)

The smelter itself would be essential to Canada in the event of war. It processes all the base metals from the great Sullivan mine at Kimberley, 200 miles away. This mine is the world's largest producer of lead and zinc and produces half of Canada's silver. The mines are also organized by the Communist-led Mine-Mill union which is organized in gold and base metal areas throughout Canada including the International Nickel Co. at Sudbury, Ont.

The significance of the atomic developments at Trail has not escaped the Communist Party. On March 10, 1950, its west coast organ, The Pacific Tribune, said editorially: "The atomic products of Chalk River and Trail can be made to serve the interests of humanity, but only if the jackals of big business within the labor movement are decisively ousted. That is why

12 Canadian writer and historian Pierre Berton visited Trail in the early 1950s to write a Cold War-style article about Local 480. Chief negotiator Harvey Murphy, self-described as the reddest rose in labour's garden, bore the brunt of the attack. Courtesy: Clipping from *Maclean's* magazine, 1 April 1951.

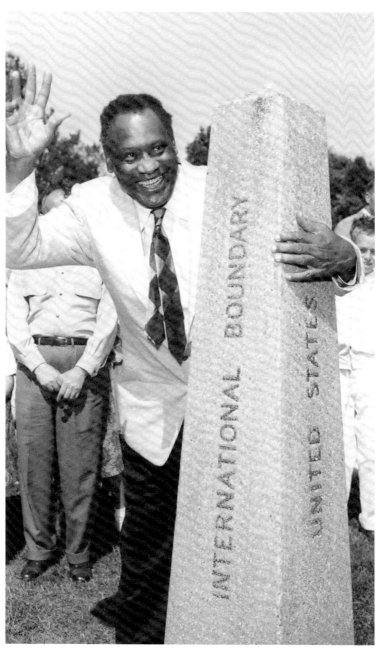

13 Popular African American singer and political activist Paul Robeson was closely associated with Mine-Mill. Credit: Courtesy Pacific Tribune Archives.

14 The Project 9 tower produced heavy water for the Manhattan Project to use in testing the atomic bomb. The Trail product was not used in the bombing of Japan. Credit: Courtesy Trail Historical Society.

15 Canadian Mine-Mill locals founded Mine-Mill Canada at a convention held in the historic Rossland Miners' Union Hall in 1955. Credit: USW Local 480.

Local 480 Continued to Win Guarded Public Support

Regardless of its pariah status, Local 480 continued to win guarded local support in its efforts at Cold War resistance. The union's cultural program exemplifies the contingent nature of its support. The four Robeson Peace Arch concerts did attempt to expose McCarthyism, but they were also entertainment. Some members who attended were fully committed to the vision of Communism, but Local 480 members who helped to organize the concerts were also fans who admired Robeson, despite widespread if false claims that he was a Communist. Conversely, Local 480's screening of *Salt of the Earth* attracted 900 out of thousands of workers and their families. This might seem like an underwhelming show of support for the Red leadership, but at the end of 1954, at the height of the McCarthyist witch-hunts, even that turnout was a positive indicator. After all, with the local police constabulary regularly spying on Local 480 and Murphy, it was perhaps a respectable indication of community support for the Red local and its fight to resist McCarthyism as practised by local anti-Communists.

The survival of Local 480 was never a given. Indeed, evidence suggests that it was just barely accepted in Trail. Close to half of the more than five thousand smelter workers and their spouses consistently rejected the Communist-led local, many preferring Blaylock's "one big happy family." And CM&S managers worked to undermine Mine-Mill by supporting internal and external attacks on the Trail local. Some attackers were class enemies; others were members of the local working class who collaborated in purging Communists. This latter group seemed to yearn for the security of the welfare capitalism that had assisted smelter families throughout the Depression, or they sided with company unionists and the Steelworker raiders, or they shared the view of the CCL and the CCF that Communism had to be expunged from the labour movement and society.

Despite divergent motivations, a significant number of smelter workers opposed Mine-Mill. Voting patterns reflected these strong anti-Local 480 sentiments. Underscoring the sustained divisions within the smelter workforce, and further bolstering the contention of divided loyalties, the 1943 LRB certification election actually favoured the company union by a thin margin of 100 votes over Mine-Mill, and the final vote in the early 1950s on the Steelworkers' bid to represent Trail smelter workers barely failed by a 300-vote margin. Thus we must reckon with a sizable minority of Trail workers who were never willing to side with Mine-Mill and its Communist leaders.

Trail workers' divided loyalties paralleled patterns in other mining and smelting communities as well as labour politics in capitalist economies more broadly. On the one hand workers tended to respect the company. It had been instrumental in establishing and transforming Trail into a relatively well-endowed city that provided steady incomes. On the other hand, and despite the many attempts to discredit their union, workers also respected Mine-Mill. It was often the only force willing to challenge the employer in the name of workers' self- and class interests. Those conflicting loyalties were in constant flux throughout most of the Second World War until Mine-Mill was certified as the legal bargaining agent. Once certified, Local 480's Communist leadership saw the union as vital to shaping the community on and below "the Hill." This had less to do with ideology than civic pride, family needs, and a city polluted with disease-causing lead.

While Trailites generally viewed Communism as a threat to national security, they varied on how serious this threat was at a local level. Police surveillance teams thought they were protecting national security by spying on the "subversive activities" of "Red" trade unionists. Writer Pierre Berton implied that Trail Communists might pass atomic secrets to the Soviets, but there is no evidence that anyone did so. Proof was never the main goal, however. Berton's innuendo was sufficient ammunition for right-wing politicians, and some on the left, who wanted to damn all Communists, especially trade unionists. So it was as well for some labour leaders seeking to oust unionists with whom they did not agree politically. Trail's smelter workers weighed these arguments and ultimately decided to accept and retain Mine-Mill.

From a collective bargaining viewpoint, it was a wise decision. Local 480's Communist leaders broke the CM&S's paternalistic hold on the lives of its workers and their families. What perhaps mattered most, however, were wage increases, providing for families, and health and safety in a notoriously unsafe industrial workplace run by a company that was as anti-union as it was anti-Communist. Local 480 won better and fairer wages by forcing the elimination of a bonus system that took wages from workers' pockets and kept them in confusion. The local also negotiated better pensions and safety measures that began to address chronic health problems such as lead accumulation, silicosis, and asbestosis.

Making Political Space in Post-War Canada

All smelter workers, regardless of their views of Local 480 and its Communist leaders, experienced gains in the workplace and the community in the 1940s and 1950s. Success in bargaining made Local 480 a force to reckon with in the CCF and the community, advocating for environmental safety measures, banning the bomb, improved health care, and better housing. It also created political space to fight against the post-war restrictions accepted by the mainstream labour movement, with Murphy using the Canadian union's new national *Mine-Mill Herald* to rail against Steelworker raiders in other towns over the next decade.

Ironically, five years after the two unions finally merged in 1967, Steelworker Local 480 was raided by a group of disgruntled smelter workers, complaining of low strike pay during a 1972 dispute. In a double irony, the Canadian Workers' Union (CWU), later subsumed by the larger Canadian Association of Industrial, Mechanical and Allied Workers, was part of a movement to oust international unions from the Canadian industrial workplace, a goal of the AUC and the ISWU two decades before. When the smelter workforce struck again in 1974, the Steelworkers ran a well-organized and well-funded strike campaign that some old-timers suggested was the union's way of telling the workers that it was going to be an effective replacement for Mine-Mill. It may also have been the

Steelworkers' way of sending the raiders packing. It worked but they would be back a decade later.

After the 1967 merger, Murphy and Al King, two of the biggest Reds in BC, took jobs with their old union nemesis, eliciting howls of disapproval from some leftists in the labour movement. Lawyer Stanton even argued that Murphy had collaborated with the employer to win the vote against Steel, and that he eventually agreed to push through the merger with Steel for his own gain. Given the history recounted here, the criticism is understandable. Long after the merger, there were still bitter memories, but the Steelworkers were determined to prove they could serve the members as well as Mine-Mill ever had. And they did gradually become one of the more progressive labour organizations in Canada. What role Murphy and King might have played in this gradual transition is not apparent. What is clear, however, is that the smelter wars they fought in the 1940s and 1950s helped shape a community and influence a movement.

Epilogue: The Smelter City Today

Memories of that eighteen-year-old kid we met in the preface to this book took me back to the smelter city of my youth, but visitors in the summer of 2021 would find it a sleepy provincial town. It was home to a growing population of pensioners who had returned for the good hunting and fishing, golf and curling, and the annual Local 480 pensioners' picnic. They could still enjoy spaghetti and chicken dinners at a local Italian family restaurant and sip locally made wine. The old Crown Point Hotel, where Murphy sometimes sidestepped police spies to hold clandestine meetings with local Reds, has been renovated and is now the Crown Columbia Hotel. Some of the old beer parlours faced competition from modern microbreweries. And low-hanging smoke from climate-change-related wild fires burning in the Columbia River Valley merged with emissions from the smelter.

Vestiges of the company town that grew from the diggings of early Kootenay prospectors are still evident in Trail. The remnants of the smelter that Butte copper king F. Augustus Heinze built in the mid-1890s are few now, having been replaced by a modern factory that still dominates the city below the Hill. Today it employs only a fraction of the more than five thousand workers who earned their living there in the 1940s. The Big Stack still towers 125 metres over the cityscape, and it still spews smoke from the zinc, lead, fertilizer, and other refineries that keep the smelter's current owner, Teck Resources Ltd., prosperous. Some of the red-roofed stairways workers used to climb – three shifts every day with a day off after a six-shift run once referred to as a "Murphy Day" – are still visible. The Smoke Eaters, albeit the juniors and not the team that was twice world champion, still play hockey at the Cominco arena, the rink the CM&S built in 1949 that is now part of the Trail Memorial Centre. Other parts of S.G. Blaylock's legacy also remain, including a hospital, gymnasium, the homes that once formed the management community of Tadanac, and the Blaylock Mansion near Nelson, BC. The mansion, whose botanical gardens were once tended by a Communist gardener named Jack Crow, is now an exclusive boutique hotel.[1]

The Cristoforo Colombo Lodge remains a solid landmark of the immigrant enclave "up the Gulch," and from the Italian families in its ranks came several notable figures. The late F.E. "Buddy" DeVito, a life-long socialist and once a Mine-Mill representative, was elected to Trail city council in December 1955 and went on to become mayor in the late 1960s. Ironically, *Times* editor Bill Curran was also elected to council in 1955. When DeVito ran for a CCF seat in a by-election, the *Times*, reminiscent of the Cold War years, suggested he "must be a secret communist," DeVito reported in his memoir *A Radical Life*.[2] Ken Georgetti, perhaps the most famous former Local 480 president, served several terms as president of the Canadian Labour Congress (CLC). Thomas D'Aquino became president of the Business Council on National Issues, the corporate lobby group that was a key promoter of the North American Free Trade Agreement, a deal the labour movement fought hard to stop.

The smoke emanating from the smelter stacks is less toxic these days, although the company still faces the occasional fine for polluting in northern Washington State. Trail's once-denuded hillsides are again mantled in green. Residents tend healthy vegetable gardens and orchards using Elephant Brand fertilizer. The Columbia River still flows wide and fast past the smelter, but upstream dams ensure that it will never again overflow its banks as it did in the Great Flood of 1948. Despite local protests, Teck demolished the Project 9 tower in the early 2000s, and with it the open secret of the smelter's role in building the first atomic bomb. A plaque now marks the site.

Today's visitor will also encounter street murals depicting cherished moments of the city's past. The south side of a building on

Bay Avenue features a colourful reminder of miners hauling ore and smelter workers pulling ingots. The north side of a building on Cedar Avenue depicts the *Trail Creek News* office, a pioneer version of Local 480's combative enemy the *Trail Daily Times*. A giant mural on the west end of Trail Memorial Centre honours the Smoke Eaters, while the east end of the building remembers First Nation fishers and the lost salmon runs. Many of these images conjure memories of Blaylock's empire and an era filled with the promise of prosperity, but with the exception of Local 480's union hall on Portland Street, there are few, if any, tangible reminders of how local Mine-Mill Communists built a union and fought for its survival during the Second World War and the Cold War.

Tellingly, there are no monuments to Harvey Murphy in today's Trail, but *Smelter Wars* would be incomplete without paying a final tribute to this most enigmatic and unsung of labour heroes. Many historians, trade union leaders, and government officials have too easily dismissed him, willingly sending him back to history's purgatory. Al King, who went on to become district secretary of Mine-Mill, would be the first to come to his defence. Although he did not always like Murphy, he saluted him as "a clever, accomplished and cagey operator and a superb strategist." But as King recalled in his memoir, he could also be "an unscrupulous bastard."[3] Others, too, had their quibbles with the man the press often dubbed the red bastion of BC labour. And yet his contribution to the labour movement and to the continuing fight for social justice begs reassessment. Murphy died on 30 April 1977 at age seventy-two, remembered by his old Alberta mining friends as "a little 'God' among the Reds," according to a secret police report.[4]

Local 480 still functions out of the union hall built after the 1950s raids ended. Above the door to the local's reception desk, a picture of labour martyr Albert "Ginger" Goodwin welcomes visitors. The local continues to be community-minded, actively participating in local social and political events. Some Local 480 members have held civic office. Some have run for mayor. But many old-timers argue that it is not like the old days when Blaylock was president. Back then, Local 480 bargaining committees met and hammered out collective agreements with locally based company management. Teck, an international conglomerate, has more distant executive managers than the ones who once lived in Tadanac houses near the Tudor-style edifice that Blaylock had constructed for himself on the banks of the Columbia.

Left-Right Battles Changed the Smelter City

Revisiting the smelter wars will revive old-timers' memories of the confrontations that tested the social fabric of the smelter city. They will meet at their favourite coffee shop or pub and reminisce about the Trail workforce. They will acknowledge that their city is a different place, diminished perhaps but still supporting an admirable level of job security. Elsewhere in North America, workplaces have continued to suffer through bouts of economic uncertainty that has seen jobs and industries downscale or even disappear since the 1970s.

During the Donald Trump era (2016–20), US workers faced even greater threats. Their unions, already long in decline, must fight even harder, as Local 480 did, to protect their memberships and stave off decertification. Just as the Taft-Hartley Act had a negative impact on unions like Mine-Mill in the 1940s and 1950s, Trump's pro-business policies undermined union organizing power. Still today, some American state governments continue pressing for right-to-work legislation that, in former president Barack Obama's view, means the right to earn less and stalls unionization efforts. In 2020, the proportion of the non-agricultural workforce that was unionized had dropped to 10.8 per cent, according to the US Bureau of Labor Statistics.[5] Still, despite unpredictable changes in government and labour-management policy shifts that can influence density, the more labour-friendly administration of President Joe Biden promises improvements.

In Canada, where union density tends to be more stable, there have also been declines, but it continued to hold its 31.3 per cent rate in 2020 and grow marginally in 2021, according to Statistics Canada figures cited in the *Toronto Star*.[6] For example, the relationship between labour and the federal government has been a mixed bag. After a decade of anti-labour rule under Conservative Prime

Minister Stephen Harper, Liberal Prime Minister Justin Trudeau basked in a comparatively positive public image. But the relationship with labour remained tenuous as he entered the fall 2021 federal election. Public sector unions, among Canada's largest, have struggled to see progress. In BC, where Murphy and other left-wing labour leaders once lobbied legislators against the pro-business ICA of the late 1940s, new hope sprang from the election in 2017 of a more labour-friendly NDP government led by former labour leader John Horgan. But support from building trades unions has seen Horgan make unpopular decisions in resource development.

Remembering Our Labour History

Many decades have passed since the smelter wars first began and much has changed. At the time of writing, the world is still in the throes of a global pandemic, and a resulting economic crisis threatens the livelihoods of millions of workers. At the same time, much has stayed the same. Women still earn less than men. Immigrants are still treated viciously by nativists and governments. Poverty and illiteracy are widespread. Canada's First Nations communities suffer the indignities of government inattention. Racism and discrimination continue to gain strength. Unions seem to be losing more battles than they are winning.

In spite of an occasional rise in political hopes, the prospect of a labour movement able to challenge modern-day capitalism seems more and more to belong to a bygone era. Although some polls show that a majority of voters favour unions, news media regularly declare the death of unions, and those that survive do not appear willing or prepared to mount any sustained resistance to the superwealthy One Per Cent. And a new Cold War seems to be unfolding as authoritarian governments increasingly pop up around the world. For organized labour to fend off the worst excesses of that war, it would do well to revisit its past, remember a labour history that seriously embraced some form of socialism as the better road to progressive social change, and rekindle the spirit of struggle and resistance that Mine-Mill Local 480 displayed in Trail so many decades ago.

Notes

Introduction

1. *Trail B.C.: A Half Century, 1901–1951*, published by Cominco Ltd. for the Trail Golden Jubilee Society, 1951, 34.
2. J.D. McDonald, *The Railways of Rossland, British Columbia* (Rossland, BC: Rossland Historical Museum Association, 1991), provides a history of the rivalry and the CPR's involvement.
3. Lance H. Whittaker, "All Is Not Gold: A Story of the Discovery, Production and Processing of the Mineral, Chemical and Power Resources of the Kootenay District of the Province of British Columbia and the Lives of the Men Who Developed and Exploited Those Resources," unpublished manuscript commissioned by S.G. Blaylock, Trail, BC, 1945, 25. Author's copy.
4. Elsie G. Turnbull, *Trail between Two Wars: The Story of the Smelter City* (Victoria, BC: Morriss Printing, 1980), 19.
5. Whittaker, "All Is Not Gold," 26.
6. Whittaker, "All Is Not Gold," 84.
7. Whittaker, "All Is Not Gold," 96.
8. *Trail Creek News* (hereafter *TCN*), untitled item, 5 August 1899, 1.
9. *TCN*, "Successful Smoker," 20 July 1907, 4.
10. *TCN*, "The Laborers of Winnipeg Have Organized," 16 September 1899, 2.
11. *TCN*, "What's the Matter with Trail?," 30 September 1899, 1.
12. *TCN*, "Trail," 3 January 1904, 4.
13. *TCN*, 30 January 1904, 2.
14. *TCN*, 1 February 1896, 3.

15. See Gerald Boucher, "The 1901 Rossland Miners' Strike: The Western Federation of Miners Responds to Industrial Capitalism" (BA graduating essay, University of Victoria, 1986).

16. Whittaker, "All Is Not Gold," 133.

17. Stanley Howard Scott, "A Profusion of Issues: Immigrant Labour, the World War, and the Cominco Strike of 1917," *Labour/Le Travail* 2 (1977): 54.

18. Scott, "Profusion of Issues," 57.

19. Scott, "Profusion of Issues," 54–5, citing *Saturday Night*, 10 April 1926.

20. A. Ross McCormack, *Reformers, Rebels, and Revolutionaries: The Western Canadian Radical Movement, 1899–1919* (Toronto: University of Toronto Press, 1977), 170.

21. Takaia Larsen, "Sowing the Seeds: Women, Work and Memory in Trail, British Columbia during and after the Second World War" (MA thesis, University of Victoria, 2007), 73.

22. Elizabeth Quinlan and Andrea Quinlan, "Textually Mediated Labour Activism: An Examination of the Ladies Auxiliary of the Canadian Mine Mill and Smelter Workers Union, 1940s–1960s," *Journal of International Women's Studies* 16, no. 3 (2015): 137–57, 150.

23. Donald Avery, *"Dangerous Foreigners": European Immigrant Workers and Labour Radicalism in Canada, 1896–1932* (Toronto: McClelland & Stewart, 1979), 46.

24. Steve Rosswurm, "The Catholic Church and Left-Led Unions: Labor Priests, Labor Schools, and the ACTU," in *The CIO's Left-Led Unions*, ed. Steve Rosswurm (New Brunswick, NJ: Rutgers University Press, 1992), 120.

25. Benjamin Isitt, *Militant Majority: British Columbia Workers and the Rise of a New Left, 1948–1972* (Toronto: University of Toronto Press, 2011), 90.

26. Al King with Kate Braid, *Red Bait!: Struggles of a Mine-Mill Local* (Vancouver: Kingbird Publishing, 1998), 74–5.

27. Laurel Sefton MacDowell, "Paul Robeson in Canada: A Border Story," *Labour/Le Travail* 51 (Spring 2003): 177.

28. See Ellen Schrecker, *Many Are the Crimes: McCarthyism in America* (New York: Little, Brown, 1998).

29. Joan Sangster, "Canada's Cold War in Fur," *Left History* 13 (Fall–Winter 2008): 11.

30. Bryan D. Palmer, *A Culture in Conflict: Skilled Workers and Industrial Capitalism in Hamilton, Ontario, 1860–1914* (Montreal/Kingston: McGill/Queen's University Press, 1979), xvi.

1 A Red Union Comes to Town

1. Evans joined the CPC in 1926, as cited in Jean Evans Sheils and Ben Swankey, *Work and Wages: A Semi-Documentary Account of the Life*

and Times of Arthur H. (Slim) Evans, 1890–1944 (Vancouver: Granville, 1977), 32.

2. *Union Bulletin,* "Miners Launch Big Union Drive – Sub-District Meet Approves Campaign," 4 July 1938, 1.

3. See Bill Waiser, *All Hell Can't Stop Us: The On-to-Ottawa Trek and Regina Riot* (Markham, ON: Fifth House Publishers, 2003).

4. Jon Bartlett and Rika Ruebsaat, *Soviet Princeton: Slim Evans and the 1932–33 Miners' Strike* (Vancouver: New Star Books, 2015), 47.

5. King with Braid, *Red Bait!,* 34.

6. Stephen L. Endicott, *Raising the Workers' Flag: The Workers' Unity League of Canada, 1930–1936* (Toronto: University of Toronto Press, 2012), 188.

7. See Roger Stonebanks, *Fighting for Dignity: The Ginger Goodwin Story* (St. John's, NL: Canadian Committee on Labour History, 2004); and Susan Mayse, *Ginger: The Life and Death of Albert Goodwin* (Madeira Park, BC: Harbour Publishing, 1990).

8. *Union Bulletin,* "From Our Organizer: Art Evans Writes a Personal Message," 4 July 1938, 4.

9. Jeffery A. Keshen, *Saints, Sinners and Soldiers: Canada's Second World War* (Vancouver: UBC Press, 2004), 5.

10. Graham Broad, *A Small Price to Pay: Consumer Culture on the Canadian Home Front, 1939–45* (Vancouver: UBC Press, 2014), 2.

11. Broad, *Small Price to Pay,* 7.

12. King with Braid, *Red Bait!,* 13.

13. King with Braid, *Red Bait!,* 11.

14. *Trail Daily Times* (hereafter *TDT*), "Trouble-Makers Foment Relief Demonstration," 11 June 1935, 4.

15. *TDT,* 20 February 1935, 4.

16. David Michael Roth, "A Union on the Hill: The International Union of Mine, Mill and Smelter Workers and the Organization of Trail Smelter and Chemical Workers, 1938–1945" (MA thesis, Simon Fraser University, 1991), 15.

17. *TDT,* "Trail Financially Is Sitting Atop of the World," 11 January 1938, 1.

18. *TDT,* "Trail Has Important Part in Dominion's Industrial Life, Canadian Club Told," 2 February 1938, 2.

19. See Mark Zuehlke, *The Gallant Cause: Canadians in the Spanish Civil War* (Toronto: John Wiley and Sons, 1996); and David Liversedge, with David Yorke, ed., *Mac-Pap: Memoirs of a Canadian in the Spanish Civil War* (Vancouver: New Star, 2013).

20. *TDT,* "Second World War Began with Ethiopia, Spanish and Japanese Campaigns, Says F.H. Soward," 31 January 1938, 8.

21. *TDT*, "Welcome Home Champions! Hail, the Smoke Eaters!," 22 April 1938, 1. See also Jamie Forbes, *50th Anniversary: A Celebration of the Trail Smoke Eaters Winning of the 1961 World Championship* (Trail: Trail Historical Society, 2011).

22. *TDT*, "CBC Feature on Air from Trail," 12 May 1938, 5.

23. *TDT*, "Business Men Not All Blaylocks so Gov't Must Direct," 18 February 1938, 1.

24. *TDT*, "S.G. Blaylock Scores Demoralizing Effect of Canada's Relief System," 7 June 1938, 2.

25. *TDT*, "Longs to See Blaylock Head of This Country," 25 June 1938, 1.

26. Sheils and Swankey, *Work and Wages*, 269.

27. *TDT*, "Evans Raps Police: Dissatisfied with Investigation into Burning of Truck," 7 October 1938, 1.

28. *TDT*, "C.M.&S. Co. Announces Bonus," 5 December 1938, 1.

29. *TDT*, "Unsettled World – But S.G. Blaylock Is Hopeful Conditions Will Hold to 1938 Level," 31 December 1938, 1.

30. Nelson Lichtenstein, *State of the Unions: A Century of American Labor* (Princeton, NJ: Princeton University Press, 2003), 267.

31. Jeremy Mouat, *Roaring Days: Rossland's Mines and the History of British Columbia* (Vancouver: UBC Press, 1995), 124, notes that Americans flooded into the interior region in those years.

32. *TDT*, "Labor's World-Wide Crusade to Free Tom Mooney Triumphed Today," 7 January 1939, 1.

33. Arthur H. (Slim) Evans, "An Open Letter to Blaylock and Guillaume," *Commentator*, 6 February 1939, 1.

34. *TDT*, "Grant Evans Use of Butler Park," 2 May 1939, 7.

35. *TDT*, "Evans Seeks Interview; Smelter Head Declines," 3 May 1939, 3.

36. *TDT*, "Organizer Arthur Evans Sees New Day for Labor," 15 May 1939, 3. The *Times* estimated the crowd at 1,200. In "The Past Year with the Drive," the *Union Bulletin*, July 1939, offered 2,000 as the true estimate. Sheils and Swankey, *Work and Wages*, 277, also cited the higher figure.

37. *TDT*, "Arthur Evans Given Remand for Eight Days," 5 June 1939, 1.

38. Sheils and Swankey, *Work and Wages*, 280.

39. *TDT*, "Arthur Evans Given Remand for Eight Days," 5 June 1939, 1.

40. *TDT*, "Evans Resigns as CIO Organizer," 3 July 1939, 1.

41. Sheils and Swankey, *Work and Wages*, 276.

42. *TDT*, "Smelter Layoff Is About Ended Says Blaylock," 24 July 1939, 1.

43. *TDT*, "Good News for Trail," 25 July 1939, 4.

44. *Commentator*, editorial, 12 July 1939, 2.

45. Jean Barman, *The West beyond the West: A History of British Columbia* (Toronto: University of Toronto Press, 1991), 197–8.
46. *TDT*, "Nazis in Trail," 5 September 1939, 1.
47. *TDT*, "Stronger Guard Placed around City Utilities," 11 September 1939, 1.
48. *TDT*, "Trail ... and War Profiteering," 15 September 1939, 4.
49. For Trailites unfamiliar with the many uses of zinc in wartime, *TDT*, "British Empire Now Produces 10 Per Cent More Zinc Than Required," 17 October 1939, 2, explained that it was essential for shell casing production, making die castings, and galvanizing metals.
50. *TDT*, "C.M.&S. Company Gives Concessions to Employees Enlisting," 12 October 1939, 1.
51. *Commentator*, "Union Declares Position on War," 16 September 1939, 1.
52. *TDT*, "The Nazi-Communist Menace to the Catholic Church," 18 October 1939, 4.
53. *TDT*, "C.I.O. Strike Is Violation of BC Law, Says Pearson," 12 October 1939, 3.
54. *TDT*, "Canadians Should Be Happy Despite War, Says Blaylock," 30 December 1939, 1.
55. *TDT*, "Nine Applications for Naturalization Are Granted at Rossland," 20 September 1939, 1.
56. *Commentator*, "The 'Yes Men' Say 'No!'," 11 January 1940, 3.
57. *TDT*, "Trail Aliens Interned," 24 January 1940, 1.
58. *TDT*, "Sabotage Attempts," 15 January 1940, 4.
59. *TDT*, "Saboteurs Deserving of Extreme Penalty," 29 January 1940, 2.
60. *TDT*, "Smelter Shares Bonuses Issued," 15 February 1940, 8.
61. *Commentator*, "Brief Presented to Company for $1.00 a Day," 2 March 1940, 1.
62. *Commentator*, "Three-Quarter Time," 9 March 1940, 3.
63. *Commentator*, "Committee Attempts Scuttle Wage Increase Drive," 9 March 1940, 4.
64. *Commentator*, editorial, 9 March 1940, 2.
65. *TDT*, "Timely Warnings," 6 May 1940, 4.
66. Constable Murray Black, "O" Division, correspondence entitled "Secret – C.P. of C. Activity in Trade Unions – Toronto, Ontario," Toronto, 9 May 1940, "Police Surveillance Files, Harvey Murphy," LAC.
67. *TDT*, "Why We Support Mr. Esling," 11 March 1940, 1. In April 1898, Esling had taken over from W.F. Thompson, who had founded the *Trail Creek News*, the city's first newspaper.

68. *TDT*, "Communists Are Backing C.C.F. Claims Burns," 20 March 1940, 3.
69. Irving Martin Abella, *Nationalism, Communism, and Canadian Labour: The CIO, the Communist Party, and the Canadian Congress of Labour, 1935–56* (Toronto: University of Toronto Press, 1973), 45.
70. *TDT*, "Subversive Groups Are Outlawed in Canada," 5 June 1940, 1.
71. *TDT*, "Smelter German Employees Sent into Northland," 5 June 1940, 9.
72. *TDT*, "Good Luck! – Trail Bids Farewell to Latest Volunteers," 18 June 1940, 1.
73. Memorandum for the minister of justice, Ernest Lapointe, Ottawa, 6 July 1940, copy included in correspondence from Inspector C. Batch, assistant intelligence officer, RCMP, Ottawa, 6 July 1940. "Police Surveillance Files, Harvey Murphy," LAC.
74. *Commentator*, "Letters to the Editor," 20 August 1940, 2.
75. *TDT*, "Trail, Picturesque City and Home of People from Many Parts of the World," 7 September 1940, 4.
76. *TDT*, "Sees No Chance for Pay Increase for Low Wage Employees," 12 September 1940, 1.
77. *TDT*, "Smelter Employees Opposed to Strike," 5 September 1940, 1.
78. *TDT*, "Christmas Bonuses for Employees of C.M.&S. Company," 5 November 1940, 1.
79. *TDT*, "Health Insurance and Proposal for Smelter Are Studied by House," 14 November 1940, 1.
80. *TDT*, "House Studies CCF Plan for Protecting Public against Profit System," 2 November 1940, 1.
81. *TDT*, "Idealistic: Smelter's Attitude to War Is Praised," 19 November 1940, 1 and 6.
82. *TDT*, "Cheery Message: Trend toward Victory Evident, Says Blaylock," 24 November 1940, 1.
83. *Commentator*, "Lessons for Labor in 1940," 21 January 1941, 1.
84. S.G. Blaylock, "A Message from One Citizen of the British Empire to Another," Trail, BC, *Empire Day*, 24 May 1941, 1.
85. Blaylock, "Message from One Citizen," 4.
86. Blaylock, "Message from One Citizen," 5.
87. *TDT*, "Blaylock Says Canadians Still Buying and Making Too Many Luxury Items," 7 May 1941, 1.
88. *Commentator*, "Slavery for Labor – War Profits for Industry," 12 August 1941, 2.
89. *TDT*, "Conscription of Wealth Urged by Labor Congress," 26 September 1941, 1.

90. *Commentator*, "Letters to the Editor," 7 October 1941, 2.
91. *Commentator*, "A Second Front for Victory," 17 October 1941, 2.
92. "In the Matter of Harvey Murphy, Recommendation of the Advisory Committee," D. O'Connell, chairman, Advisory Committee, Defence of Canada Regulations, Toronto, 9 February 1942, "Police Surveillance Files, Harvey Murphy," LAC.
93. "Notice of Release," signed by Captain D. Davison for H.N. Streight, Lt.-Colonel, commissioner of internment operations, 10 September 1942, "Police Surveillance Files, Harvey Murphy," LAC. See also Gerald Tulchinsky, *Joe Salsberg: A Life of Commitment* (Toronto: University of Toronto Press, 2013).
94. *TDT*, "Union Claims That Production Stopped at Kirkland Lake," 19 November 1941, 1.
95. *TDT*, "Union Officials Disclaim Idea of Saturday 'Holiday,'" 28 November 1941, 1.
96. Laurel Sefton MacDowell, *"Remember Kirkland Lake": The Gold Miners' Strike of 1941–42* (Toronto: University of Toronto Press, 1983), 236.
97. *TDT*, "Christmas Is a Challenge This Year, Says Blaylock," 24 December 1941, 1.
98. *TDT*, "About Town," 6 December 1941, 10.
99. *TDT*, advertisement, 26 September 1941, 3.
100. *TDT*, "Peek at the Week," 22 November 1941, 1.
101. *TDT*, "Increase Old Age Pensions," 23 January 1942, 1.
102. *TDT*, "Conscription Plebiscite to Be Held," 22 January 1942, 4.
103. *TDT*, "Japs in B.C. Areas to Lose Cars, Radios," 27 February 1942, 1.
104. *Commentator*, "This Plebiscite," 16 March 1942, 2.
105. *Commentator*, "Communication," 16 March 1942, 2.
106. *TDT*, "New Dominion Labor Program Starts at Once," 1 April 1942, 4.
107. *TDT*, "Labor and Plebiscite," 4 April 1942, 4.
108. *TDT*, "Strong Challenge for 'Yes' Vote Is Sounded at Rally," 25 April 1942, 1–2. See also *Commentator*, "Trail Unites on National Question," 17 April 1942, 1.
109. *TDT*, "Kootenay West Votes 'Yes' by 10,364 to 3,653," 28 April 1942, 1.
110. *Commentator*, "War Effort Demands Unity," 17 August 1942, 2.
111. *TDT*, "Canadian Labor to Celebrate Fourth Wartime Labor Day," 5 September 1942, 1.
112. *TDT*, "Canuck Labor Must Not Endanger Effort Says Congress Head," 14 September 1942, 1.
113. *TDT*, "Industries to Be Pruned Says Elliott Little," 15 September 1942, 1.
114. *TDT*, "AFL Convention Is Opened in Toronto," 5 October 1942, 1.

115. *TDT*, "Mackenzie King Speaks at Annual Meet of AFL," 9 October 1942, 1.
116. *TDT*, "Primate Is Interviewed: Believes Anglo-American Friendship Is First Need," 28 October 1942, 1.
117. *TDT*, "General Canvass in Trail Reaches Total of $372,900," 27 October 1942, 1.
118. *Commentator*, "Tribute to Our Russian Ally," 16 November 1942, 1–2.
119. *Commentator*, "On Collective Bargaining," 16 November 1942, 4.
120. *TDT*, "Horizons Brighter This Christmas Says Blaylock," 14 December 1942, 4.
121. *TDT*, "The Steel Strikers," 15 January 1943, 4.
122. *Commentator*, "Support the Steelworkers," 22 February 1943, 4; *TDT*, "Government Plan Rejected by Steel Men," 21 January 1943, 1.
123. *TDT*, "Labor Congress Suspends Union at Vancouver," 26 January 1943, 1.

2 Battling Blaylock's Company Union

1. *Commentator*, "New Labor Legislation Great Triumph for British Columbia Unions," 22 April 1943, 2–3.
2. *TDT*, "Protection of Company Union Asked," 5 February 1943, 1.
3. Roth, "Union on the Hill," 62.
4. *Commentator*, "Why Company Unions Should Be Outlawed," 22 February 1943, 2.
5. Roth, "Union on the Hill," 62.
6. *Commentator*, "Committee Executive Action Causes Furure [*sic*]," 15 March 1943, 1.
7. *TDT*, "It's Tops with the War Worker Girls," 6 April 1943, 2.
8. *TDT*, "30 Per Cent Liquor Cut Is Met by Canada," 15 April 1943, 4.
9. *TDT*, "Billion Dollar Security Plan Offered," 16 March 1943, 1. Lord William Beveridge wrote the British report.
10. *TDT*, "Draft of Health Insurance Bill Is Submitted," 16 March 1943, 1. For further details on Marsh's recommendations, see *Canadians in and out of Work: A Survey of Economic Classes and Their Relation to the Labour Market* (London: Oxford University Press, 1940), a respected class analysis.
11. *TDT*, "Knowles Demands New Labor Minister, Change in Policy," 4 February 1943, 1.
12. *TDT*, "S.H. Kyle States His Position in Tadanac Situation," 6 April 1943, 5.

13. *TDT*, "Herridge Asks Investigation of Tadanac," 11 March 1943, 1.
14. *TDT*, "Is It a Political Smoke Screen?," 13 March 1943, 1.
15. Jonathan Levy, *Freaks of Fortune: The Emerging World of Capitalism and Risk in America* (Cambridge, MA: Harvard University Press, 2012), 2.
16. Author unknown, "A Portrait of Progress: The Story of Cominco," unpublished manuscript, 84–96, provides a detailed account of the development of Sullivan Mine and the process of separating lead and zinc from the extracted ore. Copy obtained from the communications office of Teck Resources Ltd., Trail, BC. Mouat, *Roaring Days,* 148–9, also explains the zinc separation process.
17. *Saturday Night*, 10 April 1926.
18. *Commentator*, "CM&S Treat 'Leaded' Employees Inhumanly [*sic*]," 30 November 1938, 1.
19. King with Braid, *Red Bait!*, 25.
20. *TDT*, "A 'Dusty' Question," 8 September 1937, 4.
21. "Director's Report," CM&S *Annual Reports,* 1935–49.
22. *Rossland Miner*, "Mr. Blaylock on Industrial Relations," June 1937.
23. S.G. Blaylock, "Presidential Address: Industrial Relationship," Annual General Meeting, Canadian Institute of Mining and Metallurgy, Winnipeg, March 1935. See H.J. Macrae-Gibson, *The Whitley System in the Civil Service* (London: Fabian Society, 1922). See also Daniel M. Vrooman, *Daniel Willard and Progressive Management on the Baltimore and Ohio Railroad* (Columbus: Ohio State University Press, 1991).
24. Allen Seager, "'A New Labour Era?': Canadian National Railways and the Railway Worker, 1919–1929," *Journal of the Canadian Historical Association*, n.s. 2 (1992): 190–2.
25. See W.L. Mackenzie King, *Industry and Humanity: A Study in the Principles Underlying Industrial Reconstruction* (Toronto: Thomas Allen, 1918).
26. Thomas G. Andrews, *Killing for Coal: America's Deadliest Labor War* (Cambridge, MA: Harvard University Press, 2008), provides a detailed account of the massacre.
27. Sheils and Swankey, *Work and Wages*, 10.
28. See Beth Thomkins Bates, *Pullman Porters and the Rise of Protest Politics in Black America, 1925–1945* (Chapel Hill: University of North Carolina Press, 2001).
29. *Nelson Daily News*, "Blaylock of C.M. & S. Dies," 20 November 1945, 1.
30. *Saturday Night*, 10 April 1926.
31. S.G. Blaylock, "A Record of Achievement: What of the Future?," address to the Rossland Junior Board of Trade, Rossland, BC, 11 January 1944, 4.

32. Whittaker, "All Is Not Gold," 257.
33. Blaylock's Mansion, "About Us," www.blaylock.ca/about-us, cites the lemon comment. See also, Charlie Hodge with Dan McGauley, *Lost Souls of Lakewood: The History and Mystery of Blaylock's Mansion* (Victoria: Friesen Press, 2021).
34. Keith A. Murray, "The Trail Smelter Case: International Air Pollution in the Columbia Valley," *BC Studies* 15 (Autumn 1972): 76–7.
35. John D. Wirth, "The Trail Smelter Dispute: Canadians and Americans Confront Transboundary Pollution, 1927–41," *Environmental History* 1, no. 2 (April 1996): 39.
36. The *Times* provided daily front-page wire service coverage of the arbitration hearings from at least 23 June 1937, when the tribunal met in Washington, DC, and later Spokane.
37. *TCN*, 19 October 1895, 1.
38. D.H. Dinwoodie, "The Politics of International Pollution Control: The Trail Smelter Case," *International Journal* 27, no. 2, Canada and the United States (Spring 1972): 235.
39. King with Braid, *Red Bait!*, 72.
40. Philip M. Glende, "Labor Makes the News: Newspapers, Journalism, and Organized Labor, 1933–1955," *Enterprise and Society* 13, no. 1 (February 2012): 48.
41. Turnbull, *Trail between Two Wars*, 67.
42. *TDT*, "A Progressive Employer," 22 September 1937, 1.
43. Whittaker, "All Is Not Gold," 224.
44. Howard W. Bayley, "Cominco: A Historical Outline," January 1976, 37. Unpublished manuscript archived at the Communications Office, Teck Resources, Trail, BC.
45. William Campbell interview, conducted by Richard Bell, Glenmerry, BC, 22 August 1983, BC Archives sound recordings, Labour Organizations at Cominco series, call numbers T4101:0014 and :0015.
46. Mike Solski and John Smaller, *Mine-Mill: The History of the International Union of Mine, Mill and Smelter Workers in Canada since 1895* (Ottawa: Steel Rail Publishing, 1984), 37.
47. King with Braid, *Red Bait!*, 27.
48. King with Braid, *Red Bait!*, 28.
49. Ralph Abram "Duke" Hyssop interview, conducted by Richard Bell, Nelson, BC, 19 October 1983, BC Archives sound recordings, Labour Organizations at Cominco series, call number T4101:0022.

50. George Bishop interview, conducted by Richard Bell, Trail, BC, August 1983, BC Archives sound recordings, Labour Organizations at Cominco series, call number T4101:0010.

51. Pat Romaine interview, conducted by Richard Bell, Castlegar, BC, 29 June 1983, BC Archives sound recordings, Labour Organizations at Cominco series, call numbers T4101:0005 and :0006.

52. *Communicator*, "Smelter Group Calls Halt to Lie Campaign," 25 February 1939, 1.

53. *Communicator*, "New Paper Answers Commentator Abuses," 25 February 1939, 1.

54. *Co-operator*, "No Thanks, Mr. Evans!," 7 March 1939, 1.

55. Roth, "Union on the Hill," 39.

56. *Commentator*, "Blaylock's Co-operator," 17 April 1939, 2.

57. *Co-operator*, "'Reds' Don't Like the Co-op Committee System," 21 March 1939, 1.

58. *Co-operator*, "No 'Bag of Tricks' in the Co-op System," 21 March 1939, 4.

59. *Co-operator*, "No Thanks, Mr. Evans!"

60. Roth, "Union on the Hill," 18–20.

61. Craig Heron, *Working in Steel: The Early Years in Canada, 1883–1935* (Toronto: University of Toronto Press, 1988), 109.

62. Margaret McCallum, "Corporate Welfarism in Canada," *Canadian Historical Review* 71, no. 1 (1990): 73.

63. See Gerald Zahavi, *Workers, Managers, and Welfare Capitalism: The Shoemakers and Tanners of Endicott Johnson, 1890–1950* (Chicago: University of Illinois Press, 1988).

64. Lizabeth Cohen, *Making a New Deal: Industrial Workers in Chicago, 1919–1939* (Cambridge, MA: Cambridge University Press, 2008), 209.

65. Andrew Parnaby, *Citizen Docker: Making a New Deal on the Vancouver Waterfront, 1919–1939* (Toronto: University of Toronto Press, 2008), 10–11.

66. *TDT*, "Co-operative Committee Is Endorsed in Sweeping Employee Vote," 12 April 1939, 1.

67. *TDT*, "The Next C.I.O. Manoeuvre," 12 April 1939, 1.

68. S.G. Blaylock, "An Address to the Annual Smoker of the Consolidated Workmen's Co-operative Committee, Trail, B.C., Friday, 26 May 1939," Trail City Archives, manuscript ascension no. 86-lib, 1.

69. *Commentator*, "Government Labor Statistics Confirm Disadvantages of Smelter Employment," 12 August 1941, 4.
70. Blaylock, "Address to the Annual Smoker," 2.
71. *TDT*, "G. Thomson New Chairman of Committee," 10 May 1939, 1.
72. The "reddest rose" reference is cited in Endicott, *Raising the Workers' Flag*, 126.
73. Murphy's release date was recorded in police files obtained through access to information legislation, "Police Surveillance Files, Harvey Murphy," LAC.
74. *TDT*, "Kenneway Was Ensured Hearing Says Murphy," 10 April 1943, 4.
75. *TDT*, "Murphy Has Splendid Record Says Writer," 10 April 1943, 4.
76. *TDT*, "Writer Urges Workers Not to Spoil Good Thing," 10 April 1943, 4.
77. *TDT*, "Labor, Liquor and Taxation," 10 April 1943, 4.
78. *TDT*, "Trail Could Be a Ghost Town Warns Smelterman," 14 April 1943, 4.
79. *TDT*, "Writer Asks Why Workers Should Turn on Committee," 15 April 1943, 4.
80. *TDT*, "Remember Cape Breton Italians Warns Writer," 15 April 1943, 4.
81. *TDT*, "Meade Replies to Bell Letter," 22 April 1943, 4.
82. *TDT*, "Anti-Union Letters Amuse Member of Local," 17 April 1943, 4.
83. *TDT*, "This Paper Has Placed Limitation on Labor Letters," 10 April 1943, 4.
84. *TDT*, "Letter: Workers Do Not Need CIO to Conduct Affairs," 24 April 1943, 4.
85. *TDT*, "Letter: Writer Discusses Financial Side of Promised Raise," 24 April 1943, 4.
86. Ron Verzuh, "Blaylock's Bomb: How a Remote British Columbia City Helped Create the World's First Weapon of Mass Destruction," *BC Studies* 186 (Summer 2015): 9–37, provides a full account of the Trail smelter's role.
87. *TDT*, "Letter: Kenneway Replies to Accusation," 27 January 1943, 4.
88. *TDT*, "Council Endorses Mayor's Action in Halting Ticket Sale," 26 February 1943, 1.
89. *Commentator*, "Fink Unions Show Hand," 25 January 1943, 1.
90. *Commentator*, "Why the Ban on the Communist Party Should Be Lifted," 22 February 1943, 2.
91. Chris Frazer, "From Pariahs to Patriots: Canadian Communists and the Second World War," *Past Imperfect* 5 (1996), 20.
92. *Commentator*, "Industrialists Attack Union," 22 February 1943, 4.
93. *TDT*, "Union Member Answers Letter by 'Contented,'" 30 March 1943, 4.
94. *TDT*, "Count Blessings Is Admonition of Trail Worker," 30 March 1943, 4.

95. *TDT*, "Committee Denies Sullivan Mine Men Accepted Union," 12 April 1943, 3.
96. *TDT*, "Contented Replies to Union Writer," 1 April 1943, 4.
97. *TDT*, "Booing Kenneway at Union Meeting Rapped by Writer," 5 April 1943, 2.
98. *TDT*, "Wealth Produced by Labor Belongs to All Says Writer," 8 April 1943, 4.
99. *TDT*, "Workers Asked to Consider These Points," 9 April 1943, 4.
100. *TDT*, "Day-Pay Employees Vote for Committee Plan 1,977 to 1,888," 20 April 1943, 1.
101. *TDT*, "A Company Reports to Its Employees," 5 April 1943, 6.
102. *Commentator*, "Contribution: Shades of the Future," 22 April 1943, 4.
103. S.G. Blaylock, "A Submission to the Enquiry Being Conducted by the National War Labour Board," Trail, BC, 15 May 1943.
104. *TDT*, "Intolerable Stoppages," 1 May 1943, 4.
105. *Commentator*, "Local 480 Attains Majority," 19 May 1943, 1.
106. Roth, "Union on the Hill," 65.
107. *Commentator*, "Poets' Corner," 19 May 1943, 2. For a detailed discussion of working-class poetry in Trail, see Ron Verzuh, "The Smelter Poets: The Inspiring Role of Worker Poetry in a BC Labour Newspaper during the 'Age of the CIO,'" *BC Studies* 177 (Spring 2013): 85–126.
108. *Commentator*, "U.S. Corporate Executives Salaries Take Joy-ride," 19 May 1943, 3.
109. *Commentator*, "Reid Robinson Speaks before Large Audience – Hundreds Parade," 21 June 1943, 3.
110. *TDT*, "War Labor Board Broadens Raise to CM&S Trades," 21 June 1943, 3.
111. *Commentator*, "Just Think What a Real Union Will Do …," 21 June 1943, 3.
112. *TDT*, "Trail's Story Gets Around," 28 June 1943, 4.
113. *TDT*, "Company and CIO Reach Agreement for Kimberley Workers," 4 November 1943, 10.
114. *Commentator*, "Kimberley Local 651 Negotiates Agreement with C.M.&S. Co.," 15 November 1943, 1.
115. *Commentator*, "Tim Buck to Give Address in Trail Thursday, Nov. 18," 15 November 1943, 2.
116. *Commentator*, "In a Den of Finks," 15 November 1943, 3.
117. *Commentator*, "Fink Convention Bars Labor Press–Scab 'Federation' Born in Hamilton," 15 November 1943, 4.
118. *Commentator*, "The Rogue's Gallery," 15 November 1943, 4.

119. *TDT*, "ISWU Gains Award," 1 December 1943, 1.
120. *TDT*, "CIO Fails to Reach Majority," 28 December 1943, 1.
121. Roth, "Union on the Hill," 68.
122. Laurel Sefton MacDowell, "The Career of a Canadian Trade Union Leader: C.H. Millard 1937–1946," *Industrial Relations* 43, no. 3 (1988): 616.
123. *TDT*, "Wage Control Order Aims at Stabilization," 9 December 1943, 1.
124. *TDT*, "S.G. Blaylock Sends Confident New Year's Message to Employees," 31 December 1943, 3.
125. *TDT*, "District Labor Progressives Meet Sunday," 11 January 1944, 3.
126. *TDT*, "Air Gunner from Trail Downs Nazi," 6 January 1944, 1.
127. *TDT*, "Trail's Bill Strachan in on Big RCAF Attack," 31 January 1944, 3.
128. *TDT*, "Socialism in Action," 4 January 1944, 4.
129. *TDT*, "Mitchell Says Labor Has Lost Confidence," 19 January 1944, 4.
130. *TDT*, "Blaylock Outlines Future of Company as Free Enterprise," 12 January 1944, 3.
131. *TDT*, "Drake Says Blaylock Made Misrepresentation," 17 January 1944, 3.
132. *Commentator*, "Harvey Murphy Gives Other Side of Blaylock's Plea for 'Free Enterprise,'" 3 February 1944, 3.
133. *Commentator*, "New Labor Code Big Step Ahead," 29 February 1944, 2.
134. *Commentator*, "Kirkland Lake Snubbs [*sic*] Amalgamated President," 29 February 1944, 3.
135. *Commentator*, editorial,15 February 1944, 2.
136. *Commentator*, "Arthur Evans Dies Following Accident," 15 February 1944, 4.
137. Roth, "Union on the Hill," 71–2.
138. *TDT*, "CIO to Bargain in Trail," 3 June 1944, 1.
139. *TDT*, "Bargaining Group for CIO Named," 5 June 1944, 1.
140. *TDT*, "S.G. Blaylock Extends Christmas Greetings," 23 December 1944, 6.
141. *TDT*, "Blaylock Says Buchanan's Retirement Is Great Loss," 30 December 1944, 3.

3 Women War Workers and Ladies Auxiliary Politics

1. *Commentator*, "Local 480 and C.M.&S. Co. Sign Collective Bargaining Agreement," 31 January 1945, 1.
2. R.E. Stavert, "Director's Report," *CM&S Annual Report*, year ending 31 December 1945.

3. *TDT*, "Blaylock Gives Up Presidency of Consolidated," 26 April 1945, 1.
4. *TDT*, "Consolidated and Union Talk Labor Agreement," 17 June 1944, 1.
5. *TDT*, "C.M.&S. to Re-Employ 2,500 Men," 27 October 1944, 1.
6. Wendy Cuthbertson, *Labour Goes to War: The CIO and the Construction of a New Social Order, 1939–45* (Vancouver: UBC Press, 2012), 124.
7. Roth, "Union on the Hill," 89n11.
8. "Letter to Assistant Deputy Minister and Chief Inspector, Department of Labour from CM&S," 5 September 1942, Cominco Fonds, MS 2500, box 419, file 6, BC Archives.
9. *TDT*, "Women's Ready Response," 6 May 1942, 4.
10. *TDT*, "Women Join Industrial Parade," 7 May 1942, 5.
11. *TDT*, "Peek at the Week," 9 May 1942, 1.
12. *TDT*, "Women Officer Is with RCAF Recruiting Unit," 7 May 1942, 4.
13. *TDT*, "Women Must Replace Men in Canadian Industries," 8 June 1942, 5.
14. *TDT*, "Kootenay West Votes 'Yes' by 10,364 to 3,653," 28 April 1941, 1.
15. *TDT*, "Labor and Plebiscite," 4 April 1942, 4.
16. Turnbull, *Trail between Two Wars*, 81–2.
17. Larsen, "Sowing the Seeds," 29–30.
18. *Commentator*, "Women's New Role," 20 October 1942, 1–2.
19. Jean Thomson, "For the Ladies: Woman Power," *Cominco*, April 1943, 25.
20. Stavert, "Director's Report."
21. *TDT*, "War over for Canadians," 5 May 1945, 1.
22. *TDT*, "Alex B. Connell Wounded," and "Ray Scott Now Back in Canada," 5 May 1945, 1.
23. *TDT*, "'Buddy' DeVito to Arrive Soon," 8 May 1945, 1.
24. *TDT*, "W.H. Watt Back from Overseas," 2 May 1945, 1.
25. *TDT*, "Thousands Mark V-E Day at Butler Park Ceremony," 8 May 1945, 1.
26. *TDT*, "Service Here Tomorrow," 7 May 1945, 1.
27. Cuthbertson, *Labour Goes to War*, 130.
28. Joan Sangster, *Transforming Labour: Women and Work in Post-War Canada* (Toronto: University of Toronto Press, 2010), 35.
29. Allen Seager, "A History of the Mine Workers' Union of Canada, 1925–1936" (MA thesis, McGill University, 1977), 160.
30. Ruth A. Frager, "Labour History and the Interlocking Hierarchies of Class, Ethnicity, and Gender: A Canadian Perspective," *International Review of Social History* 44 (1999): 222.
31. Roth, "Union on the Hill," 58.
32. *Commentator*, editorial, 12 May 1941, 2.

33. *Commentator*, "Women and the CIO," 12 May 1941, 4.
34. Larsen, "Sowing the Seeds," 73.
35. *Commentator*, "I Heard on the Hill That," 12 August 1941, 1.
36. "Director's Report," *CM&S Annual Report*, 1944.
37. Roth, "Union on the Hill," 89n11, cites BC Department of Labour figures showing that there were 52 women war workers for the five smelting companies surveyed. The figure rose to 207 in 1944.
38. Eric W. Sager, "Women in the Industrial Labour Force: Evidence for British Columbia, 1921–53," *BC Studies* 149 (Summer 2006): 39–62, advised caution regarding the accuracy of Labour Department survey figures.
39. Larsen, "Sowing the Seeds," 72.
40. Stavert, "Director's Report."
41. Larsen, "Sowing the Seeds," 23–4.
42. *Commentator*, "Poets' Corner: To the Ladies," 20 October 1942, 4.
43. *Commentator*, "Women on the Hill," 20 October 1942, 3.
44. Roth, "Union on the Hill," 63.
45. *TDT*, "British Compliment the Work of Canadian Girls," 22 April 1942, 4.
46. *TDT*, "Chicago Women Train to Work in War Plants," 22 April 1942, 4.
47. Stavert, "Director's Report."
48. Cuthbertson, *Labour Goes to War*, 143.
49. *Commentator*, "Women in Industry," 17 May 1942, 1.
50. King with Braid, *Red Bait!*, 53.
51. Larsen, "Sowing the Seeds," 73.
52. Dorothy Sue Cobble, *The Other Women's Movement: Workplace Justice and Social Rights in Modern America* (Princeton, NJ: Princeton University Press, 2004), 13.
53. Joanne Pepper, interviews conducted while employed at CM&S/Cominco, 1977, tape T4350: 1–35, BC Archives, Cominco fonds MS 2500, cited in Larsen, "Sowing the Seeds," 65.
54. King with Braid, *Red Bait!*, 52.
55. Cobble, *Other Women's Movement*, 16.
56. Cobble, *Other Women's Movement*, 18.
57. Roth, "Union on the Hill," 89–90n11.
58. King with Braid, *Red Bait!*, 53.
59. Larsen, "Sowing the Seeds," 72.
60. Jean Stainton, interview conducted by the author, Trail, BC, 10 May 2010.
61. *TDT*, "Smelterwoman Urges Fight for the Truth," 15 April 1943, 4.

62. *TDT*, "Smelterwoman Disappointed by Union Silence," 21 April 1943, 4.

63. *TDT*, "Wherein the Times Is Severely Reprimanded," 17 March 1939, 4.

64. Cuthbertson, *Labour Goes to War*, 144.

65. Larsen, "Sowing the Seeds," 63.

66. Janis Nairne, "Smelterwomen," *Arrow*, July 1973, 9.

67. *Trail Ad-News*, "A Women's Appeal," 29 July 1943.

68. Joy Parr, *The Gender of Breadwinners: Women, Men, and Change in Two Industrial Towns* (Toronto: University of Toronto Press, 1990), 7.

69. Laurie Mercier and Jaclyn Gier, eds., *Mining Women: Gender in the Development of a Global Industry, 1670 to 2005* (New York: Palgrave Macmillan, 2006), 239.

70. Ruth Milkman, *Women, Work, and Protest: A Century of US Women's Labor History* (New York: Routledge, 1985), 5.

71. Cuthbertson, *Labour Goes to War*, 144.

72. Larsen, "Sowing the Seeds," 104.

73. *TDT*, "Legislature Told Women Industrial Workers Feel Decrease in Production," 6 March 1945, 5.

74. *Union Bulletin*, 18 April 1945.

75. *Commentator*, "Smelter Queen Contest," 3 April 1945, 1.

76. *BC District Union News*, "Bonus Won," 15 December 1945, 1.

77. *TDT*, "Ladies Only," 21 September 1946, 4; and *BC District Union News*, "Locals Condemn Disruption, Send Back Petitions," 21 January 1946, 8.

78. Laurie Mercier, "Gender, Labor, and Place: Reconstructing Women's Spaces in Industrial Communities of the Canadian and U.S. Wests," draft for an article submitted to *Labor History* 53, no. 3 (August 2012): 403.

79. Sager, "Women in the Industrial Labour Force," 59, notes that in the 1950s, married women in Canada represented 39 per cent of wage-earning women and in "manufacturing it was even higher." However, this was not reflected in Trail.

80. Ruth Roach Pierson, *They're Still Women after All: The Second World War and Canadian Womanhood* (Toronto: McClelland & Stewart, 1986), 220.

81. Donna Belisle, *Retail Nation: Department Stores and the Making of Modern Canada* (Vancouver: UBC Press, 2011), 179.

82. Susanne Klausen, "The Plywood Girls: Women and Gender Ideology at the Port Alberni Plywood Plant, 1942–1991," *Labour/Le Travail* 41 (Spring 1998): 200.

83. *TDT*, "Union Had Money for Booze, But Not Food during Mine Strike," 8 March 1939, 4.

84. *TDT*, "No Happiness from C.I.O., Asserts Smelterman's Wife," 8 March 1939, 4.

85. *TDT*, "Smelterman's Wife Tells Tragic Story of Unionism," 16 March 1939, 4.

86. *TDT*, "Worker's Wife Says There Is Much to Be Grateful For," 5 September 1940, 7.

87. *TDT*, "Catholic Church Clear on Labor Stand," 18 March 1939, 4.

88. *TDT*, "Silence Is Golden," 7 May 1942, 4.

89. Woodie Guthrie, "The Ladies Auxiliary," on *Hard Travellin'*, recorded by Moses "Moe" Asch, 1944.

90. *BC District Union News*, "Trail Ladies Get Charter," 10 July 1944, 6.

91. Larsen, "Sowing the Seeds," 79–80, quoting *Commentator*, "Smelter Women and the Union," 15 March 1943, 3.

92. Laurie Mercier, "Borders, Gender, and Labor: Canadian and U.S. Mining Towns during the Cold War Era," in *Company Towns in the Americas: Landscape, Power, and Working-Class Communities*, ed. Oliver J. Dinius and Angela Vergara (Athens: University of Georgia Press, 2011), 162, quoting from the *Report of the Proceedings of the 38th Convention*, Joplin, MO, August 1941, 9–10, 84–5.

93. *Commentator*, "Ladies Form Auxiliary," 29 April 1944, 3.

94. Mary Biner, "Wartime Regulations Have Begun to Affect Mrs. Trail's Household," *TDT*, 10 June 1942, 5.

95. Constable Black, 6 March 1950.

96. *Union*, "Calls Raiders 'Vultures,'" 24 April 1950, 4.

97. *Commentator*, "What Local 480 Means to Our Town," 29 April 1944, 3.

98. Rolf Knight, "Harvey Murphy Reminiscences 1918–1943," October 2014, unpublished interview manuscript, 51, Rare Books and Special Collections, University of British Columbia.

99. Larsen, "Sowing the Seeds," 72.

100. King with Braid, *Red Bait!*, 52.

101. Larsen, "Sowing the Seeds," 72.

102. Quinlan and Quinlan, "Textually Mediated Labour Activism," 137.

103. Quinlan and Quinlan, "Textually Mediated Labour Activism," 150.

104. Mercier, "Gender, Labor, and Place," 403.

105. Mercier, "Gender, Labor, and Place," 399.

106. Mercedes Steedman, "The Red Petticoat Brigade: Mine Mill Women's Auxiliaries and the Threat from Within, 1940s–70s," in *Whose National Security?: Canadian State Surveillance and the Creation of Enemies*, ed. G. Kinsmen, D. Buse, and M. Steedman (Toronto: Between the Lines, 2000), 55.

107. Steedman, "Red Petticoat Brigade," 68.

108. *Union*, "Prize-Winning Essay: What Being a Member of an MMSW Auxiliary Means to Me," 24 April 1950, 6.

109. Laurie Mercier, "'A Union without Women Is Only Half Organized':
     Mine Mill Women's Auxiliaries, and Cold War Politics in the North
     American Wests," in *One Step over the Line: Towards a History of
     Women in the North American Wests*, ed. Elizabeth Jameson and Sheila
     McManus (Edmonton: Athabasca University Press/University of
     Alberta Press, 2008), 7.

110. *Saturday Evening Post*, "Miner's Wife Fights Off Red Invasion of
     Union," 18 January 1947, 132.

111. Mercier, "Union without Women," 7.

112. *B.C. District Union News*, "More for Mary," 3 March 1947, 4; *B.C.
     District Union News*, "Demand Resignation," 24 March 1947, 2.

113. *B.C. District Union News*, "Auxiliary Activities," 14 April 1947, 7.

114. *TDT*, "Miner's Wife Fights Red Invasion," 16 January 1947, 4. Mary
     Orlich was married to Dan, an executive member of Local 1 in Butte
     and its one-time president.

115. *B.C. District Union News*, "An Open Letter to Mrs Mary Orlich,"
     17 January 1947, 3. Note that Murphy identifies the Tired Mucker as
     Ted Ward, "the tired-looking man with the pipe who taught me almost
     everything I know about newspaper work": *B.C. District Union News*,
     "Around the District," July 1955, 5.

116. *B.C. District Union News*, "Mason Knows the Score on This,"
     4 February 1947, 4.

117. Mercier, "Gender, Labor, and Place," 403.

118. Joan Sangster, *Dreams of Equality: Women on the Canadian Left,
     1920–1950* (Toronto: McClelland & Stewart, 1989), 236.

119. Murphy to Betty Donaldson, 13 November 1962, box 62, folder 16,
     IUMMSW Western District Union Files 1955–67, Ladies Auxiliaries,
     1962–64, Rare Books and Special Collections, University of British
     Columbia.

120. *Commentator*, "The Red Bogey," 4 June 1945, 2.

121. *TDT*, "Trail Helped in Atomic Bomb," 13 August 1945, 1.

4 Mine-Mill Courts Trail's Immigrant Enclave

1. *TDT*, "Headache for the Bankers," 21 July 1945, 4.

2. *TDT*, "A Word of Advice," 12 October 1945, 4. At the time, Laski, a
   political theorist and economist, served as chair of the British Labour
   Party. See Michael Newman, *Harold Laski: A Political Biography*
   (London: Merlin, 2010).

3. *Canada Census*, vol. 2 (1941), table 38, 637.

4. King with Braid, *Red Bait!*, 31.

5. See John Butler, *The Red Dean of Canterbury: The Public and Private Faces of Hewlett Johnson* (London: Scala Publishers, 2011).

6. See *London Free Press*, "Archbishop Seager Dies," 10 September 1948.

7. Allen Seager, "The Pass Strike of 1932," *Alberta History* 25, no. 1 (Winter 1977): 7.

8. Lynne Marks, *Infidels and the Damn Churches: Irreligion and Religion in Settler British Columbia* (Vancouver: UBC Press, 2017), 47.

9. King with Braid, *Red Bait!*, 31.

10. Norman Knowles, "'A Manly, Commonsense Religion': Revivalism and the Kootenay Campaign of 1909 in the Crowsnest Pass," in *A World Apart*, eds. Wayne Norton and Tom Langford (Kamloops, BC: Plateau, 2002), 8.

11. Knowles, "'Manly, Commonsense Religion,'" 11.

12. Jamie Forbes, "Churches," in *Trail of Memories: Trail, BC 1895–1945* (Trail, BC: Trail History and Heritage Committee, 1997), 43.

13. *Canada Census*, vol. 1 (1951), "Population: General Characteristics," table 41, 489; *Canada Census*, vol. 2 (1941), "Religious Denominations in Canada," table 38, 637.

14. *Canada Census*, vol. 2 (1941), table 38, 637.

15. Macdowell, "Career of a Canadian Trade Union Leader," 611, details Millard's religious upbringing.

16. Richard Allen, *The Social Passion: Religion and Social Reform in Canada, 1914–28* (Toronto: University of Toronto Press, 1990), 4.

17. Allen, *Social Passion*, 159.

18. *TDT*, "Communist: This Is it," 29 September 1948, 3.

19. Elsie G. Turnbull, *Trail: A Smelter City* (Langley, BC: Sunfire Publications, 1985), 13.

20. Scott, "Profusion of Issues," 61.

21. "Director's Report," *CM&S Annual Report*, 1939.

22. David Roediger, *The Wages of Whiteness: Race and the Making of the American Working Class* (London: Verso, 1999), 179.

23. Richard Hofstadter, *The Age of Reform* (New York: Vintage Books, 1955), 150.

24. *Commentator*, "The Church Speaks Out for Organized Labor," 2 November 1938, 4.

25. *Commentator*, "'Join a Union,' Priest Tells Workers," 12 July 1939, 4.

26. *Commentator*, "Catholic Priest Hits Co. Unions," 6 February 1939, 1.

27. *Commentator*, "It Is the Duty of Every Catholic to Join the Union," 23 March 1939, 3.

28. *Commentator*, "Do Your Share," 13 March 1939, 4.

29. *Commentator*, "'Join a Union,'" 4. See also Father John P. Monaghan, *Towards the Reconstruction and Christian Social Order* (Washington, DC: National Council of Catholic Men, 1939).

30. Rosswurm, "Catholic Church and Left-Led Unions," 122.

31. Rosswurm, "Catholic Church and Left-Led Unions," 120.

32. Rick Stow, interview with Robert Asher, *The Battle Within* (DVD-CD ROM), New Liskeard, ON, 1996, rev. 2010, 51.

33. Rosswurm, "Catholic Church and Left-Led Unions," 121–33.

34. Rosswurm, "Catholic Church and Left-Led Unions," 132.

35. Rosswurm, "Catholic Church and Left-Led Unions," 129.

36. Ronald W. Schatz, "'I Know My Way Around a Little Bit': Bishop Joseph Donnelly and American Labor, 1941–1977," *Labor* 12, no. 2 (2016): 37.

37. Roth, "Union on the Hill," 63.

38. *CIO News*, "CIO Wins Praise of Oregon Priest" (Mine-Mill edition), 1 May 1939, 6.

39. Rosswurm, "Catholic Church and Left-Led Unions," 130.

40. *Commentator*, "A Bishop Answers," 29 February 1944, 3.

41. *TDT*, "Catholic Church Clear on Labor Stand," 18 March 1939, 4.

42. Richard Polenberg, *One Nation Divisible: Class, Race, and Ethnicity in the United States since 1938* (New York: Viking, 1980), 38–40.

43. Avery, *"Dangerous Foreigners,"* 46.

44. King with Braid, *Red Bait!*, 37.

45. King with Braid, *Red Bait!*, 12.

46. "History of St. Andrews," St. Andrews Anglican Church, Trail, BC, https://cifpc.ca/st-andrews-united/.

47. See A.E. Smith, *All My Life – Crusade for Freedom: An Autobiography* (Toronto: Progress Books, 1949).

48. J. Petryshyn, "Class Conflict and Civil Liberties: The Origins and Activities of the Canadian Labour Defense League, 1925–1940," *Labour/Le Travailleur* 10 (Autumn 1982), 39.

49. See Stephen L. Endicott, *James G. Endicott: Rebel out of China* (Toronto: University of Toronto Press, 1980).

50. *TDT*, "A Pledge to Sabotage," 11 August 1950, 4.

51. *TDT*, "Endicott Draws Big City Group," 8 June 1950, 2.

52. *TDT*, "Catholics Cannot Vote for Communists," 43 March 1948, 4.

53. Garfield Belanger interview, conducted by Richard Bell, Kaslo, BC, 29 June 1983, BC Archives sound recordings, Labour Organizations at Cominco series, Victoria, BC, call numbers T4101:0003 and :0004. See also Sheils and Swankey, *Work and Wages*, 280.

54. Eric A. Christensen, *Labour History in British Columbia and the Right to Strike: A Case Study as Portrayed by the Labour Dispute between the International Mine, Mill and Smeltermen's Union and the Consolidated Mining and Smelting Co. Ltd. on November 15, 1917 in the City of Trail, B.C.* (Nelson, BC: Notre Dame University, 1976), 51.

55. Mercier and Gier, *Mining Women*, 173.

56. George Pozzetta, "Italian Americans: History, Early Migration, the Emergence of Little Italies, Acculturation and Assimilation," Countries and Their Cultures, https://www.everyculture.com/multi/Ha-La/Italian-Americans.html.

57. Avery, *"Dangerous Foreigners,"* 48.

58. Avery, *"Dangerous Foreigners,"* 62.

59. Avery, *"Dangerous Foreigners,"* 49.

60. *Trail News*, "Labor Meeting Brings Out a Large Crowd," 6 June 1919, 1.

61. Avery, *"Dangerous Foreigners,"* 143.

62. Polenberg, *One Nation Divisible*, 38.

63. King with Braid, *Red Bait!*, 10.

64. King with Braid, *Red Bait!*, 28.

65. C. Nelson Sparks, "Why Akron Is a Ghost City: How Strikes Brought Ruin," *Liberty*, 24 September 1938, 15.

66. *TDT*, "'I Was Yellow' D'Andrea Tells Court: Tormented by Opinion Intimidation Trial Witness Explains His Inconsistent Actions," 31 October 1938, 1.

67. *TDT*, "Twelve Beers: Louis D'Andrea, Harassed by Conflicting Emotions, Hoists a Few for Moral Support," 31 October 1938, 1.

68. Roth, "Union on the Hill," 33.

69. *TDT*, "Intimidation Case Dismissed – No Evidence – Great Mistake in the Cause of Labor Asserts MacDonald," 1 November 1938, 1.

70. *Labour Truth*, "Plight of Evans a Desperate One," December 1938, 5.

71. Harvey A. Levenstein, *Communism, Anticommunism, and the CIO* (Westport, CT: Greenwood, 1981), 332.

72. *B.C. District Union News*, "Mine Bosses' Paper, in Amazing Story, Reveals D.P. Exploitation Plans," 12 March 1948, 1.

73. Steve Rosswurm, "The Contextualisation of a Moment in CIO History: The Mine-Mill Battle in the Connecticut Brass Valley during World War II," in *Rethinking U.S. Labor History: Essays on the Working-Class Experience, 1756–2009*, ed. Donna T. Haverty-Stacke and Daniel J. Walkowiz (New York: Continuum, 2010), 169.

74. Rosswurm, "Contextualisation," 171.

75. Rosswurm, "Contextualisation," 184.

76. *Canada Census*, vol. 7 (1941), table 32, 498–9.

77. CM&S, *Book of Severances*, A Registry of Dismissals and Severances, 1928–1932, copy available at the Trail Historical Society, Trail, BC.

78. Gabriele Scardellato and Marin Sopta, eds., *Unknown Journey: A History of Croatians in Canada*, Polyphony Series 14 (Toronto: Multicultural History Society of Ontario, 1994), 16.

79. Ervin Dubrovic, *Merika: Emigration from Central Europe to America 1880–1914* (based on an exhibition at the City Museum of Rijeka, Croatia, 2008), 185, http://muzej-rijeka.hr/merika/merika.pdf.

80. Dubrovic, *Merika*, 186.

81. Anthony W. Rasporich, *For a Better Life: A History of Croatians in Canada* (Toronto: McClelland & Stewart, 1982), 69.

82. Rasporich, *Better Life*, 69.

83. Anthony W. Rasporich, "Three Generations of Croatian Immigrants in Canada: A Hartzian Perspective," in Scardellato and Sopta, *Unknown Journey*, 15.

84. Dubrovic, *Merika*, 191. See also John P. Enyeart, *Death to Fascism: Louis Adamic's Fight for Democracy* (Chicago: University of Chicago Press, 2019).

85. Rasporich, *Better Life*, 126.

86. Polenberg, *One Nation Divisible*, 55.

87. Avery, "*Dangerous Foreigners*," 117.

88. Avery, "*Dangerous Foreigners*," 140–1.

89. Greg Nesteroff, email correspondence with the author, 14 October 2011.

90. CM&S, *Book of Severances*, 1928–32.

91. *Columbian*, "They May Take the Law in Their Own Hands," 13 March 1962.

92. Despite their isolation from other groups, *Canada Census*, vol. 2 (1941), table 32, 498–9, reveals that 176 individuals of Russian descent resided in Trail in 1941, some of whom might have been former members of the radical Doukhobor sect.

93. Jeremy Mouat, *The Business of Power: Hydro-Electricity in Southeastern British Columbia, 1897–1997* (Victoria: Sono Nis, 1997), 156.

94. *TDT*, "Legion in B.C. Protesting Army Exemption Given Doukhs," 7 August 1940, 2.

95. CM&S, *Book of Severances*, notes that three Chinese cooks were dismissed in 1930 for having poor cooking skills. Others recorded their reason for leaving as poor working conditions.

96. Ronald A. Shearer, "The Chinese and Chinatown of Rossland," Rossland Museum, https://www.rosslandmuseum.ca/essays/rs-chineseofrossland?rq=shearer.

97. Patricia E. Roy, *The Triumph of Citizenship: The Japanese and Chinese in Canada, 1941–1967* (Vancouver: UBC Press, 2011), 103–4.

98. *TDT*, "Eighteen Relief Camp Workers Sentenced to One Day," 11 April 1935, 1.

99. *TDT*, "Trouble-Makers Foment Relief Demonstration," 11 June 1935, 4.

100. *Commentator*, "Canada's Debt to Russia," 25 January 1943, 2.

101. *TDT*, "Trail Italo-Canadians Reaffirm Their Loyalty," 10 June 1940, 1.

102. *TDT*, "Trail Italo-Canadians," 1.

103. *TDT*, "Trail Italians to Form Branch of Red Cross," 11 June 1940, 8.

104. Patricia K. Wood, *Nationalism from the Margins: Italians in Alberta and British Columbia* (Montreal and Kingston: McGill-Queen's University Press, 2002), 53.

105. *TDT*, "Italian Citizens Demonstrate Their Patriotism to Canada," 31 May 1940, 3.

106. *Commentator*, "Doesn't Mr. Blaylock Agree with Ernest LaPointe?" 10 June 1940, 2.

107. Belanger interview.

108. Virginio Tesolin, "*Chi siamo e chi sono*," *Commentator*, 10 April 1939, 4.

109. Leonard Tenisci in Ray Culos, *Injustice Served: The Story of British Columbia's Italian Enemy Aliens during World War II* (Vancouver: Cusmano Books, 2012), 207, describes his father's involvement with the Fascists.

110. *TDT*, "Fascist Activities in Trail?" 27 June 1941, 1.

111. *TDT*, "C.M.&S. Reports on Activities in 1945," 11 April 1946, 2. See also Stavert, "Director's Report."

112. Fred Rinaldo, "Defending Foreign Born Workers," in *The Cold War against Labor: An Anthology*, ed. Anne Fagan Ginger and David Christiano (Berkeley, CA: Meiklejohn Civil Liberties Institute, 1987), 2: 553.

113. Peter Howard, *The World Rebuilt: True Story of Frank Buchman and the Achievements of Moral Re-Armament* (New York: Duell, Sloan and Pearce, 1951), 232.

114. Daniel Sack, *Moral Re-Armament: The Reinventions of an American Religious Movement* (New York: Palgrave MacMillan, 2009), 159.

115. *TDT*, "Moral Re-Armament," 23 March 1953, 4.

116. *TDT*, "Bishop of Kootenay Tells Rotarians of Communist Weak Spot," 17 March 1949, 2.

117. *TDT*, "Churchmen Versus Communism," 19 March 1949, 4.

118. Rinaldo, "Defending Foreign Born Workers," 553.

119. Jason A. Miller, "Divided We Stand: A Study of the Development of the Conflict between the International Union of Mine, Mill and Smelter Workers and the United Steelworkers of America in Sudbury, Ontario (1942–1969)" (MA thesis, McMaster University, 2003), 135.

5 A Clash of Ideologies in the Kootenays

1. *TDT*, "Canadian Labor Clouds Are Gathering," 3 October 1945, 2; "Current Labor Unrest Is Similar to 1919 Pattern," 31 October 1945, 3.
2. *TDT*, "Canada Made War Supplies Worth $1,100,000,000," 23 January 1946, 1.
3. *TDT*, "Rose Preliminary Hearing Finishes," and "Carr Was Paid by U.S. Red Party," 26 March 1946, 1.
4. See June Callwood, *Emma: The Story of Treason* (New York: Beaufort Books, 1984).
5. *B.C. District Union News*, "Spy Scare," 1 April 1946, 4.
6. Unnamed officer, correspondence entitled "Extract – Murphy, Harvey – Strike – International Union of Mine, Mill & Smelter Workers," "E" Division, Vancouver, 19 September 1946, "Police Surveillance Files, Harvey Murphy," LAC.
7. *TDT*, "General Strike Is the Aim," 23 September 1946, 4.
8. *TDT*, "How Communist Are Unions?" 24 September 1946, 4.
9. King with Braid, *Red Bait!*, 58.
10. *Commentator*, "R.C. Billingsley Appointed Int. Rep.," and "New Organizer Asks Co-operation in Letter to Workers on the Hill," 31 January 1945, 1.
11. Claire Richard Billingsley oral history interview, conducted by Richard Bell, Trail, BC, 17 August 1983, BC Archives sound recordings, Labour Organizations at Cominco series, call numbers T4101:0011-0012.
12. King with Braid, *Red Bait!*, 54. See also Donald William Muldoon, "Capitalism Unchallenged: A Sketch of Canadian Communism, 1939–1949" (MA thesis, Simon Fraser University, 1977), for a discussion of political opportunism.
13. *B.C. District Union News*, "Don Berry," 4 February 1947, 3.
14. *TDT*, "Consolidated Employees Eat 40 Tons of Turkey," and "Trail Welcomes New Year in Gala Form," 2 January 1947, 2.
15. *TDT*, "Canadian Labor Stoppages Hit New High, 1946," 28 January 1947, 1.
16. Inspector Officer R.S.S. Wilson, "Murphy, Harvey Re: Unrest among Organized Labour in British Columbia," "E" Division, Vancouver, 2 January 1947, "Police Surveillance Files, Harvey Murphy," LAC.
17. *TDT*, "Father [Wilfrid] Brazeau Says Communism Is Society's Greatest Evil ... " 16 January 1947, 2.
18. *TDT*, "World Greets 1947 with Hope, Cheer," 2 January 1947, 2.
19. *TDT*, "Communism Splits Miners' Union" (reprinted from *Northern Miner*), 14 February 1947, 4.

20. Vernon H. Jensen, *Nonferrous Metals Industry Unionism, 1932–1954: A Story of Leadership Controversy* (New York: Cornell University Press, 1954), 51.
21. *B.C. District Union News*, "Sullivan Finds His Level," 24 March 1947, 4.
22. *TDT*, "Revolt against the Communists," 26 March 1947, 4.
23. Jack Scott, with Bryan D. Palmer, ed., *A Communist Life: Jack Scott and the Canadian Workers Movement, 1927–1985* (St. John's, NL: Committee on Canadian Labour History, 1988), 82.
24. Scott, with Palmer, *Communist Life*, 83.
25. Scott, with Palmer, *Communist Life*, 84.
26. Scott, with Palmer, *Communist Life*, 87.
27. Scott, with Palmer, *Communist Life*, 83–4.
28. Scott, with Palmer, *Communist Life*, 87.
29. *TDT*, "Communists Thrive on Apathy," 23 June 1947, 4.
30. *TDT*, "Sullivan to Release Bigger Expose of Reds," 24 July 1947, 1.
31. David Caute, *The Great Fear: The Anti-Communist Purge under Truman and Eisenhower* (New York: Simon and Schuster, 1978), 249.
32. Robert W. Cherny, William Issel, and Kieran Walsh Taylor, eds., *American Labor and the Cold War: Grassroots Politics and Postwar Political Culture* (New Brunswick, NJ: Rutgers University Press, 2004), 2.
33. Billingsley interview.
34. *Commentator*, "Fink Convention Bars Labor Press-Scab 'Federation' Born in Hamilton," 15 November 1943, 4.
35. *TDT*, "Red Tentacles Threaten Labor," 7 April 1947, 4. It is unclear whether Don Berry was a Communist, but Fred Henne was a CPC member.
36. King with Braid, *Red Bait!*, 69.
37. King with Braid, *Red Bait!*, 68.
38. John Hladun, "They Taught Me Treason," *Maclean's*, 1 October to 1 November 1947.
39. *TDT*, "Murphy Belittles McLean's [sic] Article on Communism," 3 November 1947, 3.
40. *TDT*, "Smelter Union Asks That Border Be Left Open," 18 February 1948, 4.
41. *TDT*, "'Ideal Society' Should Be Goal Says Diamond," 11 September 1947, 2.
42. King with Braid, *Red Bait!*, 71, includes quotations from the Kirkpatrick pamphlet.
43. *TDT*, "Strengthened Union Could Hit Communists," 12 February 1948, 2.
44. *TDT*, "Kirkpatrick 'Red-Baiter,'" 23 February 1948, 4.

45. *TDT*, "Get the Facts, Mr. Adamache!," 25 February 1948, 5.

46. *TDT*, "Businessman vs. Adamache," 25 February 1948, 5.

47. *TDT*, "Adamache Hits Back," 25 February 1948, 5.

48. King with Braid, *Red Bait!*, 70.

49. *TDT*, "John Hladun Looks Forward to Trail Visit," 10 March 1948, 1.

50. *TDT*, "Reds Will Find It Hard to Enter Canadian Labor," 12 March 1948, 1.

51. Abella, *Nationalism, Communism, and Canadian Labour*, 121.

52. Jack Webster, *Webster! An Autobiography by Jack Webster* (Vancouver: Douglas & McIntyre, 1990), 37.

53. Jack Webster, "Labor Lobby Split by Murphy Speech," *Vancouver Sun*, 9 April 1948, 1.

54. *TDT*, "Harvey Murphy to Face Trade Union Charges," 10 April 1948, 1–2.

55. *TDT*, "Labor Censures Harvey Murphy," 14 April 1948, 1. See William Rodney, *Soldiers of the International: A History of the Communist Party of Canada 1919–1929* (Toronto: University of Toronto Press, 1968), 162, for a short biographical note on Bruce. See also Ron Verzuh, "Proletarian Cromwell: Two Found Poems Offer Insights into One of Canada's Long-Forgotten Communist Labour Leaders," *Labour/Le Travail* 79 (Spring 2017): 185–227, which discusses in detail an early critique of Murphy by Bruce. Bruce eventually became a Trotskyite.

56. King with Braid, *Red Bait!*, 76.

57. Scott, with Palmer, *Communist Life*, 252.

58. Howard White, *A Hard Man to Beat: The Story of Bill White, Labour Leader, Historian, Shipyard Worker, Raconteur: An Oral History* (Vancouver: Pulp, 2011), 168.

59. White, *Hard Man to Beat*, 171.

60. Stephen Charles Gray, "Woodworkers and Legitimacy: The IWA in Canada, 1937–1957" (PhD diss., Simon Fraser University, 1989), 10.

61. John Stanton, *My Past Is Now: Further Memoirs of a Labour Lawyer* (St. John's, NL: Canadian Committee on Labour History, 1994), 119.

62. Bryan D. Palmer, *Working-Class Experience: The Rise and Reconstitution of Canadian Labour, 1800–1980* (Toronto: Butterworth, 1983), 245.

63. Palmer, *Working-Class Experience*, 246.

64. Palmer, *Working-Class Experience*, 252.

65. Reg Whitaker and Gary Marcuse, *Cold War Canada: The Making of a National Insecurity State, 1945–1957* (Toronto: University of Toronto Press, 1994), 316.

66. Gad Horowitz, *Canadian Labour in Politics* (Toronto: University of Toronto Press, 1968), 26.

67. Horowitz, *Canadian Labour in Politics*, 26.
68. Horowitz, *Canadian Labour in Politics*, 125.
69. See James Naylor, *The Fate of Labour Socialism: The Co-operative Commonwealth Federation and the Dream of a Working-Class Future* (Toronto: University of Toronto Press, 2016).
70. See Elections British Columbia, *Electoral History of British Columbia 1871–1986*, http://www.elections.bc.ca/docs/rpt/1871-1986_ElectoralHistoryofBC .pdf.
71. Austin F. Cross, "Tribute to a Great Canadian: An Appreciation of the Great Services Rendered to Canada by an Adopted Son ... W.K. Esling, MP," *Cominco*, November 1944, 2 and 30.
72. James Naylor, "The British Columbia CCF's Working-Class Moment: Socialism Not Populism," *Labour/Le Travail* 71 (Spring 2014): 101–21, analyses the 1933 CCF electoral victories.
73. See Parliament of Canada, *History of Federal Ridings since 1867*, http:// www.lop.parl.gc.ca/About/Parliament/FederalRidingsHistory/HFER.asp.
74. See Elections British Columbia, *Electoral History of British Columbia, 1971–1986*. See Parliament of Canada, *History of Federal Ridings since 1867*.
75. *TDT*, "Colin Cameron's Impressions of Trail," 29 May 1939, 4.
76. *TDT*, "Tim Buck Party Organizes Branch at Trail Meeting," 7 October 1943, 1.
77. *TDT*, "CCF Plus CCL," 17 September 1943, 4.
78. *TDT*, "Revolution Unnecessary," 18 September 1943, 4.
79. *TDT*, "CCF Promises," 5 October 1943, 4.
80. *TDT*, "'Orthodox' Socialism," 8 October 1943, 4.
81. *TDT*, "The Profit Motive," 9 October 1943, 4.
82. *TDT*, "Labor and the CCF," 6 October 1943, 4.
83. *TDT*, "Rossland Rejects United Labor," 17 December 1943, 4.
84. *TDT*, "Writer Raps CCF for Failure to Stop Red-Baiting," 9 December 1943, 4.
85. *Commentator*, "The Union and Political Action," 31 January 1945, 2.
86. *Commentator*, "Unions and Politics," 13 January 1944, 4.
87. *TDT*, "CCF Attacks Preference for Soldiers," 25 October 1944, 4.
88. *Commentator*, "A Popular Candidate," 27 November 1944, 2.
89. *TDT*, "Drake Presents Labor Progressive Stand on Herridge," 6 November 1944, 4.
90. *TDT*, "Mr. Winch Is Persuasive," 16 May 1945, 4.
91. See Maurice Hodgson, *The Squire of Kootenay West: The Biography of Bert Herridge* (Surrey, BC: Hancock House, 1976), for details on Herridge's long political career.

92. *TDT*, "Communist Party Backs Herridge in June 11 Election," 22 May 1945, 1. Thomas Alsbury would become Mayor of Vancouver in 1959.
93. *TDT*, "Mr. Herridge Has Been Tagged," 23 May 1945, 4.
94. Naylor, *Fate of Labour Socialism*, 244.
95. *TDT*, "Which Serves Our Country Best? – Fear Based on Slander or Reason Based on Facts," 29 May 1945, 3.
96. *TDT*, "Angus MacInnis Says Herridge Defiance Was Repudiation of the CCF," 31 May 1945, 3. See King with Braid, *Red Bait!*, 48.
97. *TDT*, "Kootenay West's Member," 13 June 1945, 4.
98. Isitt, *Militant Majority*, 92.
99. *TDT*, "CCF No Longer Political Voice of Trail's Local 480," 10 March 1949, 1.
100. Walter Stewart, *The Life and Political Times of Tommy Douglas* (Toronto: McArthur, 2003), 179–83.
101. *TDT*, "CCF Breaks with People's Group," 16 July 1945, 1.
102. *TDT*, "Expelled Members of CCF Reply to B.C. Executive," 21 July 1945, 4.
103. *TDT*, "It's up to Business Men," 31 July 1945, 4.
104. Naylor, *Fate of Labour Socialism*, 314.
105. *TDT*, "The Communists Win in Defeat," 31 October 1945, 4.
106. Remo Morandini interview, conducted by Richard Bell, Castlegar, BC, 10 October 1983, BC Archives sound recordings, Labour Organizations at Cominco series, call numbers T4101:0020 and :0021.
107. *TDT*, "CCFers Strong for Soviet," 19 October 1946, 4.
108. Isitt, *Militant Majority*, 90.
109. Al Warrington interview, conducted by Richard Bell, Kaslo, BC, 29 June 1983, BC Archives sound recordings, Labour Organizations at Cominco series, call numbers T4101:0017, :0018, and :0019.
110. Tom Langford and Chris Frazer, "The Cold War and Working-Class Politics in the Coal Mining Communities of the Crowsnest Pass, 1945–1958," *Labour/Le Travail* 49 (Spring 2002): 48.
111. King with Braid, *Red Bait!*, 35.
112. Horowitz, *Canadian Labour in Politics*, 129.
113. Issit, *Militant Majority*, 87.
114. See Jerry Lembcke, "The International Woodworkers of America in British Columbia, 1942–1953," *Labour/Le Travailleur* 6 (Autumn 1980): 113–48, for a detailed account of the split.
115. Stephen Charles Gray, "Woodworkers and Legitimacy: The IWA in Canada, 1937–1957" (PhD diss., Simon Fraser University, 1989), 222.
116. Gray, "Woodworkers and Legitimacy," 14–15.
117. Issit, *Militant Majority*, 55, discusses the Red Wars in detail.

118. Gray, "Woodworkers and Legitimacy," 403.
119. Elaine Bernard, "The Rod Young Affair in the British Columbia Co-operative Commonwealth Federation" (MA thesis, University of British Columbia, 1979), 79.
120. Isitt, *Militant Majority*, 93.
121. *TDT*, "Controversial CCF'er Rod Young Resigns," 12 July 1954, 3.
122. David Lewis, *The Good Fight: Political Memoirs, 1909–1958* (Toronto: Macmillan, 1981), 150.
123. Lewis, *Good Fight*, 150.
124. Leo Panitch and Donald Swartz, "Towards Permanent Exceptionalism: Coercion and Consent in Canadian Industrial Relations," *Labour/Le Travail* 13 (Spring 1984): 133–57.
125. Naylor, *Fate of Labour Socialism*, 133.
126. Isitt, *Militant Majority*, 94.
127. See Judith Stepan-Norris and Maurice Zeitlin, *Left Out: Reds and America's Industrial Unions* (Cambridge, MA: Cambridge University Press, 2003), 14–15.
128. Unnamed agent, "Harvey Murphy," secret police report, 1 October 1948, includes *Pacific Tribune*, "Murphy Blasts 'CCF News' Smear on IWA Conciliation Board Award," 1 October 1948.
129. Corporal J.S. Connors, "Harvey Murphy," "K" Division, Lethbridge, AB, 16 June 1948.
130. *TDT*, "5000 Workers Removed from Fold of C.C.L.," 25 August 1948, 1.
131. *TDT*, "Harvey Murphy Says 'Reinstatement Should Not Be Too Difficult,'" 26 August 1948, 1.
132. Billingsley interview.
133. *TDT*, "Harvey Murphy All Washed Up," 16 September 1948, 4.
134. *TDT*, "23 Powerful TLC Unions Guarantee to Back Drive against Communists," 3 September 1948, 1.
135. *TDT*, "Trail Man Refused U.S. Entry," 15 September 1948, 1.
136. *TDT*, "Reds Feel the Pinch: Industrial Relations Harmonious as Canadian Wages Hit New Peaks," 30 December 1948, 5.
137. Jensen, *Nonferrous Metals Industry Unionism*, 296.
138. *TDT*, "Unions and Politics," 18 August 1953, 4.
139. *Commentator*, "Unions and Politics," 1 September 1953, 1.

6 Steel's Cold Warriors Raid Trail's Red Union

1. *TDT*, "Margarine Hitting Butter Price," 3 March 1949, 1.
2. *TDT*, "World Premiere of Cominco Film All Set for April 19," 5 April 1949, 2.

3. *TDT*, "Do Reds Run Local 480?," 10 February 1949, 4.
4. *TDT*, "Be an Active Union Member," 14 February 1949, 3.
5. *TDT*, "An Active Union Member Speaks," 14 February 1949, 3.
6. *TDT*, "Is Local 480 Commie Tool?," 16 February 1949, 2.
7. *TDT*, "Weed Again," 18 February 1949, 2.
8. *TDT*, "Trail Times Clouds Issue," 21 February 1949, 4.
9. *TDT*, "Re-stating the Issue," 28 February 1949, 1.
10. See Bruce Mickleburgh, "Consolidated Prepares an Inside Job," *Pacific Tribune*, 11 March 1949, 5; and Mickleburgh, "The War Scare Pays Off – For Consolidated," *Pacific Tribune*, 18 March 1949, 5.
11. *TDT*, "The Threat Is Ominous," 31 March 1949, 1.
12. *TDT*, "C.M.&S. Sacks Four Local Employees; Union Orders Probe," 1 April 1949, 1.
13. King with Braid, *Red Bait!*, 73.
14. *TDT*, "Reds Condemned by Kimberley Workers in Protest Ballot," 4 April 1949, 2.
15. *B.C. District Union News*, "Fear Rule Back to Trail with Board Decision," 27 June 1949, 1.
16. *B.C. District Union News*, "Fear Rule Back to Trail," 1.
17. King with Braid, *Red Bait!*, 70.
18. Billingsley interview.
19. *B.C. District Union News*, "Billingsley Is President and McGhee Secretary in B.C. Ballot Results," 17 May 1949, 1.
20. *TDT*, "Murphy Ouster Is Foreseen as Result of Vote," 25 April 1949, 1.
21. *B.C. District Union News*, "From Our Mistakes, Too," 27 May 1949, 4.
22. *TDT*, "Communists Licked in Union Election," 7 July 1949, 1.
23. King with Braid, *Red Bait!*, 69.
24. *TDT*, "Crucial Days for Local 480," 4 October 1949, 4.
25. *TDT*, "Smelter Union Loses Good Standing in CIO," 17 December 1949, 1.
26. *TDT*, "Industrial Relations Harmonious as Canadian Wages Hit New Peak," 30 December 1949, 5.
27. *TDT*, "W.A. Curran Named Managing Director of Nelson Daily News," 31 December 1949, 1.
28. King with Braid, *Red Bait!*, 72.
29. *TDT*, "H-Bomb Is Approved by Truman," 31 January 1950, 1.
30. *TDT*, "Democrats Retain Control Despite Republican Gains: Slim Margin May Hamper Program of Harry Truman," 8 November 1950, 1.
31. *TDT*, "Atomic Mystery Man," 11 January 1950, 4.
32. *TDT*, "'You Can Survive!': Civilians Receive Tips on A-Bomb Precautions," 30 October 1950, 1.

33. *TDT*, "Steel Union Would Oust Mine-Mill: CCL Plans to Organize Unemployed," 20 January 1950, 1.
34. Solski and Smaller, *Mine-Mill*, 126.
35. Abella, *Nationalism, Communism, and Canadian Labour*, 67.
36. Abella, *Nationalism, Communism, and Canadian Labour*, 163.
37. Abella, *Nationalism, Communism, and Canadian Labour*, 221.
38. See John Stanton, *The Life and Death of the Canadian Seamen's Union* (Toronto: Steel Rail Educational Publishing, 1978).
39. Judith Stepan-Norris, "Strangers to Their Own Class?" *Sociological Inquiry* 68, no. 3 (August 1998): 340.
40. Stanton, *My Past Is Now*, 116.
41. Solski and Smaller, *Mine-Mill*, 126.
42. John B. Lang, "A Lion in a Den of Daniels: A History of the International Union of Mine, Mill and Smelter Workers in Sudbury, Ontario 1942–1962" (MA thesis, University of Guelph, 1970), 129.
43. King with Braid, *Red Bait!*, 70.
44. King with Braid, *Red Bait!*, 75.
45. Billingsley interview.
46. King with Braid, *Red Bait!*, 75.
47. Solski and Smaller, *Mine-Mill*, 126.
48. Billingsley interview.
49. King with Braid, *Red Bait!*, 81.
50. King with Braid, *Red Bait!*, 79.
51. *TDT*, "Local President Praises CIO Action in Expelling Mine, Mill," 16 February 1950, 2.
52. *TDT*, "Mine-Mill," 16 February 1950, 4.
53. *TDT*, "Murphy Replies," 9 February 1950, 1.
54. King with Braid, *Red Bait!*, 80.
55. King with Braid, *Red Bait!*, 82–3.
56. *B.C. District Union News*, "Same Old Company Union Gang Goes Steel, Where They Must Feel at Home," 7 March 1950, 3.
57. *B.C. District Union News*, "Percy Berry Broadcasts [*sic*] Reflects General Opinion of Trail Populace," 14 August 1950, 8.
58. *B.C. District Union News*, "Loyal Workers Repulse Trail Seceders, Raiders, New Officers Take Over," 7 March 1950, 1.
59. *B.C. District Union News*, "Trail Meeting Blasts CIO-CCL Policy of Ruin," 7 March 1950, 1.
60. *B.C. District Union News*, "Kimberley Knows the Score," 7 March 1950, 4.
61. *TDT*, "Consistency Thou Art a Jewel," 22 February 1950, 6.
62. *TDT*, "'Raider' Tactics Blasted at Mass Meeting," 20 February 1950, 3.

63. *TDT*, "Why the C.I.O. Expelled Mine, Mill," 21 February 1950, 6.
64. Billingsley interview.
65. Constable J.G.E. Murray, "Subversive Activities of I.U.M.M.& S.W.," RCMP Detachment, Grand Forks, BC, 12 April 1950, "Police Surveillance Files, Harvey Murphy," LAC.
66. *TDT*, "The Cat's out of the Bag," 24 March 1950, 1.
67. *TDT*, "King Convicted after Assault," 17 March 1950, 6.
68. *TDT*, "Cominco Profits Hit $41,588,033," 13 April 1950, 1. Allowing for inflation, that figure would become $448,534,066 in 2021.
69. *TDT*, "Organized Labor Supports Mine-Mill," 6 April 1950, 5.
70. Constable Murray's report, 12 April 1950; Endicott, *Raising the Workers' Flag*, on Buhay, 161.
71. Constable Murray's report, 6 March 1950.
72. *B.C. District Union News*, "Auxiliary Activities," 23 October 1950, 7.
73. Constable Murray's report, 14 March 1950.
74. Constable Murray's report, 13 March 1950.
75. *Pacific Tribune*, "Byrnes [sic] Backs Mine-Mill in House, 7 April 1950, 4.
76. *TDT*, "Steel Wins 13¢ an Hour Increase!," 3 May 1950, 6.
77. *TDT*, "Beat Them at Their Own Game!," 29 May 1950, 4.
78. *TDT*, "Steel Certification Refused: Membership Said Not in Good Standing," 6 May 1950, 1.
79. *TDT*, "Some Companies Dealing with Reds to Save a Few Cents, Say Steelmen," 12 May 1950, 2
80. *B.C. District Union News*, "Refuge of Scoundrels," 11 July 1950, 4.
81. *TDT*, "Appeal by Steel Is Ordered," 9 May 1950, 2.
82. King with Braid, *Red Bait!*, 83. See also *B.C. District Union News*, "Local 480 Case against Bolters up in Fall," 11 July 1950, 1.
83. *Union*, "Auxiliaries: Trail," 5 June 1950, 5.
84. *B.C. District Union News*, "Trail Celebration Is Unqualified Success," 11 July 1950, 1.
85. *TDT*, "TLC Orders Affiliates to Oust Red Officers," 16 September 1950, 5.
86. *TDT*, "Canadian Reds Claimed Set to Wage Underground Fight," 10 November 1950, 1.
87. *TDT*, "Canadian Underground," 13 November 1950, 4.
88. *TDT*, "Cominco Boosts Wages 7½¢," 22 December 1950, 1; *TDT*, "Contracts and Unions," 17 November 1950, 4, in which the *Times* argues against such an increase.
89. See Katherine G. Aiken, *Idaho's Bunker Hill: The Rise and Fall of a Great Mining Company, 1885–1981* (Norman: University of Oklahoma Press, 2005).

90. Jensen, *Nonferrous Metals Industry Unionism*, 277–8.
91. Jensen, *Nonferrous Metals Industry Unionism*, 293.
92. Stepan-Norris and Zeitlin, *Left Out*, 320.
93. Laurie Mercier, "Instead of Fighting the Common Enemy": Mine-Mill versus the Steelworkers in Montana, 1950–1967," *Labor History* 40, no. 4 (1999): 473.
94. Mercier, "Instead of Fighting the Common Enemy," 478.
95. Jensen, *Nonferrous Metals Industry Unionism*, 275.
96. Robert S. Keitel, "The Merger of the International Union of Mine, Mill and Smelter Workers into the United Steelworkers of America," *Labor History* (Winter 1974): 37.
97. Joseph Robert Starobin, *American Communism in Crisis, 1943–1957* (Oakland: University of California Press, 1975), 203.
98. *B.C. District Union News*, "Around the District Union," 13 July 1951, 7.
99. *TDT*, "Trail's Buying Power Is Shown 51% above Average for Canada," 13 August 1951, 1.
100. *B.C. District Union News*, "It's the Steelworkers and Company vs. Mine, Mill," 26 February 1951, 6.
101. *TDT*, "They Flee the Reds," 8 January 1951, 4.
102. *TDT*, "Denies Nonsense," 2 March 1951, 4.
103. *B.C. District Union News*, "It's the Steelworkers and Company vs. Mine, Mill," 26 February 1951, 6.
104. This note covers this and all other quotations from the *Maclean's* article by Pierre Berton, "How a Red Union Bosses Atom Workers at Trail, B.C.," *Maclean's*, 1 April 1951, 7–10.
105. Pierre Berton, "How a Red Union Bosses Atom Workers at Trail, B.C.," *Maclean's*, 1 April 1951, 8.
106. Morris Wright, "Raiding Mine-Mill," in Ginger and Christiano, *Cold War against Labor*, 612.
107. This note covers this and all further references to *B.C. District Union News*, "The Cheerful Cynic," and "Maclean's Mistake," 30 April 1951, 2.
108. *TDT*, "Labor Board Refuses to Rehear Steel Application," 7 May 1951, 1.
109. *TDT*, "CCL Says Ruling Denial of Rights," 10 May 1951, 2.
110. *B.C. District Union News*, "They Got Their Due," 28 May 1951, 1.
111. *TDT*, "Wages Are Your Business," 1 June 1951, 2.
112. *TDT*, "Cominco and Union Agree on 17.5-Cent Hourly Boost," 30 June 1951, 1.
113. *TDT*, "Gargrave Replies," 26 July 1951, 4.
114. *TDT*, "CCL Floors Red Fringe in Opening Meet Tussle," 18 September 1951, 3.

115. *TDT*, "Steel Statement Hits Labor Relations Board," 7 September 1951, 3.
116. *TDT*, "Cominco Would Bar Reds from Union Office," 6 September 1951, 1.
117. *TDT*, "A Blow for Mr. Murphy," 10 September 1951, 4.
118. *TDT*, "Murphy Blasts Cominco's Proposals to ICA Board," 7 September 1951, 1 and 4.
119. *TDT*, "Steel's Opinion," 13 September 1951, 4.
120. *Vancouver Sun*, "Battle with Murphy Costs Half-Million," 22 September 1951, 25, acknowledges the payment.
121. *B.C. District Union News*, "The Truth Is Out," 28 September 1951, 5.
122. Sangster, "Canada's Cold War in Fur," 18.
123. *TDT*, "Steel Union Plans Intensive Campaign; Mine-Mill Unconcerned," 29 October 1951, 2.
124. *B.C. District Union News*, "A New Deal for Steel?," 31 October 1951, 4.
125. *Pacific Tribune*, "Arbitration Board Deals with Firing of Trail Workers," 23 November 1951, 6.
126. *TDT*, "Unionist Hurt, Slander Suit Threatened," 13 November 1951, 1.
127. *TDT*, "The Labor Board," 29 November 1951, 4.
128. *TDT*, "Einstein Renews Plea for Authority to Protect Mankind against A-Bomb," 6 March 1952, 6.
129. *TDT*, "Communism," 26 January 1951, 5.
130. *TDT*, "No Communists," 28 January 1952, 4.
131. *TDT*, "To All Workers on the Hill," 16 January 1952, 8.
132. *TDT*, "To the Workers on the Hill," 18 April 1952, 2.
133. *TDT*, "The Hollinger Story," 3 May 1952, 3.
134. *TDT*, "A Statement," 11 March 1952, 5.
135. *TDT*, "CCF Compromised," 15 May 1952, 4.
136. *TDT*, "Mine-Mill Wins Union Vote in Trail," 15 May 1952, 1.
137. *TDT*, "Decisive Vote," 16 May 1952, 4.
138. Fred McNeil, "Mine Mill Keeps Trail," *Vancouver Sun*, 15 May 1952, 1.
139. *TDT*, "Union Issue Flares Anew; Mine-Mill Pickets Wrong Spot," 4 June 1952, 1.
140. King with Braid, *Red Bait!*, 114.
141. Stanton, *My Past Is Now*, 102.
142. Stanton, *My Past Is Now*, 103.
143. Stanton, *My Past Is Now*, 106.
144. Stanton, *My Past Is Now*, 115–16.
145. See interview with Charles Millard, conducted by Jack Spiese, 13 February 1968, 25. Copy obtained from the Pennsylvania State University, Historical Collections and Labor Archives.

146. *Vancouver Sun,* "Mine and Smelter Workers Urged to Oust Red Leaders," 30 December 1952, 1.

147. H. Keith Ralston, review of Maurice Hodgson, *The Squire of Kootenay West: A Biography of Bert Herridge* (Saanichton, BC: Hancock House Publishers, 1976), *BC Studies* 38 (Summer 1978): 71.

148. Gerald Zahavi, "'Who's Going to Dance with Somebody Who Calls You a Mainstreeter?': Communism, Culture, and Community in Sheridan County, Montana, 1918–1934," *Great Plains Quarterly* 16 (Fall 1996): 272.

149. *Pacific Tribune,* "LPP Candidates Contest Kootenay West, East Seats," 17 July 1953, 7.

150. *Pacific Tribune,* "How British Columbia Voted," 14 August 1953, 6.

7 Resisting Canadian McCarthyism in British Columbia

1. *Commentator,* "Jottings from Ottawa," February 1954, 5.

2. *Commentator,* "Keep McCarthyism out of Canada!," February 1954, 6.

3. *TDT,* "Wives Help," 3 December 1953, 4.

4. *TDT,* "Labor Front Is Rocked by Major Strike Wave," 2 October 1953, 1.

5. *TDT,* "Pill Gives Protection against A-bomb Death," 7 April 1953, 2.

6. *TDT,* "Walsh Tells of Red Sabotage Plans," 28 February 1953, 1.

7. *TDT,* "Full-Scale War on Communists by RC Church Set Off by Laborite," 23 March 1953, 4.

8. See David Lethbridge, "Jew-Haters and Red-Baiters: The Canadian League of Rights," *AntiFa Info-Bulletin,* 2 February 1999, 1–6.

9. *TDT,* "Canada's Last Red-Led Union Is Suspended by Congress," 22 August 1953, 1.

10. *Commentator,* "Harry Bridges Calls for Political Action," 13 March 1939, 4.

11. *Vancouver Sun,* "Paul Robeson 'under Domestic Arrest,'" 1 February 1952, 2.

12. *Pacific Tribune,* "Robeson to Sing at Peace Arch on May 18," 3 February 1952, 12.

13. *B.C. District Union News,* "Slap at Freedom," 11 February 1952, 3.

14. *Vancouver Sun,* "Ban on Robeson Trip Here Strictly Matter for U.S.," 1 February 1952, 1.

15. Mari Jo Buhle, Paul Buhle, and Dan Georgakas, eds., *Encyclopedia of the American Left* (Chicago: University of Illinois Press, 1990), 655.

16. Martin Duberman, *Paul Robeson: A Biography* (New York: New Press, 1989), 394 and 391.

17. Mark Kristmanson, *Plateaus of Freedom: Nationality, Culture, and State Security in Canada, 1940–1960* (Toronto: Oxford University Press, 2003), 212.

18. Reg Whitaker, *Double Standard: The Secret History of Canadian Immigration* (Toronto: Lester and Orpen Denys, 1987), 169.

19. See Raymond Arsenault, *The Sound of Freedom: Marian Anderson, the Lincoln Memorial, and the Concert That Awakened America* (New York: Bloomsbury, 2010).

20. Karl Evanzz, *The Messenger: The Rise and Fall of Elijah Muhammad* (New York: Knopf Doubleday, 2011), 224–5.

21. Buhle, Buhle, and Georgakas, *Encyclopedia*, 656.

22. Laurel Sefton MacDowell, "Paul Robeson in Canada: A Border Story," *Labour/Le Travail* 51 (Spring 2003): 177.

23. Buhle, Buhle, and Georgakas, *Encyclopedia*, 601.

24. See Ryan Bernard Porth, "Why Clarence Clemons Died: Power, Narrative, and the Death of a 'Negro Longshoreman' in Vancouver, 1952–1953" (MA thesis, University of British Columbia, 2003).

25. *TDT*, "Union Official Refused Admission to Canada," 15 October 1953, 1.

26. Ginger and Christiano, *The Cold War against Labor*, 2:653.

27. Ginger and Christiano, *Cold War against Labor*, 2:657.

28. *B.C. District Union News*, "Victory at Trail Gives Fresh Impetus to CM&S Mine, Mill Negotiations," 6 June 1952, 1.

29. *B.C. District Union News*, "Victory," citing the *Pacific Tribune* article.

30. *Union*, "30,000 Hear Robeson Border Concert Sponsored by Canadian Mine-Mill," 2 June 1952, 3.

31. *TDT*, "Paul Robeson Sings at Border," 19 May 1952, 1.

32. Videotaped interview with Elmer Pontius conducted by the author, 19 July 2010, in Trail, BC.

33. See Ron Verzuh, "Mine-Mill's Peace Arch Concerts: How a 'Red' Union and a Famous Singer-Activist Fought for Peace and Social Justice during the Cold War," *BC Studies* 174 (Summer 2012): 61–99.

34. Album cover notes, "I Came to Sing: Paul Robeson Peace Arch Program."

35. *Commentator*, "Paul Robeson Sings," June 1954, 8.

36. *Commentator*, "Why the Annual Robeson Concerts Sponsored by Mine Mill in Canada?" July 1954, 8.

37. MacDowell, "Paul Robeson," 10.

38. Isitt, *Militant Majority*, 67.

39. See Judy Fudge and Eric Tucker, *Labour before the Law: The Regulation of Workers' Collective Action in Canada, 1900–1948* (Toronto: Oxford University Press, 2001).

40. *Vancouver Province*, "Steel Union to Battle Mine-Mill," 19 December 1953, 1.

41. *TDT*, "Senator Wants McCarthy Spending Budget Slashed," 5 January 1954, 1.

42. *TDT*, "Red Debate Challenge Accepted by Murphy," 21 January 1954, 1.

43. Among many others, see Paul Buhle and Patrick McGilligan, *Tender Comrades: A Backstory of the Hollywood Blacklist* (New York: St. Martin's, 1997).

44. See Ron Verzuh, "Remembering Salt: How a Blacklisted Hollywood Movie Brought the Spectre of McCarthyism to a Small Canadian Town," *Labour/Le Travail* 76 (Fall 2015): 165–98.

45. *B.C. District Union News*, "Anita Torres Tells of Jencks' Battle to Free Her People," 29 January 1954, 3.

46. *Commentator*, "Anita Torres," *February* 1954, 5.

47. Whitaker and Marcuse, *Cold War Canada*, 348.

48. Larry Hannant, *The Infernal Machine: Investigating the Loyalty of Canada's Citizens* (Toronto: University of Toronto Press, 1995), 85.

49. David MacKenzie, *Canada's Red Scare 1945–1957*, Historical Booklet No. 61 (Ottawa: Canadian Historical Association, 2001), 10.

50. Caute, *Great Fear*, 368.

51. Gregory D. Black, *Hollywood Censored: Morality Codes, Catholics, and the Movies* (Cambridge, MA: Cambridge University Press, 1994), 1.

52. Black, *Hollywood Censored*, 7, quoting Kay Solan, *The Loud Silents: Origins of the Social Problem Film* (Chicago: University of Illinois Press, 1988).

53. See Thomas Doherty, *Hollywood's Censor: Joseph I. Breen and the Production Code Administration* (New York: Columbia University Press, 2007).

54. Buhle, Buhle, and Georgakas, *Encyclopedia*, 846.

55. Ellen Schrecker, *Many Are the Crimes: McCarthyism in America* (New York: Little, Brown, 1998), 331.

56. James J. Lorence, *The Suppression of Salt of the Earth: How Hollywood, Big Labor, and Politicians Blacklisted a Movie in Cold War America* (Albuquerque: University of New Mexico Press, 1999), 1.

57. Ellen R. Baker, *On Strike and on Film: Mexican American Families and Blacklisted Filmmakers in Cold War America* (Chapel Hill: University of North Carolina Press, 2007), 251.

58. See Paul Buhle and Dave Wagner, *Radical Hollywood: The Untold Story behind America's Favorite Movies* (New York: New Press, 2002).

59. *TDT*, "Vigilante Action Proposed by W. Kootenay Trainmen," 4 August 1953, 3; *Commentator*, "Track Blasting: Who's to Blame," 5 October 1953, 3.

60. Lorence, *Suppression of Salt of the Earth*, back cover.

61. *Union*, "'Salt of the Earth' Finally on Screen! Packs N.Y. Theater Every Performance," 29 March 1954, 4.

62. Herbert Biberman, *Salt of the Earth: The Story of a Film* (Boston: Beacon, 1965), 184.

63. Biberman, *Salt of the Earth*, 184.

64. *Commentator*, "When Is It Coming?," June 1954, 6.

65. See Glenn Frankel, *High Noon: The Hollywood Blacklist and the Making of an American Classic* (New York: Bloomsbury, 2017).

66. *Union*, "Canadians Like 'Salt of the Earth': UAW Float, Legion Band Hail Picture," 27 September 1954, 12.

67. *B.C. District Union News*, "Around the District Union," September 1954, 4–5.

68. *B.C. District Union News*, "Veteran MLA Praises 'Salt of the Earth,'" September 1954, 5.

69. Michael Denning, *The Cultural Front: The Laboring of American Culture in the Twentieth Century* (New York: Verso, 1997), xvii.

70. Promotional brochure circulated before the film's New York premiere at the Grande Theater in Manhattan.

71. Carl R. Weinberg, "*Salt of the Earth*: Labor, Film, and the Cold War," *Magazine of History*, 24, no. 4 (October 2010): 43. https://doi.org /10.1093/maghis/24.4.41.

72. Weinberg, "*Salt of the Earth*," 44.

73. Baker, *On Strike*, 244.

74. John Clark, "The President's Corner: I Tasted 'Salt of the Earth,'" *Union*, 4 January 1954, 2.

75. George B. Casey, "The Open Forum: Thanks from an Old-Timer," *Union*, 12 October 1953, 5.

76. King with Braid, *Red Bait!*, 66–7.

77. *B.C. District Union News*, "Around the District Union," November 1954, 4–5.

78. *Commentator*, "'Salt of the Earth,'" November 1954, 4.

79. *TDT*, "Salt of the Earth" (ad), 13 December 1954, 9.

80. *Commentator*, "Local 480 Mine-Mill Presents" (ad), December 1954, 5.

81. *Union*, "Castlegar Movie Packed for 'Salt of the Earth,'" 3 January 1955, 12.

82. *Commentator*, "'Salt of the Earth,'" *September* 1954, 6. For more on Nobes and other worker poets, see Verzuh, "Smelter Poets."

83. See Aaron Leonard, "The Bureau and the Journalist: Victor Riesel's Secret Relationship with the FBI," *Truthout*, 14 February 2014.

84. Lorence, *Suppression*, 78.

85. See Victor Navasky, *Naming Names* (New York: Viking, 1980). For specific details on the Dmytryk betrayal, see Larry Ceplair and Steven Englund, *The Inquisition in Hollywood: Politics in the Film Community 1930–1960* (Garden City, NY: Anchor/Doubleday, 1980). See also Ron Verzuh, "Hollywood Turncoat," *Boundary Historical Society Report*, Grand Forks Historical Society, Grand Forks, BC, 2015, 79–83.

86. *Commentator*, "Butler-Brownell-Humphrey," October 1954, 7. For a brief outline of the act, see Carl Auerbach, "Communist Control Act of 1954," Encyclopedia.com, 9 March 2014, https://www.encyclopedia.com/history/encyclopedias-almanacs-transcripts-and-maps/communist-control-act-1954.

87. "Subversive Activities in I.U.M.M.&S.W. Trail, B.C.," secret police report by Constable J.J.E.R. Boissonneault, Nelson Special Branch, 3 December 1954, "Police Surveillance Files, Harvey Murphy," LAC.

88. *Vancouver Province*, "Steel Union to Battle Mine Mill," 19 January 1955, 1.

89. *TDT*, "U.S. Should Use Atom Bomb If Attacked," 3 January 1955, 2.

90. *TDT*, "Bomb Test Danger Point Has Scientists Worried," 7 March 1955, 2.

91. *TDT*, "Communist Change of Nature Doesn't Render It Harmless," 21 January 1955, 4.

92. *B.C. District Union News*, "He Likes 'Salt,'" May 1955, 5.

93. *B.C. District Union News* "Delegates Unanimously Endorse Canadian Autonomy Proposal," March 1955, 1.

94. *Labour Organization in Canada*, 44th Annual Report, Department of Labour, table X, 1 January 1955, 17.

95. *B.C. District Union News*, "Rossland Hall Again Throbs to History as Canadian Autonomy Becomes Fact," July 1955, 1.

96. Schrecker, *Many Are the Crimes*, 334.

97. *TDT*, "Union Leader School Urged by Convention," 20 July 1955, 1.

Conclusion

1. King with Braid, *Red Bait!*, 132.

2. Endicott, *Raising the Workers' Flag*, 126.

3. See transcript of "Debate btw Harvey Murphy & Larry Sefton," Northern Ontario Labour Industrial Relations Archives, file P009, Laurentian University Archives, 15.

4. Jensen, *Nonferrous Metals Industry Unionism*, 121.

5. Allen Seager, "Memorial to a Departed Friend of the Working Man," *Bulletin of the Committee on Canadian Labour History* 4 (Autumn 1977): 12.

6. Denning, *The Cultural Front*, 21.

7. E.P. Thompson, *The Making of the English Working Class* (London: Penguin, 1963), 8.

8. Daisy de Jong Webster, *Growth of the NDP in BC, 1900–1970* (Vancouver: Broadway Printers, 1970), 26.

9. Robert H. Zieger, *The CIO 1935–1955* (Chapel Hill: University of North Carolina Press, 1995), 374.

10. Michael Petrou, *Renegades: Canadians in the Spanish Civil War* (Vancouver: UBC Press, 2008), provides new information on the enlistments to be found in Soviet files. However, none were identified as coming from Trail.

11. Jensen, *Nonferrous Metals Industry Unionism*, 297.

12. Randi Storch, *Red Chicago: American Communism at Its Grassroots, 1928–35* (Chicago: University of Illinois Press, 2007).

13. See Bert Cochran, *Labor and Communism: The Conflict That Shaped American Labor Unions* (Princeton, NJ: Princeton University Press, 1977).

14. Levenstein, *Communism, Anticommunism, and the CIO*, 335.

15. Ian Angus, *Canadian Bolsheviks: The Early Years of the Communist Party of Canada* (Montreal: Trafford Publishing, 1981); Ivan Avakumovic, *The Communist Party in Canada: A History* (Toronto: McClelland & Stewart, 1975); Norman Penner, *Canadian Communism: The Stalin Years and Beyond* (Toronto: Methuen, 1988); and Rodney, *Soldiers of the International*.

16. See John Stanton, *Never Say Die!: The Life and Times of John Stanton – A Pioneer Labour Lawyer* (Ottawa: Steel Rail Publishing, 1987). See also White, *Hard Man to Beat*.

17. Lita-Rose Betcherman, *A Little Band: The Clashes between the Communists and the Political and Legal Establishment in Canada, 1928–1932* (Toronto: Deneau, 1982), 216.

18. Jensen, *Nonferrous Metals Industry Unionism*, ix.

19. Videotaped interview with Bill King, conducted by the author, Fruitvale, BC, 19 November 2014.

20. Levenstein, *Communism, Anticommunism, and the CIO*, 331.
21. See Fudge and Tucker, *Labour before the Law*.

Epilogue

1. Interview with Judy Davidson (née Judith Ann Hall), S.G. Blaylock's granddaughter, conducted by author 6 August 2018, in which she recalls Crow being "fairly active in some local communist party."
2. F.E. "Buddy" DeVito, *A Radical Life* (Tadanac, BC: Stony Creek, 2010), 29.
3. King with Braid, *Red Bait!*, 57.
4. Sergeant J.A. Cawsey, Blairmore, AB, RCMP Detachment, in secret report, 20 November 1934, author's copy.
5. "Economic News Release," U.S. Bureau of Statistics, 22 January 2021, https://www.bls.gov/news.release/union2.nr0.htm.
6. *Toronto Star*, "We've Never Been Busier...," 21 January 2021, https://www.thestar.com/business/2021/01/16/unions-say-more-workers-looking-to-organize-during-the-pandemic.html.

Sources

To gain a more in-depth understanding of the historical events recounted in *Smelter Wars*, I consulted and heavily cited several primary sources to better grasp a sense of the community below the giant Trail smelter in the 1940s and early 1950s. These sources also provide a guide to the relationship between Mine-Mill and the CM&S, helping to situate them in a local, provincial, national, and international setting. Pivotal to obtaining a workers' perspective were the many publications – daily, weekly, and periodical – that added vibrancy to the debates about the labour movement, corporate culture, and social relations. Other sources offered a glimpse of the personalities that populated that conflicted territory in the Kootenays. Finally, and here the going gets tougher as a result of the huge number of redactions, are the thousands of pages of secret police files that contribute an often biased official view of left and labour politics in Canada during the turbulent years examined.

Another key primary source was the labour movement and Mine-Mill press of the period. There we find the union's history recorded in the coverage of events, statements of leaders, and serialized accounts of union political activity. The *Union*, for example, published Morris Wright's "Takes More Than Guns," a book-length history that appeared in journals circulated in the Kootenays. The large holdings on Mine-Mill housed at the University of British Columbia offer great detail on the union's policies and functions. There is also much to be mined in local union newspapers such as the *Commentator* and the *B.C. District Union News*, both of which offer Local 480's side of the seemingly endless fight to build and then defend the union. They were aided – some might say hindered at times – by the equally strident *Canadian Tribune, Pacific Tribune*, and its predecessors. Here we find unabashed, unashamed, and often tongue-in-cheek rebuttals and rebukes to the anti-union and anti-Communist forces that set upon Local 480 and harassed it for its Communist leadership. Other labour publications as well as those of the Co-operative Commonwealth Federation fed the intense confrontational political scene in the Trail of the period.

Smelter Wars also tapped primary sources to provide a historical view of the CM&S through four unpublished book-length manuscripts written by company staff members. Of particular interest is Lance Whittaker's "All Is Not Gold." Whittaker was Blaylock's public relations director and an early editor of *Cominco* magazine. The other three documents examine the corporation's history from a strictly business perspective, offering insights into decisions that affected smelter workers and their families. The CM&S annual reports provide the company's fiduciary details without embellishment and detail corporate developments affecting the base metals and fertilizer markets. Blaylock's "Director's Reports" also comment on labour-management relations. The BC Archives offers another source on company history in its weighty CM&S holdings, including a restricted section that requires patience and persistence to access, since the guardians of the company's past require historians to be exacting in their requests, and they review them with judiciary care.

For a record of local events and opinions, there can be no more valuable primary source than the *Trail Times* (and later *Trail Daily Times*) published from 28 April 1928 to the present. The *Rossland Miner*, the *Nelson Daily News*, as well as dailies in Vancouver and other parts of Canada furnished further news and opinions. Here we find the raw material with which editors like William Curran, who edited the *Times* for most of the period covered in *Smelter Wars*, attempted to shape public opinion with often strident front-page views on socialism, Communism, and trade unionism. Here, too, one finds a rich vein of information and opinion in the letters to the editor. Of course these were carefully selected, but a nugget of hard truth occasionally appeared, mixed with venomous attacks on Local 480, the CIO, or occasionally even the CM&S. The letters could also reveal a humorous side to how Trailites viewed the many debates that came with the union drive and the numerous conflicts that followed legal certification in 1944. Primary sources also included the periodical press of the day: among the titles consulted were *British Columbia Labor Truth, Canadian Forum, Liberty, Saturday Night,* and *Saturday Evening Post. Cominco Magazine* and *Cominco Orbit* provide insights into company policy, although these are decidedly corporate propaganda vehicles.

Many theses and dissertations also serve as primary sources for the broader labour movement and Mine-Mill's place in it. Of special value in tracking the events of the organizing drive, for example, is David Michael Roth's unpublished Simon Fraser University master's thesis, "A Union on the Hill." Also of importance as a primary source covering the many figures in Local 480's history is oral historian Richard Bell's 1983 interview series held at the BC Archives in Victoria. Takaia Larsen's oral history interviews with some of Trail's women war workers offer insights into the smelter work world and its union from a female perspective. Stanley Scott, Eric Christensen, and Mary McRoberts provide detailed accounts of the 1917 Trail smelter strike. Other sources document the history of Trail's Ladies Auxiliary Local 131, citing newsletters, correspondence and meeting minutes.

Historians will find few complete biographies or autobiographies on any of the prominent participants referred to in *Smelter Wars.* One exception is Local 480 president Al King's memoir *Red Bait!* However, some biographical sources are useful in painting a partial portrait of the individuals involved. The biography of Arthur "Slim" Evans, for example, is a collection of news clippings and personal memoirs that document the struggles of this pioneer CIO organizer. A rough biography of Harvey Murphy's life emerges from several interviews. The most extensive of these is sociologist Rolf Knight's unpublished transcript based on extensive interviews with Murphy in 1976 and 1977. Included is a short biographical memoir written by Murphy's daughter MaryAnn, then a student of

Knight's at the University of Toronto. David Millar, Alice M. Hoff-
man, Allen Seager, David Chudnovsky, Jack Webster, and Doug
Collins also interviewed Murphy, and these tapes and transcripts
provide further insights into the man and his work as a union
organizer and Communist activist. Also useful are comments from
son Rae and daughter MaryAnn obtained by the author in one
in-person interview and various telephone interviews. Rae, now
deceased, also completed a questionnaire.

In addition, helpful information was gleaned from the lengthy
interview conducted prior to his wartime internment when Murphy gave almost one hundred pages of sworn testimony before a
Defence of Canada Regulations advisory committee chaired by
Daniel O'Connell. Shortly afterwards, the committee recommended
that he be interned as a national security risk. For a tongue-in-cheek
biographical sketch, Murphy's fellow Communist Malcolm Bruce
offers a highly sarcastic look at the reddest rose's formative political
years in the unpublished poem "Wilde Harvie's Pilgrimage."

Perhaps even more shocking than the absence of a Murphy biography is the absence of one on Selwyn G. Blaylock, a true captain
of industry and an essential contributor to Allied success during
both world wars. At his death on 19 November 1945 extensive
obituaries appeared in the local press, and these included much
biographical detail. The newspapers also supplied remembrances
from Blaylock's company colleagues and fellow mining industrialists. The company histories noted above contain remembrances
and provide rich detail about this extraordinary corporate giant.
Extant speeches, many of them published in the local press, also
render clues about the man, his social values, and his views on all
matters concerning his company and the union. Mining journals,
although uncritical, offer another source of information on the
CM&S president.

Finally, *Smelter Wars* benefitted from the secret police reports
and personal profiles on Murphy, dating back to 1929 and extend-
ing past his death in 1977. The reports, obtained through access to
information legislation, also provide impressions of meetings, conferences, political debates, union confrontations, and personalities.
There are literally thousands of such reports, containing extracts,

news clippings, speeches, and other documents that police agents collected on all aspects of Mine-Mill in Trail. Regrettably, Canadian Security and Intelligence Service staff members have redacted much that might have been useful in piecing together this history. That such documents are available at all is perhaps surprising, since they reveal a stunningly costly surveillance program that was secretly conducted for half a century and yielded little of value in the pursuit of national security threats.

Research for *Smelter Wars* also depended on the published work of many historians and other scholars whose learned views on North American labour history allowed for comparisons with the Trail experience. Here is a selection of some of the secondary source materials that were consulted.

Books

Abella, Irving Martin. *Nationalism, Communism, and Canadian Labour: The CIO, the Communist Party, and the Canadian Congress of Labour, 1935–56.* Toronto: University of Toronto Press, 1973.

Adachi, Ken. *The Enemy That Never Was: A History of the Japanese Canadians.* Toronto: McClelland & Stewart, 1991.

Allen, James B. *The Company Town in the American West.* Norman: University of Oklahoma Press, 1966.

Allen, Richard. *The Social Passion: Religion and Social Reform in Canada, 1914–28.* Toronto: University of Toronto Press, 1990.

Andrews, Thomas G. *Killing for Coal: America's Deadliest Labor War.* Cambridge, MA: Harvard University Press, 2008.

Angus, Ian. *Canadian Bolsheviks: The Early Years of the Communist Party in Canada.* Montreal: Trafford Publishing, 1981.

Avery, Donald. *"Dangerous Foreigners": European Immigrant Workers and Labour Radicalism in Canada, 1896–1932.* Toronto: McClelland & Stewart, 1979.

Baker, Ellen R. *On Strike and on Film: Mexican American Families and Blacklisted Filmmakers in Cold War America.* Chapel Hill, NC: University of North Carolina Press, 2007.

Barman, Jean. *The West beyond the West: A History of British Columbia.* Toronto: University of Toronto Press, 1991.

Bartlett, Jon, and Rika Ruebsaat. *Soviet Princeton: Slim Evans and the 1932–33 Miners' Strike.* Vancouver: New Star Books, 2015.

Belshaw, John Douglas. *Colonization and Community: The Vancouver Island Coalfield and the Making of the British Columbian Working Class*. Montreal and Kingston: McGill-Queen's University Press, 2002.

Bercuson, David J. *Fools and Wise Men: The Rise and Fall of the One Big Union*. Toronto: McGraw-Hill Ryerson, 1978.

Berman, David R. *Radicalism in the Mountain West, 1890–1920: Socialists, Populists, Miners and Wobblies*. Boulder: University Press of Colorado, 2007.

Betchermen, Lita-Rose. *The Little Band: The Clashes between the Communists and the Political and Legal Establishment in Canada, 1928–1932*. Toronto: Deneau, 1982.

Biberman, Herbert. *Salt of the Earth: The Story of a Film*. Boston: Beacon, 1965.

Black, Gregory D. *Hollywood Censored: Morality Codes, Catholics, and the Movies*. Cambridge, MA: Cambridge University Press, 1994.

Broad, Graham. *A Small Price to Pay: Consumer Culture on the Canadian Home Front, 1939–45*. Vancouver: UBC Press, 2014.

Brody, David. *Steelworkers in America: The Nonunion Era*. Cambridge, MA: Harvard University Press, 1960.

Buhle, Paul, Mari Jo Buhle, and Dan Georgakas, eds. *Encyclopedia of the American Left*. Chicago: University of Illinois Press, 1990.

Burr, Christina. *Spreading the Light: Work and Labour Reform in Late Nineteenth-Century Toronto*. Toronto: University of Toronto Press, 1999.

Calvert, Jerry W. *The Gibraltar: Socialism and Labor in Butte, Montana, 1895–1920*. Helena: Montana Historical Society, 1993.

Campbell, Peter. *Canadian Marxists and the Search for a Third Way*. Montreal and Kingston: McGill-Queen's University Press, 1999.

Carlson, Linda. *Company Towns of the Pacific Northwest*. Seattle: University of Washington Press, 2003.

Caute, David. *The Great Fear: The Anti-Communist Purge under Truman and Eisenhower*. New York: Simon & Schuster, 1978.

Cavell, Richard, ed. *Love, Hate, and Fear in Canada's Cold War*. Toronto: University of Toronto Press, 2004.

Ceplair, Larry, and Steven Englund. *The Inquisition in Hollywood: Politics in the Film Community 1930–1960*. Garden City, NY: Anchor/Doubleday, 1980.

Cherny, Robert W., William Issel, and Kieran Walsh Taylor, eds. *American Labor and the Cold War: Grassroots Politics and Postwar Political Culture*. New Brunswick, NJ: Rutgers University Press, 2004.

Cobble, Dorothy Sue. *The Other Women's Movement: Workplace Justice and Social Rights in Modern America*. Princeton, NJ: Princeton University Press, 2004.

Cochran, Bert. *Labor and Communism: The Conflict That Shaped American Unions*. Princeton, NJ: Princeton University Press, 1977.

Cohen, Lizabeth. *Making a New Deal: Industrial Workers in Chicago, 1919–1939*. Cambridge, MA: Cambridge University Press, 2008.

Cowell, Jenny. *Trail of Memories: Trail, B.C., 1895–1945*. Trail, BC: Trail History and Heritage Committee, 1997.

Creese, Gillian. *Contracting Masculinity: Gender, Class and Race in a White-Collar Union 1944–1994*. Cary, NC: Oxford University Press, 1999.

Culos, Ray. *Injustice Served: The Story of British Columbia's Italian Enemy Aliens during World War II*. Vancouver: Cusmano Books, 2012.

Cuthbertson, Wendy. *Labour Goes to War: The CIO and the Construction of a New Social Order, 1939–1945*. Vancouver: UBC Press, 2012.

Dahl, Per F. *Heavy Water and the Wartime Race for Nuclear Energy*. Bristol, UK: Institute of Physics, 1999.

D'Arcangelo, John. *A Trail to Remember*. Trail, BC: Trail Historical Society, 2015.

Denning, Michael. *The Cultural Front: The Labouring of American Culture in the Twentieth Century*. New York: Verso, 1997.

DeVito, F.E. *"Buddy." A Radical Life*. Tadanac, BC: Stoney Creek Press, 2010.

Duberman, Martin. *Paul Robeson: A Biography*. New York: New Press, 1989.

Dubrovic, Ervin. *Merika: Emigration from Central Europe to America 1880–1914*. Rijeka, Croatia: City Museum, 2008.

Emmons, David M. *The Butte Irish: Class and Ethnicity in an American Mining Town, 1875–1925*. Urbana: University of Illinois Press, 1989.

Endicott, Stephen L. *Raising the Workers' Flag: The Workers' Unity League of Canada 1930–1936*. Toronto: University of Toronto Press, 2011).

Francis, Daniel. *Seeing Reds: The Red Scare of 1918–1919, Canada's First War on Terror*. Vancouver: Arsenal Pulp, 2010.

Fudge, Judy, and Eric Tucker. *Labour before the Law: The Regulation of Workers' Collective Action in Canada, 1900–1948*. Toronto: Oxford University Press, 2001.

Ginger, Ann Fagin, and David Christiano, eds. *The Cold War against Labor*. 2 vols. Berkeley, CA: Meiklejohn Civil Liberties Institute, 1987.

Goodman, Jordan. *Paul Robeson: A Watched Man*. New York: Verso, 2013.

Goutor, David. *Guarding the Gates: The Canadian Labour Movement and Immigration, 1872–1934*. Vancouver: UBC Press, 2007.

Hak, Gordon. *The Left in British Columbia: A History of Struggle*. Vancouver: Ronsdale, 2013.

Hannant, Larry. *The Infernal Machine: Investigating the Loyalty of Canada's Citizens*. Toronto: University of Toronto Press, 1995.

Heron, Craig. *Working in Steel: The Early Years in Canada, 1883–1935*. Toronto: University of Toronto Press, 1988.

Hinde, John Roderick. *When Coal Was King: Ladysmith and the Coal-Mining Industry on Vancouver Island*. Vancouver: UBC Press, 2003.

Hodgson, Maurice. *The Squire of Kootenay West: The Biography of Bert Herridge*. Surrey, BC: Hancock House, 1976.

Iacovetta, Franca. *Such Hardworking People: Italian Immigrants in Postwar Toronto*. Montreal and Kingston: McGill-Queen's University Press, 1992.

Isitt, Benjamin. *Militant Minority: British Columbia Workers and the Rise of the New Left, 1948–1972*. Toronto: University of Toronto Press, 2011.

Jameson, Elizabeth. *All That Glitters: Class, Conflict, and Community in Cripple Creek*. Urbana: University of Illinois Press, 1998.

Jensen, Vernon H. *Heritage of Conflict: Labor Relations in the Nonferrous Metals Industry up to 1930*. Ithaca, NY: Cornell University Press, 1950.

– *Nonferrous Metals Industry Unionism, 1932–1954: A Story of Leadership Controversy*. New York: Cornell University Press, 1954.

Kealey, Gregory S. *Spying on Canadians: The Royal Canadian Mounted Police Security Service and the Origins of the Long Cold War*. Toronto: University of Toronto Press, 2017.

Keshen, Jeffery A. *Saints, Sinners and Soldiers: Canada's Second World War*. Vancouver: UBC Press, 2004.

King, Al, with Kate Braid. *Red Bait!: Struggles of a Mine-Mill Local*. Vancouver: Kingbird Publishing, 1998.

Kinsman, G., D. Buse, and M. Steedman, eds. *Whose National Security?: Canadian State Surveillance and the Creation of Enemies* (Toronto: Between the Lines, 2000). See especially Mercedes Steedman, "The Red Petticoat Brigade: Mine Mill Women's Auxiliaries and the Threat from Within, 1940s–70s"; and Julie Guard, "Women Worth Watching: Radical Housewives in Cold War Canada."

Kristmanson, Mark. *Plateau of Freedom: Nationality, Culture, and State Security in Canada, 1940–1960*. Toronto: Oxford University Press, 2003.

Levenstein, Harvey A. *Communism, Anticommunism, and the CIO*. Westport, CT: Greenwood, 1981.

Levy, David. *Stalin's Man in Canada: Fred Rose and Soviet Espionage*. New York: Enigma Books, 2011.

Lichtenstein, Nelson. *Labor's War at Home: The CIO in World War II.* Cambridge, MA: Cambridge University Press, 1982.

Lingenfelter, Richard. *The Hardrock Miners: A History of the Mining Labor Movement in the American West, 1863–1893.* Berkeley: University of California Press, 1974.

Liversedge, Ronald. *Recollections of the On-To-Ottawa Trek, 1935.* Toronto: McClelland & Stewart and the Carleton Library, 1973.

Liversedge, Ronald, with David Yorke, ed. *Mac-Pap: Memoirs of a Canadian in the Spanish Civil War.* Vancouver: New Star Books, 2013.

Lorence, James L. *The Suppression of Salt of the Earth: How Hollywood, Big Labor, and Politicians Blacklisted a Movie in the American Cold War.* Albuquerque: University of New Mexico Press, 1999.

Lukas, J. Anthony. *Big Trouble: A Murder in a Small Western Town Sets Off a Struggle for the Soul of America.* New York: Simon & Schuster, 1997.

MacDowell, Laurel Sefton. *"Remember Kirkland Lake": The Gold Miners' Strike of 1941–42.* Toronto: University of Toronto Press, 1983.

Marks, Lynne. *Infidels and the Damn Churches: Irreligion and Religion in Settler British Columbia.* Vancouver: UBC Press, 2017.

Mayse, Susan. *Ginger: The Life and Death of Albert Goodwin.* Madeira Park, BC: Harbour Publishing, 1990.

McCormack, A. Ross. *Reformers, Rebels, and Revolutionaries: The Western Radical Movement 1899–1919.* Toronto: University of Toronto Press, 1991.

McInnis, Peter S. *Harnessing Labour Confrontation: Shaping the Postwar Settlement in Canada, 1943–1950.* Toronto: University of Toronto Press, 2002.

McNelis, Sarah. *Copper King at War: The Biography of F. Augustus Heinze.* Missoula: University of Montana Press, 1969.

Melady, John. *Korea: Canada's Forgotten War.* Toronto: Macmillan, 1983.

Mercier, Laurie. *Anaconda: Labor, Community, and Culture in Montana's Smelter City.* Urbana: University of Illinois Press, 2001.

Mercier, Laurie, and Jaclyn Gier, eds. *Mining Women: Gender in the Development of a Global Industry, 1670 to 2005.* New York: Palgrave Macmillan, 2006.

Milkman, Ruth. *Gender at Work: The Dynamics of Job Segregation by Sex during World War II.* Urbana: University of Illinois Press, 1987.

– *Women, Work, and Protest: A Century of US Women's Labor History.* New York: Routledge, 1985.

Montgomery, David. *The Fall of the House of Labor: The Workplace, the State and American Labor Activism.* New York: University of Cambridge Press, 1987.

Morse, Kathryn. *The Nature of Gold: An Environmental History of the Klondike Gold Rush*. Seattle: University of Washington Press, 2003.

Mosby, Ian. *Food Will Win the War: The Politics, Culture, and Science of Food on Canada's Home Front*. Vancouver: UBC Press, 2014.

Mouat, Jeremy. *The Business of Power: Hydro-Electricity in Southeastern British Columbia, 1897–1997*. Victoria: Sono Nis, 1997.

– *Roaring Days: Rossland's Mines and the History of British Columbia*. Vancouver: UBC Press, 1995.

Navasky, Victor. *Naming Names*. New York: Viking, 1980.

Naylor, James. *The Fate of Labour Socialism: The Co-operative Commonwealth Federation and the Dream of a Working-Class Future*. Toronto: University of Toronto Press, 2016.

– *The Western Federation of Miners and the International Union of Mine, Mill and Smelter Workers of America*. Winnipeg: n.p., 1993.

Palmer, Bryan D. *Working-Class Experience: The Rise and Reconstitution of Canadian Labour, 1800–1980*. Toronto: Butterworth, 1983.

Parr, Joy. *The Gender of Breadwinners: Women, Men, and Change in Two Industrial Towns*. Toronto: University of Toronto Press, 1990.

Peck, Gunther. *Reinventing Free Labor: Padrones and Immigrant Workers in the North American West, 1880–1930*. New York: Cambridge University Press, 2000.

Pierson, Ruth Roach. *They're Still Women after All: The Second World War and Canadian Womanhood*. Toronto: McClelland & Stewart, 1986.

Preis, Art. *Labor's Giant Step: Twenty Years of the CIO 1936–55*. New York: Pathfinder, 1994.

Rasporich, Anthony W. *For a Better Life: A History of Croatians in Canada*. Toronto: McClelland & Stewart, 1982.

Robin, Martin. *Radical Politics and Canadian Labour, 1880–1930*. Research Series. Kingston, ON: Industrial Relations Centre, Queen's University, 1968.

Rodney, William. *Soldiers of the International: A History of the Communist Party of Canada 1919–1929*. Toronto: University of Toronto Press, 1968.

Roediger, David. *The Wages of Whiteness: Race and the Making of the American Working Class*. London: Verso, 1999.

Rosswurm, Steve, ed. *The CIO's Left-Led Unions*. New Brunswick, NJ: Rutgers University Press, 1992.

Roy, Patricia E. *The Triumph of Citizenship: The Japanese and Chinese in Canada, 1941–1967*. Vancouver: UBC Press, 2011.

Sangster, Joan. *Dreams of Equality: Women on the Canadian Left, 1920–1950*. Toronto: McClelland & Stewart, 1989.

– *Transforming Labour: Women and Work in Post-War Canada*. Toronto: University of Toronto Press, 2010.

Scardellato, Gabriele, and Marin Sopta, eds. *Unknown Journey: A History of Croatians in Canada*. Polyphony Series 14. Toronto: Multicultural History Society of Ontario, 1994.

Schrecker, Ellen. *Many Are the Crimes: McCarthyism in America*. New York: Little, Brown, 1998.

Schwantes, Carlos A. *Radical Heritage: Labor, Socialism, and Reform in Washington and British Columbia, 1885–1917*. Vancouver: Douglas & McIntyre, 1979.

Scott, Jack, with Bryan D. Palmer, ed. *A Communist Life: Jack Scott and the Canadian Workers Movement, 1927–1985*. St. John's, NL: Committee on Canadian Labour History, 1988.

Solski, Mike, and John Smaller. *Mine-Mill: The History of the International Union of Mine, Mill and Smelter Workers in Canada since 1895*. Ottawa: Steel Rail Publishing, 1984.

Stanton, John. *The Life and Death of the Canadian Seamen's Union*. Toronto: Steel Rail Educational Publishing, 1978.

– *My Past Is Now: Further Memoirs of a Labour Lawyer*. St. John's, NL: Canadian Committee on Labour History, 1994.

– *Never Say Die!: The Life and Times of John Stanton, a Pioneer Labour Lawyer*. Ottawa: Steel Rail Publishing, 1987.

Steedman, Mercedes, Peter Suschnigg, and Kieter K. Buse, eds. *Hard Lessons: The Mine-Mill Union in the Canadian Labour Movement*. Toronto: Dundurn, 1995.

Stepan-Norris, Judith, and Maurice Zeitlin. *Left Out: Reds and America's Industrial Unions*. Cambridge, MA: Cambridge University Press, 2003.

Stonebanks, Roger. *Fighting for Dignity: The Ginger Goodwin Story*. St. John's, NL: Canadian Committee on Labour History, 2004.

Storch, Randi. *Red Chicago: American Communism at Its Grassroots, 1928–35*. Chicago: University of Illinois Press, 2007.

Swankey, Ben, and Jean Evans Sheils. *"Work and Wages"!: A Semi-Documentary Account of the Life and Times of Arthur H. (Slim) Evans, 1890–1944, Carpenter, Miner, Labour Leader*. Vancouver: Trade Union Research Bureau and Granville Press, 1977.

Thompson, E.P. *The Making of the English Working Class*. London: Penguin, 1963.

Tulchinsky, Gerald. *Joe Salsberg: A Life of Commitment*. Toronto: University of Toronto Press, 2013.

Turnbull, Elsie G. *Topping's Trail*. Vancouver: Mitchell, 1964.

– *Trail between Two Wars: The Story of a Smelter City*. Self-published, 1980.

– *Trail: A Smelter City*. Langley, BC: Sunfire Publications, 1985.

Verzuh, Ron. *Remembering Salt: A Brief History of How a Blacklisted Hollywood Movie Brought the Spectre of McCarthyism to Rural British Columbia*. San Bernardino, CA: CreateSpace, 2014.

Whitaker, Reg. *Double Standard: The Secret History of Canadian Immigration*. Toronto: Lester and Orpen Denys, 1987.

Whitaker, Reg, and Gary Marcuse. *Cold War Canada: The Making of a National Insecurity State, 1947–1957*. Toronto: University of Toronto Press, 1994.

White, Howard. *A Hard Man to Beat: The Story of Bill White, Labour Leader, Historian, Shipyard Worker, Raconteur: An Oral History*. Vancouver: Pulp, 1983.

Whitfield, Stephen J. *The Culture of the Cold War*. Baltimore, MD: Johns Hopkins University Press, 1991.

Whyte, Bert, with Larry Hannant. *Champagne and Meatballs: Adventures of a Canadian Communist*. Edmonton: Athabasca University Press, 2011.

Wood, Patricia K. *Nationalism from the Margins: Italians in Alberta and British Columbia*. Montreal and Kingston: McGill-Queen's University Press, 2002.

Woodcock, George, and Ivan Avakumovic. *The Doukhobors*. Toronto: McClelland & Stewart, 1977.

Wright, Morris. *Takes More Than Guns: A Brief History of the International Union of Mine, Mill and Smelter Workers*. Denver, CO: International Union of Mine, Mill and Smelter Workers, 1944.

Zieger, Robert H. *The CIO 1935–1955*. Chapel Hill, NC: University of Carolina Press, 1995.

Zuehlke, Mark. *The Gallant Cause: Canadians in the Spanish Civil War*. Toronto: John Wiley and Sons, 1996.

Articles

Andrews, Craig D. "Cominco and the Manhattan Project." *BC Studies* 11 (Fall 1971): 51–62.

Auerbach, Carl. "Communist Control Act of 1954." Encyclopedia.com, 2014. https://www.encyclopedia.com.

Berton, Pierre. "How a Red Union Bosses Atom Workers at Trail, B.C." *Maclean's*, 1 April 1951, 7–10.

Dinwoodie, D.H. "The Politics of International Pollution Control: The Trail Smelter Case." *International Journal* 27, no. 2 (Spring 1972): 219–35.

English, Richard. "What Makes a Hollywood Communist?" *Saturday Evening Post*, 19 May 1951, 30–1 and 147–52.

Frager, Ruth A. "Labour History and the Interlocking Hierarchies of Class, Ethnicity, and Gender: A Canadian Perspective." *International Review of Social History* 44 (1999): 197–215.

Frazer, Chris. "From Pariahs to Patriots: Canadian Communists in the Second World War." *Past Imperfect* 5 (1996): 3–36.

Guard, Julie. "Fair Play or Fair Pay? Gender Relations, Class Consciousness, and Union Solidarity in the Canadian UE." *Labour/Le Travail* 37 (Spring 1997): 149–77.

Harney, Robert F. "Montreal's King of Italian Labour: A Case Study of Padronism." *Labour/Le Travailleur* 4 (1979): 57–84.

Keitel, Robert S. "The Merger of the International Union of Mine, Mill and Smelter Workers into the United Steelworkers of America." *Labor History* (Winter 1974): 36–43.

Klausen, Susanne. "The Plywood Girls: Women and Gender Ideology at the Port Alberni Plywood Plant, 1942–1991." *Labour/Le Travail* 41 (Spring 1998): 199–235.

Krislov, Joseph. "The Extent and Trends of Raiding among American Unions." *Quarterly Journal of Economics* 69, no. 1 (February 1955): 145–52.

Langford, Tom, and Chris Frazer. "The Cold War and Working-Class Politics in the Coal Mining Community of the Crowsnest Pass, 1945–1958." *Labour/Le Travail* 49 (Spring 2002): 43–81.

Manley, John. "Canadian Communists, Revolutionary Unionism, and the 'Third Period': The Workers' Unity League, 1929–1935." *Journal of the Canadian Historical Association* 5 (1994): 167–91.

Marcuse, Gary. "Labour's Cold War: The Story of a Union That Was Not Purged." *Labour/Le Travail* 22 (Fall 1988): 199–210.

McCallum, Margaret E. "Corporate Welfarism in Canada." *Canadian Historical Review* 71, no. 1 (1990): 46–79.

McDowell, Laurel Sefton. "The Career of a Canadian Trade Union Leader: C.H. Millard 1937–1946." *Industrial Relations* 43, no. 3 (1988): 609–32.

– "Paul Robeson in Canada: A Border Story." *Labour/Le Travail* 51 (Spring 2003): 177–221.

McRoberts, Mary L. "The Routing of Radicalism: The 1917 Cominco Strike." *Ascendant Historian* 3 (April 1985): 66–107.

Mercier, Laurie. "Gender, Labor, and Place: Reconstructing Women's Spaces in Industrial Communities of the Canadian and U.S. Wests," *Labor History* 53, no. 3 (August 2012): 389–407.

– "Instead of Fighting the Common Enemy": Mine-Mill versus the Steelworkers in Montana, 1950–1967." *Labor History* 40, no. 4 (1999): 459–80.

– "'We Are Women Irish': Gender, Class, Religious, and Ethnic Identity
   in Anaconda, Montana." *Montana, the Magazine of Western History* 44
   (Winter 1994): 28–41.

Mickleburgh, Bruce. "Consolidated Prepares an Inside Job" and "War Scare
   Pays Off for Consolidated." *Pacific Tribune*, 11 and 18 March 1949.

Panitch, Leo, and Donald Swartz. "Towards Permanent Exceptionalism:
   Coercion and Consent in Canadian Industrial Relations." *Labour/Le
   Travail* 13 (Spring 1984): 133–57.

Petryshyn, J. "Class Conflict and Civil Liberties: The Origins and Activities of
   the Canadian Labour Defense League, 1925–1940." *Labour/Le Travailleur*
   10 (Autumn 1982): 39–63.

Pozzetta, George. "Italian Americans." n.d. http://www.everyculture.com
   /multi/Ha-La/Italian-Americans.html.

Quinlan, Elizabeth, and Andrea Quinlan. "Textually Mediated Labour
   Activism: An Examination of the Ladies Auxiliary of the Canadian Mine
   Mill and Smelter Workers Union, 1940s–1960s." *Journal of International
   Women's Studies* 16, no. 3 (2015): 137–57.

Sangster, Joan. "Canada's Cold War in Fur." *Left History* 13, no. 2
   (Fall–Winter 2008): 10–36.

Scott, Stanley Howard. "A Profusion of Issues: Immigrant Labour, the World
   War, and the Cominco Strike of 1917." *Labour/Le Travail* 2 (1977): 54–78.

Seager, Allen. "Company Towns." *The Canadian Encyclopedia*. Edmonton:
   Historica Foundation of Canada, 2008.

– "Socialists and Workers: The Western Canadian Coal Miners, 1900–21."
   Labour/Le Travail 16 (Fall 1985): 23–59.

Shearer, Ronald A. "The Chinese and Chinatown of Rossland: Fragments
   from Their Early History." In "Fragments: Essays on Neglected Aspects of
   Rossland's History," 2010. http://www.rosslandmuseum.ca/.

Weinberg, Carl R. "*Salt of the Earth*: Labor, Film, and the Cold War."
   Magazine of History 24, no. 4 (October 2010): 41–5.

Wilson, D.M. "Trail, B.C.: History." 2009. http://www.crowsnest-highway.ca
   /cgi-bin/citypage.pl?city=TRAIL#5.

Wood, Rachel. "What Being a Member of an MMSW Auxiliary Means to
   Me." *Union*, 24 April 1950, 9.

Other Sources

Bernard, Elaine. "The Rod Young Affair in the British Columbia
   Co-operative Commonwealth Federation." MA thesis, UBC, 1979.

Blaylock, S.G. "A Message to the Associated Boards of Trade of Southeastern
   British Columbia," Kimberley, BC, 27 May 1941 and Trail, BC,

28 May 1941, broadcast on radio stations CJAT in Trail and CKLN in Nelson, BC.

- "Presidential Address: Industrial Relationship." Annual General Meeting, Canadian Institute of Mining and Metallurgy, Winnipeg, Manitoba, March 1935. CM&S Company Annual Report, 1920, BC Archives MSS 2500, Cominco files, box 427, files 1–8, "Misc: C.M. & S. Co."

- "A Record of Achievement: What of the Future?" Address to the Rossland Junior Board of Trade, Rossland, BC, 11 January 1944.

- "A Submission to the Enquiry Being Conducted by the National War Labour Board." Trail, BC, 15 May 1943.

Blaylock, S.G. Correspondence, UBC, Main Library, Rare Books and Special Collections, Vancouver, BC.

Boucher, Gerald. "The 1901 Rossland Miners' Strike: The Western Federation of Miners Responds to Industrial Capitalism." BA graduating essay, University of Victoria, 1986.

Christensen, Eric A. *Labour History in British Columbia and the Right to Strike: A Case Study as Portrayed by the Labour Dispute between the International Mine, Mill and Smeltermen's Union and the Consolidated Mining and Smelting Co. Ltd. on November 15, 1917 in the city of Trail, B.C.* Nelson, BC: Notre Dame University, 1976. Author's copy.

Cominco Ltd. Fonds. British Columbia Archives, MS 2500, Originals, 1896–1985, 50 m; microfilm (neg.), 1898–1975, 16 mm, 119 reels (A01502–A01622); microfilm (neg.), ca. 1910–60 and 1987, 35 mm, 1 reel (A01285[7]). Records presented by Cominco Ltd. in 1985 and 1987.

Gray, Stephen Charles. "Woodworkers and Legitimacy: The IWA in Canada, 1937–1957." PhD diss., Simon Fraser University, 1989.

Knight, Rolf. "Harvey Murphy Reminiscences 1918–1943," October 2014, unpublished interview manuscript. Rare Books and Special Collections, University of British Columbia.

Knox, Paul Graham. "The Passage of Bill 39: Reform and Repression in British Columbia's Labour Policy." MA thesis, University of British Columbia, 1974.

Lang, John B. "A Lion in a Den of Daniels: A History of the International Union of Mine, Mill and Smelter Workers in Sudbury, Ontario 1942–1962." MA thesis, University of Guelph, 1970.

Larsen, Takaia. "Sowing the Seeds: Women, Work and Memory in Trail, British Columbia during and after the Second World War." MA thesis, University of Victoria, 2007.

Miller, Jason A. "Divided We Stand: A Study of the Development of the Conflict between the International Union of Mine, Mill and Smelter Workers and the United Steelworkers of America in Sudbury, Ontario (1942–1969)." MA thesis, McMaster University, 2003.

Mine-Mill Fonds (boxes 62, 68–84), UBC, Main Library, Rare Books and
   Special Collections, Vancouver, BC.
Murphy, Harvey. "The 1946 Strike." Compilation of seven CJAT radio station
   broadcasts in support of a miners' strike, Trail, BC, 3 July to 5 December
   1946, BC Archives, Tape T4306:1.
"Police Surveillance Files, Harvey Murphy." RG 146, 1929–1942, Library and
   Archives Canada (LAC), Secret police files on Harvey Murphy obtained
   through access to information legislation from the Canadian Security and
   Intelligence Service. Ten CDs containing thousands of pages of reports,
   official documents, news clippings, and photographs.

Index

Abella, Irving, 36; CCL leadership, 176; underpants speech, 148
Aldridge, Walter H. (first Trail smelter manager), 4
Allan Cup (national amateur hockey trophy), 24, 196
All-Canadian Congress of Labour (ACCL), xix; anti-Communist, 36
Allies, Allied war effort, 40; advance to victory, 110; conscription vote, 85; failure to open second front, 40; lead supply, 5; Local 480's role, 237; Local 480 support, 92, 98; Soviets join, 64; women's role, 85
Amalgamated Union of Canada (AUC), xix; *The Amalgamator* (AUC national newspaper), 7; anti-Mine-Mill campaign, 144; *Pacific Tribune*, 75; Trail affiliate, 142
American Federation of Labor (AFL), xix; annual convention in Toronto, 44; legal compliance, 210
American Institute of Mining and Metallurgy (AIMM), xix, 51; AIMM medal, 52
Anaconda, 5; Irish workers, 5; leftist community, 237; rejected Steel raiders, 188

Anderson, Marian (1939 Lincoln Memorial concert), 210
Anglican (Church of England), 4; percentage of population, 113; Rev. Henry "Father Pat" Irwin, 121; Thomas Blaylock, 4
anti-Communism, 11; Al King, Harvey Murphy, 221; Blaylock, 11; Catholic Church, 13, 117; CCF, 156; churches, 114, 118; Cold War, 135, 162; dominance, 117; forces of, 17; immigrants, 115; Jim Crow South, 211; Local 480, 147; national labour movement, 26; ostracism, 241; post-war period, 240; smelter, vanguard, 14; Steelworkers' stridency, 242; Trail views, 234, 177, 188; voices of, 46
anti-Reds; African American organizing, 21; anger at CCL and CCF, 13; Billingsley, 14; CIO campaign, 168, 211; CM&S, 197; company union, 66; crusade, 137, 147; Hladun, 148; hysteria, 225; immigrants, 109; John L. Lewis, 36; manoeuvres, China, 166; McCarthy, propaganda,

THE CANADIAN SOCIAL HISTORY SERIES

Terry Copp,
*The Anatomy of Poverty: The Condition of the Working Class
in Montreal, 1897–1929,* 1974.
ISBN 0-7710-2252-2

Alison Prentice,
*The School Promoters: Education and Social Class
in Mid-Nineteenth Century Upper Canada,* 1977.
ISBN 0-8020-8692-6

John Herd Thompson,
The Harvests of War: The Prairie West, 1914–1918, 1978.
ISBN 0-7710-8560-5

Joy Parr, Editor,
Childhood and Family in Canadian History, 1982.
ISBN 0-7710-6938-3

**Alison Prentice and Susan Mann-Trofimenkoff,
Editors,**
*The Neglected Majority: Essays in Canadian Women's
History, Volume 2,* 1985.
ISBN 0-7710-8583-4

Ruth Roach Pierson,
*'They're Still Women After All': The Second World War
and Canadian Womanhood,* 1986.
ISBN 0-7710-6958-8

Bryan D. Palmer,
*The Character of Class Struggle: Essays in Canadian
Working-Class History, 1850–1985,* 1986.
ISBN 0-7710-6946-4

Alan Metcalfe,
*Canada Learns to Play: The Emergence of Organized Sport,
1807–1914,* 1987.
ISBN 0-7710-5870-5

Marta Danylewycz,
Taking the Veil: An Alternative to Marriage, Motherhood,
and Spinsterhood in Quebec, 1840–1920, 1987.
ISBN 0-7710-2550-5

Craig Heron,
Working in Steel: The Early Years in Canada, 1883–1935, 1988.
ISBN 978-1-4426-0984-6

Wendy Mitchinson and Janice Dickin McGinnis, Editors,
Essays in the History of Canadian Medicine, 1988.
ISBN 0-7710-6063-7

Joan Sangster,
Dreams of Equality: Women on the Canadian Left,
1920–1950, 1989.
ISBN 0-7710-7946-X

Angus McLaren,
Our Own Master Race: Eugenics in Canada, 1885–1945, 1990.
ISBN 0-7710-5544-7

Bruno Ramirez,
On the Move: French-Canadian and Italian Migrants
in the North Atlantic Economy, 1860–1914, 1991.
ISBN 0-7710-7283-X

Mariana Valverde,
The Age of Light, Soap and Water: Moral Reform
in English Canada, 1885–1925, 1991.
ISBN 978-0-8020-9595-4

Bettina Bradbury,
Working Families: Age, Gender, and Daily Survival
in Industrializing Montreal, 1993.
ISBN 978-0-8020-8689-1

Andrée Lévesque,
Making and Breaking the Rules: Women in Quebec,
1919–1939, 1994.
ISBN 978-1-4426-1138-2

Cecilia Danysk,
Hired Hands: Labour and the Development of Prairie Agriculture, 1880–1930, 1995.
ISBN 0 7710-2552-1

Kathryn McPherson,
Bedside Matters: The Transformation of Canadian Nursing, 1900–1990, 1996.
ISBN 978-0-8020-8679-2

Edith Burley,
Servants of the Honourable Company: Work, Discipline, and Conflict in the Hudson's Bay Company, 1770–1870, 1997.
ISBN 0-19-541296-6

Mercedes Steedman,
Angels of the Workplace: Women and the Construction of Gender Relations in the Canadian Clothing Industry, 1890–1940, 1997.
ISBN 978-1-4426-0982-2

Angus McLaren and Arlene Tigar McLaren,
The Bedroom and the State: The Changing Practices and Politics of Contraception and Abortion in Canada, 1880–1997, 1997.
ISBN 0-19-541318-0

Kathryn McPherson, Cecilia Morgan, and Nancy M. Forestell, Editors,
Gendered Pasts: Historical Essays in Femininity and Masculinity in Canada, 1999.
ISBN 0-978-0-8020-8690-7

Gillian Creese,
Contracting Masculinity: Gender, Class, and Race in a White-Collar Union, 1944–1994, 1999.
ISBN 0-19-541454-3

Geoffrey Reaume,
Remembrance of Patients Past: Patient Life at the Toronto Hospital for the Insane, 1870–1940, 2000.
ISBN 978-1-4426-1075-0

Miriam Wright,
A Fishery for Modern Times: The State and the Industrialization of the Newfoundland Fishery, 1934–1968, 2001.
ISBN 0-19-541620-1

Judy Fudge and Eric Tucker,
Labour Before the Law: The Regulation of Workers' Collective Action in Canada, 1900–1948, 2001.
ISBN 978-0-8020-3793-0

Mark Moss,
Manliness and Militarism: Educating Young Boys in Ontario for War, 2001.
ISBN 0-19-541594-9

Joan Sangster,
Regulating Girls and Women: Sexuality, Family, and the Law in Ontario, 1920–1960, 2001.
ISBN 0-19-541663-5

Reinhold Kramer and Tom Mitchell,
Walk Towards the Gallows: The Tragedy of Hilda Blake, Hanged 1899, 2002.
ISBN 978-0-8020-9542-8

Mark Kristmanson,
Plateaus of Freedom: Nationality, Culture, and State Security in Canada, 1940–1960, 2002.
ISBN 0-19-541866-2 (cloth)
ISBN 0-19-541803-4 (paper)

Robin Jarvis Brownlie,
A Fatherly Eye: Indian Agents, Government Power, and Aboriginal Resistance in Ontario, 1918–1939, 2003.
ISBN 0-19-541891-3 (cloth)
ISBN 0-19-541784-4 (paper)

Steve Hewitt,
Riding to the Rescue: The Transformation of the RCMP in Alberta and Saskatchewan, 1914–1872, 2006.
ISBN 978-0-8020-9021-8 (cloth)
ISBN 978-0-8020-4895-0 (paper)

Robert K. Kristofferson,
Craft Capitalism: Craftworkers and Early Industrialization in Hamilton, Ontario, 1840–1871, 2007.
ISBN 978-0-8020-9127-7 (cloth)
ISBN 978-0-8020-9408-7 (paper)

Andrew Parnaby,
Citizen Docker: Making a New Deal on the Vancouver Waterfront, 1919–1939, 2008.
ISBN 978-0-8020-9056-0 (cloth)
ISBN 978-0-8020-9384-4 (paper)

J.I. Little,
Loyalties in Conflict: A Canadian Borderland in War and Rebellion, 1812–1840, 2008.
ISBN 978-0-8020-9773-6 (cloth)
ISBN 978-0-8020-9525-1 (paper)

Pauline Greenhill,
Make the Night Hideous: Four English Canadian Charivaris, 1881–1940, 2010.
ISBN 978-1-4426-4077-1 (cloth)
ISBN 978-1-4426-1015-6 (paper)

Rhonda L. Hinther and Jim Mochoruk,
Re-imagining Ukrainian-Canadians: History, Politics, and Identity, 2010.
ISBN 978-1-4426-4134-1 (cloth)
ISBN 978-1-4426-1062-0 (paper)

Reinhold Kramer and Tom Mitchell,
When the State Trembled: How A.J. Andrews and the Citizens' Committee Broke the Winnipeg General Strike, 2010.
ISBN 978-1-4426-4219-5 (cloth)
ISBN 978-1-4426-1116-0 (paper)

Barrington Walker,
Race on Trial: Black Defendants in Ontario's Criminal Courts, 1858–1958, 2010.
ISBN 978-0-8020-9909-9 (cloth)
ISBN 978-0-8020-9610-4 (paper)

Lara Campbell, Dominique Clément, and Greg Kealey,
Debating Dissent: Canada and the 1960s, 2012.
ISBN 978-1-4426-4164-8 (cloth)
ISBN 978-1-4426-1078-1 (paper)

Janis Thiessen,
*Manufacturing Mennonites: Work and Religion
in Post-War Manitoba,* 2013.
ISBN 978-1-4426-4213-3 (cloth)
ISBN 978-1-4426-1113-9 (paper)

Don Nerbas,
*Dominion of Capital: The Politics of Big Business
and the Crisis of the Canadian Bourgeoisie,
1914–1947,* 2013.
ISBN 978-1-4426-4545-5 (cloth)
ISBN 978-1-4426-1352-2 (paper)

Kirk Niergarth,
*"The Dignity of Every Human Being": New Brunswick Artists
and Canadian Culture between the Great Depression
and the Cold War,* 2015.
ISBN 978-1-4426-4560-8 (cloth)
ISBN 978-1-4426-1389-8 (paper)

Dennis G. Molinaro,
*An Exceptional Law: Section 98 and the Emergency State,
1919–1936,* 2017.
ISBN 978-1-4426-2957-8 (cloth)
ISBN 978-1-4426-2958-5 (paper)

Ruth Bleasdale,
*Rough Work: Labourers on the Public Works of British North
America and Canada, 1842–1982,* 2018.
ISBN 978-1-4875- 0248-5 (cloth)
ISBN 978-1-4875-2199-8 (paper)

Ruth Compton Brouwer,
*All Things in Common: A Canadian Family and Its Island
Utopia,* 2021.
ISBN 978-1-4875-0797-8 (cloth)
ISBN 978-1-4875-2556-9 (paper)

Ron Verzuh,
Smelter Wars: A Rebellious Red Trade Union Fights for Its Life in Wartime Western Canada, 2021.
ISBN 978-1-4875-4111-8 (cloth)
ISBN 978-1-4875-4112-5 (paper)